Brief Contents

Contents

A Framework for Marketing Management

Philip Kotler

Northwestern University

Prentice
Hall

Upper Saddle River, New Jersey 07458

Acquisitions Editor: Whitney Blake
Managing Editor (Editorial): Bruce Kaplan
Editor-in-Chief: Jim Boyd
Marketing Manager: Shannon Moore
Marketing Assistant: Kathleen Mulligan
Managing Editor (Production): John Roberts
Permissions Coordinator: Suzanne Grappi
Production Manager: Arnold Vila
Associate Director, Manufacturing: Vincent Scelta
Design Manager: Patricia Smythe
Interior Design: Jill Little
Cover Design: Lorraine Castellano
Cover Illustration: Margie Nay Graves
Composition: Carlisle Communications

Library of Congress Cataloging-in-Publication Data
Kotler, Philip.
 A framework for marketing management/Philip Kotler.
  p. cm.
 "'A framework for marketing management' is a condensed version of 'Marketing management'"—Preface.
 Includes bibliographical references and index.
 ISBN 0-13-018525-6
 1. Marketing—Management. I. Kotler, Philip. Marketing management. II. Title.

HF5415.13 .K636 2001
658.8–dc21   00-039180

Printed in the United States of America
10 9 8 7 6 5 4 3 2 1
ISBN 0-13-018525-6

Preface

A *Framework for Marketing Management* is a significantly shorter version of *Marketing Management*, Tenth Edition, a classic in the discipline. It will appeal to those professors who want an authoritative account of what is going on in the field of marketing management yet want a text that is short enough to let them spend more class time on such things as cases and simulations.

A Framework for Marketing Management retains all of the strengths of the larger book.

1. *A managerial orientation.* This book focuses on the major decisions that marketing managers and top management face in their efforts to harmonize the organization's objectives, capabilities, and resources with marketplace needs and opportunities.

2. *An analytical approach.* This book presents a framework for analyzing recurrent problems in marketing management. Cases and examples illustrate effective marketing principles, strategies, and practices.

3. *A basic disciplines perspective.* This book draws on the rich findings of various scientific disciplines—economics, behavioral science, management theory, and mathematics—for fundamental concepts and tools.

4. *Universal applications.* This book applies marketing thinking to the complete spectrum of marketing: products and services, consumer and business markets, profit and non-profit organizations, domestic and foreign companies, small and large firms, manufacturing and intermediary businesses, and low- and high-tech industries.

5. *Comprehensive and balanced coverage.* This book covers all the topics an informed marketing manager needs to understand: it covers the major issues in strategic, tactical, and administrative marketing.

A Framework for Marketing Management was designed to provide the major concepts of marketing management in a concise way. Each chapter ends with an executive summary. Boxed material from the larger parent text has been either excised or incorporated into the text. Examples necessarily are shorter or less numerous, but still broad in scope.

The brevity of *A Framework for Marketing Management* gives instructors the flexibility to add cases and simulations in class, if they want to do this. Featured in-class supplements include the following.

MARKETING PLAN PRO

This highly rated software is totally interactive, featuring ten sample marketing plans, excellent help, customizable charts, and professional-looking color printouts. The plan wizards enable you to easily customize your marketing plan to fit your marketing needs. You then follow the clearly outlined steps—define, plan, budget, forecast, track, and measure—to progress from strategy to implementation. Click to print and your text, spreadsheet, and charts come together to create a powerful marketing plan. Available shrinkwrapped with the text for an additional $10.00.

PHOTOWARS CD-ROM

PhotoWars is a brand-new simulation by Mohan Sawhney and Raj Malhotra, together with PowerSim and Arthur Andersen. It provides a software-based learning environment to help users improve their skills for navigating in high-change digital markets. PhotoWars is designed to be an "action learning" exercise where students will learn concepts and apply what they learn based on the Digistrat management framework. The PhotoWars environment allows repeated plays and provides instant feedback by employing powerful system dynamics models based on a PowerSim simulation software engine. This allows managers to learn by doing, and to learn by failing safely. Observing and experimenting with such interactions allows the user to grasp the model's structure. Available at a nominal cost, PhotoWars can be assigned outside of class or incorporated into two- to three-class sessions.

CUSTOM CASES

Choose from an extensive and growing database of diverse, high-quality cases to best suit your course curriculum. For more information, please contact your Prentice Hall sales representative.

A Framework for Marketing Management is accompanied by a full supplement package.

➤ A comprehensive, extensively revised Instructor's Resource Manual includes chapter summary overviews, key teaching objectives, answers to all end-of-chapter application exercises, supplementary resource suggestions, exercises, and transparency lecture notes. Detailed lecture outlines integrate video material and transparency notes. Portions of the manual may be downloaded as an electronic file from the Prentice Hall Web site at www.prenhall.com/kotler.

➤ The Test Item File, prepared by Andrew Yap, contains over 1,500 multiple-choice, true/false, and essay questions. Each question is rated by level of difficulty and includes a text section reference. In electronic format, it is available in Mac and Windows in Prentice Hall Test Manager; it is also available in print. Instructors without access to computers can use Prentice Hall's complimentary test preparation service. Just call 1-800-842-2958 and tell the customer service representative which questions from the test item file you want on the test. A ready-to-administer test will be faxed to you within 24 hours.

➤ PowerPoint Presentations, 10 to 20 slides per chapter, highlight key concepts. Each transparency is accompanied by a full page of teaching notes that include relevant key terms and discussion points from the chapters as well as additional material from supplementary sources. The electronic transparencies may be downloaded as an electronic file from the Prentice Hall Web site at www.prenhall.com/kotler.

➤ Broadcast television and marketing education have joined forces to create the most exciting and valuable video series ever produced for business education: ON LOCATION! Custom Case Videos for Marketing. Each of the 6- to 8-minute ON LOCATION! clips is issue oriented and holds students' attention by linking video to all the major conceptual elements of the text. Each clip weaves facilities, advertisements, product shots, text illustrations, and interviews with marketing managers and customers. With ON LOCATION! you can take your class on these marketing field trips without leaving the classroom. The videos available include House of Blues, Kodak, Levi's, NASCAR, Sputnik, Forum Shops, the WNBA, Yahoo!, Ericsson, the *Blair Witch Project*, and the U.S. Miltary Academy at West Point.

CW/PHLIP

Keep your course updated throughout the year with the most advanced and text-specific site available on the Web today! Developed by professors for professors and their students, this is a content-rich, multidisciplinary business Web site updated every two weeks by the CW/PHLIP Team of 40 Ph.D. professors. This resource is available at no extra cost to professors and students. Our Web site has been vastly improved to include electronic study guides for students, additional Internet exercises and links for students, and a complete array of teaching material including downloadable versions of many components. (Try syllabus builder to plan your course!) Go as fast as you can to www.prenhall.com/phlip to preview this fantastic resource!

WEBCT

What is a Business Publishing WebCT course?

A full featured, Internet-based, complete course management and distance learning solution. Instructors with little or no technical experience can use a point-and-click navigation system to design their own on-line course components, including setting up a course calendar, quizzes, assignments, lectures, and self-paced study help.

Who developed the courses, and what are their backgrounds?

These courses were developed by educators for educators. The same team that developed our feature-rich Web sites hired 40 experienced college professors to produce our WebCT courses in teams of three.

Pricing

$12 as a shrink-wrap with a Prentice Hall text. This includes the price of a site license for WebCT.

How do you place an order?

The student purchases a package consisting of the text plus the access code (PIN) at the bookstore. The instructor receives the content cartridge and the WebCT program, which is downloaded to the school's server.

For more information on any of these ancillaries, please speak to your Prentice Hall sales representative or visit the Kotler *Framework for Marketing Management* Web site at: www.prenhall.com/kotler.

ACKNOWLEDGMENTS

This concise edition of *Marketing Management* bears the imprint of many people who have contributed to editions of *Marketing Management*. Marian Wood is owed the gratitude and credit for editing and developing this shorter version and her painstaking efforts in working on *Framework* are gratefully acknowledged. In addition, the authors of the supplements for both *Marketing Management* and *A Framework for Marketing Management* have provided a comprehensive set of teaching materials; for *Marketing Management,* Tenth Edition, we extend our thanks to Betty Pritchett, Eric Karson, and Dale N. Shook. For *Framework,* we thank Andrew Yap, Craig A. Hollingshead, Barbara R. Oates, and Jimidene Murphey.

Philip Kotler
S. C. Johnson Distinguished Professor of International Marketing
J. L. Kellogg Graduate School of Management
Northwestern University
Evanston, Illinois
May 2000

C h a p t e r   1

Marketing in the Twenty-First Century

In this chapter, we will address the following questions:

- What are the tasks of marketing?
- What are the major concepts and tools of marketing?
- What orientations do companies exhibit in the marketplace?
- How are companies and marketers responding to the new challenges?

Change is occurring at an accelerating rate; today is not like yesterday, and tomorrow will be different from today. Continuing today's strategy is risky; so is turning to a new strategy. Therefore, tomorrow's successful companies will have to heed three certainties:

➤ Global forces will continue to affect everyone's business and personal life.

➤ Technology will continue to advance and amaze us.

➤ There will be a continuing push toward deregulation of the economic sector.

These three developments—globalization, technological advances, and deregulation—spell endless opportunities. But what is marketing and what does it have to do with these issues?

Marketing deals with identifying and meeting human and social needs. One of the shortest definitions of marketing is "meeting needs profitably." Whether the marketer is Procter & Gamble, which notices that people feel overweight and want tasty but less fatty food and invents Olestra; or CarMax, which notes that people want more certainty when they buy a used automobile and invents a new system for selling used cars; or IKEA, which notices that people want good furniture at a substantially lower price and creates knock-down furniture—all illustrate a drive to turn a private or social need into a profitable business opportunity through marketing.

MARKETING TASKS

A recent book, *Radical Marketing*, praises companies such as Harley-Davidson for succeeding by breaking all of the rules of marketing.[1] Instead of commissioning expensive marketing research, spending huge sums on advertising, and operating large market-

1

ing departments, these companies stretch their limited resources, live close to their customers, and create more satisfying solutions to customers' needs. They form buyers clubs, use creative public relations, and focus on delivering quality products to win long-term customer loyalty. It seems that not all marketing must follow the P&G model.

In fact, we can distinguish three stages through which marketing practice might pass:

1. *Entrepreneurial marketing:* Most companies are started by individuals who visualize an opportunity and knock on every door to gain attention. Jim Koch, founder of Boston Beer Company, whose Samuel Adams beer has become a top-selling "craft" beer, started out in 1984 carrying bottles of Samuel Adams from bar to bar to persuade bartenders to carry it. For 10 years, he sold his beer through direct selling and grassroots public relations. Today his business pulls in nearly $200 million, making it the leader in the U.S. craft beer market.[2]

2. *Formulated marketing:* As small companies achieve success, they inevitably move toward more formulated marketing. Boston Beer recently began a $15 million television advertising campaign. The company now employs more that 175 salespeople and has a marketing department that carries on market research, adopting some of the tools used in professionally run marketing companies.

3. *Intrepreneurial marketing:* Many large companies get stuck in formulated marketing, poring over the latest ratings, scanning research reports, trying to fine-tune dealer relations and advertising messages. These companies lack the creativity and passion of the guerrilla marketers in the entrepreneurial stage.[3] Their brand and product managers need to start living with their customers and visualizing new ways to add value to their customers' lives.

The bottom line is that effective marketing can take many forms. Although it is easier to learn the formulated side (which will occupy most of our attention in this book), we will also see how creativity and passion can be used by today's and tomorrow's marketing managers.

The Scope of Marketing

Marketing people are involved in marketing 10 types of entities: goods, services, experiences, events, persons, places, properties, organizations, information, and ideas.

Goods. Physical goods constitute the bulk of most countries' production and marketing effort. The United States produces and markets billions of physical goods, from eggs to steel to hair dryers. In developing nations, goods—particularly food, commodities, clothing, and housing—are the mainstay of the economy.

Services. As economies advance, a growing proportion of their activities are focused on the production of services. The U.S. economy today consists of a 70–30 services-to-goods mix. Services include airlines, hotels, and maintenance and repair people, as well as professionals such as accountants, lawyers, engineers, and doctors. Many market offerings consist of a variable mix of goods and services.

Experiences. By orchestrating several services and goods, one can create, stage, and market experiences. Walt Disney World's Magic Kingdom is an experience; so is the Hard Rock Cafe.

Events. Marketers promote time-based events, such as the Olympics, trade shows, sports events, and artistic performances.

Persons. Celebrity marketing has become a major business. Artists, musicians, CEOs, physicians, high-profile lawyers and financiers, and other professionals draw help from celebrity marketers.[4]

Places. Cities, states, regions, and nations compete to attract tourists, factories, company headquarters, and new residents.[5] Place marketers include economic development specialists, real estate agents, commercial banks, local business associations, and advertising and public relations agencies.

Properties. Properties are intangible rights of ownership of either real property (real estate) or financial property (stocks and bonds). Properties are bought and sold, and this occasions a marketing effort by real estate agents (for real estate) and investment companies and banks (for securities).

Organizations. Organizations actively work to build a strong, favorable image in the mind of their publics. Philips, the Dutch electronics company, advertises with the tag line, "Let's Make Things Better." The Body Shop and Ben & Jerry's also gain attention by promoting social causes. Universities, museums, and performing arts organizations boost their public images to compete more successfully for audiences and funds.

Information. The production, packaging, and distribution of information is one of society's major industries.[6] Among the marketers of information are schools and universities; publishers of encyclopedias, nonfiction books, and specialized magazines; makers of CDs; and Internet Web sites.

Ideas. Every market offering has a basic idea at its core. In essence, products and services are platforms for delivering some idea or benefit to satisfy a core need.

A Broadened View of Marketing Tasks

Marketers are skilled in stimulating demand for their products. However, this is too limited a view of the tasks that marketers perform. Just as production and logistics professionals are responsible for supply management, marketers are responsible for demand management. They may have to manage negative demand (avoidance of a product), no demand (lack of awareness or interest in a product), latent demand (a strong need that cannot be satisfied by existing products), declining demand (lower demand), irregular demand (demand varying by season, day, or hour), full demand (a satisfying level of demand), overfull demand (more demand than can be handled), or unwholesome demand (demand for unhealthy or dangerous products). To meet the organization's objectives, marketing managers seek to influence the level, timing, and composition of these various demand states.

The Decisions That Marketers Make

Marketing managers face a host of decisions in handling marketing tasks. These range from major decisions such as what product features to design into a new product, how many salespeople to hire, or how much to spend on advertising, to minor decisions such as the wording or color for new packaging.

Among the questions that marketers ask (and will be addressed in this text) are: How can we spot and choose the right market segment(s)? How can we differentiate our offering? How should we respond to customers who press for a lower price? How can we compete against lower-cost, lower-price rivals? How far can we go in customizing our offering for each customer? How can we grow our business? How can we build stronger brands? How can we reduce the cost of customer acquisition and keep customers loyal? How can we tell which customers are more important? How can we measure the payback from marketing communications? How can we improve sales-force productivity? How can we manage channel conflict? How can we get other departments to be more customer-oriented?

Marketing Concepts and Tools

Marketing boasts a rich array of concepts and tools to help marketers address the decisions they must make. We will start by defining marketing and then describing its major concepts and tools.

Defining Marketing

We can distinguish between a social and a managerial definition for marketing. According to a social definition, **marketing** is a societal process by which individuals and groups obtain what they need and want through creating, offering, and exchanging products and services of value freely with others.

As a managerial definition, marketing has often been described as "the art of selling products." But Peter Drucker, a leading management theorist, says that "the aim of marketing is to make selling superfluous. The aim of marketing is to know and understand the customer so well that the product or service fits him and sells itself. Ideally, marketing should result in a customer who is ready to buy."[7]

The American Marketing Association offers this managerial definition: **Marketing (management)** is the process of planning and executing the conception, pricing, promotion, and distribution of ideas, goods, and services to create exchanges that satisfy individual and organizational goals.[8]

Coping with exchange processes—part of this definition—calls for a considerable amount of work and skill. We see marketing management as the art and science of applying core marketing concepts to choose target markets and get, keep, and grow customers through creating, delivering, and communicating superior customer value.

Core Marketing Concepts

Marketing can be further understood by defining the core concepts applied by marketing managers.

Target Markets and Segmentation

A marketer can rarely satisfy everyone in a market. Not everyone likes the same soft drink, automobile, college, and movie. Therefore, marketers start with *market segmentation*. They identify and profile distinct groups of buyers who might prefer or require varying products and marketing mixes. Market segments can be identified by examining demographic, psychographic, and behavioral differences among buyers. The firm then decides which segments present the greatest opportunity—those whose needs the firm can meet in a superior fashion.

For each chosen target market, the firm develops a *market offering*. The offering is *positioned* in the minds of the target buyers as delivering some central benefit(s). For example, Volvo develops its cars for the target market of buyers for whom automobile safety is a major concern. Volvo, therefore, positions its car as the safest a customer can buy.

Traditionally, a "market" was a physical place where buyers and sellers gathered to exchange goods. Now marketers view the sellers as the *industry* and the buyers as the *market* (see Figure 1.1). The sellers send goods and services and communications (ads, direct mail, e-mail messages) to the market; in return they receive money and information (attitudes, sales data). The inner loop in the diagram in Figure 1.1 shows

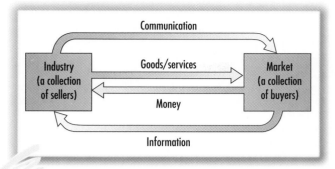

Figure 1.1 A Simple Marketing System

an exchange of money for goods and services; the outer loop shows an exchange of information.

A *global industry* is one in which the strategic positions of competitors in major geographic or national markets are fundamentally affected by their overall global positions. Global firms—both large and small—plan, operate, and coordinate their activities and exchanges on a worldwide basis.

Today we can distinguish between a *marketplace* and a *marketspace*. The marketplace is physical, as when one goes shopping in a store; marketspace is digital, as when one goes shopping on the Internet. E-commerce—business transactions conducted on-line—has many advantages for both consumers and businesses, including convenience, savings, selection, personalization, and information. For example, on-line shopping is so convenient that 30 percent of the orders generated by the Web site of REI, a recreational equipment retailer, is logged from 10 P.M. to 7 A.M., sparing REI the expense of keeping its stores open late or hiring customer service representatives. However, the e-commerce marketspace is also bringing pressure from consumers for lower prices and is threatening intermediaries such as travel agents, stockbrokers, insurance agents, and traditional retailers. To succeed in the on-line marketspace, marketers will need to reorganize and redefine themselves.

The *metamarket,* a concept proposed by Mohan Sawhney, describes a cluster of complementary products and services that are closely related in the minds of consumers but are spread across a diverse set of industries. The automobile metamarket consists of automobile manufacturers, new and used car dealers, financing companies, insurance companies, mechanics, spare parts dealers, service shops, auto magazines, classified auto ads in newspapers, and auto sites on the Internet. Car buyers can get involved in many parts of this metamarket. This has created an opportunity for *metamediaries* to assist buyers to move seamlessly through these groups. One example is Edmund's (www.edmunds.com), a Web site where buyers can find prices for different cars and click to other sites to search for dealers, financing, and accessories. Metamediaries can serve various metamarkets, such as the home ownership market, the parenting and baby care market, and the wedding market.[9]

Marketers and Prospects

Another core concept is the distinction between marketers and prospects. A marketer is someone who is seeking a response (attention, a purchase, a vote, a donation) from another party, called the *prospect.* If two parties are seeking to sell something to each other, both are marketers.

Needs, Wants, and Demands

The successful marketer will try to understand the target market's needs, wants, and demands. *Needs* describe basic human requirements such as food, air, water, clothing, and shelter. People also have strong needs for recreation, education, and entertainment. These needs become wants when they are directed to specific objects that might satisfy the need. An American *needs* food but *wants* a hamburger, French fries, and a soft drink. A person in Mauritius *needs* food but *wants* a mango, rice, lentils, and beans. Clearly, wants are shaped by one's society.

Demands are wants for specific products backed by an ability to pay. Many people want a Mercedes; only a few are able and willing to buy one. Companies must measure not only how many people want their product, but also how many would actually be willing and able to buy it.

However, marketers do not create needs: Needs preexist marketers. Marketers, along with other societal influences, influence wants. Marketers might promote the idea that a Mercedes would satisfy a person's need for social status. They do not, however, create the need for social status.

Product or Offering

People satisfy their needs and wants with products. A *product* is any offering that can satisfy a need or want, such as one of the 10 basic offerings of goods, services, experiences, events, persons, places, properties, organizations, information, and ideas.

A *brand* is an offering from a known source. A brand name such as McDonald's carries many associations in the minds of people: hamburgers, fun, children, fast food, golden arches. These associations make up the brand image. All companies strive to build a strong, favorable brand image.

Value and Satisfaction

In terms of marketing, the product or offering will be successful if it delivers value and satisfaction to the target buyer. The buyer chooses between different offerings on the basis of which is perceived to deliver the most value. We define *value* as a ratio between what the customer *gets* and what he *gives*. The customer gets *benefits* and assumes *costs*, as shown in this equation:

$$\text{Value} = \frac{\text{Benefits}}{\text{Costs}} = \frac{\text{Functional benefits} + \text{emotional benefits}}{\text{Monetary costs} + \text{time costs} + \text{energy costs} + \text{psychic costs}}$$

Based on this equation, the marketer can increase the value of the customer offering by (1) raising benefits, (2) reducing costs, (3) raising benefits and reducing costs, (4) raising benefits by more than the raise in costs, or (5) lowering benefits by less than the reduction in costs. A customer choosing between two value offerings, V_1 and V_2, will examine the ratio V_1/V_2. She will favor V_1 if the ratio is larger than one; she will favor V_2 if the ratio is smaller than one; and she will be indifferent if the ratio equals one.

Exchange and Transactions

Exchange, the core of marketing, involves obtaining a desired product from someone by offering something in return. For exchange potential to exist, five conditions must be satisfied:

1. There are at least two parties.
2. Each party has something that might be of value to the other party.
3. Each party is capable of communication and delivery.

4. Each party is free to accept or reject the exchange offer.

5. Each party believes it is appropriate or desirable to deal with the other party.

Whether exchange actually takes place depends upon whether the two parties can agree on terms that will leave them both better off (or at least not worse off) than before. Exchange is a value-creating process because it normally leaves both parties better off.

Note that exchange is a process rather than an event. Two parties are engaged in exchange if they are negotiating—trying to arrive at mutually agreeable terms. When an agreement is reached, we say that a transaction takes place. A *transaction* involves at least two things of value, agreed-upon conditions, a time of agreement, and a place of agreement. Usually a legal system exists to support and enforce compliance among transactors. However, transactions do not require money as one of the traded values. A barter transaction, for example, involves trading goods or services for other goods or services.

Note also that a transaction differs from a transfer. In a *transfer*, A gives a gift, a subsidy, or a charitable contribution to B but receives nothing tangible in return. Transfer behavior can also be understood through the concept of exchange. Typically, the transferer expects something in exchange for his or her gift—for example, gratitude or seeing changed behavior in the recipient. Professional fund-raisers provide benefits to donors, such as thank-you notes. Contemporary marketers have broadened the concept of marketing to include the study of transfer behavior as well as transaction behavior.

Marketing consists of actions undertaken to elicit desired responses from a target audience. To effect successful exchanges, marketers analyze what each party expects from the transaction. Suppose Caterpillar, the world's largest manufacturer of earth-moving equipment, researches the benefits that a typical construction company wants when it buys such equipment. The items shown on the prospect's want list in Figure 1.2 are not equally important and may vary from buyer to buyer. One of Caterpillar's marketing tasks is to discover the relative importance of these different wants to the buyer.

As the marketer, Caterpillar also has a want list. If there is a sufficient match or overlap in the want lists, a basis for a transaction exists. Caterpillar's task is to formulate an offer that motivates the construction company to buy Caterpillar equipment. The construction company might, in turn, make a counteroffer. This process of negotiation leads to mutually acceptable terms or a decision not to transact.

Relationships and Networks

Transaction marketing is part of a larger idea called relationship marketing. *Relationship marketing* aims to build long-term mutually satisfying relations with key parties—customers, suppliers, distributors—in order to earn and retain their long-term preference and business.[10] Effective marketers accomplish this by promising and delivering high-quality products and services at fair prices to the other parties over time. Relationship marketing builds strong economic, technical, and social ties among the parties. It cuts down on transaction costs and time. In the most successful cases, transactions move from being negotiated each time to being a matter of routine.

The ultimate outcome of relationship marketing is the building of a unique company asset called a marketing network. A *marketing network* consists of the company and its supporting *stakeholders* (customers, employees, suppliers, distributors, university scientists, and others) with whom it has built mutually profitable business relationships. Increasingly, competition is not between companies but rather between marketing networks, with the profits going to the company that has the better network.[11]

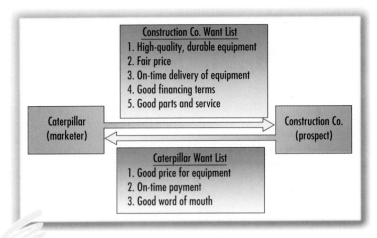

Figure 1.2   Two-Party Exchange Map Showing Want Lists of Both Parties

Marketing Channels

To reach a target market, the marketer uses three kinds of marketing channels. *Communication channels* deliver messages to and receive messages from target buyers. They include newspapers, magazines, radio, television, mail, telephone, billboards, posters, fliers, CDs, audiotapes, and the Internet. Beyond these, communications are conveyed by facial expressions and clothing, the look of retail stores, and many other media. Marketers are increasingly adding *dialogue channels* (e-mail and toll-free numbers) to counterbalance the more normal *monologue channels* (such as ads).

The marketer uses *distribution channels* to display or deliver the physical product or service(s) to the buyer or user. There are physical distribution channels and service distribution channels, which include warehouses, transportation vehicles, and various *trade channels* such as distributors, wholesalers, and retailers. The marketer also uses *selling channels* to effect transactions with potential buyers. Selling channels include not only the distributors and retailers but also the banks and insurance companies that facilitate transactions. Marketers clearly face a design problem in choosing the best mix of communication, distribution, and selling channels for their offerings.

Supply Chain

Whereas marketing channels connect the marketer to the target buyers, the *supply chain* describes a longer channel stretching from raw materials to components to final products that are carried to final buyers. For example, the supply chain for women's purses starts with hides, tanning operations, cutting operations, manufacturing, and the marketing channels that bring products to customers. This supply chain represents a *value delivery system*. Each company captures only a certain percentage of the total value generated by the supply chain. When a company acquires competitors or moves upstream or downstream, its aim is to capture a higher percentage of supply chain value.

Competition

Competition, a critical factor in marketing management, includes all of the actual and potential rival offerings and substitutes that a buyer might consider. Suppose an automobile company is planning to buy steel for its cars. The car manufacturer can buy from U.S. Steel or other U.S. or foreign integrated steel mills; can go to a minimill such as Nucor to buy steel at a cost savings; can buy aluminum for certain parts of the car to lighten the car's weight; or can buy some engineered plastics parts instead of steel.

Clearly U.S. Steel would be thinking too narrowly of competition if it thought only of other integrated steel companies. In fact, U.S. Steel is more likely to be hurt in the long run by substitute products than by its immediate steel company rivals. U.S. Steel also must consider whether to make substitute materials or stick only to those applications in which steel offers superior performance.

We can broaden the picture by distinguishing four levels of competition, based on degree of product substitutability:

1. *Brand competition:* A company sees its competitors as other companies that offer similar products and services to the same customers at similar prices. Volkswagen might see its major competitors as Toyota, Honda, and other manufacturers of medium-price automobiles, rather than Mercedes or Hyundai.

2. *Industry competition:* A company sees its competitors as all companies that make the same product or class of products. Thus, Volkswagen would be competing against all other car manufacturers.

3. *Form competition:* A company sees its competitors as all companies that manufacture products that supply the same service. Volkswagen would see itself competing against manufacturers of all vehicles, such as motorcycles, bicycles, and trucks.

4. *Generic competition:* A company sees its competitors as all companies that compete for the same consumer dollars. Volkswagen would see itself competing with companies that sell major consumer durables, foreign vacations, and new homes.

Marketing Environment

Competition represents only one force in the environment in which all marketers operate. The overall marketing environment consists of the task environment and the broad environment.

The *task environment* includes the immediate actors involved in producing, distributing, and promoting the offering, including the company, suppliers, distributors, dealers, and the target customers. Material suppliers and service suppliers such as marketing research agencies, advertising agencies, Web site designers, banking and insurance companies, and transportation and telecommunications companies are included in the supplier group. Agents, brokers, manufacturer representatives, and others who facilitate finding and selling to customers are included with distributors and dealers.

The *broad environment* consists of six components: *demographic environment, economic environment, natural environment, technological environment, political-legal environment,* and *social-cultural environment.* These environments contain forces that can have a major impact on the actors in the task environment, which is why smart marketers track environmental trends and changes closely.

Marketing Mix

Marketers use numerous tools to elicit the desired responses from their target markets. These tools constitute a marketing mix:[12] **Marketing mix** is the set of marketing tools that the firm uses to pursue its marketing objectives in the target market. As shown in Figure 1.3, McCarthy classified these tools into four broad groups that he called the four Ps of marketing: product, price, place, and promotion.[13]

Marketing-mix decisions must be made to influence the trade channels as well as the final consumers. Typically, the firm can change its price, sales-force size, and advertising expenditures in the short run. However, it can develop new products and modify its distribution channels only in the long run. Thus, the firm typically makes fewer

Figure 1.3   The Four P Components of the Marketing Mix

period-to-period marketing-mix changes in the short run than the number of market-ing-mix decision variables might suggest.

Robert Lauterborn suggested that the sellers' four Ps correspond to the cus-tomers' four Cs.[14]

Four Ps	Four Cs
Product	Customer solution
Price	Customer cost
Place	Convenience
Promotion	Communication

Winning companies are those that meet customer needs economically and conve-niently and with effective communication.

COMPANY ORIENTATIONS TOWARD THE MARKETPLACE

Marketing management is the conscious effort to achieve desired exchange outcomes with target markets. But what philosophy should guide a company's marketing efforts? What relative weights should be given to the often conflicting interests of the organi-zation, customers, and society?

For example, one of Dexter Corporation's most popular products was a prof-itable grade of paper used in tea bags. Unfortunately, the materials in this paper accounted for 98 percent of Dexter's hazardous wastes. So while Dexter's product was popular with customers, it was also detrimental to the environment. Dexter assigned an employee task force to tackle this problem. The task force succeeded, and the com-pany increased its market share while virtually eliminating hazardous waste.[15]

Clearly, marketing activities should be carried out under a well-thought-out philosophy of efficient, effective, and socially responsible marketing. In fact, there are five competing concepts under which organizations conduct marketing activities: production concept, product concept, selling concept, marketing concept, and societal marketing concept.

The Production Concept

The **production concept,** one of the oldest in business, holds that consumers prefer products that are widely available and inexpensive. Managers of production-oriented businesses concentrate on achieving high production efficiency, low costs, and mass distribution. This orientation makes sense in developing countries, where consumers are more interested in obtaining the product than in its features. It is also used when a company wants to expand the market. Texas Instruments is a leading exponent of this concept. It concentrates on building production volume and upgrading technology in order to bring costs down, leading to lower prices and expansion of the market. This orientation has also been a key strategy of many Japanese companies.

The Product Concept

Other businesses are guided by the **product concept,** which holds that consumers favor those products that offer the most quality, performance, or innovative features. Managers in these organizations focus on making superior products and improving them over time, assuming that buyers can appraise quality and performance.

Product-oriented companies often design their products with little or no customer input, trusting that their engineers can design exceptional products. A General Motors executive said years ago: "How can the public know what kind of car they want until they see what is available?" GM today asks customers what they value in a car and includes marketing people in the very beginning stages of design.

However, the product concept can lead to *marketing myopia.*[16] Railroad management thought that travelers wanted trains rather than transportation and overlooked the growing competition from airlines, buses, trucks, and automobiles. Colleges, department stores, and the post office all assume that they are offering the public the right product and wonder why their sales slip. These organizations too often are looking into a mirror when they should be looking out of the window.

The Selling Concept

The **selling concept,** another common business orientation, holds that consumers and businesses, if left alone, will ordinarily not buy enough of the organization's products. The organization must, therefore, undertake an aggressive selling and promotion effort. This concept assumes that consumers must be coaxed into buying, so the company has a battery of selling and promotion tools to stimulate buying.

The selling concept is practiced most aggressively with unsought goods—goods that buyers normally do not think of buying, such as insurance and funeral plots. The selling concept is also practiced in the nonprofit area by fund-raisers, college admissions offices, and political parties.

Most firms practice the selling concept when they have overcapacity. Their aim is to sell what they make rather than make what the market wants. In modern industrial economies, productive capacity has been built up to a point where most markets are buyer markets (the buyers are dominant) and sellers have to scramble for customers. Prospects are bombarded with sales messages. As a result, the public often identifies marketing with hard selling and advertising. But marketing based on hard selling carries high risks. It assumes that customers who are coaxed into buying a product will like it;

and if they don't, that they won't bad-mouth it or complain to consumer organizations and will forget their disappointment and buy it again. These are indefensible assumptions. In fact, one study showed that dissatisfied customers may bad-mouth the product to 10 or more acquaintances; bad news travels fast, something marketers that use hard selling should bear in mind.[17]

The Marketing Concept

The marketing concept, based on central tenets crystallized in the mid-1950s, challenges the three business orientations we just discussed.[18] The **marketing concept** holds that the key to achieving organizational goals consists of the company being more effective than its competitors in creating, delivering, and communicating customer value to its chosen target markets.

Theodore Levitt of Harvard drew a perceptive contrast between the selling and marketing concepts: "Selling focuses on the needs of the seller; marketing on the needs of the buyer. Selling is preoccupied with the seller's need to convert his product into cash; marketing with the idea of satisfying the needs of the customer by means of the product and the whole cluster of things associated with creating, delivering and finally consuming it."[19]

The marketing concept rests on four pillars: *target market, customer needs, integrated marketing,* and *profitability.* The selling concept takes an inside-out perspective. It starts with the factory, focuses on existing products, and calls for heavy selling and promoting to produce profitable sales. The marketing concept takes an outside-in perspective. It starts with a well-defined market, focuses on customer needs, coordinates activities that affect customers, and produces profits by satisfying customers.

Target Market

Companies do best when they choose their target market(s) carefully and prepare tailored marketing programs. For example, when cosmetics giant Estee Lauder recognized the increased buying power of minority groups, its Prescriptives subsidiary launched an "All Skins" line offering 115 foundation shades for different skin tones. Prescriptives credits All Skins for a 45 percent sales increase since this product line was launched.

Customer Needs

A company can carefully define its target market yet fail to correctly understand the customers' needs. Clearly, understanding customer needs and wants is not always simple. Some customers have needs of which they are not fully conscious; some cannot articulate these needs or use words that require some interpretation. We can distinguish among five types of needs: (1) stated needs, (2) real needs, (3) unstated needs, (4) delight needs, and (5) secret needs.

Responding only to the stated need may shortchange the customer. For example, if a customer enters a hardware store and asks for a sealant to seal glass window panes, she is stating a solution, not a need. If the salesperson suggests that tape would provide a better solution, the customer may appreciate that the salesperson met her need and not her stated solution.

A distinction needs to be drawn between *responsive marketing, anticipative marketing,* and *creative marketing.* A responsive marketer finds a stated need and fills it, while an anticipative marketer looks ahead to the needs that customers may have in the near future. In contrast, a creative marketer discovers and produces solutions that customers did not ask for, but to which they enthusiastically respond. Sony exemplifies a creative marketer because it has introduced many successful new products that customers never asked for or even thought were possible: Walkmans, VCRs, and so on. Sony goes beyond customer-led marketing: It is a *market-driving* firm, not just a market-driven firm. Akio Morita, its founder, proclaimed that he doesn't serve markets; he creates markets.[20]

Why is it supremely important to satisfy the needs of target customers? Because a company's sales come from two groups: new customers and repeat customers. One estimate is that attracting a new customer can cost five times as much as pleasing an existing one.[21] And it might cost 16 times as much to bring the new customer to the same level of profitability as that of the lost customer. *Customer retention* is thus more important than *customer attraction*.

Integrated Marketing

When all of the company's departments work together to serve the customers' interests, the result is *integrated marketing*. Integrated marketing takes place on two levels. First, the various marketing functions—sales force, advertising, customer service, product management, marketing research—must work together. All of these functions must be coordinated from the customer's point of view.

Second, marketing must be embraced by the other departments. According to David Packard of Hewlett-Packard: "Marketing is far too important to be left only to the marketing department!" Marketing is not a department so much as a company-wide orientation. Xerox, for example, goes so far as to include in every job description an explanation of how each job affects the customer. Xerox factory managers know that visits to the factory can help sell a potential customer if the factory is clean and efficient. Xerox accountants know that customer attitudes are affected by Xerox's billing accuracy.

To foster teamwork among all departments, the company must carry out internal marketing as well as external marketing. *External marketing* is marketing directed at people outside the company. *Internal marketing* is the task of hiring, training, and motivating able employees who want to serve customers well. In fact, internal marketing must precede external marketing. It makes no sense to promise excellent service before the company's staff is ready to provide it.

Managers who believe the customer is the company's only true "profit center" consider the traditional organization chart—a pyramid with the CEO at the top, management in the middle, and front-line people and customers at the bottom—obsolete. Master marketing companies invert the chart, putting customers at the top. Next in importance are the front-line people who meet, serve, and satisfy the customers; under them are the middle managers, who support the front-line people so they can serve the customers; and at the base is top management, whose job is to hire and support good middle managers.

Profitability

The ultimate purpose of the marketing concept is to help organizations achieve their objectives. In the case of private firms, the major objective is profit; in the case of non-profit and public organizations, it is surviving and attracting enough funds to perform useful work. Private firms should aim to achieve profits as a consequence of creating superior customer value, by satisfying customer needs better than competitors. For example, Perdue Farms has achieved above-average margins marketing chicken—a commodity if there ever was one! The company has always aimed to control breeding and other factors in order to produce tender-tasting chickens for which discriminating customers will pay more.[22]

How many companies actually practice the marketing concept? Unfortunately, too few. Only a handful of companies stand out as master marketers: Procter & Gamble, Disney, Nordstrom, Wal-Mart, Milliken & Company, McDonald's, Marriott Hotels, American Airlines, and several Japanese (Sony, Toyota, Canon) and European companies (IKEA, Club Med, Nokia, ABB, Marks & Spencer). These companies focus on the customer and are organized to respond effectively to changing customer needs. They all have well-staffed marketing departments, and all of their other departments—manufacturing, finance, research and development, personnel, purchasing—accept the customer as king.

Most companies do not embrace the marketing concept until driven to it by circumstances. Various developments prod them to take the marketing concept to heart, including sales declines, slow growth, changing buying patterns, more competition, and higher expenses. Despite the benefits, firms face three hurdles in converting to a marketing orientation: organized resistance, slow learning, and fast forgetting.

Some company departments (often manufacturing, finance, and research and development) believe a stronger marketing function threatens their power in the organization. Resistance is especially strong in industries in which marketing is being introduced for the first time—for instance, in law offices, colleges, deregulated industries, and government agencies. In spite of the resistance, many companies manage to introduce some marketing thinking into their organization. Over time, marketing emerges as the major function. Ultimately, the customer becomes the controlling function, and with that view, marketing can emerge as the integrative function within the organization.

The Societal Marketing Concept

Some have questioned whether the marketing concept is an appropriate philosophy in an age of environmental deterioration, resource shortages, explosive population growth, world hunger and poverty, and neglected social services. Are companies that successfully satisfy consumer wants necessarily acting in the best, long-run interests of consumers and society? The marketing concept sidesteps the potential conflicts among consumer wants, consumer interests, and long-run societal welfare.

Yet some firms and industries are criticized for satisfying consumer wants at society's expense. Such situations call for a new term that enlarges the marketing concept. We propose calling it the **societal marketing concept,** which holds that the organization's task is to determine the needs, wants, and interests of target markets and to deliver the desired satisfactions more effectively and efficiently than competitors in a way that preserves or enhances the consumer's and the society's well-being.

The societal marketing concept calls upon marketers to build social and ethical considerations into their marketing practices. They must balance and juggle the often conflicting criteria of company profits, consumer want satisfaction, and public interest. Yet a number of companies have achieved notable sales and profit gains by adopting and practicing the societal marketing concept.

Some companies practice a form of the societal marketing concept called *cause-related marketing*. Pringle and Thompson define this as "activity by which a company with an image, product, or service to market builds a relationship or partnership with a 'cause,' or a number of 'causes,' for mutual benefit."[23] They see it as affording an opportunity for companies to enhance their corporate reputation, raise brand awareness, increase customer loyalty, build sales, and increase press coverage. They believe that customers will increasingly look for demonstrations of good corporate citizenship. Smart companies will respond by adding "higher order" image attributes than simply rational and emotional benefits. Critics, however, complain that cause-related marketing might make consumers feel they have fulfilled their philanthropic duties by buying products instead of donating to causes directly.

HOW BUSINESS AND MARKETING ARE CHANGING

We can say with some confidence that "the marketplace isn't what it used to be." It is changing radically as a result of major forces such as technological advances, globalization, and deregulation. These forces have created new behaviors and challenges:

Customers increasingly expect higher quality and service and some customization. They perceive fewer real product differences and show less brand loyalty. They can obtain extensive product information from the Internet and other sources, permitting them to shop more intelligently. They are showing greater price sensitivity in their search for value.

Brand manufacturers are facing intense competition from domestic and foreign brands, which is resulting in rising promotion costs and shrinking profit margins. They are being further buffeted by powerful retailers who command limited shelf space and are putting out their own store brands in competition with national brands.

Store-based retailers are suffering from an oversaturation of retailing. Small retailers are succumbing to the growing power of giant retailers and "category killers." Store-based retailers are facing growing competition from direct-mail firms; newspaper, magazine, and TV direct-to-customer ads; home shopping TV; and the Internet. As a result, they are experiencing shrinking margins. In response, entrepreneurial retailers are building entertainment into stores with coffee bars, lectures, demonstrations, and performances, marketing an "experience" rather than a product assortment.

Company Responses and Adjustments

Given these changes, companies are doing a lot of soul-searching, and many highly respected firms are adjusting in a number of ways. Here are some current trends:

- ➤ *Reengineering:* From focusing on functional departments to reorganizing by key processes, each managed by multidiscipline teams.

- ➤ *Outsourcing:* From making everything inside the company to buying more products from outside if they can be obtained cheaper and better. *Virtual companies* outsource everything, so they own very few assets and, therefore, earn extraordinary rates of return.

- ➤ *E-commerce:* From attracting customers to stores and having salespeople call on offices to making virtually all products available on the Internet. Business-to-business purchasing is growing fast on the Internet, and personal selling can increasingly be conducted electronically.

- ➤ *Benchmarking:* From relying on self-improvement to studying world-class performers and adopting best practices.

- ➤ *Alliances:* From trying to win alone to forming networks of partner firms.[24]

- ➤ *Partner–suppliers:* From using many suppliers to using fewer but more reliable suppliers who work closely in a "partnership" relationship with the company.

- ➤ *Market-centered:* From organizing by products to organizing by market segment.

- ➤ *Global and local:* From being local to being both global and local.

- ➤ *Decentralized:* From being managed from the top to encouraging more initiative and "intrepreneurship" at the local level.

Marketer Responses and Adjustments

As the environment changes and companies adjust, marketers also are rethinking their philosophies, concepts, and tools. Here are the major marketing themes at the start of the new millennium:

- ➤ *Relationship marketing:* From focusing on transactions to building long-term, profitable customer relationships. Companies focus on their most profitable customers, products, and channels.

➤ *Customer lifetime value:* From making a profit on each sale to making profits by managing customer lifetime value. Some companies offer to deliver a constantly needed product on a regular basis at a lower price per unit because they will enjoy the customer's business for a longer period.

➤ *Customer share:* From a focus on gaining market share to a focus on building customer share. Companies build customer share by offering a larger variety of goods to their existing customers and by training employees in cross-selling and up-selling.

➤ *Target marketing:* From selling to everyone to trying to be the best firm serving well-defined target markets. Target marketing is being facilitated by the proliferation of special-interest magazines, TV channels, and Internet newsgroups.

➤ *Individualization:* From selling the same offer in the same way to everyone in the target market to individualizing and customizing messages and offerings.

➤ *Customer database:* From collecting sales data to building a data warehouse of information about individual customers' purchases, preferences, demographics, and profitability. Companies can "data-mine" their proprietary databases to detect different customer need clusters and make differentiated offerings to each cluster.

➤ *Integrated marketing communications:* From reliance on one communication tool such as advertising to blending several tools to deliver a consistent brand image to customers at every brand contact.

➤ *Channels as partners:* From thinking of intermediaries as customers to treating them as partners in delivering value to final customers.

➤ *Every employee a marketer:* From thinking that marketing is done only by marketing, sales, and customer support personnel to recognizing that every employee must be customer-focused.

➤ *Model-based decision making:* From making decisions on intuition or slim data to basing decisions on models and facts on how the marketplace works.

These major themes will be examined throughout this book to help marketers and companies sail safely through the rough, but promising, waters ahead. Successful companies will change their marketing as fast as their marketplaces and marketspaces change, so they can build customer satisfaction, value, and retention, the subject of Chapter 2.

EXECUTIVE SUMMARY

All marketers need to be aware of the effect of globalization, technology, and deregulation. Rather than try to satisfy everyone, marketers start with market segmentation and develop a market offering that is positioned in the minds of the target market. To satisfy the target market's needs, wants, and demands, marketers create a product, one of the 10 types of entities (goods, services, experiences, events, persons, places, properties, organizations, information, and ideas). Marketers must search hard for the core need they are trying to satisfy, remembering that their products will be successful only if they deliver value (the ratio of benefits and costs) to customers.

Every marketing exchange requires at least two parties—both with something valued by the other party, both capable of communication and delivery, both free to accept or reject the offer, and both finding it appropriate or desirable to deal with the other. One agreement to exchange constitutes a transaction, part of the larger idea of relationship marketing. Through relationship marketing, organizations aim to build enduring, mutually satisfying bonds with customers and other key parties to earn and retain their long-term business. Reaching out to a target market entails communication channels, distribution channels, and selling channels. The supply chain, which stretches from raw materials to the final products for final buyers, represents a value delivery system. Marketers can capture more of the supply chain value by acquiring competitors or expanding upstream or downstream.

In the marketing environment, marketers face brand, industry, form, and generic competition. The marketing environment can be divided into the task environment (the immediate actors in producing, distributing, and promoting the product offering) and the broad environment (forces in the demographic, economic, natural, technological, political-legal, and social-cultural environment). To succeed, marketers must pay close attention to the trends and developments in these environments and make timely adjustments to their marketing strategies. Within these environments, marketers apply the marketing mix—the set of marketing tools used to pursue marketing objectives in the target market. The marketing mix consists of the four Ps: product, price, place, and promotion.

Companies can adopt one of five orientations toward the marketplace. The production concept assumes that consumers want widely available, affordable products; the product concept assumes that consumers want products with the most quality, performance, or innovative features; the selling concept assumes that customers will not buy enough products without an aggressive selling and promotion effort; the marketing concept assumes the firm must be better than competitors in creating, delivering, and communicating customer value to its chosen target markets; and the societal marketing concept assumes that the firm must satisfy customers more effectively and efficiently than competitors while still preserving the consumer's and the society's well-being. Keeping this concept in mind, smart companies will add "higher order" image attributes to supplement both rational and emotional benefits.

The combination of technology, globalization, and deregulation is influencing customers, brand manufacturers, and store-based retailers in a variety of ways. Responding to the changes and new demands brought on by these forces has caused many companies to make adjustments. In turn, savvy marketers must also alter their marketing activities, tools, and approaches to keep pace with the changes they will face today and tomorrow.

NOTES

1. Sam Hill and Glenn Rifkin, *Radical Marketing* (New York: HarperBusiness, 1999).
2. "Boston Beer Reports Barrelage Down, But Net Sales Stable," *Modern Brewery Age,* March 1, 1999, accessed on www.hoovers.com.
3. Jay Conrad Levinson and Seth Grodin, *The Guerrilla Marketing Handbook* (Boston: Houghton Mifflin, 1994).
4. See Irving J. Rein, Philip Kotler, and Martin Stoller, *High Visibility* (Chicago: NTC Publishers, 1998).
5. See Philip Kotler, Irving J. Rein, and Donald Haider, *Marketing Places: Attracting Investment, Industry, and Tourism to Cities, States, and Nations* (New York: Free Press, 1993).
6. See Carl Shapiro and Hal R. Varian, "Versioning: The Smart Way to Sell Information," *Harvard Business Review,* November–December 1998, pp. 106–14.
7. Peter Drucker, *Management: Tasks, Responsibilities, Practices* (New York: Harper & Row, 1973), pp. 64–65.
8. *Dictionary of Marketing Terms,* 2d ed., ed. Peter D. Bennett (Chicago: American Marketing Association, 1995).
9. From a lecture by Mohan Sawhney, faculty member at Kellogg Graduate School of Management, Northwestern University, June 4, 1998.

10. See Regis McKenna, *Relationship Marketing* (Reading, MA: Addison-Wesley, 1991); Martin Christopher, Adrian Payne, and David Ballantyne, *Relationship Marketing: Bringing Quality, Customer Service, and Marketing Together* (Oxford, UK: Butterworth-Heinemann, 1991); and Jagdish N. Sheth and Atul Parvatiyar, eds., *Relationship Marketing: Theory, Methods, and Applications,* 1994 Research Conference Proceedings, Center for Relationship Marketing, Roberto C. Goizueta Business School, Emory University, Atlanta, GA.

11. See James C. Anderson, Hakan Hakansson, and Jan Johanson, "Dyadic Business Relationships Within a Business Network Context," *Journal of Marketing,* October 15, 1994, pp. 1–15.

12. See Neil H. Borden, The Concept of the Marketing Mix, Journal of Advertising Research, 4 (June): 2–7. For another framework, see George S. Day, "The Capabilities of Market-Driven Organizations," *Journal of Marketing,* 58, no. 4 (October 1994): 37–52.

13. E. Jerome McCarthy, *Basic Marketing: A Managerial Approach,* 13th ed. (Homewood, IL: Irwin, 1999). Two alternative classifications are worth noting. Frey proposed that all marketing decision variables could be categorized into two factors: the offering (product, packaging, brand, price, and service) and methods and tools (distribution channels, personal selling, advertising, sales promotion, and publicity).

14. Robert Lauterborn, "New Marketing Litany: 4Ps Passe; C-Words Take Over," *Advertising Age,* October 1, 1990, p. 26. Also see Frederick E. Webster Jr., "Defining the New Marketing Concept," *Marketing Management* 2, no. 4 (1994), 22–31; and Frederick E. Webster Jr., "Executing the New Marketing Concept," *Marketing Management* 3, no. 1 (1994): 8–16. See also Ajay Menon and Anil Menon, "Enviropreneurial Marketing Strategy: The Emergence of Corporate Environmentalism as Marketing Strategy," *Journal of Marketing* 61, no. 1 (January 1997): 51–67.

15. Kathleen Dechant and Barbara Altman, "Environmental Leadership: From Compliance to Competitive Advantage," *Academy of Management Executive* 8, no. 3 (1994): 7–19. Also see Gregory R. Elliott, "The Marketing Concept: Necessary, but Sufficient? An Environmental View," *European Journal of Marketing* 24, no. 8 (1990): 20–30.

16. See Theodore Levitt's classic article, "Marketing Myopia," *Harvard Business Review,* July–August 1960, pp. 45–56.

17. See Karl Albrecht and Ron Zemke, *Service America!* (Homewood, IL: Dow Jones-Irwin, 1985), pp. 6–7.

18. See John B. McKitterick, "What Is the Marketing Management Concept?" *The Frontiers of Marketing Thought and Action* (Chicago: American Marketing Association, 1957), pp. 71–82; Fred J. Borch, *The Marketing Philosophy as a Way of Business Life, The Marketing Concept: Its Meaning to Management,* Marketing series, no. 99 (New York: American Management Association, 1957), pp. 3–5; and Robert J. Keith, "The Marketing Revolution," *Journal of Marketing,* January 1960, pp. 35–38.

19. Levitt, "Marketing Myopia," p. 50.

20. Akio Morita, *Made in Japan* (New York: Dutton, 1986), ch. 1.

21. See Patricia Sellers, "Getting Customers to Love You," *Fortune,* March 13, 1989, pp. 38–49.

22. Suzanne L. MacLachlan, "Son Now Beats Perdue Drumstick," *Christian Science Monitor,* March 9, 1995, p. 9; Sharon Nelton, "Crowing over Leadership Succession," *Nation's Business,* May 1995, p. 52.

23. See Hanish Pringle and Marjorie Thompson, *Brand Soul: How Cause-Related Marketing Builds Brands* (New York: John Wiley & Sons, 1999). Also see Marilyn Collins, "Global Corporate Philanthropy—Marketing Beyond the Call of Duty?" *European Journal of Marketing* 27, no. 2 (1993): 46–58.

24. See Leonard L. Berry, *Discovering the Soul of Service* (New York: Free Press, 1999), especially ch. 7.

C h a p t e r   2

Building Customer Satisfaction, Value, and Retention

In this chapter, we will address the following questions:

- What are customer value and satisfaction, and how do leading companies produce and deliver them?
- What makes a high-performance business?
- How can companies both attract and retain customers?
- How can companies improve customer profitability?
- How can companies practice total quality management to create value and customer satisfaction?

How can companies go about winning customers and outperforming competitors? The answer lies in doing a better job of meeting and satisfying customer needs. Only customer-centered companies are adept at building customers, not just products. They are skilled in market engineering, not just product engineering.

Too many companies think that it is the marketing or sales department's job to procure customers. In fact, marketing is only one factor in attracting and keeping customers. The best marketing department in the world cannot sell products that are poorly made or fail to meet anyone's need. The marketing department can be effective only in companies whose departments and employees have designed and implemented a competitively superior customer value-delivery system.

For example, people do not swarm to McDonald's solely because they love the food. People are actually flocking to a fine-tuned system that delivers a high standard of what McDonald's calls QSCV—quality, service, cleanliness, and value. Thus, McDonald's is effective because it works with its suppliers, franchise owners, employees, and others to deliver exceptionally high value to its customers.[1] This chapter describes and illustrates the philosophy of the customer-focused firm and value marketing.

DEFINING CUSTOMER VALUE AND SATISFACTION

Today's customers face a vast array of product and brand choices, prices, and suppliers. How do they make their choices? We believe that customers estimate which offer will deliver the most value. Customers are value-maximizers, within the bounds of search costs and limited knowledge, mobility, and income. They form an expectation of value and act on it. Whether or not the offer lives up to the value expectation affects both satisfaction and repurchase probability.

Customer Value

Our premise is that customers will buy from the firm that they perceive offers the highest customer delivered value. **Customer delivered value** is the difference between total customer value and total customer cost. **Total customer value** is the bundle of benefits that customers expect from a given product or service, as shown in Figure 2.1. **Total customer cost** is the bundle of costs that customers expect to incur in evaluating, obtaining, using, and disposing of the product or service.

As an example, suppose the buyer for a residential construction company wants to buy a tractor from either Caterpillar or Komatsu. After evaluating the two tractors, he decides that Caterpillar has a higher product value, based on perceived reliability, durability, performance, and resale value. He also decides that Caterpillar's personnel are more knowledgeable, and perceives that the company will provide better services, such as maintenance. Finally, he places higher value on Caterpillar's corporate image. He adds all of the values from these four sources—*product, services, personnel,* and *image*—and perceives Caterpillar as offering more total customer value.

The buyer also examines his total cost of transacting with Caterpillar versus Komatsu. In addition to the *monetary cost;* the total customer cost includes the buyer's *time, energy,* and *psychic costs.* Then the buyer compares Caterpillar's total customer cost to its total customer value and compares Komatsu's total customer cost to its total customer value. In the end, the buyer will buy from the company that he perceives is offering the highest delivered value.

According to this theory of buyer decision making, Caterpillar can succeed in selling to this buyer by improving its offer in three ways. First, it can increase total customer value by improving product, services, personnel, and/or image benefits. Second, it can reduce the buyer's nonmonetary costs by lessening the time, energy, and psychic costs. Third, it can reduce its product's monetary cost to the buyer. If Caterpillar wants to win the sale, it must offer more delivered value than Komatsu does. Delivered value can be measured as a difference or a ratio. If total customer value is $20,000 and total customer

Figure 2.1   Determinants of Customer Delivered Value

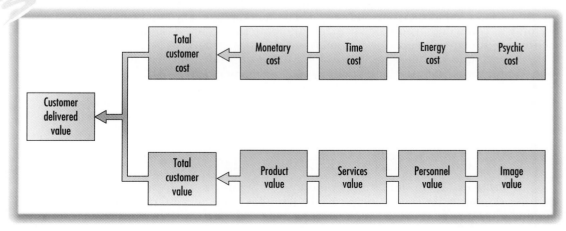

cost is \$16,000, then the delivered value is \$4,000 (measured as a difference), or 1.25 (measured as a ratio). Ratios used to compare offers are often called *value-price ratios*.[2]

Some marketers might argue that this process is too rational, because buyers do not always choose the offer with the highest delivered value. Suppose the customer chose the Komatsu tractor. How can we explain this choice? Here are three possibilities:

1. The buyer might be under orders to buy at the lowest price, regardless of delivered value. To win this sale, Caterpillar must convince the buyer's manager that buying only on price will result in lower long-term profits.

2. The buyer will retire before the company realizes that the Komatsu tractor is more expensive to operate than the Caterpillar tractor. To win this sale, Caterpillar must convince other people in the construction company that its offer delivers greater long-term value.

3. The buyer enjoys a long-term friendship with the Komatsu salesperson. Here, Caterpillar must show the buyer that the Komatsu tractor will draw complaints from the tractor operators when they discover its high fuel cost and need for frequent repairs.

Still, delivered-value maximization is a useful framework that applies to many situations and yields rich insights for marketers. Here are its implications: First, the seller must assess the total customer value and total customer cost associated with each competitor's offer to know how his or her own offer rates in the buyer's mind. Second, the seller who is at a delivered-value disadvantage can either try to increase total customer value or try to decrease total customer cost.

Customer Satisfaction

Whether the buyer is satisfied after making a purchase depends on the offer's performance in relation to the buyer's expectations. **Satisfaction** is a person's feelings of pleasure or disappointment resulting from comparing a product's perceived performance (or outcome) in relation to his or her expectations.

As this definition makes clear, satisfaction is a function of *perceived performance* and *expectations*. If the performance falls short of expectations, the customer is dissatisfied. If performance matches expectations, the customer is satisfied; if it exceeds expectations, the customer is highly satisfied or delighted.

Many companies aim for high customer satisfaction, which creates an emotional bond with the brand, not just a rational preference. The result is high customer loyalty. The most successful companies go a step further, aiming for *total customer satisfaction*. Xerox's senior management believes that a very satisfied or delighted customer is worth 10 times as much to the company as a satisfied customer. A very satisfied customer is likely to stay with Xerox many more years and buy more than a satisfied customer will. This is why Xerox guarantees "total satisfaction" and will replace, at its expense, any dissatisfied customer's equipment within three years after purchase.

Clearly, the key to generating high customer loyalty is to deliver high customer value. Michael Lanning, in *Delivering Profitable Value*, says a firm must develop a competitively superior *value proposition* and a superior *value-delivery system*.[3] A firm's value proposition is much more than its positioning on a single attribute; it is a statement about the *resulting experience* customers will have from the offering and their relationship with the supplier. The brand must represent a promise about the total resulting experience that customers can expect. Whether the promise is kept depends upon the firm's ability to manage its value-delivery system, including all of the communications and channel experiences that customers will have as they obtain the offering.

Simon Knox and Stan Maklan emphasize a similar theme in *Competing on Value*.[4] Too many companies fail to align *brand value* with *customer value*. Brand marketers try to distinguish their brand from others by a *slogan,* by a *unique selling proposition,* or by *augmenting* the basic offering with added services. But they are less successful in delivering customer value, primarily because their marketers are focus on brand development. Knox and Maklan want marketers to spend as much time influencing the company's core processes as the time spent designing the brand profile.

For customer-centered companies, customer satisfaction is both a goal and a marketing tool. Companies that achieve high customer satisfaction ratings make sure that their target market knows it. Dell Computer's meteoric growth in personal computers can be partly attributed to achieving and advertising its number-one rank in customer satisfaction. Dell's direct-to-customer business model enables it to be extremely responsive to customers while keeping costs and prices low. The company's service capability is based on "the Dell vision," which states that a customer "must have a quality experience and must be pleased, not just satisfied."[5]

Note that the main goal of the customer-centered firm is not to maximize customer satisfaction. If the company increases satisfaction by lowering its price or increasing its services, the result may be lower profits. The company might be able to increase its profitability by means other than increased satisfaction (for example, by improving manufacturing processes or investing more in R&D). Also, the company has many stakeholders, including employees, dealers, suppliers, and stockholders. Spending more to increase customer satisfaction might divert funds from increasing the satisfaction of other "partners." Ultimately, the company is aiming to deliver high customer satisfaction subject to delivering acceptable levels of satisfaction to other stakeholders within the constraints of its total resources.

Companies that navigate all of these pitfalls to reach their customer value and satisfaction goals are high-performance businesses.

THE NATURE OF HIGH-PERFORMANCE BUSINESSES

The consulting firm of Arthur D. Little proposed a four-factor model of the characteristics of a high-performance business (see Figure 2.2). According to this model, the four keys to success are stakeholders, processes, resources, and organization.[6]

Stakeholders

As its first step on the road to high performance, the business must define its stakeholders and their needs. Although businesses have traditionally paid the most attention to their stockholders, today they recognize that unless they nourish other *stakeholders;*—customers, employees, suppliers, distributors—the business may never earn sufficient profits for the stockholders.

A business must strive to satisfy the minimum expectations of each stakeholder group while delivering above-minimum satisfaction levels for different stakeholders. For example, the company might aim to delight its customers, perform well for its employees, and deliver a threshold level of satisfaction to its suppliers. In setting these levels, the company must be careful not to violate the various stakeholder groups' sense of fairness about the relative treatment they are getting.[7]

Processes

A company can accomplish its satisfaction goals only by managing and linking *work processes,* the second focus for high-performance businesses. Leading firms of all sizes

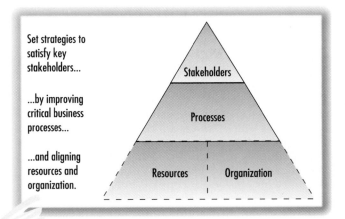

Set strategies to satisfy key stakeholders...

...by improving critical business processes...

...and aligning resources and organization.

Figure 2.2   The High-Performance Business

are increasingly focusing on the need to manage core business processes such as new-product development, customer attraction and retention, and order fulfillment. As a result, they are *reengineering* the work flows and building *cross-functional teams* that are responsible for each process.[8]

At Xerox, for example, a Customer Operations Group links sales, shipping, installation, service, and billing so that these activities flow smoothly into one another. AT&T and Custom Research are just some of the companies that have reorganized their workers into cross-functional teams. Cross-functional teams are also becoming more common in government agencies and in nonprofits. For example, as its mission changed from exhibition to conservation to education, the San Diego Zoo eliminated traditional departmental boundaries. In their place, the zoo established cross-functional teams of gardeners, groundskeepers, and animal care experts to care for the flora and fauna in new bioclimatic zones.[9]

Resources

To carry out its work processes, a company needs to own, lease, or rent *resources*—the labor power, materials, machines, information, energy, and other resources that make up the third focus of a high-performance business. Traditionally, companies owned and controlled most of the resources that entered their business. Many companies today have decided to *outsource* less critical resources if they can be obtained at better quality or lower cost from outside the organization. Frequently outsourced resources include cleaning services, lawn care, and auto fleet management. Recently, Kodak turned over the management of its data processing department to IBM.

For high-performance companies, the key is to own and nurture the resources and competences that make up the essence of the business. Nike, for example, does not manufacture its own shoes, because its Asian manufacturers are more competent in this task. But Nike nurtures its superiority in shoe design and shoe merchandising, its two core competencies. A *core competence* has three characteristics: (1) It is a source of competitive advantage in that it makes a significant contribution to perceived customer benefits; (2) it has a potential breadth of applications to a wide variety of markets; and (3) it is difficult for competitors to imitate.[10]

Competitive advantage also accrues to companies that possess *distinctive capabilities*. Whereas core competencies tend to refer to areas of special technical and production expertise, capabilities tend to describe excellence in broader business processes. For example, Wal-Mart has a distinctive capability in product replenishment based on its core competencies of information system design and logistics.

Organization and Organizational Culture

A company's *organization,* the fourth focus of a high-performance business, consists of its structures, policies, and corporate culture, all of which can become dysfunctional in a rapidly changing business environment. Whereas structures and policies can be changed (with difficulty), the firm's culture is very hard to change. Yet changing the culture is often the key to implementing a new strategy successfully.

What exactly is a *corporate culture?* This elusive concept has been defined as "the shared experiences, stories, beliefs, and norms that characterize an organization." Sometimes corporate culture develops organically and is transmitted directly from the CEO's personality and habits to the company employees. Such is the case with computer giant Microsoft. Even as a multi-billion dollar company, Microsoft hasn't lost the hard-driving culture perpetuated by founder Bill Gates, exemplified by a take-no-prisoners competitive drive and its employees' dedication to the company. This culture may be the biggest key to Microsoft's success and to its much-criticized dominance in the computing industry.[11]

In high-performance businesses, the organization and the corporate culture are focused on delivering customer value and satisfaction. Let's see how this is done.

DELIVERING CUSTOMER VALUE AND SATISFACTION

Given the importance of customer value and satisfaction, what does it take to produce and deliver them? To answer this question, we need to discuss the concepts of a value chain and value-delivery systems.

Value Chain

Michael Porter of Harvard proposed the *value chain* as a tool for identifying ways to create more customer value.[12] Every firm is a collection of activities that are performed to design, produce, market, deliver, and support its product. The value chain identifies nine strategically relevant activities that create value and cost in a specific business. These nine value-creating activities consist of five primary activities and four support activities, as shown in Figure 2.3.

The firm's task is to examine the value chain and look for ways to improve its costs and performance in each value-creating activity. The firm should estimate its competitors' costs and performances as *benchmarks* against which to compare its own costs and performances. To the extent that it can perform certain activities better than its competitors, it can achieve a competitive advantage.

Many companies today are *reengineering* their businesses, creating cross-disciplinary teams to more smoothly manage these five *core business processes:*[13]

➤ *New-product realization:* Researching, developing, and launching new, high-quality products.

➤ *Inventory management:* Developing and managing cost-effective inventory levels of raw materials, semifinished materials, and finished goods.

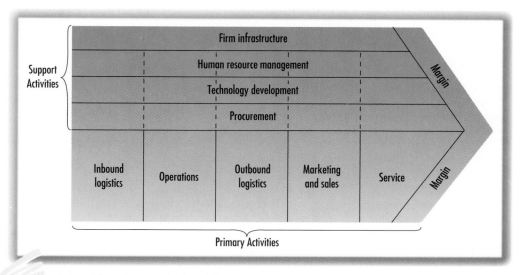

Figure 2.3   The Generic Value Chain

➤ *Customer acquisition and retention:* Effectively attracting, developing, and retaining customers.

➤ *Order-to-remittance:* Efficiently receiving and approving orders, shipping goods, and collecting payment.

➤ *Customer service:* Providing quick, satisfactory customer service, answers, and problem resolution.

Strong companies develop superior capabilities in managing these core processes. For example, one of Wal-Mart's greatest strengths is its efficiency in moving goods from suppliers to individual stores, which gives it a competitive advantage in inventory management.

Value Delivery Network

To be successful, the firm also needs to look for competitive advantages beyond its own operations, into the value chains of its suppliers, distributors, and customers. Many companies today have partnered with specific suppliers and distributors to create a superior *value-delivery network.* For example, Bailey Controls, which makes control systems for big factories, plugs some of its suppliers directly into its electronic inventory-management system, treating them as if they were departments within Bailey. This way, suppliers can check Bailey's inventory levels and forecasts and then gear up to provide the materials the firm will need for the coming 6 months.[14]

Another excellent example of a value-delivery network is the one that connects Levi Strauss & Company, the famous maker of blue jeans, with its suppliers and distributors, including Sears. Every night, Levi's receives electronic notification of the sizes and styles of its blue jeans sold through Sears. Levi's then electronically orders more fabric for next-day delivery from Milliken & Company, its fabric supplier. Milliken, in turn, orders more fiber from DuPont, its fiber supplier. In this *quick response system,* the goods are pulled by demand rather than pushed by supply. Thus, Levi's performance depends upon the quality of its *marketing network,* not just its own operations.

ATTRACTING AND RETAINING CUSTOMERS

In addition to improving relations with supply-chain partners, many companies are developing stronger bonds and loyalty with their ultimate customers. In the past, many companies took their customers for granted. However, today's customers are smarter, more price conscious, more demanding, less forgiving, and approached by more competitors with equal or better offers. The challenge now, says Jeffrey Gitomer, is not to produce satisfied customers, but to produce loyal customers.[15]

Attracting Customers

Companies seeking to grow their sales and profits must spend considerable time and resources searching for new customers. *Customer acquisition* requires substantial skills in *lead generation, lead qualification,* and *account conversion.* The company can use ads, Web pages, direct mail, telemarketing, and personal selling to generate leads and produce a list of suspects. The next task is to qualify the suspects as prospects, rank them in priority order, and initiate sales activities to convert prospects into customers. After they are acquired, however, some of these customers will not be retained.

Computing the Cost of Lost Customers

Too many companies suffer from high customer *churn*—namely, they gain new customers only to lose many of them. Today's companies must pay closer attention to their *customer defection rate* (the rate at which they lose customers). Cellular carriers, for example, lose 25 percent of their subscribers each year at a cost estimated at $2 billion to $4 billion.

Companies can take four steps to reduce defection. First, the firm must define and measure its retention rate. For a magazine, the renewal rate is a good retention measure. For a college, it could be the first- to second-year retention rate, or the class graduation rate.

Second, the company must distinguish the causes of customer attrition and identify those that can be managed better. The Forum Corporation analyzed the customers lost by 14 major companies for reasons other than leaving the area or going out of business: 15 percent switched to a better product; 15 percent found a cheaper product; and 70 percent left because of poor or little attention from the supplier. Clearly, firms can take steps to retain customers who leave because of poor service, shoddy products, or high prices.[16]

Third, the company needs to estimate how much profit it loses when it loses customers. In the case of an individual customer, the lost profit is equal to the customer's *lifetime value*—that is, the present value of the profit stream that the company would have realized if the customer had not defected prematurely. Suppose a company annually loses 5 percent of its 64,000 customers due to poor service (3,200 customers). If each lost account averages $40,000 in revenue, the company loses $128 million in revenue (3,200 × $40,000). On a 10 percent profit margin, this is $12.8 million in lost profits every year.

Fourth, the company needs to figure out how much it would cost to reduce the defection rate. As long as the cost is less than the lost profit, the company should spend that amount to reduce the defection rate. Nothing beats plain old listening to customers. MBNA, the credit-card giant, asks every executive to listen in on telephone conversations in the customer service area or customer recovery units. This keeps MBNA managers tuned into front-line customer feedback about problems and opportunities.[17]

The Need for Customer Retention

Unfortunately, most marketing theory and practice center on the art of attracting new customers rather than on retaining existing ones. The emphasis traditionally has been on making sales rather than building relationships; on selling rather than caring for the customer afterward. Some companies, however, have always cared passionately about customer loyalty and retention.[18] Lexus, for example, has constructed a model to calculate how much more each auto dealership could earn by achieving higher levels of repurchase and service loyalty. One Lexus executive told the author: "Our company's aim goes beyond satisfying the customer. Our aim is to delight the customer."

The key to customer retention is *customer satisfaction.* A highly satisfied customer stays loyal longer, buys more, talks favorably about the company and its products, pays less attention to competitors, is less price-sensitive, offers product or service ideas, and costs less to serve than new customers because transactions are routinized. Thus, a company would be wise to measure customer satisfaction regularly and try to exceed customer expectations, not merely meet them.

Some companies think they are getting a sense of customer satisfaction by tallying customer complaints. However, 95 percent of dissatisfied customers do not complain; many just stop buying.[19] The best thing a firm can do is to make it easy for customers to complain via toll-free phone numbers, suggestion forms, and e-mail—and then listen. 3M, for example, encourages customers to submit suggestions, inquiries, and complaints. The company says that over two-thirds of its product-improvement ideas come from listening to customer complaints.

Listening is not enough, however. The company must respond quickly and constructively to the complaints. As Albrecht and Zemke observe: "The company must respond quickly and constructively to the complaints. Of the customers who register a complaint, between 54 and 70% will buy again if their complaint is resolved. The figure goes up to a staggering 95% if the customer feels the complaint was resolved quickly. And customers whose complaints were satisfactorily resolved tell an average of five people about the good treatment they received."[20]

One company long recognized for its emphasis on customer satisfaction is L.L. Bean, which runs a mail-order and Internet catalog business in clothing and equipment for rugged living. L.L. Bean has carefully blended its external and internal marketing programs. To its customers, it offers the following:[21]

100% Guarantee

All of our products are guaranteed to give 100% satisfaction in every way. Return anything purchased from us at any time if it proves otherwise. We will replace it, refund your purchase price or credit your credit card, as you wish. We do not want you to have anything from L.L. Bean that is not completely satisfactory.

To motivate its employees to serve customers well, it displays the following poster prominently around its offices:[22]

What Is a Customer?

A Customer is the most important person ever in this office . . . in person or by mail.

A Customer is not dependent on us . . . we are dependent on him.

A Customer is not an interruption of our work . . . he is the purpose of it. We are not doing a favor by serving him . . . he is doing us a favor by giving us the opportunity to do so.

> A Customer is not someone to argue or match wits with. Nobody ever won an argument with a Customer.
>
> A Customer is a person who brings us his wants. It is our job to handle them profitably to him and to ourselves.

Today, more and more companies are, like L.L. Bean, recognizing the benefits of satisfying and retaining current customers. Remember, acquiring new customers can cost five times more than the cost of satisfying and retaining current customers. On average, companies lose 10 percent of their customers each year. Yet by reducing the customer defection rate by 5 percent, companies can increase profits by 25 percent to 85 percent, depending on the industry. And the customer profit rate tends to increase over the life of the retained customer, another compelling reason to satisfy customers so they remain loyal.[23]

We can work out an example to support the case for emphasizing customer retention. If a company requires four sales calls (at $300 per call) to convert a prospect into a new customer, its cost of acquisition is $1,200 (4 × 300). Now suppose each customer generates $5,000 in annual revenues and remains loyal for 2 years, yielding $10,000 (5,000 × 2) in revenues. At a 10 percent profit margin, the customer lifetime value is $1,000 (10,000 × .10). This company is spending more to attract new customers than they are worth—a recipe for disaster unless the company can change its acquisition costs or its customer lifetime value.

Companies can strengthen customer retention in two ways. One way is to erect high switching barriers. Customers are less inclined to switch to another supplier when this would involve high capital costs, high search costs, or the loss of loyal-customer discounts. The better approach is to deliver high customer satisfaction. This makes it harder for competitors to overcome switching barriers by simply offering lower prices or switching inducements. The task of creating strong customer loyalty is called *relationship marketing*. Relationship marketing embraces all of those steps that customer-centered companies undertake to better know and serve their valued customers.

Relationship Marketing: The Key

To understand customer relationship marketing, we must review the process involved in attracting and keeping customers. Figure 2.4 shows the main steps in the *customer-development process*.

The starting point is *suspects,* everyone who might conceivably buy the product or service. The company examines suspects to determine who are its most likely *prospects*—the people who have a strong potential interest and ability to pay for the product. *Disqualified prospects* are those the company rejects because they have poor credit or would be unprofitable. The company hopes to convert many *qualified prospects* into first-time customers, and then to convert those satisfied first-time customers into *repeat customers.* Once the company acts to convert repeat customers into *clients*—people whom the company treats very specially—the next challenge is to turn clients into *members,* by starting a membership program offering benefits to customers who join. The goal here is to turn members into *advocates* who recommend the company and its offerings to others. The ultimate challenge is to turn advocates into *partners,* where the customer and the company work together actively.

Of course, some customers will inevitably become inactive or drop out because of financial reasons, moves to other locations, dissatisfaction, and so on. Here the

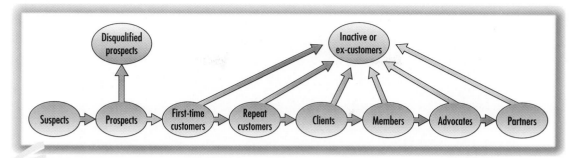

Figure 2.4   The Customer-Development Process

company's challenge is to reactivate these former customers through win-back strategies. This is easier than finding new customers because the company knows former customers' names and histories.

How much should a company invest in relationship building, so that the costs do not exceed the gains? We need to distinguish five levels of investment in customer-relationship building:

1. *Basic marketing:* Simply selling the product.

2. *Reactive marketing:* Selling the product and encouraging customers to offer questions, comments, or complaints.

3. *Accountable marketing:* Following up after the sale to see whether the product meets expectations and to ask for improvement suggestions and any specific disappointments.

4. *Proactive marketing:* Contacting customers periodically with suggestions about improved product uses or helpful new products.

5. *Partnership marketing:* Working continuously with customers to find ways to perform better.

Most companies practice only basic marketing when their markets contain many customers and their unit profit margins are small. Heinz is not going to phone each ketchup buyer to express appreciation. At best, Heinz will set up a customer hot line. At the other extreme, in markets with few customers and high profit margins, most sellers will move toward partnership marketing. Boeing, for example, works closely with American Airlines in designing Boeing airplanes that fully satisfy American's requirements. As Figure 2.5 shows, the likely level of relationship marketing depends on the number of customers and the profit margin level.

The best relationship marketing going on today is driven by technology. GE Plastics, for example, could not target its customer newsletter so effectively without advances in database software. And Dell Computer could not customize on-line computer ordering for its global corporate customers without advances in Internet technology. Companies are using e-mail, Web sites, call centers, databases, and database software to foster continuous contact with their customers. For example, Logistix, a California-based technology company, is testing software that synchronizes the Web screens viewed by its employees and its customers as they talk by

	HIGH MARGIN	MEDIUM MARGIN	LOW MARGIN
Many customers/ distributors	Accountable	Reactive	Basic or reactive
Medium number of customers/ distributors	Proactive	Accountable	Reactive
Few customers/ distributors	Partnership	Proactive	Accountable

Figure 2.5   Levels of Relationship Marketing

phone. This "teleweb" arrangement allows Logistix and other companies that sell complicated high-tech products to better communicate and build stronger relationships with customers.

What specific marketing tools can a company use to develop stronger customer bonding and satisfaction? Berry and Parasuraman have distinguished three value-building approaches: adding financial benefits, adding social benefits, and adding structural ties.[24]

Adding Financial Benefits

Two financial benefits that companies can offer to bond customers more closely are frequency marketing programs and club marketing programs. *Frequency marketing programs (FMPs)* reward customers who buy frequently and/or in substantial amounts. Frequency marketing programs acknowledge the fact that 20 percent of a company's customers might account for 80 percent of its business.

American Airlines was one of the first companies to pioneer a frequency marketing program when it began offering free mileage credit to its customers in the early 1980s. Hotels next adopted FMPs, with frequent guests receiving room upgrades or free rooms after earning so many points. Car rental firms soon started FMPs, then credit-card companies began to offer points and rebates for card usage. Today most supermarket chains offer "price club cards," which provide member customers with discounts on particular items. Typically, the first company to introduce an FMP gains the most benefit. After competitors respond, FMPs can become a financial burden to all of the offering companies.

Many companies have created *club membership programs* to strengthen bonds with customers. Club membership can be open to everyone who purchases a product or service, such as a frequent flier or frequent diners club, or it can be limited to an *affinity group* or to those willing to pay a small fee. Although open clubs are good for building a database or snagging customers from competitors, limited membership clubs are more powerful long-term loyalty builders. Fees and membership conditions prevent those with only a fleeting interest in a company's products from joining. Limited membership clubs attract and keep those customers who are responsible for the largest portion of business. For example, the IKEA Family, the club formed by the $5 billion Swedish furniture company, has members in nine countries. Some of IKEA's club benefits include furniture transportation, insurance, and a program for members to swap holiday homes.[25]

Similarly, Telepizza S.A. was able to eclipse multinational Pizza Hut in Spain through the skillful use of marketing to children via a magic club. So far Telepizza boasts the largest membership club in Spain, with 3 million children enrolled. The magic club offers children small prizes, usually simple magic tricks, with every order. Telepizza now has nearly 500 restaurants in Spain, where its market share is 65 percent compared to less than 20 percent for Pizza Hut.[26]

Adding Social Benefits

In this value-building technique, the company increases its social bonds with customers by individualizing and personalizing customer relationships. In essence, thoughtful companies turn their customers into clients. Donnelly, Berry, and Thompson draw this distinction: "Customers may be nameless to the institution; clients cannot be nameless. Customers are served as part of the mass or as part of larger segments; clients are served on an individual basis. Customers are served by anyone who happens to be available; clients are served by the professional assigned to them."[27] Harley-Davidson and other companies go further, building *brand communities* to bring their customers together.

Adding Structural Ties

Another value-building technique used by companies is to supply special equipment or computer linkages to help customers manage their orders, payroll, inventory, and so on. A good example is McKesson Corporation, a leading pharmaceutical wholesaler, which invested millions of dollars in electronic capabilities to help independent pharmacies manage inventory, order entry processes, and shelf space. Another example is Milliken & Company, which provides proprietary software programs, marketing research, sales training, and sales leads to loyal customers. The goal of these structural ties is to add value and strengthen bonds with customers.

CUSTOMER PROFITABILITY: THE ULTIMATE TEST

Ultimately, marketing is the art of attracting and keeping profitable customers. According to James Vander Putten of American Express, the best customers outspend others by ratios of 16 to 1 in retailing, 13 to 1 in the restaurant business, 12 to 1 in the airline business, and 5 to 1 in the hotel and motel industry.[28] Carl Sewell, who runs one of the best-managed auto dealerships in the world, estimates that a typical auto buyer represents a potential lifetime value of over $300,000 in car purchases and services.[29]

Yet every company loses money on some of its customers. The well-known *20–80 rule* says that the top 20 percent of the customers may generate as much as 80 percent of the company's profits. Sherden suggested amending the rule to read 20–80–30, to reflect the idea that the top 20 percent of customers generate 80 percent of the company's profits, half of which is lost serving the bottom 30 percent of unprofitable customers.[30] The implication is that a company could improve its profits by "firing" its worst customers. However, there are two other alternatives: Raise the prices or lower the costs of serving the less profitable customers.

Furthermore, it is not necessarily the company's largest customers who are yielding the most profit. The largest customers demand considerable service and receive the deepest discounts. The smallest customers pay full price and receive minimal service, but transaction costs reduce small customers' profitability. The midsize customers receive good service, pay nearly full price, and are often the most profitable. This is why many large firms are now invading the middle market. Major air express carriers, for instance, are finding that it does not pay to ignore the small and midsize international shippers. Programs geared toward smaller customers provide a network of drop boxes, which allow for substantial discounts over letters and packages picked up at the shipper's place of business. In addition to putting more drop boxes in place, United Parcel Service (UPS) conducts seminars to instruct exporters in the finer points of shipping overseas.[31]

A company should not try to pursue and satisfy all customers, because this would confuse the positioning of its products and services. Lanning and Phillips make this point well: "Some organizations try to do anything and everything customers suggest. . . . Yet, while customers often make many good suggestions, they also suggest many courses of action that are unactionable or unprofitable. Randomly following these suggestions is fundamentally different from market-focus—making a disciplined choice of which customers to serve and which specific combination of benefits and price to deliver to them (and which to deny them)."[32]

What makes a customer profitable? A **profitable customer** is a person, household, or company that over time yields a revenue stream that exceeds by an acceptable amount the company's cost stream of attracting, selling, and servicing that customer. Note that the emphasis is on the lifetime stream of revenue and cost, not on one transaction's profitability. For example, executives at Taco Bell have determined that a repeat customer is worth as much as $11,000. By sharing such estimates of lifetime value, Taco Bell's managers help employees understand the value of keeping customers satisfied.[33]

Although many companies measure customer satisfaction, most fail to measure individual customer profitability. Banks claim that this is difficult because a customer uses different banking services and the transactions are logged in different departments. However, banks that have succeeded in linking customer transactions have been appalled by the number of unprofitable customers in their customer base. Some banks report losing money on over 45 percent of their customers. It is not surprising that banks are increasingly charging fees for services they formerly supplied free.

Figure 2.6   Customer-Product Profitability Analysis

Products		Customers			
		C_1	C_2	C_3	
	P_1	+	+	+	Highly profitable product
	P_2	+			Profitable product
	P_3		−	−	Losing product
	P_4	+		−	Mixed-bag product
		High-profit customer	Mixed-bag customer	Losing customer	

Figure 2.6 shows a useful type of profitability analysis.[34] In this figure, customers are arrayed along the columns and products are arrayed along the rows. Each cell contains a symbol standing for the profitability of selling that product to that customer. Customer 1 is very profitable, buying three profitable products. Customer 2 represents mixed profitability, buying one profitable and one unprofitable product. Customer 3 is a losing customer, buying one profitable and two unprofitable products. What can the company do about customers 2 and 3? It can either (1) raise the price of its less profitable products or eliminate them, or (2) try to sell profitable products to the unprofitable customers. In fact, this company would benefit by encouraging unprofitable customers to switch to competitors.

In general, the higher the company's value-creation ability, the more efficient its internal operations; and the greater its competitive advantage, the higher its profits will be. Successful companies must not only be able to create high absolute value but also high value relative to competitors at a sufficiently low cost. *Competitive advantage* is a company's ability to perform in one or more ways that competitors cannot or will not match. Note that if the customer does not care about the company's competitive advantage, it is not a *customer advantage*. However, companies that build sustainable and meaningful customer advantages to deliver high customer value and satisfaction will enjoy high repeat purchases and, therefore, high company profitability.

IMPLEMENTING TOTAL QUALITY MANAGEMENT

One of the major values that customers expect from suppliers is high product and service quality. Today's executives therefore set the improvement of product and service quality as a top priority. If companies want to stay in the race, let alone be profitable, they must adopt total quality management.

Total quality management (TQM) is an organizationwide approach to continuously improving the quality of all of the organization's processes, products, and services. Market-leading firms see TQM as a key component of customer satisfaction and, ultimately, of profitability. According to General Electric's chairman, John F. Welch Jr.: "Quality is our best assurance of customer allegiance, our strongest defense against foreign competition, and the only path to sustained growth and earnings."[35]

The drive to produce goods of superior quality for world markets has led some countries—and groups of countries—to recognize or award prizes to companies that exemplify the best quality practices. In 1951, Japan became the first country to award a national quality prize, the Deming prize (named after W. Edwards Deming, the American statistician who taught quality improvement to postwar Japan).

In the mid-1980s, the United States established the Malcolm Baldrige National Quality Award in honor of the late secretary of commerce. The Baldrige award criteria consist of seven measures: customer focus and satisfaction, quality and operational results, management of process quality, human resource development and management, strategic quality planning, information and analysis, and senior executive leadership. Federal Express, Ritz-Carlton hotels, and Custom Research are some past winners.

The European Quality Award was established in 1993 by the European Foundation for Quality Management and the European Organization for Quality. It is awarded to companies that have achieved high grades on quality leadership, people management, policy and strategy, resources, processes, people satisfaction, customer satisfaction, impact on society, and business results. Europe also initiated an exacting set of international quality standards called ISO 9000, which has become a set of generally accepted principles for documenting quality. Earning the ISO 9000 certification involves a quality audit every 6 months from a registered ISO (International Standards Organization) assessor.[36]

There is an intimate connection among product and service quality, customer satisfaction, and company profitability. Higher levels of quality result in higher levels of customer satisfaction while supporting higher prices and (often) lower costs. Therefore, *quality improvement programs (QIPs)* normally increase profitability. In fact, the PIMS (Profit Impact of Market Strategy) studies have shown a high correlation between relative product quality and company profitability.[37]

But what exactly is quality? According to the American Society for Quality Control's definition, which has been adopted worldwide, *quality* is the totality of features and characteristics of a product or service that bear on its ability to satisfy stated or implied needs.[38] This is clearly a customer-centered definition. We can say that the seller has delivered quality whenever the seller's product or service meets or exceeds the customers' expectations. A company that satisfies most of its customers' needs most of the time is called a *quality company*.

It is important to distinguish between conformance quality and performance quality (or grade). A Mercedes provides higher *performance quality* than a Hyundai: The Mercedes rides smoother, goes faster, and lasts longer. Yet both a Mercedes and a Hyundai can be said to deliver the same *conformance quality* if all of the units deliver their respective promised quality.

Because total quality is key to value creation and customer satisfaction, it is everyone's job, just as marketing is everyone's job. This idea was expressed well by Daniel Beckham: "Marketers who don't learn the language of quality improvement, manufacturing, and operations will become as obsolete as buggy whips. The days of functional marketing are gone. We can no longer afford to think of ourselves as market researchers, advertising people, direct marketers, strategists—we have to think of ourselves as customer satisfiers—customer advocates focused on whole processes."[39]

Marketing managers, in particular, have two responsibilities in a quality-centered company. First, they must participate in formulating strategies and policies designed to help the company win through total quality excellence. Second, they must deliver marketing quality alongside production quality. This means that every marketing activity—marketing research, sales training, advertising, customer service, and so on—must be performed to high standards.

Marketers actually play six roles in helping their company define and deliver high-quality goods and services to target customers. First, they bear the major responsibility for correctly identifying the customers' needs and requirements. Second, they must communicate customer expectations properly to product designers. Third, they must make sure that customers' orders are filled correctly and on time. Fourth, they must check that customers have received proper instructions, training, and technical assistance in the product's use. Fifth, they must stay in touch with customers after the sale to ensure that they are—and remain—satisfied. Sixth, they must gather customer ideas for product and service improvements and convey them to the appropriate company departments. When marketers do all of this, they are making substantial contributions to total quality management and customer satisfaction.

One implication of TQM is that marketing people must spend time and effort not only to improve *external marketing* but also to improve *internal marketing*. The marketer must complain like the customer complains when the product or the service is not right. Marketing must be the customer's watchdog or guardian, constantly holding up the standard of "giving the customer the best solution." In customer-centered companies, this attitude permeates every aspect of the planning process, the subject of the next chapter.

EXECUTIVE SUMMARY

Customers are value-maximizers. They will buy from the firm they perceive offers the highest *customer delivered value,* defined as the difference between total customer value and total customer cost. Sellers who are at a delivered-value disadvantage can either try to increase total customer value or decrease total customer cost.

Satisfaction is a function of the product's perceived performance and the buyer's expectations. The key to high customer loyalty is to deliver higher customer satisfaction, so many companies are aiming for total customer satisfaction. Companies that reach their customer value and satisfaction goals are high-performance businesses. These firms recognize the dynamic relationship connecting their stakeholder groups and the need for managing core business processes. They also own and nurture their core competencies, which lead to distinctive capabilities that build competitive advantage. Finally, their structures, policies, and corporate culture are focused on delivering customer value and satisfaction.

The value chain identifies nine strategically relevant activities that create value and cost in a business. The five core business processes are new-product realization, inventory management, customer acquisition and retention, order-to-remittance, and customer service. Managing these core processes means creating a value-delivery network or marketing network in which the company works with the value chains of its suppliers and distributors. Companies no longer compete—marketing networks do.

Losing profitable customers can dramatically affect profits, so companies need to examine the percentage of customers who defect. Winning back lost customers is an important marketing activity, and often costs less than attracting first-time customers. In addition, the cost of attracting a new customer is estimated to be five times the cost of keeping a current customer happy. They key to retaining customers is relationship marketing. Five levels of investment in customer-relationship building are basic, reactive, accountable, proactive, and partnership marketing. Three ways to build stronger customer bonds are by adding financial benefits, adding social benefits, and adding structural benefits.

Marketing is the art of attracting and keeping profitable customers, but companies should not aim to pursue and satisfy all customers. Building sustainable and meaningful customer advantages to deliver high customer value and satisfaction helps firms strengthen customer loyalty and boost profitability.

Total quality management (TQM) is an organizationwide approach to continually improving the quality of all processes, products, and services. Quality is the totality of features and characteristics of a product that bear on its ability to satisfy stated or implied needs. Today's companies must implement TQM to remain profitable, because total quality is vital to value creation and customer satisfaction. Marketing managers must participate in formulating strategies and policies for quality excellence; they must also deliver marketing quality alongside production quality.

NOTES

1. "Mac Attacks," *USA Today;* March 23, 1998, p. B1; David Leonhardt, "Getting Off Their McButts," *Business Week,* February 22, 1999, bwarchive.businessweek.com.
2. See Irwin P. Levin and Richard D. Johnson, "Estimating Price-Quality Tradeoffs Using Comparative Judgments," *Journal of Consumer Research,* June 11, 1984, pp. 593–600.
3. Michael J. Lanning, *Delivering Profitable Value* (Oxford, UK: Capstone, 1998).

4. Simon Knox and Stan Maklan, *Competing on Value: Bridging the Gap Between Brand and Customer Value* (London, UK: Financial Times, 1998). See also Richard A. Spreng, Scott B. MacKenzie, and Richard W. Olshawskiy, "A Reexamination of the Determinants of Consumer Satisfaction," *Journal of Marketing,* no. 3 (July 1996): 15–32.

5. Evan Ramstad, "Dell Fights PC Wars by Emphasizing Customer Service," *Wall Street Journal,* 15 August 1997, p. B4.

6. See Tamara J. Erickson and C. Everett Shorey, "Business Strategy: New Thinking for the 90s," *Prism,* Fourth Quarter 1992, pp. 19–35.

7. See Robert S. Kaplan and David P. Norton, *The Balanced Scorecard: Translating Strategy Into Action* (Boston: Harvard Business School Press, 1996), as a tool for monitoring stakeholder satisfaction.

8. See Jon R. Katzenbach and Douglas K. Smith, *The Wisdom of Teams: Creating the High-Performance Organization* (Boston: Harvard Business School Press, 1993) and Michael Hammer and James Champy, *Reengineering the Corporation* (New York: HarperBusiness, 1993).

9. Leonard L. Berry, *Discovering the Soul of Service* (New York: Free Press, 1999), pp. 188–89; David Glines, "Do You Work in a Zoo?" *Executive Excellence,* 11, no. 10 (October 1994): 12–13.

10. C. K. Prahalad and Gary Hamel, "The Core Competence of the Corporation," *Harvard Business Review,* May-June 1990, pp. 79–91.

11. "Business: Microsoft's Contradiction," *The Economist,* January 31, 1998, pp. 65–67; Andrew J. Glass, "Microsoft Pushes Forward, Playing to Win the Market," *Atlanta Constitution,* June 24, 1998, p. D12; Ron Chernow, "The Burden of Being a Misunderstood Monopolist," *Business Week,* November 22, 1999, p. 42.

12. Michael E. Porter, *Competitive Advantage: Creating and Sustaining Superior Performance* (New York: Free Press, 1985).

13. Hammer and Champy, *Reengineering the Corporation.*

14. Myron Magnet, "The New Golden Rule of Business," *Fortune,* November 28, 1994, pp. 60–64.

15. See Jeffrey Gitomer, *Customer Satisfaction Is Worthless: Customer Loyalty Is Priceless: How to Make Customers Love You, Keep Them Coming Back and Tell Everyone They Know* (Austin, TX: Bard Press, 1998).

16. See Frederick F. Reichheld, "Learning from Customer Defections," *Harvard Business Review,* March-April 1996, pp. 56–69.

17. Ibid.

18. Ibid.

19. See *Technical Assistance Research Programs (TARP),* U.S. Office of Consumer Affairs Study on Complaint Handling in America, 1986.

20. Karl Albrecht and Ron Zemke, *Service America!* (Homewood IL: Dow Jones-Irwin, 1985), pp. 6–7.

21. Courtesy L.L. Bean, Freeport, Maine.

22. Ibid.

23. See Frederick F. Reichheld, *The Loyalty Effect* (Boston: Harvard Business School Press, 1996).

24. Leonard L. Berry and A. Parasuraman, *Marketing Services: Competing Through Quality* (New York: Free Press, 1991), pp. 136–42. See also Richard Cross and Janet Smith, *Customer Bonding: Pathways to Lasting Customer Loyalty* (Lincolnwood, IL: NTC Business Books, 1995).

25. Stephan A. Butscher, "Welcome to the Club: Building Customer Loyalty," *Marketing News,* September 9, 1996, p. 9; Justin Doebele, "In Privacy They Thrive," *Forbes Global,* December 13, 1999, www.forbes.com/forbesglobal/99/1213/0225076a.htm.

26. Constance L. Hays, "What Companies Need to Know Is in the Pizza Dough," *New York Times,* July 26, 1998, p. 3.

27. James H. Donnelly Jr., Leonard L. Berry, and Thomas W. Thompson, *Marketing Financial Services—A Strategic Vision* (Homewood, IL: Dow Jones-Irwin, 1985), p. 113.

28. Quoted in Don Peppers and Martha Rogers, *The One to One Future: Building Relationships One Customer at a Time* (New York: Currency Doubleday, 1993), p. 108.

29. Carl Sewell and Paul Brown, *Customers for Life* (New York: Pocket Books, 1990), p. 162.

30. William A. Sherden, *Market Ownership: The Art & Science of Becoming #1* (New York: Amacom, 1994), p. 77.

31. Robert J. Bowman, "Good Things, Smaller Packages," *World Trade* 6, no. 9 (October 1993): 106–10.

32. Michael J. Lanning and Lynn W. Phillips, "Strategy Shifts Up a Gear," *Marketing,* October 1991, p. 9.

33. Lynn O'Rourke Hayes, "Quality Is Worth 11,000 in the Bank," *Restaurant Hospitality,* March 1993, p. 68.

34. See Thomas M. Petro, "Profitability: The Fifth P of Marketing," *Bank Marketing,* September 1990, pp. 48–52; and Petro, "Who Are Your Best Customers?" *Bank Marketing,* October 1990, pp. 48–52.

35. "Quality: The U.S. Drives to Catch Up," Business Week, November 1982, pp. 66–80, here p. 68. For a more recent assessment of progress, see "Quality Programs Show Shoddy Results," *Wall Street Journal,* May 14, 1992, p. B1. See also Roland R. Rust, Anthony J. Zahorik, and Timothy L. Keiningham, "Return on Quality (ROQ): Making Service Quality Financially Accountable," *Journal of Marketing* 59, no. 2 (April 1995): 58–70.

36. See "Quality in Europe," *Work Study,* January-February 1993, p. 30; Ronald Henkoff, "The Hot New Seal of Quality," *Fortune,* June 28, 1993, pp. 116–20; Amy Zukerman, "One Size Doesn't Fit All," *Industry Week,* January 9, 1995, pp. 37–40; and "The Sleeper Issue of the 90s," *Industry Week,* August 15, 1994, pp. 99–100, 108.

37. Robert D. Buzzell and Bradley T. Gale, *The PIMS Principles: Linking Strategy to Performance* (New York: Free Press, 1987), ch. 6.

38. See Cyndee Miller, "U.S. Firms Lag in Meeting Global Quality Standards," *Marketing News,* February 15, 1993.

39. J. Daniel Beckham, "Expect the Unexpected in Health Care Marketing Future," *The Academy Bulletin,* July 1992, p. 3.

Winning Markets Through Strategic Planning, Implementation, and Control

In this chapter, we will address the following questions:

- How is strategic planning carried out at the corporate, division, and business-unit levels?
- What are the major steps in planning the marketing process?
- How can a company effectively manage the marketing process?

In chapters 1 and 2, we addressed the question: How do companies compete in a global marketplace? One part of the answer is a commitment to creating and retaining satisfied customers. We can now add a second part: Successful companies know how to adapt to a continuously changing marketplace through strategic planning and careful management of the marketing process.

In most large companies, corporate headquarters is responsible for designing a corporate *strategic plan* to guide the whole enterprise and deciding about resource allocations as well as starting and eliminating particular businesses. Guided by the corporate strategic plan, each division establishes a *division plan* for each business unit within the division; in turn, each business unit develops a *business unit strategic plan*. Finally, the managers of each product line and brand within a business unit develop a *marketing plan* for achieving their objectives.

However, the development of a marketing plan is not the end of the marketing process. High-performance firms must hone their expertise in organizing, implementing, and controlling marketing activities as they follow marketing results closely, diagnose problems, and take corrective action when necessary. In today's fast-paced business world, the ability to effectively manage the marketing process—beginning to end—has become an extremely important competitive advantage.

CORPORATE AND DIVISION STRATEGIC PLANNING

Marketing plays a critical role in corporate strategic planning within successful companies. **Market-oriented strategic planning** is the managerial process of developing and maintaining a viable fit among the organization's objectives, skills, and resources and its changing market opportunities. The aim of strategic planning is to shape the company's businesses and products so that they yield target profits and growth and keep the company healthy despite any unexpected threats that may arise.

Strategic planning calls for action in three key areas. The first area is managing a company's businesses as an investment portfolio. The second area involves assessing each business's strength by considering the market's growth rate and the company's position and fit in that market. And the third area is the development of *strategy*, a game plan for achieving long-term objectives. The complete strategic planning, implementation, and control cycle is shown in Figure 3.1.

Corporate headquarters starts the strategic planning process by preparing statements of mission, policy, strategy, and goals, establishing the framework within which the divisions and business units will prepare their plans. Some corporations allow their business units a great deal of freedom in setting sales and profit goals and strategies. Others set goals for their business units but let them develop their own strategies. Still others set the goals and get involved heavily in the individual business unit strategies.[1] Regardless of the degree of involvement, all strategic plans are based on the corporate mission.

Defining the Corporate Mission

An organization exists to accomplish something: to make cars, lend money, provide a night's lodging, and so on. Its specific mission or purpose is usually clear when the business starts. Over time, however, the mission may lose its relevance because of changed market conditions or may become unclear as the corporation adds new products and markets.

When management senses that the organization is drifting from its mission, it must renew its search for purpose. According to Peter Drucker, it is time to ask some fundamental questions.[2] *What is our business? Who is the customer? What is of value to the customer? What will our business be? What should our business be?* Successful companies continuously raise these questions and answer them thoughtfully and thoroughly.

Figure 3.1   The Strategic Planning, Implementation, and Control Process

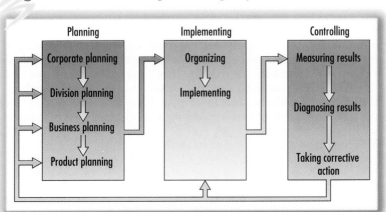

A well-worked-out mission statement provides employees with a shared sense of purpose, direction, and opportunity. It also guides geographically dispersed employees to work independently and yet collectively toward realizing the organization's goals. The mission statement of Motorola, for example, is "to honorably serve the needs of the community by providing products and services of superior quality at a fair price to our customers; to do this so as to earn an adequate profit which is required for the total enterprise to grow; and by so doing provide the opportunity for our employees and shareholders to achieve their reasonable personal objectives."

Good mission statements focus on a limited number of goals, stress the company's major policies and values, and define the company's major *competitive scopes.* These include:

➤ *Industry scope:* The industry or range of industries in which a company will operate. For example, DuPont operates in the industrial market; Dow operates in the industrial and consumer markets; and 3M will go into almost any industry where it can make money.

➤ *Products and applications scope:* The range of products and applications that a company will supply. St. Jude Medical aims to "serve physicians worldwide with high-quality products for cardiovascular care."

➤ *Competence scope:* The range of technological and other core competencies that a company will master and leverage. Japan's NEC has built its core competencies in computing, communications, and components to support production of laptop computers, televisions, and other electronics items.

➤ *Market-segment scope:* The type of market or customers a company will serve. For example, Porsche makes only expensive cars for the upscale market and licenses its name for high-quality accessories.

➤ *Vertical scope:* The number of channel levels from raw material to final product and distribution in which a company will participate. At one extreme are companies with a large vertical scope; at the other extreme are firms with low or no vertical integration that may outsource design, manufacture, marketing, and physical distribution.[3]

➤ *Geographical scope:* The range of regions or countries in which a company will operate. At one extreme are companies that operate in a specific city or state. At the other extreme are multinationals such as Unilever and Caterpillar, which operate in almost every one of the world's countries.

A company must redefine its mission if that mission has lost credibility or no longer defines an optimal course for the company.[4] Kodak redefined itself from a film company to an image company so that it could add digital imaging;[5] Sara Lee redefined itself by outsourcing manufacturing and becoming a marketer of brands. The corporate mission provides direction for the firm's various business units.

Establishing Strategic Business Units

A business can be defined in terms of three dimensions: *customer groups, customer needs,* and *technology.*[6] For example, a company that defines its business as designing incandescent lighting systems for television studios would have television studios as its customer group; lighting as its customer need; and incandescent lighting as its technology.

In line with Levitt's argument that market definitions of a business are superior to product definitions,[7] these three dimensions describe the business in terms of a customer-satisfying process, not a goods-producing process. Thus, Xerox's product definition would be "We make copying equipment," while its market definition would be "We help improve office productivity." Similarly, Missouri-Pacific Railroad's product definition would be "We run a railroad," while its market definition would be "We are a people-and-goods mover."

Large companies normally manage quite different businesses, each requiring its own strategy; General Electric, as one example, has established 49 *strategic business units (SBUs)*. An SBU has three characteristics: (1) It is a single business or collection of related businesses that can be planned separately from the rest of the company; (2) it has its own set of competitors; and (3) it has a manager responsible for strategic planning and profit performance who controls most of the factors affecting profit.

Assigning Resources to SBUs

The purpose of identifying the company's strategic business units is to develop separate strategies and assign appropriate funding to the entire business portfolio. Senior managers generally apply analytical tools to classify all of their SBUs according to profit potential. Two of the best-known business portfolio evaluation models are the Boston Consulting Group model and the General Electric model.[8]

The Boston Consulting Group Approach

The Boston Consulting Group (BCG), a leading management consulting firm, developed and popularized the *growth-share matrix* shown in Figure 3.2. The eight circles represent the current sizes and positions of eight business units in a hypothetical company. The dollar-volume size of each business is proportional to the circle's area. Thus, the two largest businesses are 5 and 6. The location of each business unit indicates its market growth rate and relative market share.

The *market growth rate* on the vertical axis indicates the annual growth rate of the market in which the business operates. *Relative market share,* which is measured on the horizontal axis, refers to the SBU's market share relative to that of its largest competitor in the segment. It serves as a measure of the company's strength in the relevant market segment. The growth-share matrix is divided into four cells, each indicating a different type of business:

➤ *Question marks* are businesses that operate in high-growth markets but have low relative market shares. Most businesses start off as question marks as the company tries to enter a high-growth market in which there is already a market leader. A question mark requires a lot of cash because the company is spending money on plant, equipment, and personnel. The term *question mark* is appropriate because the company has to think hard about whether to keep pouring money into this business.

➤ *Stars* are market leaders in a high-growth market. A star was once a question mark, but it does not necessarily produce positive cash flow; the company must still spend to keep up with the high market growth and fight off competition.

➤ *Cash cows* are former stars with the largest relative market share in a slow-growth market. A cash cow produces a lot of cash for the company (due to economies of scale and higher profit margins), paying the company's bills and supporting its other businesses.

➤ *Dogs* are businesses with weak market shares in low-growth markets; typically, these generate low profits or even losses.

After plotting its various businesses in the growth-share matrix, a company must determine whether the portfolio is healthy. An unbalanced portfolio would have too many

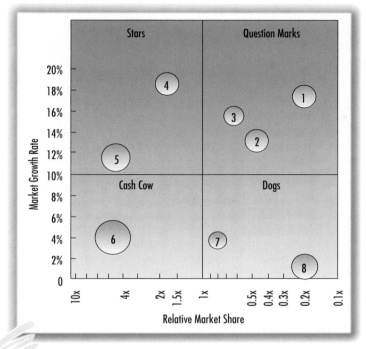

Figure 3.2   The Boston Consulting Group's Growth-Share Matrix

dogs or question marks or too few stars and cash cows. The next task is to determine what objective, strategy, and budget to assign to each SBU. Four strategies can be pursued:

1. *Build:* The objective here is to increase market share, even forgoing short-term earnings to achieve this objective if necessary. Building is appropriate for question marks whose market shares must grow if they are to become stars.

2. *Hold:* The objective in a hold strategy is to preserve market share, an appropriate strategy for strong cash cows if they are to continue yielding a large positive cash flow.

3. *Harvest:* The objective here is to increase short-term cash flow regardless of long-term effect. Harvesting involves a decision to withdraw from a business by implementing a program of continuous cost retrenchment. The hope is to reduce costs faster than any potential drop in sales, thus boosting cash flow. This strategy is appropriate for weak cash cows whose future is dim and from which more cash flow is needed. Harvesting can also be used with question marks and dogs.

4. *Divest:* The objective is to sell or liquidate the business because the resources can be better used elsewhere. This is appropriate for dogs and question marks that are dragging down company profits.

Successful SBUs move through a life cycle, starting as question marks and becoming stars, then cash cows, and finally dogs. Given this life-cycle movement, companies should be aware not only of their SBUs' current positions in the growth-share matrix (as in a snapshot), but also of their moving positions (as in a motion picture). If an SBU's expected future trajectory is not satisfactory, the corporation will need to work out a new strategy to improve the likely trajectory.

The General Electric Model

An SBU's appropriate objective cannot be determined solely by its position in the growth-share matrix. If additional factors are considered, the growth-share matrix can be seen as a special case of a multifactor portfolio matrix that General Electric (GE) pioneered. In this model, each business is rated in terms of two major dimensions—*market attractiveness* and *business strength*. These two factors make excellent marketing sense for rating a business. Companies are successful to the extent that they enter attractive markets and possess the required business strengths to succeed in those markets. If one of these factors is missing, the business will not produce outstanding results. Neither a strong company operating in an unattractive market nor a weak company operating in an attractive market will do well.

Using these two dimensions, the GE matrix is divided into nine cells, as shown in Figure 3.3. The three cells in the upper-left corner indicate strong SBUs suitable for investment or growth. The diagonal cells stretching from the lower left to the upper right indicate SBUs of medium attractiveness; these should be pursued selectively and managed for earnings. The three cells in the lower-right corner indicate SBUs low in overall attractiveness, which the company may want to harvest or divest.[9]

In addition to identifying each SBU's current position on the matrix, management should also forecast its expected position over the next 3 to 5 years. Making this determination involves analyzing product life cycle, expected competitor strategies,

Figure 3.3   Market-Attractiveness Portfolio Strategies

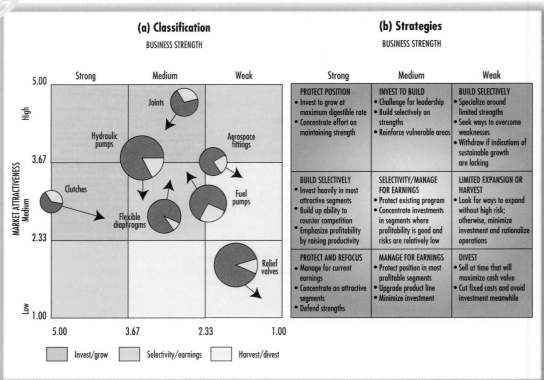

new technologies, economic events, and so on. Again, the purpose is to see where SBUs are as well as where they appear to be headed.

Critique of Portfolio Models

Both the BCG and GE portfolio models have a number of benefits. They can help managers think more strategically, better understand the economics of their SBUs, improve the quality of their plans, improve communication between SBU and corporate management, identify important issues, eliminate weaker SBUs, and strengthen their investment in more promising SBUs.

However, portfolio models must be used cautiously. They may lead a firm to overemphasize market-share growth and entry into high-growth businesses or to neglect its current businesses. Also, the models' results are sensitive to ratings and weights and can be manipulated to produce a desired location in the matrix. Finally, the models fail to delineate the synergies between two or more businesses, which means that making decisions for one business at a time might be risky. There is a danger of terminating a losing SBU that actually provides an essential core competence needed by several other business units. Overall, though, portfolio models have improved managers' analytical and strategic capabilities and allowed them to make better decisions than they could with mere impressions.[10]

Planning New Businesses, Downsizing Older Businesses

Corporate management often desires higher sales and profits than indicated by the projections for the SBU portfolio. The question then becomes how to grow much faster than the current businesses will permit. One option is to identify opportunities to achieve further growth within the company's current businesses (*intensive growth opportunities*). A second option is to identify opportunities to build or acquire businesses that are related to the company's current businesses (*integrative growth opportunities*). A third option is to identify opportunities to add attractive businesses that are unrelated to the company's current businesses (*diversification growth opportunities*).

➤ *Intensive growth.* Ansoff has proposed the *product–market expansion grid* as a framework for detecting new intensive growth opportunities.[11] In this grid, the company first considers whether it could gain more market share with its current products in current markets (*market-penetration strategy*) by encouraging current customers to buy more, attracting competitors' customers, or convincing nonusers to start buying its products. Next it considers whether it can find or develop new markets for its current products (*market-development strategy*). Then it considers whether it can develop new products for its current markets (*product-development strategy*). Later it will also review opportunities to develop new products for new markets (*diversification strategy*).

➤ *Integrative growth.* Often a business's sales and profits can be increased through *backward integration* (acquiring a supplier), *forward integration* (acquiring a distributor), or *horizontal integration* (acquiring a competitor).

➤ *Diversification growth.* This makes sense when good opportunities exist outside the present businesses. Three types of diversification are possible. The company could seek new products that have technological or marketing synergies with existing product lines, even though the new products themselves may appeal to a different group of customers (*concentric diversification strategy*). Second, the company might search for new products that appeal to its current customers but are technologically unrelated to the current product line (*horizontal diversification strategy*). Finally, the company might seek new businesses that have no relationship to the company's current technology, products, or markets (*conglomerate diversification strategy*).

Of course, companies must not only develop new businesses, but also prune, harvest, or divest tired, old businesses in order to release needed resources and reduce costs. Weak businesses require a disproportionate amount of managerial attention; managers should therefore focus on growth opportunities rather than wasting energy and resources trying to save hemorrhaging businesses.

BUSINESS STRATEGIC PLANNING

Below the corporate level, the strategic-planning process for each business or SBU consists of the eight steps shown in Figure 3.4. We examine each step in the sections that follow.

Business Mission

Each business unit needs to define its specific mission within the broader company mission. Thus, a television studio-lighting-equipment company might define its mission as "The company aims to target major television studios and become their vendor of choice for lighting technologies that represent the most advanced and reliable studio lighting arrangements."

SWOT Analysis

The overall evaluation of a business's strengths, weaknesses, opportunities, and threats is called *SWOT analysis*. SWOT analysis consists of an analysis of the external and internal environments.

External Environment Analysis

In general, a business unit has to monitor key *macroenvironment forces* (demographic-economic, technological, political-legal, and social-cultural) and *microenvironment actors* (customers, competitors, distributors, and suppliers) that affect its ability to earn profits (see Chapter 4 for more detail). Then, for each trend or development, management needs to identify the associated marketing opportunities and threats.

A **marketing opportunity** is an area of buyer need in which a company can perform profitably. Opportunities can be classified according to their *attractiveness* and their *success probability*. The company's success probability depends on whether its busi-

Figure 3.4   The Business Strategic-Planning Process

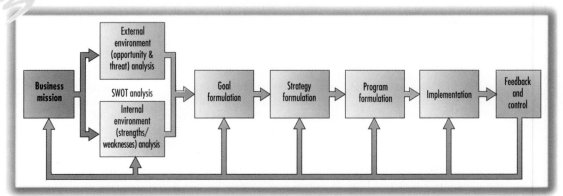

ness strengths not only match the key success requirements for operating in the target market, but also exceed those of its competitors. Mere competence does not constitute a competitive advantage. The best-performing company will be the one that can generate the greatest customer value and sustain it over time.

An **environmental threat** is a challenge posed by an unfavorable external trend or development that would lead, in the absence of defensive marketing action, to deterioration in sales or profit. Threats should be classified according to *seriousness* and *probability of occurrence.* Minor threats can be ignored; somewhat more serious threats must be carefully monitored; and major threats require the development of contingency plans that spell out changes the company can make if necessary.

Internal Environment Analysis

It is one thing to discern attractive opportunities and another to have the competencies to succeed in these opportunities. Thus, each business needs to periodically evaluate its internal strengths and weaknesses in marketing, financial, manufacturing, and organizational competencies. Clearly, the business does not have to correct all of its weaknesses, nor should it gloat about all of its strengths. The big question is whether the business should limit itself to those opportunities in which it possesses the required strengths or consider better opportunities to acquire or develop certain strengths.

Sometimes a business does poorly because its departments do not work together well as a team. It is therefore critically important to assess interdepartmental working relationships as part of the internal environmental audit. Honeywell, for example, asks each department to annually rate its own strengths and weaknesses and those of the other departments with which it interacts. The notion is that each department is a "supplier" to some departments and a "customer" of other departments. If one department has weaknesses that hurt its "internal customers," Honeywell wants to correct them.

Goal Formulation

Once the company has performed a SWOT analysis of the internal and external environments, it can proceed to develop specific goals for the planning period in a process called *goal formulation.* Managers use the term *goals* to describe objectives that are specific with respect to magnitude and time. Turning objectives into measurable goals facilitates management planning, implementation, and control.

To be effective, goals must (1) be arranged *hierarchically* to guide the businesses in moving from broad to specific objectives for departments and individuals; (2) be stated *quantitatively* whenever possible; (3) be *realistic;* and (4) be *consistent.* Other important trade-offs in setting goals include: balancing short-term profit versus long-term growth; balancing deep penetration of existing markets with development of new markets; balancing profit goals versus nonprofit goals; and balancing high growth versus low risk. Each choice in this set of goal trade-offs calls for a different marketing strategy.

Strategy Formulation

Goals indicate what a business unit wants to achieve; *strategy* describes the game plan for achieving those goals. Every business strategy consists of a marketing strategy plus a compatible technology strategy and sourcing strategy. Although many types of marketing strategies are available, Michael Porter has condensed them into three generic types that provide a good starting point for strategic thinking: overall cost leadership, differentiation, or focus.[12]

> ➤ *Overall cost leadership:* Here the business works to achieve the lowest production and distribution costs so that it can price lower than competitors and win more market

share. Firms pursuing this strategy must be good at engineering, purchasing, manufacturing, and physical distribution; they need less skill in marketing. Texas Instruments uses this strategy. The problem is that rivals may emerge with still lower costs, hurting a firm that has rested its whole future on cost leadership.

➤ *Differentiation:* Here the business concentrates on achieving superior performance in an important customer benefit area, such as being the leader in service, quality, style, or technology—but not leading in all of these things. Intel, for instance, differentiates itself through leadership in technology, coming out with new microprocessors at breakneck speed.

➤ *Focus:* Here the business focuses on one or more narrow market segments, getting to know these segments intimately and pursuing either cost leadership or differentiation within the target segment. Airwalk shoes, for instance, came to fame by focusing on the very narrow extreme-sports segment.

Firms that do not pursue a clear strategy—"middle-of-the-roaders"—do the worst. International Harvester fell upon hard times because it did not stand out as lowest in cost, highest in perceived value, or best in serving some market segment. Middle-of-the-roaders try to be good on all strategic dimensions, but because strategic dimensions require different and often inconsistent ways of organizing the firm, these firms end up being not particularly excellent at anything.

Strategy formulation in the age of the Internet is particularly challenging. The chemical company Solutia, a Monsanto spinoff, copes by creating four different, possible short-term scenarios for each strategy. This allows the firm to act quickly when it sees a scenario unfolding. Sun Microsystems holds a weekly meeting with the firm's top decision makers to brainstorm strategies for handling new threats. By revisiting strategic plans frequently, both companies are able to stay ahead of environmental changes.[13]

Program Formulation

Once the business unit has developed its principal strategies, it must work out detailed supporting programs. Thus, if the business has decided to attain technological leadership, it must plan programs to strengthen its R&D department, gather technological intelligence, develop leading-edge products, train the technical sales force, and develop ads to communicate its technological leadership.

After these marketing programs have been tentatively formulated, the marketing people must estimate their costs. Questions arise: Is participating in a particular trade show worth it? Will a specific sales contest pay for itself? Will hiring another salesperson contribute to the bottom line? Activity-based cost (ABC) accounting should be applied to each marketing program to determine whether it is likely to produce sufficient results to justify the cost.[14]

Implementation

A clear strategy and well-thought-out supporting programs may be useless if the firm fails to implement them carefully. Indeed, strategy is only one of seven elements, according to McKinsey & Company, that the best-managed companies exhibit.[15] In the McKinsey 7-S framework for business success, strategy, structure, and systems are considered the "hardware" of success, and style (how employees think and behave), skills (to carry out the strategy), staff (able people who are properly trained and assigned), and shared values (values that guide employees' actions) are the "software." When these software elements are present, companies are usually more successful at strategy implementation.[16] Implementation is vital to effective management of the marketing process, as discussed later in this chapter.

Feedback and Control

As it implements its strategy, the firm needs to track the results and monitor new developments in the internal and external environments. Some environments are fairly stable from year to year. Other environments evolve slowly in a fairly predictable way. Still other environments change rapidly in significant and unpredictable ways. Nonetheless, the company can count on one thing: The marketplace will change. And when it does, the company will need to review and revise its implementation, programs, strategies, or even objectives.

A company's strategic fit with the environment will inevitably erode because the market environment changes faster than the company's 7-Ss. Thus a company might remain efficient while it loses effectiveness. Peter Drucker pointed out that it is more important to "do the right thing" (effectiveness) than "to do things right" (efficiency). The most successful companies excel at both.

Once an organization fails to respond to a changed environment, it has difficulty recapturing its lost position. This happened to the once-unassailable Motorola when it was slow to respond to the new digital technology used by Nokia and others, and kept rolling out analog phones.[17] Similarly, Barnes & Noble did not immediately recognize the threat posed by Amazon.com's Internet-based book retailing model; then, as a latecomer to e-commerce, it had more of a struggle establishing itself. Clearly, the key to organizational health is the firm's willingness to examine the changing environment and to adopt appropriate new goals and behaviors. High-performance organizations continuously monitor the environment and use flexible strategic planning to maintain a viable fit with the evolving environment.

THE MARKETING PROCESS

Planning at the corporate, division, and business levels is an integral part of planning for the marketing process. To understand that process fully, we must first look at how a company defines its business.

The task of any business is to deliver value to the market at a profit. There are at least two views of the *value-delivery process*.[18] The traditional view is that the firm makes something and then sells it (Figure 3.5a). In this view, marketing takes place in the second half of the value-delivery process. The traditional view assumes that the company knows what to make and that the market will buy enough units to produce profits for the company.

Companies that subscribe to this traditional view have the best chance of succeeding in economies marked by goods shortages in which consumers are not fussy about quality, features, or style. But the traditional view of the business process will not work in more competitive economies in which people face abundant choices. The "mass market" is actually splintering into numerous micromarkets, each with its own wants, perceptions, preferences, and buying criteria. The smart competitor therefore must design the offer for well-defined target markets.

The Value-Delivery Sequence

This belief is at the core of the new view of business processes, which places marketing at the beginning of the planning process. Instead of emphasizing making and selling, companies see themselves involved in a three-phase value creation and delivery sequence (Figure 3.5b).

The first phase, choosing the value, represents the strategic "homework" that marketing must do before any product exists. The marketing staff must segment the market, select the appropriate market target, and develop the offer's value position-

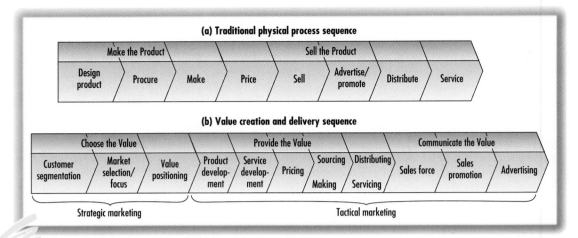

Figure 3.5 Two Views of the Value-Delivery Process

ing. In the second phase, providing the value, marketers detail the product's specifications and services, set a target price, then make and distribute the product. Developing specific product features, prices, and distribution occurs at this stage and is part of *tactical marketing.* The task in the third phase is communicating the value. Here, further tactical marketing occurs in utilizing the sales force, sales promotion, advertising, and other promotional tools to inform the market about the product. Thus, as Figure 3.5b shows, the marketing process actually begins before there is a product and continues while it is being developed and after it becomes available.

Steps in the Marketing Process

The **marketing process** consists of analyzing market opportunities, researching and selecting target markets, designing marketing strategies, planning marketing programs, and organizing, implementing, and controlling the marketing effort. The four steps in the marketing process are:

1. *Analyzing market opportunities.* The marketer's initial task is to identify potential long-run opportunities given the company's market experience and core competencies. To evaluate its various opportunities, assess buyer wants and needs, and gauge market size, the firm needs a marketing research and information system (see Chapter 4). Next, the firm studies consumer markets (Chapter 5) or business markets (Chapter 6) to find out about buying behavior, perceptions, wants, and needs. Smart firms also pay close attention to competitors (Chapter 7) and look for major segments within each market that they can profitably serve (Chapter 8).

2. *Developing marketing strategies.* In this step, the marketer prepares a *positioning* strategy for each new and existing product's progress through the life cycle (Chapter 9), makes decisions about product lines and branding (Chapter 10), and designs and markets its services (Chapter 11).

3. *Planning marketing programs.* To transform marketing strategy into marketing programs, marketing managers must make basic decisions on marketing expenditures, marketing mix, and marketing allocation. The first decision is about the level of marketing expenditures needed to achieve the firm's marketing objectives. The second

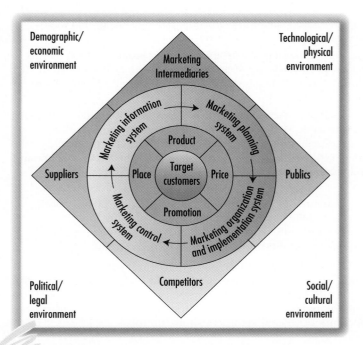

Figure 3.6   Factors Influencing Company Marketing Strategy

decision is how to divide the total marketing budget among the various tools in the marketing mix: *product, price, place,* and *promotion* (Chapters 9 through 17).[19] And the third decision is how to allocate the marketing budget to the various products, channels, promotion media, and sales areas.

4. *Managing the marketing effort.* In this step (discussed later in this chapter), marketers organize the firm's marketing resources to implement and control the marketing plan. Because of surprises and disappointments as marketing plans are implemented, the company also needs feedback and control.

Figure 3.6 presents a grand summary of the marketing process and the factors that shape the company's marketing strategy.

The Nature and Contents of a Marketing Plan

The *marketing plan* created for each product line or brand is one of the most important outputs of planning for the marketing process. A typical marketing plan has eight sections:

➤ *Executive summary and table of contents:* This brief summary outlines the plan's main goals and recommendations; it is followed by a table of contents.

➤ *Current marketing situation:* This section presents relevant background data on sales, costs, profits, the market, competitors, distribution, and the macroenvironment, drawn from a fact book maintained by the product manager.

➤ *Opportunity and issue analysis:* This section identifies the major opportunities and threats, strengths and weaknesses, and issues facing the product line or brand.

➤ *Objectives:* This section spells out the financial and marketing objectives to be achieved.

➤ *Marketing strategy:* This section explains the broad marketing strategy that will be implemented to accomplish the plan's objectives.

➤ *Action programs:* This section outlines the broad marketing programs for achieving the business objectives. Each marketing strategy element must be elaborated to answer these questions: What will be done? When will it be done? Who will do it? How much will it cost?

➤ *Projected profit-and-loss statement:* Action plans allow the product manager to build a supporting budget with forecasted sales volume (units and average price), costs (production, physical distribution, and marketing), and projected profit. Once approved, the budget is the basis for developing plans and schedules for material procurement, production scheduling, employee recruitment, and marketing operations.

➤ *Controls:* This last section outlines the controls for monitoring the plan. Typically, the goals and budget are spelled out for each month or quarter so senior management can review the results each period. Sometimes contingency plans for handling specific adverse developments are included.

No two companies handle marketing planning and marketing plan content exactly the same way. Most marketing plans cover one year and vary in length; some firms take their plans very seriously, while others use them as only a rough guide to action. The most frequently cited shortcomings of marketing plans, according to marketing executives, are lack of realism, insufficient competitive analysis, and a short-run focus.

MANAGING THE MARKETING PROCESS

In addition to updating their marketing plans, companies often need to restructure business and marketing practices in response to major environmental changes such as globalization, deregulation, computer and telecommunications advances, and market fragmentation. Against this dynamic backdrop, the role of marketing in the organization must change as well. Now that the enterprise is fully networked, every functional area can interact directly with customers. This means that marketing no longer has sole ownership of customer interactions; rather, marketing needs to integrate all the customer-facing processes so that customers see a single face and hear a single voice when they interact with the firm. To accomplish this requires careful structuring of the marketing organization.

Organization of the Marketing Department

Modern marketing departments take numerous forms. The marketing department may be organized according to function, geographic area, products, or customer markets. Global organization is another consideration for firms that market goods or services in other countries.

Functional Organization

The most common form of marketing organization consists of functional specialists (such as the sales manager and marketing research manager) who report to a marketing vice president, who coordinates their activities. The main advantage of a functional marketing organization is its administrative simplicity. However, this form loses effectiveness as products and markets increase. First, a functional organization often leads to inadequate planning for specific products and markets because products that are not favored by anyone are neglected. Second, each functional group competes with the other functions for budget and status. Therefore, the marketing vice president constantly has to weigh the claims of competing functional specialists and faces a difficult coordination problem.

Geographic Organization

A company selling in a national market often organizes its sales force (and sometimes other functions, including marketing) along geographic lines. The national sales manager may supervise four regional sales managers, who each supervise six zone managers, who in turn supervise eight district sales managers, who supervise 10 sales people. Several companies are now adding *area market specialists* (regional or local marketing managers) to support the sales efforts in high-volume, distinctive markets. For example, McDonald's now spends about 50 percent of its advertising budget regionally, and Anheuser-Bush has subdivided its regional markets into ethnic and demographic segments, with different ad campaigns for each.

Product- or Brand-Management Organization

Companies that produce a variety of products and brands often establish a product- (or brand-) management organization as another layer of management within the marketing function. A product manager supervises product category managers, who in turn supervise specific product and brand managers. A product-management organization makes sense if the firm's products are quite different, or if the sheer number of products is beyond the ability of a functional marketing organization to handle.

In both consumer and industrial markets, product and brand managers are responsible for product planning and strategy; preparing annual marketing plans and sales forecasts; working with advertising and merchandising agencies to create programs and campaigns; stimulating support among sales reps and distributors; ongoing research into product performance, customer and dealer attitudes, opportunities and threats; and initiating product improvements to meet changing market needs.

The product-management organization allows the product manager to concentrate on developing a cost-effective marketing mix for each product, to react more quickly to marketplace changes, and to watch over smaller brands. On the other hand, it can lead to conflict and frustration when product managers are not given enough authority to carry out their responsibilities effectively. In addition, product managers become experts in their product but rarely achieve functional expertise. And appointing product managers and associate product managers for even minor products can bloat payroll costs. Finally, brand managers normally move up in a few years to another brand or transfer to another company, leading to short-term thinking that plays havoc with long-term brand building.

To counter these disadvantages, some companies have switched from product managers to product teams. For example, Hallmark uses a triangular marketing team consisting of a market manager (the leader), a marketing manager, and a distribution manager; 3M uses a horizontal product team consisting of a team leader and representatives from sales, marketing, laboratory, engineering, accounting, and marketing research.

Another alternative is to introduce *category management,* in which a company focuses on product categories to manage its brands. Kraft has changed from a classic brand-management structure, in which each brand competed for resources and market share, to a category-based structure in which category business directors (or "product integrators") lead cross-functional teams of representatives from marketing, R&D, consumer promotion, and finance. These category teams work with process teams dedicated to each product category and with customer teams dedicated to each major customer.[20] Still, category management is essentially product-driven, which is why Colgate recently moved from brand management (Colgate toothpaste) to category management (toothpaste category) to a new stage called "customer-need management" (mouth care). This last step finally focuses the organization on a basic customer need.[21]

Market-Management Organization

Many companies sell their products to a diverse set of markets; Canon, for instance, sells fax machines to consumer, business, and government markets. When customers fall into different user groups with distinct buying preferences and practices, a market management organization is desirable. A *markets manager* supervises several *market managers* (also called *market-development managers, market specialists,* or *industry specialists*). The market managers draw upon functional services as needed or may even have functional specialists reporting to them.

Market managers are staff (not line) people, with duties similar to those of product managers. This system has many of the same advantages and disadvantages of product management systems. Its strongest advantage is that the marketing activity is organized to meet the needs of distinct customer groups. This is why Xerox converted from geographic selling to selling by industry, as did IBM, which recently reorganized its employees into 14 customer-focused divisions. In fact, several studies have confirmed the value of market-centered organization: Slater and Narver found a substantial positive effect of market orientation on both commodity and noncommodity businesses.[22]

Product-Management/Market-Management Organization

Companies that produce many products that flow into many markets tend to adopt a *matrix organization.* Consider DuPont, a pioneer in developing the matrix structure. Its textile fibers department consists of separate product managers for rayon and other fibers plus separate market managers for menswear and other markets. The product managers plan the sales and profits for their respective fibers, each seeking to expand the use of his or her fiber; the market managers seek to meet their market's needs rather than push a particular fiber. Ultimately, the sales forecasts from the market managers and the product managers should add to the same grand total.

A matrix organization would seem desirable in a multiproduct, multimarket company. However, this system is costly and often creates conflicts as well as questions about authority and responsibility. By the early 1980s, a number of companies had abandoned matrix management. But matrix management has resurfaced and is again flourishing in the form of "business teams" staffed with full-time specialists reporting to one team boss. The major difference is that companies today provide the right context in which a matrix can thrive—an emphasis on flat, lean team organizations focused around business processes that cut horizontally across functions.[23]

Corporate-Divisional Organization

As multiproduct-multimarket companies grow, they often convert their larger product or market groups into separate divisions with their own departments and services. This raises the question of what marketing services and activities should be retained at corporate headquarters. Some corporations leave marketing to each division; some have a small corporate marketing staff; and some prefer to maintain a strong corporate marketing staff.

The potential contribution of a corporate marketing staff varies in different stages of the company's evolution. Most companies begin with weak marketing in their divisions and often establish a corporate staff to bring stronger marketing into the divisions through training and other services. Some members of corporate marketing might be transferred to head divisional marketing departments. As divisions become strong in their marketing, corporate marketing has less to offer them. Some companies then decide corporate marketing has done its job and proceed to eliminate the department.[24]

Global Organization

Companies that market internationally can organize in three ways. Those just going global may start by establishing an *export department* with a sales manager and a few assistants (and limited marketing services). As they go after global business more aggressively, they can create an *international division* with functional specialists (including marketing) and operating units structured geographically, according to product, or as international subsidiaries. Finally, companies that become truly *global organizations* have top corporate management and staff plan worldwide operations, marketing policies, financial flows, and logistical systems. In these organizations, the global operating units report directly to top management, not to the head of an international division.

Building a Companywide Marketing Orientation

Many companies are beginning to realize that their organizations are not really market- and customer-driven—they are product or sales driven. Companies such as Baxter, General Motors, and Shell are working hard to reorganize themselves into true market-driven companies. The task is not easy: it requires changes in job and department definitions, responsibilities, incentives, and relationships.

To create a market- and customer-focused company, the CEO must: convince senior managers of the need to be more customer-focused; appoint a senior marketing officer and marketing task force; get outside help and guidance; change reward measurement and system to encourage actions that build long-term customer satisfaction; hire strong marketing talent; develop strong in-house marketing training programs; install a modern marketing planning system; establish an annual marketing excellence recognition program; consider restructuring as a market-centered organization; and shift from a department focus to a process-outcome focus.

DuPont successfully made the transition from an inward-looking to an outward-looking orientation when it began building a "marketing community" by reorganizing divisions along market lines and holding marketing management training seminars for thousands of managers and employees. The company also established a marketing excellence recognition program and honored employees from around the world who had developed innovative marketing strategies and service improvements.[25] It takes a great deal of planning and patience to get managers to accept customers as the foundation and future of the business—but it can be done, as the DuPont example shows.

Marketing Implementation

Organization is one factor contributing to effective **marketing implementation,** the process that turns marketing plans into action assignments and ensures that such assignments are executed in a manner that accomplishes the plan's stated objectives.[26] This part of the marketing process is critical, because a brilliant strategic marketing plan counts for little if it is not implemented properly. Whereas strategy addresses the *what* and *why* of marketing activities, implementation addresses the *who, where, when,* and *how.* Strategy and implementation are closely related in that one layer of strategy implies certain tactical implementation assignments at a lower level. For example, top management's strategic decision to "harvest" a product must be translated into specific actions and assignments.

Bonoma identified four sets of skills for implementing marketing programs: (1) diagnostic skills (the ability to determine what went wrong); (2) identification of company level (the ability to discern whether problems occurred in the marketing function, the marketing program, or the marketing policy); (3) implementation skills (the ability to budget resources, organize effectively, motivate others); and (4) evaluation skills (the ability to evaluate results).[27] These skills are as vital for nonprofits as they are for businesses, as the Alvin Ailey Dance Theater has discovered.

Like many nonprofit cultural organizations, the company founded by Alvin Ailey in 1958 always seemed to be operating in the red—despite its ability to attract full houses—because of the high costs of mounting a production. But Judith Jameson, the principal dancer who succeeded Ailey as director after his death, has been able to keep the company in the black, thanks largely to her skill at motivating others to carry out marketing efforts. The nonprofit implements its marketing plan through a high-powered board of directors and a group of businesses that want to associate with the Ailey company for their own marketing purposes. For example, Healthsouth Corporation provides free physical therapy to the dancers and benefits from the association when marketing its sports medicine clinics. With an audience that is almost half African American and 43 percent of which is between the ages of 19 and 39, Ailey provides access to an important market for its corporate partners, earning their enthusiastic support.[28]

Evaluating and Controlling the Marketing Process

To deal with the many surprises that occur during the implementation of marketing plans, the marketing department has to monitor and control marketing activities continuously. Table 3.1 lists four types of marketing control needed by companies: annual-plan control, profitability control, efficiency control, and strategic control.

Annual-Plan Control

The purpose of annual-plan control is to ensure that the company achieves the sales, profits, and other goals established in its annual plan. The heart of annual-plan control is the four-step *management by objectives* process in which management (1) sets monthly or quarterly goals; (2) monitors the company's marketplace performance; (3) determines the causes of serious performance deviations; and (4) takes corrective action to close the gaps between goals and performance.

This control model applies to all levels of the organization. Top management sets sales and profit goals for the year that are elaborated into specific goals for each lower level. In turn, each product manager commits to attaining specified levels of sales and costs; each regional district and sales manager and each sales representative also commits to specific goals. Each period, top management reviews and interprets performance results at all levels, using these five tools:

➤ *Sales analysis. Sales analysis* consists of measuring and evaluating actual sales in relation to goals, using two specific tools. *Sales-variance analysis* measures the relative contribution of different factors to a gap in sales performance. *Microsales analysis* looks at specific products, territories, and other elements that failed to produce expected sales. The point of these analyses is to determine what factors (pricing, lower volume, specific territories, etc.) contributed to a failure to meet sales goals.

➤ *Market-share analysis.* Company sales do not reveal how well the company is performing relative to competitors. To do this, management needs to track its market share. Overall market share is the company's sales expressed as a percentage

Table 3.1   Types of Marketing Control

Type of Control	Prime Responsibility	Purpose of Control	Approaches
I. Annual-plan control	Top management Middle management	To examine whether the planned results are being achieved	▪ Sales analysis ▪ Market-share analysis ▪ Marketing expense-to-sales analysis ▪ Financial analysis ▪ Market-based scorecard analysis
II. Profitability control	Marketing controller	To examine where the company is making and losing money	Profitability by: ▪ product ▪ territory ▪ customer ▪ segment ▪ trade channel ▪ order size
III. Efficiency control	Line and staff management Marketing controller	To evaluate and improve the spending efficiency and impact of marketing expenditures	Efficiency of: ▪ sales force ▪ advertising ▪ sales promotion ▪ distribution
IV. Strategic control	Top management Marketing auditor	To examine whether the company is pursuing its best opportunities in markets, products, and channels	▪ Marketiing-effectiveness review ▪ Marketing audit ▪ Marketing excellence review ▪ Company ethical and social responsibility review

of total market sales. Served market share is its sales expressed as a percentage of the total sales to its *served market*—all of the buyers who are able and willing to buy the product. Relative market share can be expressed as market share in relation to the largest competitor; a rise in relative market share means a company is gaining on its leading competitor. A useful way to analyze market-share movements is in terms of customer penetration, customer loyalty, customer selectivity, and price selectivity.

➤ *Marketing expense-to-sales analysis.* This is a key ratio because it allows management to be sure that the company is not overspending to achieve sales goals. Minor fluctuations in the expense-to-sales ratio can be ignored, but major fluctuations are cause for concern.

➤ *Financial analysis.* Management uses financial analysis to identify the factors that affect the company's *rate of return on net worth.*[29] The main factors are shown in Figure 3.7, along with illustrative numbers for a large chain-store retailer. To improve its return on net worth, the company must increase its ratio of net profits to its assets or increase the ratio of its assets to its net worth. The company should analyze the composition of its assets (i.e., cash, accounts receivable, inventory, and plant and equipment) and see if it can improve its asset management.[30]

➤ *Market-based scorecard analysis.* Companies should also prepare two market-based scorecards that reflect performance and provide possible early warning signals of problems. A *customer-performance scorecard* records how well the company is doing on such customer-based measures as new customers, dissatisfied customers, lost customers, target market awareness, target market preference, relative product quality, and relative service quality. A *stakeholder-performance scorecard* tracks the satisfaction of constituencies who have a critical interest in and impact on the company's performance: employees, suppliers, banks, distributors, retailers, and stockholders.[31]

Profitability Control

Successful companies also measure the profitability of their products, territories, customer groups, segments, trade channels, and order sizes. This information helps management determine whether any products or marketing activities should be expanded, reduced, or eliminated. The first step in marketing-profitability analysis is to identify the functional expenses (such as advertising and delivery) incurred for each activity. Next, the firm measures how much functional expense was associated with selling through each type of channel. Third, the company prepares a profit-and-loss statement for each type of channel.

In general, marketing-profitability analysis indicates the relative profitability of different channels, products, territories, or other marketing entities. However, it does not prove that the best course of action is to drop the unprofitable marketing entities,

Figure 3.7   Financial Model of Return on Net Worth

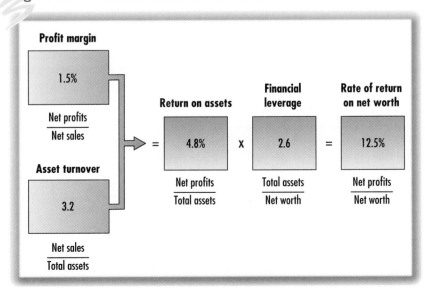

nor does it capture the likely profit improvement if these marginal marketing entities are dropped. Therefore, the company must examine its alternatives closely before taking corrective action.

Efficiency Control

Suppose a profitability analysis reveals poor profits for certain products, territories, or markets. This is when management must ask whether there are more efficient ways to manage the sales force, advertising, sales promotion, and distribution in connection with these marketing entities. Some companies have established a *marketing controller* position to work on such issues and improve marketing efficiency.

Marketing controllers work out of the controller's office but specialize in the marketing side of the business. At companies such as General Foods, DuPont, and Johnson & Johnson, they perform a sophisticated financial analysis of marketing expenditures and results, analyzing adherence to profit plans, helping prepare brand managers' budgets, measuring the efficiency of promotions, analyzing media production costs, evaluating customer and geographic profitability, and educating marketing personnel on the financial implications of marketing decisions.[32]

Strategic Control

From time to time, companies need to undertake a critical review of overall marketing goals and effectiveness. Each company should periodically reassess its strategic approach to the marketplace with marketing-effectiveness reviews and marketing audits.

➤ *The marketing-effectiveness review.* Marketing effectiveness is reflected in the degree to which a company or division exhibits the five major attributes of a marketing orientation: *customer philosophy* (serving customers' needs and wants), *integrated marketing organization* (integrating marketing with other key departments), *adequate marketing information* (conducting timely, appropriate marketing research), *strategic orientation* (developing formal marketing plans and strategies), and *operational efficiency* (using marketing resources effectively and flexibly). Unfortunately, most companies and divisions score in the fair-to-good range on measures of marketing effectiveness.[33]

➤ *The marketing audit.* Companies that discover marketing weaknesses should undertake a **marketing audit,** a comprehensive, systematic, independent, and periodic examination of a company's (or SBU's) marketing environment, objectives, strategies, and activities to identify problem areas and opportunities and recommend a plan of action for improving the company's marketing performance.[34] The marketing audit examines six major marketing components: (1) the macroenvironment and task environment, (2) marketing strategy, (3) marketing organization, (4) marketing systems, (5) marketing productivity, and (6) marketing function (the 4 Ps).

Highly successful companies also perform marketing excellence reviews and ethical-social responsibility reviews to gain an outside-in perspective on their marketing activities.

➤ *The marketing excellence review.* This best-practices excellence review rates a firm's performance in relation to the best marketing and business practices of high-performing businesses. The resulting profile exposes weaknesses and strengths and highlights where the company might change to become a truly outstanding player in the marketplace.

➤ *The ethical and social responsibility review.* In addition, companies need to evaluate whether they are truly practicing ethical and socially responsible marketing. Business success and continually satisfying customers and other stakeholders are intimately tied to adoption and implementation of high standards of business and marketing conduct. The most admired companies abide by a code of serving people's interests, not only their own. Thus, the ethical and social responsibility review allows management to determine how the firm is grappling with ethical issues and exhibiting a "social conscience" in its business dealings.

Effective control of the marketing process ultimately depends on accurate, timely, and complete information about markets, demand, and the marketing environment—the subject of the next chapter.

EXECUTIVE SUMMARY

Market-oriented strategic planning is the managerial process of developing and maintaining a viable fit among the organization's objectives, skills, and resources and its changing market opportunities. The aim of strategic planning is to shape the company's businesses and products to yield the targeted profits and growth. Strategic planning takes place at four levels: corporate, division, business unit, and product.

The corporate strategy establishes the framework within which the divisions and business units prepare their strategic plans. Setting a corporate strategy entails defining the corporate mission; establishing strategic business units (SBUs), assigning resources to each SBU based on its market attractiveness and business strength, and planning new businesses and downsizing older businesses. Strategic planning for SBUs entails defining the business mission, analyzing external opportunities and threats, analyzing internal strengths and weaknesses, formulating goals, formulating strategy, formulating programs, implementing the programs, and gathering feedback and exercising control.

The marketing process consists of four steps: analyzing market opportunities, developing marketing strategies, planning marketing programs, and managing marketing effort. Each product level within a business unit must develop a marketing plan for achieving its goals. The marketing plan is one of the most important outputs of the marketing process. It should contain an executive summary and table of contents, an overview of the marketing situation, an analysis of opportunities and threats, a summary of financial and marketing objectives, an overview of marketing strategy, a description of action programs, a projected profit-and-loss statement, and a summary of the controls for monitoring the plan's progress.

In managing the marketing process, companies can organize the marketing department according to function, geographic area, products, or customer markets. Companies that market in other countries can create an export department, an international division, or a global organization. Marketing implementation is the process that turns marketing plans into action assignments and ensures that such assignments are executed in a manner that accomplishes the plan's stated objectives. To manage the marketing process, companies can apply four types of control: annual-plan control, profitability control, efficiency control, and strategic control.

NOTES

1. See "The New Breed of Strategic Planning," *Business Week,* September 7, 1984, pp. 62–68.
2. See Peter Drucker, *Management: Tasks, Responsibilities and Practices* (New York: Harper & Row, 1973), ch. 7.
3. See "The Hollow Corporation," *Business Week,* March 3, 1986, pp. 57–59. Also see William H. Davidow and Michael S. Malone, *The Virtual Corporation* (New York: HarperBusiness, 1992).

4. For more discussion, see Laura Nash, "Mission Statements—Mirrors and Windows," *Harvard Business Review,* March–April 1988, pp. 155–56.

5. For more on Kodak's imaging strategy, see Irene M. Kunii, "Fuji: Beyond Film," *Business Week,* November 22, 1999, pp. 132–38.

6. Derek Abell, *Defining the Business: The Starting Point of Strategic Planning* (Upper Saddle River, NJ: Prentice-Hall, 1980), ch. 3.

7. Theodore Levitt, "Marketing Myopia," *Harvard Business Review,* July–August 1960, pp. 45–56.

8. See Roger A. Kerin, Vijay Mahajan, and P. Rajan Varadarajan, *Contemporary Perspectives on Strategic Planning* (Boston: Allyn & Bacon, 1990).

9. A hard decision must be made between harvesting and divesting a business. Harvesting a business will strip it of its long-run value, in which case it will be difficult to find a buyer. Divesting, on the other hand, is facilitated by maintaining a business in a fit condition in order to attract a buyer.

10. For a contrary view, however, see J. Scott Armstrong and Roderick J. Brodie, "Effects of Portfolio Planning Methods on Decision Making: Experimental Results," *International Journal of Research in Marketing* (1994), pp. 73–84.

11. The same matrix can be expanded into nine cells by adding modified products and modified markets. See S. J. Johnson and Conrad Jones, "How to Organize for New Products," *Harvard Business Review,* May–June 1957, pp. 49–62.

12. See Michael E. Porter, *Competitive Strategy: Techniques for Analyzing Industries and Competitors* (New York: Free Press, 1980), ch. 2.

13. Marcia Stepanek, "How Fast Is Net Fast?" *Business Week,* November 1, 1999, pp. EB52–EB54.

14. See Robin Cooper and Robert S. Kaplan, "Profit Priorities from Activity-Based Costing," *Harvard Business Review,* May–June 1991, pp. 130–35.

15. See Thomas J. Peters and Robert H. Waterman, Jr., *In Search of Excellence: Lessons from America's Best-Run Companies* (New York: Harper & Row, 1982), pp. 9–12. The same framework is used in Richard Tanner Pascale and Anthony G. Athos, *The Art of Japanese Management: Applications for American Executives* (New York: Simon & Schuster, 1981).

16. See Terrence E. Deal and Allan A. Kennedy, *Corporate Cultures: The Rites and Rituals of Corporate Life* (Reading, MA: Addison-Wesley, 1982); "Corporate Culture," *Business Week,* October 27, 1980, pp. 148–60; Stanley M. Davis, *Managing Corporate Culture* (Cambridge, MA: Ballinger, 1984); and John P. Kotter and James L. Heskett, *Corporate Culture and Performance* (New York: Free Press, 1992).

17. Stephen Baker, "The Future Goes Cellular," *Business Week,* November 8, 1999, p. 74.

18. Michael J. Lanning and Edward G. Michaels, "Business Is a Value Delivery System," *McKinsey Staff Paper,* no. 41, June 1988 (McKinsey & Co., Inc.).

19. Perrault and McCarthy, *Basic Marketing: A Global Managerial Approach,* 13th ed. (Burr Ridge, IL: 1996).

20. Michael George, Anthony Freeling, and David Court, "Reinventing the Marketing Organization," *The McKinsey Quarterly,* no. 4 (1994): 43–62.

21. For further reading, see Robert Dewar and Don Shultz, "The Product Manager, an Idea Whose Time Has Gone," *Marketing Communications,* May 1998, pp. 28–35; "The Marketing Revolution at Procter and Gamble," *Business Week,* July 25, 1988, pp. 72–76; Kevin T. Higgins, "Category Management: New Tools Changing Life for Manufacturers, Retailers," *Marketing News,* September 25, 1989, pp. 2, 19; George S. Low and Ronald A. Fullerton, "Brands, Brand Management, and the Brand Manager System: A Critical Historical Evaluation," *Journal of Marketing Research,* May 1994, pp. 173–90; and Michael J. Zanor, "The Profit Benefits of Category Management," *Journal of Marketing Research,* May 1994, pp. 202–13.

22. Stanley F. Slater and John C. Narver, "Market Orientation, Customer Value, and Superior Performance," *Business Horizons,* March–April 1994, pp. 22–28. See also Frederick E.

Webster, *Market-Driven Management* (New York: John Wiley, 1994); John C. Narver and Stanley F. Slater, "The Effect of a Market Orientation on Business Profitability, "*Journal of Marketing,* October 1990, pp. 20–35; Bernard Jaworski and Ajay K. Kohli, "Market Orientation: Antecedents and Consequences," *Journal of Marketing,* July 1993, pp. 53–70; and Rohit Deshpande and John U. Farley, "Measuring Market Orientation. "*Journal of Market-Focused Management* 2 (1998): 213–32.

23. Richard E. Anderson, "Matrix Redux," *Business Horizons,* November–December 1994, pp. 6–10.

24. For further reading on marketing organization, see Nigel Piercy, *Marketing Organization: An Analysis of Information Processing, Power and Politics* (London: George Allen & Unwin, 1985); Robert W. Ruekert, Orville C. Walker, and Kenneth J. Roering, "The Organization of Marketing Activities: A Contingency Theory of Structure and Performance," *Journal of Marketing,* Winter 1995, pp. 13–25; Tyzoon T, Tyebjee, Albert V. Bruno, and Shelly H. McIntyre, "Growing Ventures Can Anticipate Marketing Stages," *Harvard Business Review,* January–February 1983, pp. 2–4; and Andrew Pollak, "Revamping Said to be Set at Microsoft," *New York Times,* February 9, 1999, p. C1.

25. Edward E. Messikomer, "DuPont's 'Marketing Community,' " *Business Marketing,* October 1987, pp. 90–94. For an excellent account of how to convert a company into a market-driven organization, see George Day, *The Market-Driven Organization: Aligning Culture, Capabilities, and Configuration to the Market* (New York: Free Press, 1989).

26. For more on developing and implementing marketing plans, see H. W. Goetsch, *Developing, Implementing, and Managing an Effective Marketing Plan* (Chicago: American Marketing Association; Lincolnwood, IL: NTC Business Books, 1993).

27. Thomas V. Bonoma, *The Marketing Edge: Making Strategies Work* (New York: Free Press, 1985). Much of this section is based on Bonoma's work.

28. Emily Denitto, "New Steps Bring Alvin Ailey into the Business of Art," *Crain's New York Business,* December, 1998, pp. 4, 33.

29. Alternatively, companies need to focus on factors affecting *shareholder value.* The goal of marketing planning is to increase shareholder value, which is the *present value* of the future income stream created by the company's present actions. *Rate-of-return analysis* usually focuses on only 1 year's results. See Alfred Rapport, *Creating Shareholder Value,* rev. ed. (New York: Free Press, 1997).

30. For additional reading on financial analysis, see Peter L. Mullins, *Measuring Customer and Product Line Profitability* (Washington, DC: Distribution Research and Education Foundation, 1984).

31. See Robert S. Kaplan and David P. Norton, *The Balanced Scorecard* (Boston: Harvard Business School Press,1996).

32. Sam R. Goodman, *Increasing Corporate Profitability* (New York: Ronald Press, 1982), ch. 1. Also see Bernard J. Jaworski, Vlasis Stathakopoulos, and H. Shanker Krishnan, "Control Combinations in Marketing: Conceptual Framework and Empirical Evidence," *Journal of Marketing,* January 1993, pp. 57–69.

33. For further discussion of this instrument, see Philip Kotler, "From Sales Obsession to Marketing Effectiveness," *Harvard Business Review,* November–December 1977, pp. 67–75.

34. See Philip Kotler, William Gregor, and William Rodgers, "The Marketing Audit Comes of Age," *Sloan Management Review,* Winter 1989, pp. 49–62.

C h a p t e r   4

Understanding Markets, Market Demand, and the Marketing Environment

In this chapter, we will address the following questions:

- What are the components of a marketing information system?
- How can marketers improve marketing decisions through intelligence systems, marketing research, and marketing decision support systems?
- How can demand be more accurately measured and forecasted?
- What are the key demographic, economic, natural, technological, political, and cultural developments in the macroenvironment?

The marketing environment is changing at an accelerating rate, and the need for real-time market information is greater than at any time in the past. Companies are expanding from local to national to global marketing; consumers are gaining buying power and becoming more selective in their choices; and sellers are shifting from price to nonprice competition. At the same time, impressive information technologies are emerging: powerful computers, DVD players, the Internet, and more.[1]

Against the backdrop of this dynamic environment, some firms have developed marketing information systems that provide managers with incredible detail about buyer wants, preferences, and behavior. Today, companies with superior information enjoy a competitive advantage: They can do a better job of choosing their markets, developing their offerings, and executing their marketing plans.

Yet many companies fail to see change as opportunity and ignore or resist changes until it is too late. Their strategies, structures, systems, and organizational culture grow increasingly obsolete and dysfunctional as the environment changes. Corporations as mighty as General Motors, IBM, and Sears passed through difficult times because they ignored macroenvironmental changes for too long. The major responsibility for identifying marketplace changes falls to marketers. More than any other group in the company, they must be the trend trackers and opportunity seekers. This and the coming chapters examine the macroenvironmental forces that affect the company, its markets, and its competitors.

SUPPORTING MARKETING DECISIONS WITH INFORMATION, INTELLIGENCE, AND RESEARCH

Every firm must organize a rich flow of information to its marketing managers for analysis, planning, implementation, and control. Competitive companies study their managers' information needs and design marketing information systems to meet these needs. A **marketing information system (MIS)** consists of people, equipment, and procedures that gather, sort, analyze, evaluate, and distribute needed, timely, and accurate information to marketing decision makers. This information is developed through internal company records, marketing intelligence, marketing research, and marketing decision support analysis.

Internal Records System

Marketing managers rely on data from internal reports about orders, sales, prices, costs, inventory levels, receivables, payables, and so on. By analyzing this information, they can spot important opportunities and problems.

> ➤ *The order-to-payment cycle.* The heart of the internal records system is the *order-to-payment cycle.* Sales representatives, dealers, and customers dispatch orders to the firm. The sales department prepares invoices and transmits copies to various departments. Out-of-stock items are back ordered. Shipped items are accompanied by shipping and billing documents that are sent to various departments. Today's companies need to perform these steps quickly and accurately, because customers favor firms that can promise timely delivery. Electronic systems and *intranets* improve the speed, accuracy, and efficiency of the order-to-payment cycle for Wal-Mart and many other firms.[2]

> ➤ *Sales information systems.* Marketing managers need up-to-the-minute reports on current sales. Sales reps armed with laptop computers can access information about prospects and customers and provide immediate feedback and sales reports. Sales force automation (SFA) software allows reps to give prospective customers more information and keep more detailed notes. For example, Alliance Health Care gives computers to hospitals so they can electronically transmit orders to the company. This has helped Alliance cut inventories, improve customer service, and increase its market share.

Marketing Intelligence System

Whereas the internal records system supplies *results data,* the marketing intelligence system supplies *happenings data.* A **marketing intelligence system** is a set of procedures and sources used by managers to obtain everyday information about developments in the marketing environment. Marketing managers collect marketing intelligence by reading books, newspapers, and trade publications; talking to customers, suppliers, and distributors; checking Internet sources; and meeting with other company managers. A company can take six steps to improve the quality of its marketing intelligence.

First, it can train and motivate the sales force to spot and report new developments. Second, the company can motivate distributors, retailers, and other intermediaries to pass along important intelligence.[3] For example, Parker Hannifin, a fluid-power-products manufacturer, asks its distributors to send in a copy of all invoices covering sales of its products. Parker's marketing research division analyzes these invoices to learn more about end users, then shares the findings with the distributors.

Third, the company can learn about competitors by purchasing their products; attending trade shows; scanning Web sites; attending stockholders' meetings; talking to employees, dealers, suppliers, and shippers; collecting rivals' ads; and reading business and trade publications. Fourth, the firm can set up a customer advisory panel. For example, Hitachi Data Systems regularly meets with its 20-member customer panel to discuss service, new technologies, and customers' requirements. While the firm learns about customer needs, its customers feel closer to a company that listens to their comments.[4]

Fifth, the company can purchase information from outside suppliers such as those identified in the commercial data portion of Table 4.1. These suppliers gather and store data at a much lower cost than the company could do internally. Sixth, some companies have established a marketing information center to collect and circulate marketing intelligence throughout the organization.

Marketing Research

Marketing managers often commission formal marketing studies of specific problems and opportunities, such as a market survey, a product-preference test, a sales forecast by region, or an advertising evaluation. We define **marketing research** as the systematic design, collection, analysis, and reporting of data and findings that are relevant to a specific marketing situation facing the company.

A company can obtain marketing research in a number of ways. Most large companies have their own marketing research departments.[5] At Procter & Gamble, one marketing research group is in charge of overall company advertising research, while another is in charge of market testing. Each group's staff consists of marketing research managers, supporting specialists (survey designers, statisticians, behavioral scientists), and in-house field representatives who conduct and supervise interviewing. Each year, P&G contacts over 1 million people in connection with about 1,000 research projects.

Small companies can hire the services of a marketing research firm or conduct research in creative and affordable ways. They can engage students or professors to design and carry out projects, they can use the Internet, and they can visit their competitors. Tom Coohill, who owns two Atlanta restaurants, gives managers a food allowance to dine out and bring back ideas. Atlanta jeweler Frank Maier Jr., who often visits out-of-town rivals, spotted and copied a dramatic way of lighting displays.[6]

Companies normally budget marketing research at 1 to 2 percent of company sales. Much of this budget is spent with outside research firms, which fall into three categories:

➤ *Syndicated-service research firms* such as Information Resources, Inc. gather consumer and trade information, which they sell for a fee.

➤ *Custom marketing research firms* design studies, carry them out, and report the findings.

➤ *Specialty-line marketing research firms* provide specialized services such as field interviewing.

Table 4.1   Selected Secondary Data Sources

Internal Sources

Company profit-loss statements, balance sheets, sales figures, sales-call reports, invoices, inventory records, and prior research reports.

Government Publications

Printed sources such as *Statistical Abstract of the United States, County and City Data Book, Industrial Outlook, Marketing Information Guide;* specialized publications such as *Annual Survey of Manufacturers, Federal Reserve Bulletin;* and Internet sources such as Census Bureau (www.census.gov), Fed World clearinghouse site (www.fedworld.gov), Thomas legislative site (www.thomas.loc.gov).

Periodicals and Books

Business Periodicals Index, Standard & Poor's Industry, Moody's Manuals, Encyclopedia of Associations; marketing journals such as *Journal of Marketing, Journal of Marketing Research, Journal of Consumer Research;* trade magazines such as *Advertising Age, Sales & Marketing Management;* and business magazines such as *Business Week, Fortune, Forbes, The Economist, Fast Company, Business 2.0, Harvard Business Review.*

Business Information

On the Internet: Bloomberg financial news (www.bloomberg.com); C/Net coverage of technology (www.cnet.com); Hoover's capsules of company data (www.hoovers.com); Company Link directory of company data (www.companylink.com); SEC public company financial data (www.sec.gov); and National Trade Data Bank of industry trends and competition (www.stat-usa.gov).

Commercial Data

Nielsen (data on sales of products/brands, media audiences); *Information Resources, Inc.* (data on supermarket purchases, impact of supermarket promotions); *Mediamark Research* (data on media audiences); *Simmons Market Research Bureau* (data on media and product/brand consumption); and *Audit Bureau of Circulation* (audit data on media audiences).

Associations

On the Internet: American Marketing Association (www.ama.org); CommerceNet association for Internet commerce (www.commerce.net); and *Gale's Encyclopedia of Associations* (www.gale.com).

International Information

On the Internet: *CIA World Factbook* (www.odic.gov/cia/publications); I-Trade information about global trading (www.itrade.com); and the Electronic Embassy links to embassy sites (www.embassy.org).

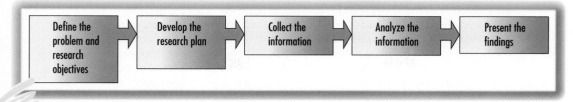

Figure 4.1   Marketing Research Process

Effective marketing research involves the five steps shown in Figure 4.1. We illustrate these steps with the following situation: American Airlines is constantly looking for new ways to serve its passengers. One marketing manager came up with the idea of offering in-flight phone service. His research indicated that the equipment would cost about $1,000 a flight. The airline could break even if it charged $25 per call and at least 40 passengers made in-flight calls. The marketing research manager was asked to find out how air travelers would respond to this service.

Step 1: Define the Problem and Research Objectives

In the first step of the marketing research process, management must carefully define the problem to be studied. American's marketing manager and marketing researcher defined the problem this way: "Will offering an in-flight phone service create enough incremental preference and profit for American Airlines to justify its cost against other possible investments?" They agreed on six objectives: Why do passengers place in-flight phone calls? What kinds of passengers would be most likely to make calls? How many passengers are likely to make calls, given different price levels? How many extra passengers might choose American because of this service? How will this add to American Airlines' image? How important is phone service relative to improving other services such as food quality?

Not all research projects are this specific. Some research is *exploratory*—its goal is to shed light on the real nature of the problem and to suggest possible solutions or new ideas. Some research is *descriptive*—it seeks to ascertain certain magnitudes, such as how many people would make an in-flight phone call at $25 a call. Some research is *causal*—to test a cause-and-effect relationship, such as whether passengers would make more calls if phones were located at their seats rather than in the aisle.

Step 2: Develop the Research Plan

The second step of the marketing research process is to design an efficient, affordable research plan. This step calls for decisions on the data sources, research approaches, research instruments, sampling plan, and contact methods.

Data Sources The researcher can gather secondary data, primary data, or both. *Secondary data* are data that were collected for another purpose and already exist somewhere. *Primary data* are data gathered for a specific purpose or a specific research project.

Researchers usually start an investigation by examining secondary data to see whether the problem can be partly or wholly solved without collecting costlier primary data. Table 4.1 shows some of the secondary-data sources available in the United States.[7] Secondary data provide a starting point for research and offer the advantages of low cost and ready availability.

One important secondary data source is the **customer** or **prospect database,** an organized collection of comprehensive data about individual customers, prospects, or suspects that is current, accessible, and actionable for marketing purposes such as lead generation, lead qualification, sales, and maintenance of customer relationships. Banks and credit-card companies are just some of the firms that have organized mountains of customer information into *data warehouses.* Then they apply *data mining,* a set of methods that allows firms to extract patterns from data warehouses.

Through data mining, firms can determine which customers may be open to upgrade offers, which might buy additional products, which might defect, and so on. By data mining its proprietary database, for example, the British grocery chain Tesco can identify discrete groups such as cheese buyers and wine buyers, then communicate with them about special sales. Similarly, American Express has collected 500 billion bytes of data on how its customers have used the firm's 35 million green, gold, and platinum charge cards. Through data mining, Amex is able to select and include precisely targeted offers in its monthly mailing of millions of customer bills.[8]

As another example, when Lands' End engaged IBM to apply data mining to cluster its customers into segments, IBM identified 5,200 different market cells. One cell consisted of 850 customers who had purchased a blue shirt and red tie. Lands' End realized that these customers might be interested in buying a dark blue jacket, so it sent them a special offer. Lands' End would expect a higher response rate to this offer than if it sent the same offer to 1 million customers independently of past purchase patterns.

Secondary data can be very valuable, but when the needed information does not exist or is dated, inaccurate, incomplete, or unreliable, the researcher will have to collect primary data.

Research Approaches   Researchers can collect primary data for marketing research in five ways: observation, focus groups, surveys, behavioral data, and experiments.

Observational research: Fresh data can be gathered by observing the relevant actors and settings. The American Airlines researchers might meander around airports and airline offices to hear travelers talk about different carriers, or they can fly on American and competitors' planes to observe in-flight service. These observations could yield some hypotheses about how travelers choose air carriers.

Focus-group research: A *focus group* is a gathering of six to ten people who spend a few hours with a skilled moderator to discuss a product, service, or other marketing entity. Many companies now conduct focus groups on the Internet to take advantage of the lower cost and faster feedback. Janice Gjersten of WPStudio, for instance, hired a research firm to hold a focus group in an on-line chat room. She was able to "watch" from her office computer and send private e-mails to the moderator. Gjersten says the on-line respondents were more honest than those in a traditional focus group; the cost was much lower; and the research report came in faster.[9] In the American Airlines research, the focus group moderator might start with a question such as "How do you feel about air travel?" and then ask about different airlines, different services, and in-flight telephone service. However, researchers must avoid generalizing on-line or traditional focus-group responses to the whole market, because the sample size is too small and is not randomly drawn.[10]

Survey research: Surveys are best suited for descriptive research such as learning about people's knowledge, beliefs, preferences, and satisfaction, and measuring these magnitudes in the general population. American Airlines researchers might want to survey how many people know about American, have flown it, prefer it, and would like telephone availability.

Behavioral data: Customers leave traces of their purchasing behavior in store scanning data, catalog and Internet purchase records, and customer databases. Much can be learned by analyzing this data. Customers' purchases reflect their preferences and often are more reliable than their statements to researchers. People often report preferences for popular brands, yet they actually buy other brands.

Experimental research: The most scientifically valid research is experimental research. The purpose of this research is to capture cause-and-effect relationships by eliminating competing explanations of the observed findings. American Airlines might experiment by introducing phone service on one flight, priced at $25 per call. On the same flight the next day, it could offer this service at $15 per call. If the plane carried the same number and type of passengers on each flight, and the day of the week made no difference, any significant difference in the number of calls made could be related to price.

Research Instruments Marketing researchers use two main research instruments in collecting primary data: questionnaires and mechanical devices. A questionnaire consists of a set of questions presented to respondents for their answers. Because of its flexibility, the questionnaire is by far the most common instrument used to collect primary data. Questionnaires need to be carefully developed, tested, and debugged before they are administered on a large scale. Questionnaires can contain closed-end and open-end questions. *Closed-end questions* prespecify all of the possible answers, so they are easy to interpret and tabulate. *Open-end questions* allow respondents to answer in their own words. These questions often reveal more because they do not constrain respondents' answers, so they are especially useful in exploratory research.

Mechanical devices are occasionally used in marketing research. Galvanometers measure the interest or emotions aroused by exposure to a specific ad or picture. User Interface Engineering, a Web design firm, uses an infrared eye-tracking system to study how consumers view Web sites: where their eyes land first, how long they linger, and so on. An audiometer attached to a participant's television registers when the set is on and to which channel it is tuned.[11]

Sampling Plan After deciding on the research approach and instruments, the marketing researcher must design a sampling plan, based on three decisions:

1. *Sampling unit: Who is to be surveyed?* The marketing researcher must define the target population to be sampled. In the American Airlines survey, should the sampling unit be business travelers, vacation travelers, or both? Once the sampling unit is determined, a sampling frame must be developed so that everyone in the target population has an equal or known chance of being sampled.

2. *Sample size: How many people should be surveyed?* Large samples give more reliable results than small samples. However, samples of less than 1 percent of a population can be reliable with a credible sampling procedure.

3. *Sampling procedure: How should the respondents be chosen?* To obtain a representative sample, a probability sample of the population should be drawn. *Probability sampling* allows the calculation of confidence limits for sampling error. When the cost or time involved in probability sampling is too high, marketing researchers will use *nonprobability sampling*.

Contact Methods Once the sampling plan has been determined, the marketing researcher must decide how to contact subjects. Choices include mail, telephone, personal, or on-line interviews. The advantages and disadvantages of these methods are summarized in Table 4.2.

Table 4.2   Marketing Research Contact Methods

Contact Method	Advantages	Disadvantages
Mail questionnaire	Ability to reach people who would not give personal interviews or whose responses might be biased or distorted by the interviewers.	Response rate is usually low or slow.
Telephone interview	Ability to gather information quickly and clarify questions respondents do not understand; higher response rate than mail questionnaires.	Interviews must be short and not too personal; contact getting more difficult because of answering machines and suspicions about telemarketing.
Personal interview	Ability to ask more questions and record additional observations.	Most expensive contact method; requires more planning and supervision and is subject to interviewer bias or distortion.
On-line interview	Ability to post a questionnaire on the Web or place a banner to quickly, easily recruit and survey participants.	Data may not be representative of a target population because respondents are self-selected.

Step 3: Collect the Information

The third step in marketing research, data collection, is generally the most expensive and the most prone to error. In the case of surveys, four major problems arise: (1) Respondents who are not at home must be recontacted or replaced; (2) some respondents will not cooperate; (3) some will give biased or dishonest answers; and (4) some interviewers will be biased or dishonest.

Yet data collection methods are rapidly improving, thanks to technology. For example, Information Resources, Inc. (IRI) recruits supermarkets equipped with scanners to read the universal product code on products purchased. The firm also recruits a panel of store customers who agree to use a special card containing personal data and allow their television-viewing habits to be monitored. Because panelists receive their programs through cable television, IRI controls the ads sent to their sets and can determine, through store purchases, which ads led to more purchasing and by which customers.[12]

Step 4: Analyze the Information

The fourth step in the marketing research process is to extract findings from the collected data. The researcher first tabulates the data and then applies various statistical techniques and decision models to analyze the results. More detailed analysis is possible through marketing decision support systems, which are discussed later in this chapter.

Step 5: Present the Findings

In the last step of the marketing research process, the researcher presents the major findings that are relevant to the key marketing decisions facing management. The main survey findings for the American Airlines case, for example, show that the chief reasons for using in-flight phone service are emergencies, urgent business deals, and mix-ups in flight times. About 20 passengers out of every 200 would make in-flight phone calls at $25 a call; about 40 would make calls at $15. Thus, a charge of $15 would produce more revenue (40 × $15 = $600) than $25 (20 × $25 = $500), still below the break-even point of $1,000. In-flight phone service would win American about two extra passengers per flight; this extra revenue would allow the airline to break even. And the service would strengthen American's innovative image, which could bring in new passengers. With these findings, American could now have more confidence in launching the telephone service.

Marketing Decision Support System

A growing number of organizations are using a marketing decision support system to help marketing managers make better decisions. According to Little, a **marketing decision support system (MDSS)** is a coordinated collection of data, systems, tools, and techniques with supporting software and hardware by which an organization gathers and interprets information from business and the environment and turns it into a basis for marketing action.[13] An MDSS may include statistical tools such as multiple regression and conjoint analysis, models such as queuing models and new-product pretest models, and optimization routines such as game theory and heuristics.

Many marketing and sales software programs can help marketers design marketing research studies, segment markets, set prices and advertising budgets, analyze media, and plan sales force activity. Some models even attempt to duplicate the way expert marketers make their decisions. Lilien and Rangaswamy's *Marketing Engineering: Computer-Assisted Marketing Analysis and Planning* discusses a number of widely used modeling software tools.[14]

AN OVERVIEW OF FORECASTING AND DEMAND MEASUREMENT

One major reason for using marketing research is to identify market opportunities. Once the research is complete, marketers must measure and forecast the size, growth, and profit potential of each market opportunity. These sales forecasts, which are based on estimates of demand, are used by finance to plan for the needed cash for investment and operations; by manufacturing to establish capacity and output levels; by purchasing to acquire the right amount of supplies; and by human resources to hire the needed number of workers. The first step is to determine which market to measure.

Which Market to Measure?

A **market** is the set of all actual and potential buyers of a market offer. The size of a market hinges on the number of buyers who might exist for a particular market offer. Although the *potential market* is the set of consumers who have a sufficient level of interest in a market offer, interest is not enough to define a market. Potential consumers must have enough income and have access to the product offer. The *available market* is thus the set of consumers who have interest, income, and access to a particular offer.

A company can go after the whole available market or concentrate on certain segments. The *target market* (also called the *served market*) is the part of the *qualified available market* (those with the interest, income, access, and qualifications to respond to a product offer) the company decides to pursue. Ultimately, the *penetrated market* is the set of consumers who buy the company's product.

These market definitions are useful tools for market planning. If the company is not satisfied with its current sales, it can (1) try to attract more buyers from its target market; (2) lower the qualifications of potential buyers; (3) expand its available market by adding distribution or lowering price; or (4) try to expand the potential market by advertising to prospects not previously targeted. Some retailers have successfully retargeted their market with new ad campaigns. When discounter Target Stores faced stiff competition from Wal-Mart and Kmart, it ran an unusual advertising campaign in the Sunday magazines of top metropolitan newspapers. With the look of department store ads, these hip spots gained Target a reputation as the "upstairs" mass retailer where department store shoppers can buy clothing along with staples such as housewares—at good prices.[15]

Demand Measurement

Once the marketer has defined its target market, the next step is to estimate market demand. **Market demand** for a product is the total volume that would be bought by a defined customer group in a defined geographical area in a defined time period in a defined marketing environment under a defined marketing program. Market demand is not a fixed number but rather a function of the stated conditions. For this reason, it can be called the *market demand function.*

The dependence of total market demand on underlying conditions is illustrated in Figure 4.2a. The horizontal axis shows different possible levels of industry marketing expenditure in a given time period. The vertical axis shows the resulting demand level. The curve represents the estimated market demand associated with varying levels of industry marketing expenditure. Some base sales (called the *market minimum,* labeled Q_1 in the figure) would take place without any such expenditures. Higher levels of industry marketing expenditures would yield higher levels of demand, first at an increasing rate, then at a decreasing rate. Marketing expenditures beyond a certain level would not stimulate much further demand, suggesting an upper limit called the *market potential* (labeled Q_2).

The total size of an *expansible market* is much affected by the level of industry marketing spending. In Figure 4.2a, the distance between Q_1 and Q_2 is relatively large.

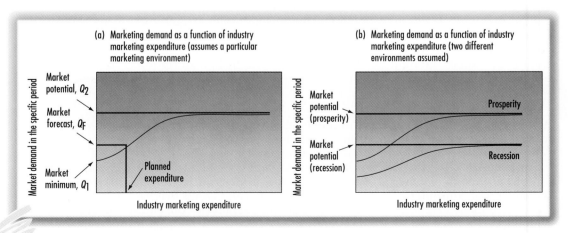

Figure 4.2 Market Demand Functions

However, in a *nonexpansible market*—one not much affected by the level of marketing expenditures—the distance between Q_1 and Q_2 would be relatively small. Organizations that sell in a nonexpansible market must accept the market's size (the level of *primary demand* for the product class) and try to win a larger market share (the level of *selective demand* for the company's product).

The market demand curve shows alternative current forecasts of market demand associated with alternative possible levels of industry marketing effort in the current period. Only one level of industry marketing expenditure will actually occur; the market demand at this level is the *market forecast*. This forecast shows expected market demand, not maximum market demand.

Market potential is the limit approached by market demand as industry marketing expenditures approach infinity for a given marketing environment. The phrase "for a given market environment" is crucial. The market potential for many products is higher during prosperity than during recession, as illustrated in Figure 4.2b. Companies cannot do anything about the position of the market demand function, but their marketing spending can influence their location on the function.

Company Demand and Sales Forecast

Company demand is the company's estimated share of market demand at alternative levels of company marketing effort in a given time period. The company's share of market demand depends on how its marketing mix is perceived relative to that of its competitors. If other things are equal, the company's market share would depend on the size and effectiveness of its market expenditures relative to competitors. Marketing model builders have developed sales-response functions to measure how a company's sales are affected by marketing expenditures, marketing mix, and marketing effectiveness.[16]

Once marketers have estimated company demand, they next choose a level of marketing effort to produce an expected level of sales. The **company sales forecast** is the expected level of company sales based on a chosen marketing plan and an assumed marketing environment. The company sales forecast is graphed with company sales on the vertical axis and company marketing effort on the horizontal axis, as in Figure 4.2. Note that the sales forecast is the *result* of an assumed marketing expenditure plan.

A **sales quota** is the sales goal set for a product line, company division, or sales representative. It is primarily a managerial device for defining and stimulating sales effort. Generally, sales quotas are set slightly higher than estimated sales to stretch the sales force's effort.

A **sales budget** is a conservative estimate of the expected sales volume, and is used primarily for making current purchasing, production, and cash-flow decisions. The sales budget considers the sales forecast and avoids excessive risk, so it is generally set slightly lower than the sales forecast.

Company sales potential is the sales limit approached by company demand as company marketing effort increases relative to competitors. The absolute limit of company demand is, of course, the market potential. In most cases, company sales potential is less than market potential, even when company marketing expenditures increase considerably, because each competitor has a core of loyal buyers who are not very responsive to other companies' efforts to woo them.

Estimating Current Demand

We are now ready to examine practical methods for estimating current market demand. Marketing executives want to estimate total market potential, area market potential, and total industry sales and market shares.

Total Market Potential

Total market potential is the maximum amount of sales that might be available to all of the firms in an industry during a given period under a given level of industry marketing effort and given environmental conditions. A common way to estimate total market potential is as follows: Estimate the potential number of buyers times the average quantity purchased by a buyer times the price.

The most difficult component to estimate is the number of buyers in the specific product or market. Companies can start with a total population, eliminate groups that obviously would not buy the product, and do research to eliminate groups without interest or money to buy. This leaves a *prospect pool* of potential buyers that companies can include in the calculation of total market potential.

Area Market Potential

Companies face the problem of selecting the best territories and allocating their marketing budget optimally among these territories. Therefore, they need to estimate the market potential of different cities, states, and nations. Business marketers primarily use the market-buildup method, while consumer marketers primarily use the multiple-factor index method.

➤ *Market-buildup method.* The market-buildup method calls for identifying all of the potential buyers in an area and estimating their potential purchases. This works well if firms have a list of all potential buyers and a good estimate of what each will buy—data that can be difficult to gather. An efficient method makes use of the North American Industry Classification System (NAICS), a six-digit code that provides statistics that are comparable across the United States, Canada, and Mexico.[17] To compute the potential for a market, the company must estimate how many products might be used in an industry. In addition to estimating the amount of products each company might buy—multiplied by the number of companies in the market—the company must also examine the extent of market saturation, the number of competitors, the market growth rate, and other variables. Then the company adds up the market potential for all markets where it will be active.

➤ *Multiple-factor index method.* Consumer companies also estimate area market potentials, but because their customers are too numerous to be listed, they often use the index method. A drug marketer, for example, might assume that the market potential for drugs is directly related to population size. If Virginia has 2.28 percent of the U.S. population, the company might assume that state will account for 2.28 percent of all drugs sold. In reality, drug sales are also influenced by other factors. Thus, it makes sense to develop a multiple-factor index with each factor assigned a specific weight. For example, if Virginia has 2.00 percent of the U.S. disposable personal income, 1.96 percent of U.S. retail sales, and 2.28 percent of U.S. population, with respective weights of 0.5, 0.3, and 0.2, the buying-power index for drugs in Virginia would be:

$$0.5 \ (2.00) + 0.3 \ (1.96) + 0.2 \ (2.28) = 2.04$$

In addition to estimating total market potential and area potential, a company needs to know the actual industry sales in its market. This means identifying its competitors and estimating their sales. Some information may be available from trade associations and marketing research firms, although not for individual competitors. Business marketers typically have a harder time estimating industry sales and market shares than consumer-goods manufacturers do.

Estimating Future Demand

Very few products or services lend themselves to easy forecasting of future demand. Those that do generally involve a product whose absolute level or trend is fairly constant and for which competition is nonexistent (public utilities) or stable (pure oligopolies). In most markets, total demand and company demand are not stable. Good forecasting becomes a key factor in company success. The more unstable the demand, the more critical is forecast accuracy, and the more elaborate is forecasting procedure.

Companies commonly use a three-stage procedure to prepare a sales forecast: They prepare a macroeconomic forecast first, then an industry forecast, then a company sales forecast. The macroeconomic forecast projects inflation, unemployment, interest rates, consumer spending, business investment, and other variables. The result is a forecast of gross domestic product, which is used, along with other indicators, to forecast industry sales. Finally, the company derives its sales forecast by assuming that it will win a certain market share. Methods for sales forecasting are shown in Table 4.3.

Table 4.3   Sales Forecast Methods

Forecast Method	Description	Use
Survey of buyers' intentions	Survey consumers or businesses about purchase probability, future finances, and expectations about the economy.	To estimate demand for industrial products, consumer durables, purchases requiring advance planning, and new products.
Composite of sales force opinions	Have sales representatives estimate how many current and prospective customers will buy the company's products.	To gather detailed forecast estimates broken down by product, territory, customer, and sales rep.
Expert opinion	Obtain forecasts from experts such as dealers, distributors, suppliers, consultants, and trade associations; can be purchased from economic-forecasting firms.	To gather estimates from knowledgeable specialists who may offer good insights.
Past-sales analysis	Use time-series analysis, exponential smoothing, statistical demand analysis, or econometric analysis to analyze past sales.	To project future demand on the basis of an analysis of past demand.
Market-test method	Conduct a direct market test to understand customer response and estimate future sales.	To better forecast sales of new products or sales in a new area.

IDENTIFYING AND RESPONDING TO MACROENVIRONMENTAL TRENDS AND FORCES

Marketers find many opportunities by identifying trends in the macroenvironment. A **trend** is a direction or sequence of events that have some momentum and durability, such as the increased participation of women in the workforce. According to futurist Faith Popcorn, a trend has longevity, is observable across several market areas and consumer activities, and is consistent with other significant indicators that occur or emerge at the same time.[18] In contrast, a *fad* is "unpredictable, short-lived, and without social, economic, and political significance."[19] A new product or marketing program is likely to be more successful if it is in line with strong trends rather than opposed to them. But detecting a new market opportunity does not guarantee its success, even if it is technically feasible.

Companies and their suppliers, marketing intermediaries, customers, and competitors all operate in a macroenvironment of forces and trends that shape opportunities and pose threats. These forces represent "noncontrollables" that the company must monitor and respond to. In the economic arena, companies and consumers are increasingly affected by global forces such as speedier transportation, communication, and financial transactions; the severe debt problems of some countries; the move toward market economies; and the growth of global brands in some product categories.

Within the rapidly changing global picture, the firm must monitor six major forces: demographic, economic, natural, technological, political-legal, and social-cultural. Although these forces will be described separately, marketers must pay attention to their interactions, because these set the stage for new opportunities as well as threats. For example, population growth (demographic) leads to resource depletion and pollution (natural environment), which leads consumers to call for more laws (political-legal). The restrictions stimulate new technological solutions and products (technology); if the solutions and products are affordable (economic forces), they may actually change attitudes and behavior (social-cultural).

Demographic Environment

Marketers monitor population trends because people make up markets. Marketers are keenly interested in the size and growth rate of the population in different cities, regions, and nations; age distribution and ethnic mix; educational levels; household patterns; and regional characteristics and movements.

Worldwide Population Growth

The world population totaled 5.4 billion in 1991; by 1999 it topped 6 billion, on its way to an estimated 8 billion by 2025.[20] This population explosion has been a source of major concern for two reasons. First, certain resources that are needed to support this much human life (fuel, foods, and minerals) are limited and may run out at some point. Second, population growth is highest in areas that can least afford it. The less developed regions of the world currently account for 76 percent of the world population and are growing at 2 percent per year, whereas the population in the more developed countries is growing at only 0.6 percent per year. Feeding, clothing, and educating children while also providing a rising standard of living is nearly impossible in the less developed areas.

The explosive world population growth has major implications for business. A growing population does not mean growing markets unless these markets have sufficient purchasing power. Nonetheless, companies that carefully analyze their markets can find major opportunities. For example, the Chinese government limits families to one child per family. Toy marketers, in particular, see that these "little emperors" are showered with everything from candy to computers by parents, grandparents, great-grandparents, aunts, and uncles. This trend has encouraged Japan's Bandai Company, Denmark's Lego Group, and Mattel to enter the Chinese market.[21]

Population Age Mix

National populations vary in their age mix. A population can be subdivided into six age groups: preschool, school-age children, teens, young adults age 25 to 40, middle-aged adults age 40 to 65, and older adults age 65 and up. The most populous age groups shape the marketing environment. In the United States, the "baby boomers," the 78 million people born between 1946 and 1964, are one of the most powerful forces shaping the marketplace. Baby boomers grew up with television ads, so they are an easier market to reach than the 45 million people who were born between 1965 and 1976, dubbed Generation X. Gen-Xers are typically cynical about hard-sell marketing pitches that promise more than they can deliver.[22] The next generation is the baby boomlet, the 72 million people who were born between 1977 and 1994, a group that is highly fluent and comfortable with computer and Internet technology.

Ethnic Markets

Countries also vary in ethnic and racial makeup. The United States was originally called a "melting pot," but people now call it a "salad bowl" society, with ethnic groups maintaining their ethnic differences, neighborhoods, and cultures. Major groups within the U.S. population include whites, African Americans, Latinos (with subgroups of Mexican, Puerto Rican, and Cuban descent), and Asian Americans (with subgroups of Chinese, Filipino, Japanese, Asian Indian, and Korean descent).

Each group has certain specific wants and buying habits. Sears, for example, is targeting Latino consumers in 130 stores in southern California, Texas, Florida, and New York. "We make a special effort to staff those stores with bilingual sales personnel, to use bilingual signage, and to support community programs," says a Sears spokesperson. Yet marketers must be careful not to overgeneralize about ethnic groups. Within each ethnic group are consumers who are as different from each other as they are from Americans of European background.

Educational Groups

The population in any society falls into five educational groups: illiterates, high school dropouts, high school degrees, college degrees, and professional degrees. In Japan, 99 percent of the population is literate, whereas in the United States up to 15 percent of the population may be functionally illiterate. However, around 36 percent of the U.S. population is college-educated, one of the world's highest percentages; this education level fuels demand for quality books, magazines, and travel.

Household Patterns

One out of eight U.S. households is "diverse" or "nontraditional," and includes single live-alones, adult live-togethers of one or both sexes, single-parent families, childless married couples, and empty nesters. More people are divorcing or separating, choosing not to marry, marrying later, or marrying without the intention to have children. Each group has a distinctive set of needs and buying habits. For example, single, separated, widowed, or divorced people need smaller apartments, smaller appliances and furniture, and food packaged in smaller sizes. Marketers must increasingly consider the special needs of nontraditional households, because they are now growing more rapidly than traditional households.

Geographical Shifts in Population

This is a period of great migratory movements between and within countries. In Eastern Europe, nationalities are reasserting themselves and forming independent countries, causing many people to seek political asylum in other nations. In many areas of the United States, people are moving from urban to rural areas, bringing new marketing opportunities. Meanwhile, an influx of immigrants from Mexico, the Caribbean, and some Asian nations is opening new opportunities for U.S. entrepreneurs. For example, 1-800-777-CLUB is a telemarketing business based in California that logs about 1,200 calls a day from Asian immigrants seeking help with electric bills and with other issues. The names of the callers go into a 1.5-million-name database that is used for highly targeted telemarketing on behalf of Sprint and other companies.[23]

Shift from a Mass Market to Micromarkets

The effect of all these changes is fragmentation of the mass market into numerous micromarkets that are differentiated by age, sex, ethnic background, education, geography, lifestyle, and other characteristics. Each group has strong preferences and is reached through increasingly targeted communication and distribution channels. More companies are shifting away from targeting a mythical "average" consumer and are instead targeting their products and marketing programs for specific micromarkets. One example is Kinko's Copy Centers, which targets the home office micromarket, offering fax machines, fast color printers, computers loaded with popular software programs, and high-speed Internet connections. The company's business model is summed up in its slogan: "Your branch office/Open 24 hours."[24]

Economic Environment

Successful companies realize that markets require purchasing power as well as people. The available purchasing power in an economy depends on current income, prices, savings, debt, and credit availability. For this reason, marketers must track the trends in income and consumer-spending patterns.

Income Distribution

Nations vary greatly in level and distribution of income and industrial structure. There are four types of industrial structures: (1) subsistence economies, which offer few marketing opportunities because most people barter excess output for simple goods and services; (2) raw-material-exporting economies, which are rich in natural resources and represent markets for trucks and other equipment; (3) industrializing economies, where growing industrialization is creating a growing middle class that demands new goods; and (4) industrial economies, which are major exporters that have a sizable middle class for all sorts of goods.

Marketers often distinguish countries with five different income-distribution patterns: (1) very low incomes; (2) mostly low incomes; (3) very low, very high incomes; (4) low, medium, high incomes; and (5) mostly medium incomes. Since 1980, the income of the wealthiest one-fifth of the U.S. population has grown by 21 percent, while wages for the bottom 60 percent have stagnated or even dipped. This is leading to a two-tier U.S. market, with affluent people buying expensive goods and working-class people spending more carefully and selecting less expensive store brands. Conventional retailers who offer medium-price goods are the most vulnerable to these changes. Companies that respond to the trend by tailoring their products and pitches to these two very different Americas stand to gain a lot.[25]

Savings, Debt, and Credit Availability

Consumer expenditures are affected by consumer savings, debt, and credit availability. The Japanese, for example, save about 13.1 percent of their income, whereas U.S. consumers save about 4.7 percent. U.S. consumers also have a high debt-to-income ratio, which slows down further expenditures on housing and large-ticket items. Credit is very available in the United States, but lower-income borrowers pay fairly high interest rates. Marketers must pay careful attention to major changes in incomes, cost of living, interest rates, savings, and borrowing patterns because these can have a high impact on business, especially for companies whose products have high income and price sensitivity.

Natural Environment

The deterioration of the natural environment is a major global concern. In many cities, air and water pollution have reached dangerous levels. In Western Europe, "green" parties have pressed for public action to reduce industrial pollution. However, legislation protecting the natural environment has hit certain industries very hard. Steel companies have had to invest in expensive pollution-control equipment and earth-friendly fuels, while automakers have had to install expensive emission controls in their vehicles. In general, marketers need to monitor these four trends closely: the shortage of raw materials, the increased cost of energy, increased pollution levels, and the changing role of governments.

Shortage of Raw Materials

The earth's raw materials consist of the infinite, the finite renewable, and the finite nonrenewable. Infinite resources, such as air and water, pose no immediate problem, although some groups see a long-run danger. Finite *renewable* resources, such as forests and food, must be used wisely. Forestry companies are required to reforest timberlands, for example. Finite *nonrenewable* resources such as oil will pose a serious problem as the point of depletion approaches. Firms that make products with these resources face substantial cost increases that they may be unable to pass along to customers.

Increased Energy Costs

One finite nonrenewable resource, oil, has created serious problems for the world economy as oil prices have gyrated, setting off a search for alternative energy forms such as coal, solar, nuclear, and wind. When oil prices go down, there is an adverse effect on the oil-exploration industry, even though oil-using industries and consumers benefit.

Increased Pollution Levels

Some industrial activity will inevitably damage the natural environment. However, because about 42 percent of U.S. consumers are willing to pay higher prices for "green" products, there is a large market for pollution-control solutions such as scrubbers, recycling centers, and landfill systems. Smart companies are initiating environment-friendly moves to show their concern. For example, 3M's Pollution Prevention Pays program substantially reduces pollution and costs, and Dow's ethylene plant in Alberta uses 40 percent less energy and releases 97 percent less wastewater.[26]

Changing Role of Governments

Governments vary in their concern and efforts to promote a clean environment. For example, the German government is vigorous in its pursuit of environmental quality, partly because of the strong green movement in Germany and partly because of the ecological devastation in the former East Germany. Many nations are doing little about pollution because they lack the funds or the political will. The major hopes are that companies around the world will accept more social responsibility and that less expensive devices will be invented to control and reduce pollution.

Technological Environment

One of the most dramatic forces shaping people's lives is technology. However, every new technology is a force for "creative destruction." For instance, autos hurt the railroads, and television hurt the newspapers. Instead of moving into the new technologies, many old industries fought or ignored them, and their businesses declined. Also, technological progress can be sporadic; for example, railroads sparked investment, and then investment petered out until the auto industry emerged. In between major innovations, the economy can stagnate. Marketers must monitor these trends in technology: the pace of change, the opportunities for innovation, varying R&D budgets, and increased regulation.

Accelerating Pace of Technological Change

Many of today's common products, such as personal computers and fax machines, were not available 40 years ago. The time lag between new ideas and their successful implementation is decreasing rapidly, and the time between introduction and peak production is much shorter. These technological changes are changing markets and needs. For example, technology enabling people to *telecommute*—work at home instead of traveling to offices—may reduce auto pollution, bring families closer, and create more home-centered activities, affecting shopping behavior as well as marketing performance.

Unlimited Opportunities for Innovation

Scientists today are working on a startling range of new technologies (such as biotechnology and robotics) that will revolutionize products and production processes. The challenge in innovation is not only technical but also commercial—to develop affordable new products. Companies are already harnessing the power of *virtual reality,* the combination of technologies that allows users to experience three-dimensional, computer-generated environments through sound, sight, and touch. Virtual reality has helped firms to gather consumer reactions to new car designs, kitchen layouts, and other potential offerings.

Varying R&D Budgets

Although the United States leads the world in R&D expenditures, most is earmarked for defense. There is a need to transfer more of this money into other types of research. Many companies are still content to put their money into copying competitors' products and making minor feature and style improvements. Even basic-research companies such as DuPont, Bell Laboratories, and Pfizer are proceeding cautiously. Thus, much research is defensive rather than offensive. Increasingly, research directed toward major breakthroughs is conducted by consortiums of companies rather than by single companies.

Increased Regulation of Technological Change

As products become more complex, the public needs to be assured of their safety. Consequently, government agencies' powers to investigate and ban potentially unsafe products have been expanded. In the United States, the Federal Food and Drug Administration must approve all drugs before they can be sold. Safety and health regulations have also increased in the areas of food, automobiles, clothing, electrical appliances, and construction. Marketers must be aware of these regulations when proposing, developing, and launching new products.

Political-Legal Environment

Marketing decisions are strongly affected by developments in the political and legal environments, which are composed of laws, government agencies, and pressure groups that influence and limit organizations and individuals. Sometimes these laws also create new opportunities for business. Mandatory recycling laws, for example, have spurred companies to make new products from recycled materials. One example is Wellman, which makes EscoSpun Squared fiber for performance apparel from recycled soda bottles.

Legislation Regulating Business

Business legislation has three main purposes: to protect firms from unfair competition, to protect consumers from unfair business practices, and to protect society from unbridled business behavior. Over the years, legislation affecting business has steadily increased. For example, the European Community has enacted laws that cover competitive behavior, product standards, product liability, and commercial transactions, and ex-Soviet nations are passing laws to promote and regulate an open market economy. The United States has many laws covering such issues as competition, product safety and liability, fair trade and credit practices, and packaging and labeling.[27]

However, at what point do the costs of regulation exceed the benefits? Although each new law may have a legitimate rationale, it may have the unintended effect of sapping initiative and retarding economic growth. Companies need a good working knowledge of business legislation, with legal review procedures and ethical standards to guide marketing managers. Internet marketers also need new parameters for doing business ethically. America Online, the most popular U.S. on-line service provider, has lost millions of dollars due to unethical tactics such as unclear explanations of free trial offers.[28]

Growth of Special-Interest Groups

The number and power of special-interest groups have increased over the past decades. *Political-action committees (PACs)* lobby government officials and pressure business executives to pay more attention to consumer rights, women's rights, senior citizen rights, minority rights, and gay rights. Many companies have public-affairs and consumer-affairs departments to deal with these groups and issues. Consumerists have won many rights, including the right to know the true interest cost of a loan and the true benefits of a product. Yet new laws and growing pressure from special-interest groups continue to add more restraints, moving many private marketing transactions into the public domain.

Social-Cultural Environment

Society shapes our beliefs, values, and norms. People absorb, almost unconsciously, a worldview that defines their relationship to themselves, others, organizations, society, nature, and the universe. Other cultural characteristics of interest to marketers include the persistence of core cultural values, the existence of subcultures, and shifts of values through time.

Views of themselves: People vary in their relative emphasis on self-gratification. Today, people are more conservative: They cannot rely on continuous employment and rising income, so they are more cautious in spending and more value-driven in purchasing.

Views of others: Some observers detect more concern about the homeless and other social problems. At the same time, people hunger for more lasting relationships with a few others. These trends portend a growing market for offerings that promote direct relations among human beings (such as health clubs) and for offerings that allow people who are alone to feel that they are not (such as video games).

Views of organizations: People vary in their attitudes toward corporations, government agencies, trade unions, and other organizations. There has been an overall decline in organizational loyalty due to downsizings. As a result, companies need to find new ways to win back consumer and employee confidence through honesty and good corporate citizenship.

Views of society: People vary in their attitudes toward their society. Some defend it, some run it, some take what they can from it, some want to change it, some look for something deeper, and some want to leave it.[29] Consumption patterns often reflect social attitude; those who want to change it, for example, may drive smaller cars and wear simpler clothes.

Views of nature: People vary in their attitude toward nature. A long-term trend has been humankind's growing mastery of nature through technology. Recently, however, people have awakened to nature's fragility and finite resources. Love of nature is leading to more activities such as camping, hiking, and boating, leading in turn to more marketing of hiking boots and related goods and services.

Views of the universe: People vary in their beliefs about the origin of the universe and their place in it. Most Americans are monotheistic, although religious conviction and practice have varied through the years.

High Persistence of Core Values

The people who live in a particular society hold many *core beliefs* and values that tend to persist. Core beliefs and values are passed on from parents to children and are reinforced by major social institutions—schools, churches, business, and government. *Secondary beliefs* and values are more open to change. Marketers may change secondary values but have little chance of changing core values. For instance, the nonprofit organization Mothers Against Drunk Drivers (MADD) does not try to stop the sale of alcohol, but it does promote the idea of appointing a designated driver who will not drink.

Existence of Subcultures

Each society contains *subcultures,* groups with shared values emerging from their special life experiences or circumstances. Star Trek fans, Black Muslims, and Hell's Angels are all subcultures whose members share common beliefs, preferences, and behaviors. To the extent that subcultural groups exhibit different wants and consumption behavior, marketers can target particular subcultures. For instance, marketers love teenagers because they are trendsetters in fashion, music, entertainment, and attitudes. Marketers know that if they attract someone as a teen, they will probably keep that customer for years. Frito-Lay, which draws 15 percent of its sales from teens, has seen more chip-snacking by grown-ups. "We think it's because we brought them in as teenagers," says a Frito-Lay marketing director.[30]

Shifts of Secondary Cultural Values Through Time

Although core values are fairly persistent, cultural swings do take place, bringing new marketing opportunities or threats. Several firms offer social-cultural forecasts. The Yankelovich Monitor interviews 2,500 people each year and tracks social trends such as "antibigness" and "living for today." It describes the percentage of the population that shares each attitude as well as the percentage that does not. For example, the percentage of people who value physical fitness and well-being has risen steadily, especially in the under-30 group, the young women and upscale groups, and people living in the West. Marketers of health foods are catering to this trend with appropriate products and communications.

EXECUTIVE SUMMARY

Three developments make the need for marketing information greater now than in the past: the rise of global marketing, the emphasis on buyers' wants, and the trend toward nonprice competition. Marketing managers therefore need a marketing information system (MIS) to assess information needs, develop the needed information, and distribute that information in a timely manner. An MIS consists of (a) an internal records system with information on the order-to-payment cycle and sales reporting systems; (b) a marketing intelligence system to obtain everyday information about pertinent developments in the marketing environment; (c) marketing research for the systematic design, collection, analysis, and reporting of data and findings that are relevant to a specific marketing situation; and (d) a computerized marketing decision support system to help marketers make and implement better decisions.

Companies can conduct their own marketing research or hire other companies to do it for them. The marketing research process consists of defining the problem and research objective, developing the research plan, collecting the information, analyzing the information, and presenting the findings to management. In conducting research, firms must decide whether to collect their own data or use data that already exist. They must also decide which research approach (observational, focus-group, survey, behavioral data, or experimental) and which research instrument (questionnaire or mechanical instruments) to use. In addition, they have to decide on a sampling plan and contact methods.

One purpose of marketing research is to discover market opportunities. Once the research is complete, the company must evaluate its opportunities carefully and decide which markets to enter. Then it must prepare sales forecasts based on estimates of market and company demand. To estimate current demand, companies look at total market potential, area market potential, industry sales, and market share. To estimate future demand, companies survey buyers' intentions, solicit sales input, gather expert opinions, or engage in market testing. Mathematical models, statistical techniques, and computerized data collection procedures are used in demand and sales forecasting.

Marketers are responsible for identifying significant macroenvironmental changes, especially opportunities and threats posed by trends in six environmental forces. In the demographic environment, they must look at population growth; changes in age, ethnic composition, and educational levels; the rise of nontraditional families; geographic shifts in population; and the move to micromarketing.

Within the economic environment, marketers should focus on income distribution and savings, debt, and credit availability. Within the natural environment, they need to watch raw-materials shortages, higher energy costs and pollution levels, and the changing role of governments in environmental protection. In the technological environment, they should note the faster pace of technological change, opportunities for innovation, varying R&D budgets, and increased governmental regulation.

Within the political-legal environment, marketers must be aware of the laws that regulate business practices and the influence of special-interest groups. Within the social-cultural environment, they must understand how people view themselves, others, organizations, society, nature, and the universe; market products that fit with core and secondary cultural values; and address the needs of different subcultures.

NOTES

1. See James C. Anderson and James A. Narus, *Business Market Management: Understanding, Creating and Delivering Value* (Upper Saddle River, NJ: Prentice-Hall, 1998), ch. 2.
2. Amy Feldman, "How Big Can It Get," *Money,* December 1999, pp. 158–64.
3. James A. Narus and James C. Anderson, "Turn Your Industrial Distributors into Partners," *Harvard Business Review,* March–April 1986, pp. 66–71.
4. Don Peppers, "How You Can Help Them," *Fast Company,* October–November 1997, pp. 128–36.
5. See *1994 Survey of Market Research,* eds. Thomas Kinnear and Ann Root (Chicago: American Marketing Association, 1994).
6. Kevin J. Clancy and Robert S. Shulman, *Marketing Myths That Are Killing Business,* (New York: McGraw-Hill, 1994), p. 58; Phaedra Hise, "Comprehensive CompuServe," *Inc.,* June 1994, p. 109; "Business Bulletin: Studying the Competition," *Wall Street Journal,* pp. A1–5.
7. For an excellent annotated reference to major secondary sources of business and marketing data, see Gilbert A. Churchill Jr., *Marketing Research: Methodological Foundations,* 6th ed. (Fort Worth, TX: Dryden, 1995).
8. Peter R. Peacock, "Data Mining in Marketing: Part 1," *Marketing Management,* Winter 1998, pp. 9–18, and "Data Mining in Marketing: Part 2," *Marketing Management,* Spring 1998, pp. 15–25; Ginger Conlon, "What the !@#!*?!! Is a Data Warehouse?" *Sales & Marketing Management,* April 1997, pp. 41–48; Skip Press, "Fool's Gold? As Companies Rush to Mine Data, They May Dig Up Real Gems—or False Trends," *Sales & Marketing Management,* April 1997, pp. 58, 60, 62.
9. Sarah Schafer, "Communications: Getting a Line on Customers," *Inc. Tech* (1996), p. 102; see also Alexia Parks, "On-Line Focus Groups Reshape Market Research Industry," *Marketing News,* May 12, l997, p. 28.
10. Thomas L. Greenbaum, *The Handbook for Focus Group Research* (New York: Lexington Books, 1993).
11. Elizabeth Millard, "Spool of Thought," *Business 2.0,* October 1999, pp. 219, 221; Roger D. Blackwell, James S. Hensel, Michael B. Phillips, and Brian Sternthal, *Laboratory Equipment for Marketing Research* (Dubuque, IA: Kendall/Hunt, 1970); and Wally Wood, "The Race to Replace Memory," *Marketing and Media Decisions,* July 1986, pp. 166–67. See also Gerald Zaltman, "Rethinking Market Research: Putting People Back In," *Journal of Marketing Research* 34, no. 4 (November 1997): 424–37.
12. For further reading, see Joanne Lipman, "Single-Source Ad Research Heralds Detailed Look at Household Habits," *Wall Street Journal,* February 16, 1988, p. 39; Joe Schwartz, "Back to the Source," *American Demographics,* January 1989, pp. 22–26; and Magid H. Abraham and Leonard M. Lodish, "Getting the Most Out of Advertising and Promotions," *Harvard Business Review,* May–June 1990, pp. 50–60.
13. John D. C. Little, "Decision Support Systems for Marketing Managers," *Journal of Marketing,* Summer 1979, p. 11.

14. Gary L. Lilien and Arvind Rangaswamy, *Marketing Engineering: Computer-Assisted Marketing Analysis and Planning* (Upper Saddle River, NJ: Prentice Hall, 1998).

15. Robert Berner, "Image Ads Catch the Imagination of Dayton Hudson's Target Unit," *Wall Street Journal,* October 3, 1997, p. B5.

16. For further discussion, see Gary L. Lilien, Philip Kotler, and K. Sridhar Moorthy, *Marketing Models* (Upper Saddle River, NJ: Prentice-Hall, 1992).

17. For more information on NAICS, check the U.S. Bureau of the Census Web site, www.census.gov/epcd/www/naics.html.

18. See Faith Popcorn, *The Popcorn Report* (New York: HarperBusiness, 1992).

19. Gerald Celente, *Trend Tracking* (New York: Warner Books, 1991).

20. See "World Population Profile: 1998—Highlights," U.S. Census Bureau, March 18, 1999, www.census.gov/ipc/www/wp98001.html.

21. Sally D. Goll, "Marketing: China's (Only) Children Get the Royal Treatment," *Wall Street Journal,* February 8, 1995, p. B1.

22. Bill Stoneman, "Beyond Rocking the Ages: An Interview with J. Walker Smith," *American Demographics,* May 1998, pp. 45–49; Margot Hornblower, "Great X," *Time,* June 9, 1997, pp. 58–59; Bruce Horowitz, "Gen X in a Class by Itself," *USA Today,* September 23, 1996, p. B1.

23. Michael Barrier, "The Language of Success," *Nation's Business,* August 1997, pp. 56–57.

24. Lauri J. Flynn, "Not Just a Copy Shop Any Longer, Kinko's Pushes Its Computer Services," *New York Times,* July 6, 1998, p. D1.

25. David Leonhardt, "Two-Tier Marketing," *Business Week,* March 17, 1997, pp. 82–90.

26. Francoise L. Simon, "Marketing Green Products in the Triad," *The Columbia Journal of World Business,* Fall and Winter 1992, pp. 268–85; and Jacquelyn A. Ottman, *Green Marketing: Responding to Environmental Consumer Demands* (Lincolnwood, IL: NTC Business Books, 1993).

27. See Dorothy Cohen, *Legal Issues on Marketing Decision Making* (Cincinnati: South-Western, 1995).

28. Rajiv Chandrasekaran, "AOL Settles Marketing Complaints," *Washington Post,* May 29, 1998, p. F1.

29. Arnold Mitchell of the Stanford Research Institute, private publication.

30. Laura Zinn, "Teens: Here Comes the Biggest Wave Yet," *Business Week,* April 11, 1994, pp. 76–86.

Analyzing Consumer Markets and Buyer Behavior

In this chapter, we will address the following questions:

■ How do cultural, social, personal, and psychological factors influence consumer buying behavior?

■ How does the consumer make a purchasing decision?

The aim of marketing is to meet and satisfy target customers' needs and wants. The field of consumer behavior studies how individuals, groups, and organizations select, buy, use, and dispose of goods, services, ideas, or experiences to satisfy their needs and desires. Understanding consumer behavior is never simple, because customers may say one thing but do another. They may not be in touch with their deeper motivations, and they may respond to influences and change their minds at the last minute.

Still, all marketers can profit from understanding how and why consumers buy. For example, Whirlpool's staff anthropologists go into people's homes, observe how they use appliances, and talk with household members. Whirlpool has found that in busy families, women are not the only ones doing the laundry. Knowing this, the company's engineers developed color-coded washer and dryer controls to make it easier for kids and men to pitch in.[1]

In fact, not understanding your customer's motivations, needs, and preferences can lead to major mistakes. This is what happened when Kodak introduced its Advanta camera—a costly bust. The company proudly touted it as a high-tech product, but the marketplace was dominated by middle-aged baby-boomers. In midlife, fancy new technology generally loses its appeal, and simplicity begins to edge out complexity in consumer preferences, so Advanta sales did not skyrocket.

Such examples show why successful marketers use both rigorous scientific procedures and more intuitive methods to study customers and uncover clues for developing new products, product features, prices, channels, messages, and other marketing-mix elements. This chapter explores individual consumers' buying dynamics; the next chapter explores the buying dynamics of business buyers.

HOW AND WHY CONSUMERS BUY

The starting point for understanding consumer buying behavior is the stimulus-response model shown in Figure 5.1. As this model shows, both marketing and environmental stimuli enter the buyer's consciousness. In turn, the buyer's characteristics and decision process lead to certain purchase decisions. The marketer's task is to understand what happens in the buyer's consciousness between the arrival of outside stimuli and the buyer's purchase decisions.

As this model indicates, a consumer's buying behavior is influenced by cultural, social, personal, and psychological factors.

Cultural Factors Influencing Buyer Behavior

Culture, subculture, and social class are particularly important influences on consumer buying behavior.

➤ *Culture. Culture* is the most fundamental determinant of a person's wants and behavior. A child growing up in the United States is exposed to these broad cultural values: achievement and success, activity, efficiency and practicality, progress, material comfort, individualism, freedom, external comfort, humanitarianism, and youthfulness.[2]

➤ *Subculture.* Each culture consists of smaller subcultures that provide more specific identification and socialization for their members. Subcultures include nationalities, religions, racial groups, and geographic regions. Many subcultures make up important market segments, leading marketers to tailor products and marketing programs to their needs. Latinos, for example, the fastest-growing U.S. subculture, are targeted by Dallas-based Carnival Food Stores, among other marketers. Dallas is one of the top 10 cities in terms of Latino population, and when the chain uses Spanish language promotions, customers are more responsive. Marketers are targeting another subculture, African Americans, because of its hefty $500 billion in purchasing power. Hallmark, for instance, created its Mahogany line of 800 greeting cards especially for African Americans. Age forms subcultures, as well; the 75 million Americans in the 50-plus market are being targeted by marketers such as Pfizer, which airs ads showing how its medications help seniors live life to the fullest.[3]

Figure 5.1   Model of Consumer Buyer Behavior

➤ *Social class.* **Social classes** are relatively homogeneous and enduring divisions in a society. They are hierarchically ordered and their members share similar values, interests, and behavior (see Table 5.1). Social classes reflect income as well as occupation, education, and other indicators. Those within each social class tend to behave more alike than do persons from different social classes. Also, within the culture, persons are perceived as occupying inferior or superior positions according to social class. Social class is indicated by a cluster of variables rather than by any single variable. Still, individuals can move from one social class to another—up or down—during their lifetime. Because social classes often show distinct product and brand preferences, some marketers focus their efforts on one social class. Neiman Marcus, for example, focuses on the upper classes, offering top-quality merchandise in upscale stores with many personal services geared to these customers' needs.

Social Factors Influencing Buyer Behavior

In addition to cultural factors, a consumer's behavior is influenced by such social factors as reference groups, family, and social roles and statuses.

Reference Groups

Reference groups consist of all of the groups that have a direct (face-to-face) or indirect influence on a person's attitudes or behavior. Groups that have a direct influence on a person are called *membership groups*. Some primary membership groups are family, friends, neighbors, and co-workers, with whom individuals interact fairly continuously and informally. Secondary groups, such as professional and trade-union groups, tend to be more formal and require less continuous interaction. Reference groups expose people to new behaviors and lifestyles, influence attitudes and self-concept, and create pressures for conformity that may affect product and brand choices.

People are also influenced by groups to which they do not belong. *Aspirational groups* are those the person hopes to join; *dissociative groups* are those whose values or behavior an individual rejects.

Although marketers try to identify target customers' reference groups, the level of reference-group influence varies among products and brands. Manufacturers of products and brands with strong group influence must reach and influence the opinion leaders in these reference groups. An *opinion leader* is the person in informal product-related communications who offers advice or information about a product or product category.[4] Marketers try to reach opinion leaders by identifying demographic and psychographic characteristics associated with opinion leadership, identifying the preferred media of opinion leaders, and directing messages at the opinion leaders. For example, the hottest trends in teenage music and fashion start in America's inner cities, then spread to youth in the suburbs. As a result, clothing companies that target teens carefully monitor the style and behavior of urban opinion leaders.

Family

The family is the most important consumer-buying organization in society, and it has been researched extensively.[5] The *family of orientation* consists of one's parents and siblings. From parents, a person acquires an orientation toward religion, politics, and economics as well as a sense of personal ambition, self-worth, and love.[6] A more direct influence on the everyday buying behavior of adults is the *family of procreation*—namely, one's spouse and children.

Marketers are interested in the roles and relative influence of the husband, wife, and children in the purchase of a large variety of products and services. These roles vary widely in different cultures and social classes. Vietnamese Americans, for example,

Table 5.1   Selected Characteristics of Major U.S. Social Classes

Social Class	Characteristics
Upper Uppers (less than 1 percent of U.S. population)	The social elite who live on inherited wealth; they give large sums to charity, maintain more than one home, and send their children to top schools. This small group serves as a reference group for other social classes.
Lower Uppers (about 2 percent of U.S. population)	People coming up from the middle class who have earned high income or wealth through professions or business; they tend to be active in social and civic affairs, buy status-symbol products, and aspire to be accepted in the upper-upper stratum.
Upper Middles (12 percent of U.S. population)	People without family status or unusual wealth who are focused on their careers as professionals, independent business persons, and corporate managers; they believe in education and are civic-minded and home-oriented.
Middle Class (32 percent of U.S. population)	Average-pay white- and blue-collar workers; they often buy popular products to keep up with trends, and they believe in spending more money on worthwhile experiences for their children and aiming them toward a college education.
Working Class (38 percent of U.S. population)	Average-pay blue-collar workers and those who lead a working-class lifestyle; they depend on relatives for economic and emotional support, job tips, and assistance, and they tend to maintain sharp sex-role divisions and stereotyping.
Upper Lowers (9 percent of U.S. population)	Workers whose living standard is just above poverty; they perform unskilled work, are poorly paid, and are educationally deficient.
Lower Lowers (7 percent of U.S. population)	People on welfare, visibly poverty stricken, and usually out of work; some are uninterested in finding permanent work, and most depend on public aid or charity for income.

Sources: Richard P. Coleman, "The Continuing Significance of Social Class to Marketing," *Journal of Consumer Research,* December 1983, pp. 265–80, and Richard P. Coleman and Lee P. Rainwater, *Social Standing in America: New Dimension of Class* (New York: Basic Books, 1978).

are more likely to adhere to the model in which the man makes large-purchase decisions. In the United States, husband-wife involvement has traditionally varied widely by product category, so marketers need to determine which member has the greater influence in choosing particular products. Today, traditional household purchasing patterns are changing, with baby-boomer husbands and wives shopping jointly for products traditionally thought to be under the separate control of one spouse or the other.[7] For this reason, marketers of products traditionally purchased by one spouse may need to start thinking of the other as a possible purchaser.

Another shift in buying patterns is an increase in the amount of money spent and influence wielded by children and teens.[8] Children age 4 to 12 spend an estimated $24.4 billion annually—three times the value of the ready-to-eat cereal market. Indirect influence means that parents know the brands, product choices, and preferences of their children without hints or outright requests; direct influence refers to children's hints, requests, and demands.

Because the fastest route to Mom and Dad's wallets may be through Junior, many successful companies are showing off their products to children—and soliciting marketing information from them—over the Internet. This has consumer groups and parents up in arms. Many marketers have come under fire for not requiring parental consent when requesting personal information and not clearly differentiating ads from games or entertainment.

One company that uses ethical tactics to market to children is Disney, which operates the popular children's site Disney Online. Disney clearly states its on-line policies on its home page and on the home pages of its other sites, including Disney's Daily Blast, a subscription-based Internet service geared to children age 3 to 12. Disney's on-line practices include alerting parents through e-mail when a child has submitted personal information to a Web site, whether it be to enter a contest, cast a vote, or register at a site. Whereas many sites and advertisers use "cookies," tiny bits of data that a Web site puts on a user's computer to enhance his or her visit, Disney does not use cookies for promotional or marketing purposes and does not share them with third parties.[9]

Roles and Statuses

A person participates in many groups, such as family, clubs, or organizations. The person's position in each group can be defined in terms of role and status. A *role* consists of the activities that a person is expected to perform. Each role carries a *status*. A Supreme Court justice has more status than a sales manager, and a sales manager has more status than an administrative assistant. In general, people choose products that communicate their role and status in society. Thus, company presidents often drive Mercedes, wear expensive suits, and drink Chivas Regal scotch. Savvy marketers are aware of the *status symbol* potential of products and brands.

Personal Factors Influencing Buyer Behavior

Cultural and social factors are just two of the four major factors that influence consumer buying behavior. The third factor is personal characteristics, including the buyer's age, stage in the life cycle, occupation, economic circumstances, lifestyle, personality, and self-concept.

Age and Stage in the Life Cycle

People buy different goods and services over a lifetime. They eat baby food in the early years, most foods in the growing and mature years, and special diets in the later years. Taste in clothes, furniture, and recreation is also age-related, which is why smart marketers are attentive to the influence of age.

Similarly, consumption is shaped by the *family life cycle.* The traditional family life cycle covers stages in adult lives, starting with independence from parents and continuing into marriage, child-rearing, empty-nest years, retirement, and later life. Marketers often choose a specific group from this traditional life-cycle as their target market. Yet target households are not always family based: There are also single households, gay households, and cohabitor households.

Some recent research has identified *psychological life-cycle stages.* Adults experience certain "passages" or "transformations" as they go through life.[10] Leading marketers pay close attention to changing life circumstances—divorce, widowhood, remarriage—and their effect on consumption behavior.

Occupation and Economic Circumstances

Occupation also influences a person's consumption pattern. A blue-collar worker will buy work clothes and lunchboxes, while a company president will buy expensive suits and a country club membership. For this reason, marketers should identify the occupational groups that are more interested in their products and services, and consider specializing their products for certain occupations. Software manufacturers, for example, have developed special programs for lawyers, physicians, and other occupational groups.

In addition, product choice is greatly affected by a consumer's economic circumstances: spendable income (level, stability, and time pattern), savings and assets (including the percentage that is liquid), debts, borrowing power, and attitude toward spending versus saving. Thus, marketers of income-sensitive goods must track trends in personal income, savings, and interest rates. If a recession is likely, marketers can redesign, reposition, and reprice their products to offer more value to target customers.

Lifestyle

People from the same subculture, social class, and occupation may actually lead quite different lifestyles. A **lifestyle** is the person's pattern of living in the world as expressed in activities, interests, and opinions. Lifestyle portrays the "whole person" interacting with his or her environment.

Successful marketers search for relationships between their products and lifestyle groups. For example, a computer manufacturer might find that most computer buyers are achievement-oriented. The marketer may then aim its brand more clearly at the achiever lifestyle.

Psychographics is the science of measuring and categorizing consumer lifestyles. One of the most popular classifications based on psychographic measurements is SRI International's Values and Lifestyles (VALS) framework. The VALS 2 system classifies all U.S. adults into eight groups based on psychological attributes drawn from survey responses to demographic, attitudinal, and behavioral questions, including questions about Internet usage.[11] The major tendencies of these groups are:

➤ *Actualizers:* Successful, sophisticated, active, "take-charge" people whose purchases often reflect cultivated tastes for relatively upscale, niche-oriented products.

➤ *Fulfilleds:* Mature, satisfied, comfortable, and reflective people who favor durability, functionality, and value in products.

➤ *Achievers:* Successful, career- and work-oriented consumers who favor established, prestige products that demonstrate success.

➤ *Experiencers:* Young, vital, enthusiastic, impulsive, and rebellious people who spend much of their income on clothing, fast food, music, movies, and video.

➤ *Believers:* Conservative, conventional, and traditional people who favor familiar products and established brands.

➤ *Strivers:* Uncertain, insecure, approval-seeking, resource constrained consumers who favor stylish products that emulate the purchases of wealthier people.

➤ *Makers:* Practical, self-sufficient, traditional, and family-oriented people who favor products with a practical or functional purpose, such as tools and fishing equipment.

➤ *Strugglers:* Elderly, resigned, passive, concerned, and resource-constrained consumers who are cautious and loyal to favorite brands.

Although psychographics is a valid and valued methodology for many marketers, social scientists are realizing that older tools for predicting consumer behavior are not always applicable to the use of the Internet or on-line services and purchases of technology products. As a result, researchers are coming up with new research methods for segmenting consumers based on technology types. Forrester Research's Technographics system segments consumers according to motivation, desire, and ability to invest in technology; SRI's iVALS system segments consumers into segments based on Internet usage.[12]

Lifestyle segmentation schemes vary by culture. McCann-Erickson London, for example, has identified these British lifestyles: Avant-Gardians (interested in change); Pontificators (traditionalists); Chameleons (follow the crowd); and Sleepwalkers (contented underachievers). The advertising agency D'Arcy, Masius, Benton & Bowles has identified these segments of Russian consumers: "Kuptsi" (merchants), "Cossacks" (ambitious and status seeking), "Students," "Business Executives," and "Russian Souls" (passive, fearful of choices).[13]

Personality and Self-Concept

Each person has a distinct personality that influences buying behavior. **Personality** refers to the distinguishing psychological characteristics that lead to relatively consistent and enduring responses to environment. Personality is usually described in terms of such traits as self-confidence, dominance, autonomy, deference, sociability, defensiveness, and adaptability.[14]

Personality can be useful in analyzing consumer behavior, provided that personality types can be classified accurately and that strong correlations exist between certain personality types and product or brand choices. For example, a computer company might discover that many prospects show high self-confidence, dominance, and autonomy, suggesting that computer ads should appeal to these traits.

Self-concept (or self-image) is related to personality. Marketers often try to develop brand images that match the target market's self-image. Yet it is possible that a person's *actual self-concept* (how she views herself) differs from her *ideal self-concept* (how she would like to view herself) and from her *others-self-concept* (how she thinks others see her). Which self will she try to satisfy in making a purchase? Because it is difficult to answer this question, self-concept theory has had a mixed record of success in predicting consumer responses to brand images.[15]

Psychological Factors Influencing Buyer Behavior

Psychological factors are the fourth major influence on consumer buying behavior (in addition to cultural, social, and personal factors). In general, a person's buying choices are influenced by the psychological factors of motivation, perception, learning, beliefs, and attitudes.

Motivation

A person has many needs at any given time. Some needs are *biogenic;* they arise from physiological states of tension such as hunger, thirst, discomfort. Other needs are *psychogenic;* they arise from psychological states of tension such as the need for recognition, esteem, or belonging. A need becomes a motive when it is aroused to a sufficient level of intensity. A *motive* is a need that is sufficiently pressing to drive the person to act.

Psychologists have developed theories of human motivation. Three of the best known—the theories of Sigmund Freud, Abraham Maslow, and Frederick Herzberg—carry quite different implications for consumer analysis and marketing strategy.

➤ *Freud's theory.* Sigmund Freud assumed that the psychological forces shaping people's behavior are largely unconscious, and that a person cannot fully understand his or her own motivations. A technique called *laddering* can be used to trace a person's motivations from the stated instrumental ones to the more terminal ones. Then the marketer can decide at what level to develop the message and appeal.[16] In line with Freud's theory, consumers react not only to the stated capabilities of specific brands, but also to other, less conscious cues. Successful marketers are therefore mindful that shape, size, weight, material, color, and brand name can all trigger certain associations and emotions.

➤ *Maslow's theory.* Abraham Maslow sought to explain why people are driven by particular needs at particular times.[17] His theory is that human needs are arranged in a hierarchy, from the most to the least pressing. In order of importance, these five categories are physiological, safety, social, esteem, and self-actualization needs. A consumer will try to satisfy the most important need first; when that need is satisfied, the person will try to satisfy the next-most-pressing need. Maslow's theory helps marketers understand how various products fit into the plans, goals, and lives of consumers.

➤ *Herzberg's theory.* Frederick Herzberg developed a *two-factor theory* that distinguishes dissatisfiers (factors that cause dissatisfaction) from satisfiers (factors that cause satisfaction).[18] The absence of dissatisfiers is not enough; satisfiers must be actively present to motivate a purchase. For example, a computer that comes without a warranty would be a dissatisfier. Yet the presence of a product warranty would not act as a satisfier or motivator of a purchase, because it is not a source of intrinsic satisfaction with the computer. Ease of use would, however, be a satisfier for a computer buyer. In line with this theory, marketers should avoid dissatisfiers that might unsell their products. They should also identify and supply the major satisfiers or motivators of purchase, because these satisfiers determine which brand consumers will buy.

Perception

A motivated person is ready to act, yet how that person actually acts is influenced by his or her perception of the situation. **Perception** is the process by which an individual selects, organizes, and interprets information inputs to create a meaningful picture of the world.[19] Perception depends not only on physical stimuli, but also on the stimuli's relation to the surrounding field and on conditions within the individual. The key word is *individual.* Individuals can have different perceptions of the same object because of three perceptual processes: selective attention, selective distortion, and selective retention.

➤ *Selective attention.* People are exposed to many daily stimuli such as ads; most of these stimuli are screened out—a process called *selective attention.* The end result is that marketers have to work hard to attract consumers' attention. Through research, marketers have learned that people are more likely to notice stimuli that relate to a current need, which is why car shoppers notice car ads but not appliance ads. Furthermore, people are more likely to notice stimuli that they anticipate—such as foods being promoted on a food Web site. And people are more likely to notice stimuli whose deviations are large in relation to the normal size of the stimuli, such as a banner ad offering $100 (not just $5) off a product's list price.

➤ *Selective distortion.* Even noticed stimuli do not always come across the way that marketers intend. *Selective distortion* is the tendency to twist information into personal meanings and interpret information in a way that fits our preconceptions. Unfortunately, marketers can do little about selective distortion.

➤ *Selective retention.* People forget much that they learn but tend to retain information that supports their attitudes and beliefs. Because of *selective retention,* we are likely to remember good points mentioned about a product we like and forget good points mentioned about competing products. Selective retention explains why marketers use drama and repetition in messages to target audiences.

Learning

When people act, they learn. **Learning** involves changes in an individual's behavior that arise from experience. Most human behavior is learned. Theorists believe that learning is produced through the interplay of drives, stimuli, cues, responses, and reinforcement. A *drive* is a strong internal stimulus that impels action. *Cues* are minor stimuli that determine when, where, and how a person responds.

Suppose you buy an IBM computer. If your experience is rewarding, your response to computers and IBM will be positively reinforced. Later, when you want to buy a printer, you may assume that because IBM makes good computers, it also makes good printers. You have now *generalized* your response to similar stimuli. A counter-tendency to generalization is *discrimination,* in which the person learns to recognize differences in sets of similar stimuli and adjust responses accordingly. Applying learning theory, marketers can build up demand for a product by associating it with strong drives, using motivating cues, and providing positive reinforcement.

Beliefs and Attitudes

Through doing and learning, people acquire beliefs and attitudes that, in turn, influence buying behavior. A **belief** is a descriptive thought that a person holds about something. Beliefs may be based on knowledge, opinion, or faith, and they may or may not carry an emotional charge. Of course, manufacturers are very interested in the beliefs that people have about their products and services. These beliefs make up product and brand images, and people act on their images. If some beliefs are wrong and inhibit purchase, the manufacturer will want to launch a campaign to correct these beliefs.[20]

Particularly important to global marketers is the fact that buyers often hold distinct beliefs about brands or products based on their country of origin. Studies have found, for example, that the impact of country of origin varies with the type of product. Consumers want to know where a car was made but not where lubricating oil came from. In addition, attitudes toward country of origin can change over time; Japan, for instance, had a poor quality image before World War II.

A company has several options when its products' place of origin turns off consumers. The company can consider co-production with a foreign company that has a better name. Another alternative is to hire a well-known celebrity to endorse the product. Or the company can adopt a strategy to achieve world-class quality in the local industry, as is the case with Belgian chocolates and Colombian coffee.

This is what South African wineries are attempting to do as their wine exports increase. South African wines have been hurt by the perception that the country's vineyards are primitive in comparison to those in other countries and that wine farmers are continuing crude labor practices. In reality, South Africa's wine farmers have improved the lives of their workers. "Wine is such a product of origin that we cannot succeed if South Africa doesn't look good," says Willem Barnard, chief executive of the Ko-operatieve Wijnbouwers Vereniging, the farmers' co-op that dominates the industry.[21]

Attitudes are just as important as beliefs for influencing buying behavior. An **attitude** is a person's enduring favorable or unfavorable evaluations, emotional feelings, and action tendencies toward some object or idea.[22] People have attitudes toward almost everything: religion, politics, clothes, music, food. Attitudes put them into a frame of mind of liking or disliking an object, moving toward or away from it. Attitudes lead people to behave in a fairly consistent way toward similar objects. Because attitudes economize on energy and thought, they are very difficult to change; to change a single attitude may require major adjustments in other attitudes.

Thus, a company would be well advised to fit its product into existing attitudes rather than to try to change people's attitudes. Of course, trying to change attitudes can pay off occasionally. Look at the milk industry. By the early 1990s, milk consumption had been in decline for 25 years, because the general perception was that milk was unhealthy, outdated, just for kids, or only good with cookies and cakes. Then the National Fluid Milk Processor Education Program kicked off a multi-million dollar print ad campaign featuring milk be-mustached celebrities like Hanson and Tyra Banks with the tag line "Where's your mustache?" The wildly popular campaign has changed attitudes and, in the process, boosted milk consumption. The milk producers have also established an on-line Club Milk (www.whymilk.com), limiting membership to people who pledge to drink three glasses of milk a day.[23]

THE CONSUMER BUYING DECISION PROCESS

Marketers have to go beyond the various influences on buyers and develop an in-depth understanding of how consumers actually make their buying decisions. Specifically, marketers must identify who makes the buying decision, the types of buying decisions, and the stages in the buying process.

Buying Roles

Marketers can identify the buyer for many products easily. In the United States, men normally choose their shaving equipment, and women choose their pantyhose. Still, marketers must be careful, because buying roles can change. After the giant British chemical firm ICI discovered that women made 60 percent of the decisions on the brand of household paint, it began advertising its DeLux brand to women.

We can distinguish five roles that people might play in a buying decision. An *initiator* first suggests the idea of buying the product or service. An *influencer* is the person whose view or advice influences the decision. A *decider* actually decides whether to buy, what to buy, how to buy, or where to buy. A *buyer* makes the actual purchase, while a *user* consumes or uses the product or service.

Buying Behavior

Marketers also need to be aware that consumer decision making varies with the type of buying decision. The decisions to buy toothpaste, a tennis racket, a personal computer, and a new car are all very different. In general, complex and expensive purchases are likely to involve more buyer deliberation and more participants. As shown in Table 5.2, Assael distinguished four types of consumer buying behavior, based on the degree of buyer involvement and the degree of differences among brands:[24]

➤ *Complex buying behavior* applies to high-involvement products such as personal computers. Buyers may not know what attributes to consider in these products, so they do research. Knowing this, marketers can help educate buyers about product

Table 5.2   Four Types of Consumer Buying Behavior

	High Involvement	Low Involvement
Significant Differences between Brands	Complex buying behavior—applies when product is expensive, bought infrequently, risky, and self-expressive; buyer first develops beliefs about the product, then develops attitudes about it, and finally makes a thoughtful choice.	Variety-seeking buying behavior—applies when buyer switches brands for the sake of variety rather than dissatisfaction; buyer has some beliefs about the product, chooses a brand with little evaluation, and evaluates the product during consumption.
Few Differences between Brands	Dissonance-reducing behavior—applies when the product is expensive, bought infrequently, and risky; buyer shops around and buys fairly quickly, then later experiences dissonance but stays alert to information supporting the purchase decision.	Habitual buying behavior—applies when the product is low-cost and frequently purchased; buyers do not pass through normal sequence of belief, attitude, and behavior but instead make decisions based on brand familiarity.

Source: Modified from Henry Assael, *Consumer Behavior and Marketing Action* (Boston: Kent Publishing Co., 1987), p. 87. Copyright © 1987 by Wadsworth, Inc. Printed by permission of Kent Publishing Co., a division of Wadsworth, Inc.

attributes, differentiate and describe the brand's features, and motivate store personnel and others to influence the final brand choice.

➤ *Dissonance-reducing buyer behavior* applies to high-involvement products such as carpeting. Carpeting is expensive and self-expressive, yet the buyer may consider most brands in a given price range to be the same. After buying, the consumer might experience dissonance after noticing certain disquieting features or hearing favorable things about other brands. Marketers should therefore supply beliefs and evaluations that help consumers feel good about their brand choices.

➤ *Habitual buying behavior* applies to low-involvement products such as salt. Consumers keep buying the same brand out of habit, not due to strong brand loyalty, because they are passive recipients of information conveyed by advertising. Ad repetition creates *brand familiarity* rather than *brand conviction*. Marketers of such products can use price and sales promotions to entice new customers to try their products.

➤ *Variety-seeking buying behavior* applies to low-involvement products such as cookies. In this category, consumers switch brands often because they want more variety. The market leader will therefore try to encourage habitual buying behavior by dominating the shelf space, keeping shelves stocked, and running frequent reminder ads. Challenger firms will encourage variety seeking by offering lower prices, coupons, free samples, and ads that offer reasons for trying something new.

The Stages of the Buying Decision Process

In addition to examining buying roles and behavior, smart companies research the buying decision process involved in their product category. They ask consumers when they first became acquainted with the product category and brands, what their brand beliefs are, how involved they are with the product, how they make their brand choices, and how satisfied they are after purchase.

Figure 5.2 shows a five-stage model of the typical buying process. Starting with problem recognition, the consumer passes through the stages of information search, evaluation of alternatives, purchase decision, and postpurchase behavior. As this model demonstrates, the consumer buying process starts long before the actual purchase and has consequences long afterward.[25] Although the model implies that consumers pass sequentially through all five stages in buying a product, consumers sometimes skip or reverse some stages. However, we use this model because it captures the full range of considerations that arise when a consumer faces a highly involving new purchase.[26]

Stage 1: Problem Recognition

The buying process starts when the buyer recognizes a problem or need. This need can be triggered by internal stimuli (such as feeling hunger or thirst) or external stimuli (such as seeing an ad) that then becomes a drive. By gathering information from a number of consumers, marketers can identify the most frequent stimuli that spark interest in a product category. They can then develop marketing strategies that trigger consumer interest and lead to the second stage in the buying process.

Stage 2: Information Search

An aroused consumer who recognizes a problem will be inclined to search for more information. We can distinguish between two levels of arousal. At the milder search state of *heightened attention,* a person simply becomes more receptive to information about a product. At the *active information search* level, a person surfs the Internet, talks with friends, and visits stores to learn more about the product. Consumer information sources include personal sources (family, friends, neighbors, acquaintances), commercial sources (advertising, Web sites, salespersons, dealers, packaging, displays), public sources (mass media, consumer-rating organizations), and experiential sources (handling, examining, using the product). The consumer usually receives the most information from commercial (marketer-dominated) sources, although the most influential information comes from personal sources.

Through gathering information, the consumer learns more and more about competing brands. The first box in Figure 5.3 shows the *total set* of brands available to the consumer. The individual consumer will come to know only a subset of these brands (*awareness set*). Some of these brands will meet initial buying criteria (*consideration set*). As the person gathers more information, only a few brands will remain as strong contenders (*choice set*). The person makes a final choice from this set.[27]

Figure 5.2   Five-Stage Model of the Consumer Buying Process

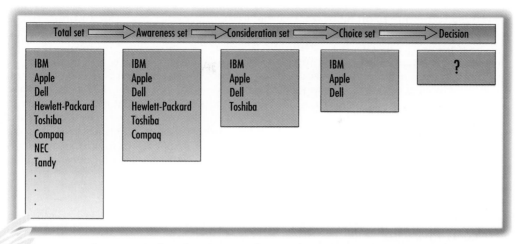

Figure 5.3   Successive Sets Involved in Consumer Decision Making

Figure 5.3 makes it clear that a company must strategize to get its brand into the prospect's awareness set, consideration set, and choice set. The company must also identify the other brands in the consumer's choice set so that it can plan competitive appeals. In addition, the company should identify the consumer's information sources and evaluate their relative importance so it can prepare a range of effective communications for the target market.

Stage 3: Evaluation of Alternatives

Once the consumer has conducted an information search, how does he or she process competitive brand information and make a final judgment? There are several evaluation processes; the most current models view the process as being cognitively oriented, meaning that consumers form judgments largely on a conscious and rational basis.

Some basic concepts underlie consumer evaluation processes. As noted earlier, the consumer is trying to satisfy a *need*. In seeking certain *benefits* from the product solution, the consumer sees each product as a *bundle of attributes* with varying abilities of delivering the benefits to satisfy this need. However, the attributes of interest to buyers vary by product. For example, the attributes sought in a camera might be picture sharpness, camera size, and price. In addition, consumers vary as to which product attributes they see as most relevant and the importance they attach to each attribute. Knowing that consumers pay the most attention to attributes that deliver the benefits they seek, many successful marketers segment their markets according to the attributes that are salient to different consumer groups.

In the course of evaluating alternatives, the consumer develops a set of *brand beliefs* about where each brand stands on each attribute. The set of beliefs about a particular brand, which make up the *brand image*, will vary with the consumer's experiences as filtered by the effects of selective perception, selective distortion, and selective retention.

Ultimately, consumers develop attitudes toward various brand alternatives through an attribute evaluation procedure.[28] Suppose, for example, that Linda Brown has narrowed her choice set to four computers (A, B, C, D) on the basis of four attributes: memory capacity, graphics capability, size and weight, and price. If one computer dominated the others on all of the criteria, we could predict that Linda would choose it. But her choice set consists of brands that vary in their appeal. She sees A as having the best memory capacity, B as having the best graphics capability, C as having the best size and weight, and D as having the best price.

Like most buyers, Linda is considering several attributes in her purchase decision, and she gives each a particular weight. She has assigned 40 percent of the importance to the computer's memory capacity, 30 percent to its graphics capability, 20 percent to its size and weight, and 10 percent to its price. To find Linda's perceived value for each computer, we multiply her weights by the scores indicating her beliefs about each computer's attributes. So for computer A, if she assigns a score of 10 for memory capacity, 8 for graphics capability, 6 for size and weight, and 4 for price, the overall score would be:

$$0.4 \ (10) + 0.3 \ (8) + 0.2 \ (6) + 0.1 \ (4) = 8$$

Calculating the scores for all of the other computers that Linda is evaluating would show which one has the highest perceived value.[29] This is critical, because a manufacturer who knows how buyers evaluate alternatives and form preferences can take steps to influence buyer decisions. In the case of computers, a manufacturer might redesign the computer (a technique called *real repositioning*), alter consumer beliefs about the brand (*psychological repositioning*), alter consumer beliefs about competitors' brands (*competitive depositioning*), alter the importance weights (to persuade buyers to attach more importance to the attributes in which the brand excels), call attention to neglected attributes (such as styling), shift the buyer's ideals (to persuade buyers to change ideal levels on one or more attributes).[30]

Stage 4: Purchase Decision

In the evaluation stage, the consumer forms preferences among the brands in the choice set and may also form an intention to buy the most preferred brand. However, two factors can intervene between the purchase intention and the purchase decision.[31]

The first factor is the *attitudes of others*. The extent to which another person's attitude reduces one's preferred alternative depends on two things: (1) the intensity of the other person's negative attitude toward the consumer's preferred alternative, and (2) the consumer's motivation to comply with the other person's wishes.[32] The influence of others becomes even more complex when several people close to the buyer hold contradictory opinions and the buyer would like to please them all.

The second factor is *unanticipated situational factors* that may erupt to change the purchase intention. A consumer could lose his job, some other purchase might become more urgent, or a store salesperson may turn him or her off, which is why preferences and even purchase intentions are not completely reliable predictors of purchase behavior.

Just as important, a consumer's decision to modify, postpone, or avoid a purchase decision is heavily influenced by *perceived risk*.[33] The amount of perceived risk varies with the amount of money at stake, the amount of attribute uncertainty, and the amount of consumer self-confidence. Consumers develop routines for reducing risk, such as decision avoidance, information gathering from friends, and preference for national brand names and warranties. Smart marketers study the factors that provoke a feeling of risk in consumers and then provide information and support to reduce the perceived risk.

Stage 5: Postpurchase Behavior

After purchasing the product, the consumer moves into the final stage of the consumer buying process, in which he or she will experience some level of satisfaction or dissatisfaction. This is why the marketer's job does not end when the product is bought. In particular, marketers must monitor postpurchase satisfaction, postpurchase actions, and postpurchase product uses.

Postpurchase Satisfaction The buyer's satisfaction with a purchase is a function of the closeness between the buyer's expectations and the product's perceived performance.[34] If performance falls short of expectations, the customer is *disappointed;* if it meets expectations, the customer is *satisfied;* if it exceeds expectations, the customer is *delighted.* These feelings of satisfaction influence whether the customer buys the product again and talks favorably or unfavorably about the product to others.

The importance of postpurchase satisfaction suggests that product claims must truthfully represent the product's likely performance. Some sellers might even understate performance levels so that consumers experience higher-than-expected satisfaction with the product.

Postpurchase Actions The consumer's satisfaction or dissatisfaction with the product after purchase will influence subsequent behavior. Satisfied consumers will be more likely to purchase the product again. This has been confirmed by the data on automobile brand choice, which show a high correlation between satisfaction with the last brand bought and intention to rebuy the brand. One survey showed that 75 percent of Toyota buyers were highly satisfied and about 75 percent intended to buy a Toyota again; 35 percent of Chevrolet buyers were highly satisfied and about 35 percent intended to buy a Chevrolet again. Satisfied customers also tend to say good things about the brand to others, which is why many marketers say: "Our best advertisement is a satisfied customer."[35]

Dissatisfied consumers, on the other hand, may abandon or return the product; seek information that confirms its high value; take public action by complaining to the company, going to a lawyer, or complaining to government agencies and other groups; or take private actions such as not buying the product or warning friends.[36] In these cases, the seller has done a poor job of satisfying the customer.[37]

Marketers can use postpurchase communications to buyers as a way to reduce product returns and order cancellations.[38] Computer companies, for example, might take a number of actions, including sending e-mail messages to new buyers congratulating them on having selected a fine computer, placing ads showing satisfied brand owners, soliciting customer suggestions for improvements, and providing channels for speedy resolution of customer complaints.

Postpurchase Use and Disposal Marketers should also monitor how buyers use and dispose of the product after purchase. The various options that are open to consumers are shown in Figure 5.4. If consumers store the product and never use it, the product is probably not very satisfying, and word-of-mouth will not be strong. If they sell or trade the product, new-product sales will be depressed.

Consumers sometimes find new uses for a product, as Avon discovered when its customers talked about Skin-So-Soft bath oil and moisturizer as an insect repellant. This prompted Avon to seek and receive Environmental Protection Agency approval so it could officially tout Skin-So-Soft as a triple-action product that provides insect repellent, waterproof sunscreen, and moisturizers.[39]

As Figure 5.4 indicates, getting rid of the product permanently leads to a new set of options. If consumers throw the product away, the marketer needs to consider how they dispose of it, especially if it can hurt the environment. For example, increased public awareness of recycling and ecological concerns as well as consumer complaints about having to throw away beautiful bottles led French perfume maker Rochas to

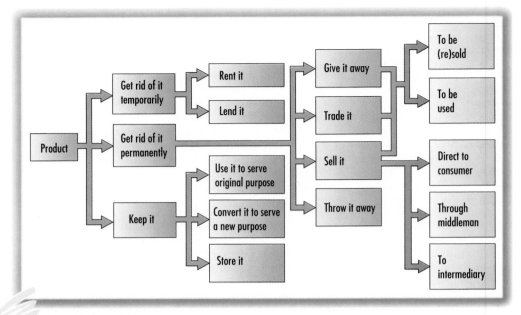

Figure 5.4   How Consumers Use or Dispose of Products

think about introducing a new, refillable bottle fragrance line. This is a more creative, satisfying response to an element that could potentially cause dissatisfaction among buyers.

Just as firms that target consumers must understand how and why consumers buy, those that target businesses and other organizations must be aware of the differences between consumer and business buying behaviors and the way that businesses make buying decisions. These topics are covered in the next chapter.

EXECUTIVE SUMMARY

Before developing their marketing plans, marketers need to use both rigorous scientific procedures and more intuitive methods to study consumer behavior, which is influenced by four factors: cultural (culture, subculture, and social class), social (reference groups, family, and social roles and statuses), personal (age, stage in the life cycle, occupation, economic circumstances, lifestyle, personality, and self-concept), and psychological (motivation, perception, learning, beliefs, and attitudes). Research into all of these factors can provide clues as to how to reach and serve consumers more effectively.

To understand how consumers actually make their buying decisions, marketers must identify who makes and influences the buying decision. People can be initiators, influencers, deciders, buyers, or users, and different marketing campaigns might be targeted to each type of person. Marketers must also examine buyers' levels of involvement and the number of brands available to determine whether consumers are engaging in complex buying behavior, dissonance-reducing buying behavior, habitual buying behavior, or variety-seeking buying behavior.

The five-stage consumer buying process consists of problem recognition, information search, evaluation of alternatives, purchase decision, and postpurchase behavior. The marketer's job is to understand the buyer's behavior at each stage and what influences are operating. The attitudes of others, unanticipated situational factors, and perceived risk may all affect the decision to buy, as will consumers' levels of post-purchase satisfaction, the company's postpurchase actions, and consumers' postpurchase use and disposal of the product. Satisfied customers will continue to purchase; dissatisfied customers will stop purchasing the product and are likely to spread the word among their friends. For this reason, smart companies work to ensure customer satisfaction in every stage of the buying process.

NOTES

1. Tobi Elkin, "Product Pampering," *Brandweek,* June 16, 1997, pp. 38–40; Tim Stevens, "Lights, Camera, Innovation!" *Industry Week,* July 19, 1999, www.industryweek.com; Rekha Balu, "Whirlpool Gets Real with Customers," *Fast Company,* December 1999, pp. 74, 76.

2. See Leon G. Schiffman and Leslie Lazar Kanuk, *Consumer Behavior,* 7th ed. (Upper Saddle River, NJ: Prentice-Hall, 2000).

3. Carole Radice, "Hispanic Consumers: Understanding a Changing Market," *Progressive Grocer,* February 1997, pp. 109–14; Dana Canedy, "The Courtship of Black Consumers," *New York Times,* August 11, 1998, p. D1; Sharon Fairley, George P. Moschis, Herbert M. Myers, and Arnold Thiesfeldt, "Senior Smarts: The Experts Sound Off," *Brandweek,* August 4, 1997, pp. 24–25; Candace Corlett, "Senior Theses," *Brandweek,* August 4, 1997, pp. 22–23.

4. Ibid.

5. See Rosann L. Spiro, "Persuasion in Family Decision Making," *Journal of Consumer Research,* March 1983, pp. 393–402; Lawrence H. Wortzel, "Marital Roles and Typologies as Predictors of Purchase Decision Making for Everyday Household Products: Suggestions for Research," in *Advances in Consumer Research,* Vol. 7, ed. Jerry C. Olson (Chicago: American Marketing Association, 1989), pp. 212–15; David J. Burns, "Husband-Wife Innovative Consumer Decision Making: Exploring the Effect of Family Power," *Psychology & Marketing,* May–June 1992, pp. 175–89; Robert Boutilier, "Pulling the Family's Strings," *American Demographics,* August 1993, pp. 44–48. For cross-cultural comparisons of husband–wife buying roles, see John B. Ford, Michael S. LaTour, and Tony L. Henthorne, "Perception of Marital Roles in Purchase-Decision Processes: A Cross-Cultural Study," *Journal of the Academy of Marketing Science,* Spring 1995, pp. 120–31.

6. George Moschis, "The Role of Family Communication in Consumer Socialization of Children and Adolescents," *Journal of Consumer Research,* March 1985, pp. 898–913.

7. Marilyn Lavin, "Husband-Dominant, Wife-Dominant, Joint: A Shopping Typology for Baby Boom Couples?" *Journal of Consumer Marketing* 10, no. 3 (1993): 33–42.

8. James U. McNeal, "Tapping the Three Kids' Markets," *American Demographics,* April 1998, pp. 37–41.

9. Rob Yoegel, "Reaching Youth on the Web," *Target Marketing,* November 1997, pp. 38–41.

10. See Lawrence Lepisto, "A Life Span Perspective of Consumer Behavior," in *Advances in Consumer Research,* Vol. 12, ed. Elizabeth Hirshman and Morris Holbrook (Provo, UT: Association for Consumer Research, 1985), p. 47. Also see Gail Sheehy, *New Passages: Mapping Your Life Across Time* (New York: Random House, 1995).

11. Arnold Mitchell, *The Nine American Lifestyles* (New York: Warner Books), pp. viii–x, 25–31; Personal communication from the VALS™ Program, Business Intelligence Center, SRI Consulting, Menlo Park, CA, February 1, 1996. See also Wagner A. Kamakura and Michel Wedel, "Lifestyle Segmentation with Tailored Interviewing," *Journal of Marketing Research* 32, no. 3 (August 1995): 308–17.

12. Paul C. Judge, "Are Tech Buyers Different?" *Business Week,* January 26, 1998, pp. 64–65, 68; Andy Hines, "Do you Know Your Technology Type?" *The Futurist,* September–October

1997, pp. 10–11; Rebecca Piirto Heath, "The Frontiers of Psychographics," *American Demographics,* July 1996, pp. 38–43; information on iVALS from www.future.sri.com (September 1999).

13. Stuart Elliott, "Sampling Tastes of a Changing Russia," *New York Times,* April 1, 1992, pp. D1, D19.

14. See Harold H. Kassarjian and Mary Jane Sheffet, "Personality and Consumer Behavior: An Update," in *Perspectives in Consumer Behavior,* ed. Harold H. Kassarjian and Thomas S. Robertson (Glenview, IL: Scott, Foresman, 1981), pp. 160–80.

15. See M. Joseph Sirgy, "Self-Concept in Consumer Behavior: A Critical Review," *Journal of Consumer Research,* December 1982, pp. 287–300.

16. See Thomas J. Reynolds and Jonathan Gutman, "Laddering Theory, Method, Analysis, and Interpretation," *Journal of Advertising Research,* February–March 1988, pp. 11–34.

17. Abraham Maslow, *Motivation and Personality* (New York: Harper & Row, 1954), pp. 80–106.

18. See Frederick Herzberg, *Work and the Nature of Man* (Cleveland, OH: William Collins, 1966); and Henk Thierry and Agnes M. Koopman-Iwerna, "Motivation and Satisfaction," in *Handbook of Work and Organizational Psychology,* ed. P. J. Drenth (New York: John Wiley, 1984), pp. 141–42.

19. Bernard Berelson and Gary A. Steiner, *Human Behavior: An Inventory of Scientific Findings* (New York: Harcourt Brace Jovanovich, 1964), p. 88.

20. See Alice M. Tybout, Bobby J. Calder, and Brian Sternthal, "Using Information Processing Theory to Design Marketing Strategies," *Journal of Marketing Research,* February 1981, pp. 73–79.

21. "International: Old Wine in New Bottles," *The Economist,* February 21, 1998, p. 45.

22. See David Krech, Richard S. Crutchfield, and Egerton L. Ballachey, *Individual in Society* (New York: McGraw-Hill, 1962), ch. 2.

23. Melanie Wells, "Got a Milk Mustache? Campaign's Popularity Staying Fresh," *USA Today Ad Track,* July 13, 1999, www.usatoday.com; Jill Venter, "Milk Mustache Campaign Is a Hit with Teens," *St. Louis Post-Dispatch,* April 1, 1998, p. E1; Dave Fusaro, "The Milk Mustache," *Dairy Foods,* April 1997, p. 75; Judann Pollack, "Milk: Kurt Graetzer," *Advertising Age,* June 30, 1997, p. S1.

24. See Henry Assael, *Consumer Behavior and Marketing Action* (Boston: Kent, 1987), ch. 4.

25. Marketing scholars have developed several models of the consumer buying process. See John A. Howard and Jagdish N. Sheth, *The Theory of Buyer Behavior* (New York: Wiley, 1969); and James F. Engel, Roger D. Blackwell, and Paul W. Miniard, *Consumer Behavior,* 8th ed. (Fort Worth, TX: Dryden, 1994).

26. See William P. Putsis, Jr. and Narasimhan Srinivasan, "Buying or Just Browsing? The Duration of Purchase Deliberation," *Journal of Marketing Research,* August 1994, pp. 393–402.

27. See Chem L. Narayana and Rom J. Markin, "Consumer Behavior and Product Performance: An Alternative Conceptualization," *Journal of Marketing,* October 1975, pp. 1–6. See also Wayne S. DeSarbo and Kamel Jedidi, "The Spatial Representation of Heterogeneous Consideration Sets," *Marketing Science* 14, no. 3, pt. 2 (1995), 326–42; and Lee G. Cooper and Akihiro Inoue, "Building Market Structures from Consumer Preferences," *Journal of Marketing Research* 33, no. 3 (August 1996), 293–306.

28. See Paul E. Green and Yoram Wind, *Multiattribute Decisions in Marketing: A Measurement Approach* (Hinsdale, IL: Dryden, 1973), ch. 2; Leigh McAlister, "Choosing Multiple Items from a Product Class," *Journal of Consumer Research,* December 1979, pp. 213–24.

29. This expectancy-value model was developed by Martin Fishbein, "Attitudes and Prediction of Behavior," in *Readings in Attitude Theory and Measurement,* ed. Martin Fishbein (New York: John Wiley, 1967), pp. 477–92. For a critical review, see Paul W. Miniard and Joel B.

Cohen, "An Examination of the Fishbein-Ajzen Behavioral-Intentions Model's Concepts and Measures," *Journal of Experimental Social Psychology,* May 1981, pp. 309–39.

30. See Harper W. Boyd Jr., Michael L. Ray, and Edward C. Strong, "An Attitudinal Framework for Advertising Strategy," *Journal of Marketing,* April 1972, pp. 27–33.

31. See Jagdish N. Sheth, "An Investigation of Relationships among Evaluative Beliefs, Affect, Behavioral Intention, and Behavior," in *Consumer Behavior: Theory and Application,* eds. John U. Farley, John A. Howard, and L. Winston Ring (Boston: Allyn & Bacon, 1974), pp. 89–114.

32. See Fishbein, "Attitudes and Prediction of Behavior."

33. See Raymond A. Bauer, "Consumer Behavior as Risk Taking," in *Risk Taking and Information Handling in Consumer Behavior,* ed. Donald F. Cox (Boston: Division of Research, Harvard Business School, 1967); and James W. Taylor, "The Role of Risk in Consumer Behavior," *Journal of Marketing,* April 1974, pp. 54–60.

34. See Priscilla A. La Barbera and David Mazursky, "A Longitudinal Assessment of Consumer Satisfaction/Dissatisfaction: The Dynamic Aspect of the Cognitive Process," *Journal of Marketing Research,* November 1983, pp. 393–404.

35. See Barry L. Bayus, "Word of Mouth: The Indirect Effects of Marketing Efforts," *Journal of Advertising Research,* June-July 1985, pp. 31–39.

36. See Albert O. Hirschman, *Exit, Voice, and Loyalty* (Cambridge, MA: Harvard University Press, 1970).

37. See Mary C. Gilly and Richard W. Hansen, "Consumer Complaint Handling as a Strategic Marketing Tool," *Journal of Consumer Marketing,* Fall 1985, pp. 5–16.

38. See James H. Donnelly Jr. and John M. Ivancevich, "Post-Purchase Reinforcement and Back-Out Behavior," *Journal of Marketing Research,* August 1970, pp. 399–400.

39. Pam Weisz, "Avon's Skin-So-Soft Bugs Out," *Brandweek,* June 6, 1994, p. 4.

Analyzing Business Markets and Buyer Behavior

In this chapter, we will address the following questions:

■ What is the business market, and how does it differ from the consumer market?

■ How do institutions and government agencies do their buying?

■ What buying situations do organizational buyers face?

■ Who participates in business buying, and what are the influences on business buying decisions?

■ How do business buyers make their decisions?

Business organizations do not only sell. They also buy vast quantities of raw materials, manufactured components, plants and equipment, supplies, and business services. Over 13 million business, institutional, and government organizations in the United States alone—plus millions more in other countries—represent a huge, lucrative buying market for goods and services purchased from both domestic and international suppliers.

Business buyers purchase goods and services to achieve specific goals, such as making money, reducing operating costs, and satisfying social or legal obligations. For example, a mini-mill steelmaker like Nucor will add another plant if it sees a chance to boost profits, upgrade its computerized accounting system to reduce operating costs, and add pollution-control equipment to meet legal requirements.

In principle, a business buyer seeks to obtain for his or her organization the best package of economic, technical, service, and social benefits in relation to a market offering's costs. In reality, a business buyer (like a consumer) will have more incentive to choose the offering with the highest ratio of perceived benefits to costs—that is, the highest perceived value. The marketer must therefore provide an offering that delivers superior customer value to the targeted business buyers and be familiar with the underlying dynamics and process of business buying.

WHAT IS ORGANIZATIONAL BUYING?

Organizational buying, according to Webster and Wind, is the decision-making process by which formal organizations establish the need for purchased products and services and identify, evaluate, and choose among alternative brands and suppliers.[1] Just as no two consumers buy in exactly the same way, no two organizations buy in exactly the same way. Therefore, as they do for the consumer market, business sellers work hard to distinguish clusters of customers that buy in similar ways and then create suitable marketing strategies for reaching those targeted business market segments. However, the business market differs from the consumer market in a number of significant ways.

The Business Market Versus the Consumer Market

The *business market* consists of all of the organizations that acquire goods and services used in the production of other products or services that are sold, rented, or supplied to other customers. The major industries making up the business market are agriculture, forestry, and fisheries; mining; manufacturing; construction; transportation; communication; public utilities; banking, finance, and insurance; distribution; and services. As discussed in Chapter 4, U.S. marketers can learn more about specific industries by consulting the North American Industry Classification System (NAICS), a categorized listing of all of the industries operating in Canada, the United States, and Mexico.

In general, more dollars and items are involved in sales to business buyers than to consumers. Consider the process of producing and selling a simple pair of shoes. Hide dealers must sell hides to tanners, who sell leather to shoe manufacturers, who sell shoes to wholesalers, who sell shoes to retailers, who finally sell them to consumers. Along the way, each party in the supply chain also has to buy many other goods and services, which means that every business seller is a business buyer, as well.

From the number and size of buyers to geographical location, demand, and buying behaviors, business markets have a number of characteristics that contrast sharply with those of consumer markets. These characteristics are described in Table 6.1.

Understanding the impact of these characteristics can help a supplier target business buyers more effectively. Pittsburgh-based Cutler-Hammer, for example, sells circuit breakers, motor starters, and other electrical equipment to industrial manufacturers such as Ford Motor. As its product line grew larger and more complex, C-H developed "pods" of salespeople that focus on a particular geographical region, industry, or market concentration. Each individual brings a degree of expertise about a product or service that the other members of the team can take to the customer. This allows the salespeople to leverage the knowledge of co-workers to sell to increasingly sophisticated buying teams, instead of working in isolation.[2]

Specialized Organizational Markets

The overall business market includes institutional and government organizations in addition to profit-seeking companies. However, the buying goals, needs, and methods of these two specialized organizational markets are generally different from those of businesses, something firms must keep in mind when planning their business marketing strategies.

The Institutional Market

The *institutional market* consists of schools, hospitals, nursing homes, prisons, and other institutions that provide goods and services to people in their care. Many of

Table 6.1   Characteristics of Business Markets

Characteristic	Description	Example
Fewer buyers	Business marketers normally deal with far fewer buyers than do consumer marketers.	Goodyear Tire Company aims to get orders from buyers for the Big Three U.S. automakers (General Motors, Ford, and Daimler-Chrysler).
Larger buyers	Buyers for a few large firms do most of the purchasing in many industries.	Major companies are big customers in industries such as aircraft engines and defense weapons.
Close supplier-customer relationship	With the smaller customer base and the importance and power of the larger customers, suppliers are frequently required to customize offerings, practices, and performance to meet the needs of individual customers.	Tooling supplier Stillwater Technologies shares office and manufacturing space with key customer Motoman, a supplier of industrial robots, to minimize delivery distances and enhance their symbiotic working relationship.[1]
Geographically concentrated buyers	More than half of U.S. business buyers are concentrated in seven states: New York, California, Pennsylvania, Illinois, Ohio, New Jersey, and Michigan, which helps to reduce selling costs.	Because the Big Three U.S. automakers have their U.S. headquarters in the Detroit area, industry suppliers head there on sales calls.
Derived demand	Demand for business goods is ultimately derived from demand for consumer goods, so business marketers must monitor the buying patterns of ultimate consumers.	The Big Three U.S. automakers are seeing higher demand for steel-bar products, mostly derived from consumers' demand for minivans and other light trucks, which consume far more steel than cars.
Inelastic demand	Total demand for many business goods and services is inelastic and not much affected by price changes, especially in the short run, because producers cannot make quick production changes.	Shoe manufacturers will not buy much more leather if the price of leather falls. Nor will they buy much less leather if the price rises unless they can find satisfactory substitutes.
Fluctuating demand	Demand for business products tends to be more volatile than demand for consumer products. An increase in consumer demand can lead to a much larger increase in demand for plant and equipment needed to produce the additional output.	An increase of only 10% in consumer demand for computers might result in a 200% increase in business demand for related parts, supplies, and services; a 10% drop in consumer demand for computers might cause a complete collapse in business demand.

Continued

Table 6.1 Characteristics of Business Markets—*Continued*

Characteristic	Description	Example
Professional purchasing	Trained purchasing agents follow organizational purchasing policies, constraints, and requirements to buy business products. Many of the buying instruments—such as proposals and purchase contracts—are not typical of consumer buying.	Programs on the Cisco Systems Web site allow purchasing agents to research, select, and price new networking systems at any hour and obtain speedy online answers about products, orders, and service.[2]
Multiple buying influences	More people typically influence business buying decisions. Buying committees are common in the purchase of major goods; marketers have to send well-trained sales reps and often sales teams to deal with these well-trained buyers.	Metal supplier Phelps Dodge uses an "account management approach" to reach all the key people who influence business buying decisions in customer organizations.[3]
Multiple sales calls	With more people involved in the process, it takes multiple sales calls to win most business orders, and the sales cycle can take years.	In the case of major capital equipment sales, customers may take multiple attempts to fund a project, and the sales cycle—between quoting a job and delivering the product—is often measured in years.[4]
Direct purchasing	Business buyers often buy directly from manufacturers rather than through intermediaries, especially items that are technically complex or expensive.	Southwest Airlines, Air Madagascar, and other airlines around the world buy airplanes directly from Boeing.
Reciprocity	Business buyers often select suppliers who also buy from them.	A paper manufacturer buys chemicals from a chemical company that buys a considerable amount of its paper.
Leasing	Many industrial buyers lease rather than buy heavy equipment to conserve capital, get the latest products, receive better service, and gain tax advantages. The lessor often makes more profit and sells to customers who could not afford outright purchase.	General Electric leases truck and car fleets, aircraft, commercial trailers, railcars, and other major equipment products to business buyers.

Sources for examples: [1]John H. Sheridan, "An Alliance Built on Trust," *Industry Week,* March 17, 1997, pp. 66–70; [2]Andy Reinhardt, "Meet Mr. Internet," *Business Week,* September 13, 1999, pp. 128–40; [3]Minda Zetlin, "It's All the Same to Me," *Sales & Marketing Management,* February 1994, pp. 71–75; [4]Michael Collins, "Breaking into the Big Leagues," *American Demographics,* January 1996, p. 24.

these organizations have low budgets and captive clienteles. For example, hospitals have to decide what quality of food to buy for their patients. The buying objective here is not profit, because the food is provided to the patients as part of the total service package. Nor is cost minimization the sole objective, because poor food will cause patients to complain and hurt the hospital's reputation. The hospital purchasing agent has to search for institutional food vendors whose quality meets or exceeds a certain minimum standard and whose prices are low. Knowing this, many food vendors set up a separate division to respond to the special needs of institutional buyers. Thus, Heinz, for example, will produce, package, and price its ketchup differently to meet the different requirements of hospitals, colleges, and prisons.

Being a supplier of choice for the nation's schools or hospitals means big business for marketers such as Allegiance Healthcare. This firm has become the largest U.S. supplier of medical, surgical, and laboratory products. Through its stockless inventory program, known as "ValueLink," Allegiance delivers ordered products to more than 150 hospitals when and where staff members need them. Under the old system, the most needed items were inevitably in short supply, while the rarely used items were available in great number. By using Allegiance's ValueLink system, hospitals save an average of $500,000 or more yearly and gain faster, easier access to the items they need.[3]

The Government Market

In most countries, government organizations are a major buyer of goods and services. The U.S. government, for example, buys goods and services valued at $200 billion, making it the largest customer in the world. The number of individual purchases is equally staggering: Over 20 million individual contract actions are processed every year. Although the cost of most items purchased is between $2,500 and $25,000, the government also makes purchases of $25,000 and up, sometimes well into the millions of dollars.

Government organizations typically require suppliers to submit bids. Normally, they award the contract to the lowest bidder, although they sometimes take into account a supplier's superior quality or reputation for completing contracts on time. Because their spending decisions are subject to public review, government organizations require considerable documentation from suppliers, who often complain about excessive paperwork, bureaucracy, regulations, decision-making delays, and shifts in procurement personnel.

Consider the experience of ADI Technology Corporation. The U.S. government has always been ADI's most important client, accounting for about 90 percent of its nearly $6 million in annual revenues. Yet managers at this professional services company often shake their heads at all of the work that goes into winning the coveted government contracts. A comprehensive bid proposal will run from 500 to 700 pages, and ADI's president estimates that the firm has spent as much as $20,000, mostly in worker hours, to prepare a single bid proposal.

Fortunately for businesses of all sizes, the federal government has been putting reforms in place to streamline buying procedures. Now the government is moving all purchasing on-line, with the use of Web-based technologies such as digital signatures.[4] Several federal agencies that act as purchasing agents for the rest of the government have already launched Web-based catalogs, allowing defense and civilian agencies to buy everything from medical and office supplies to clothing through on-line purchasing. State and local governments are following suit: The city of Fort Collins, Colorado, for example, announces its buying needs, posts requests for proposals, and offers downloads of standard supplier documents on its Web site. Internet-based purchasing has enabled Fort Collins to more efficiently buy computers, flooring, and an ever-widening range of goods for city use.

A number of major companies, such as Gateway, Rockwell, Kodak, and Goodyear, make a special effort to anticipate the needs and projects of the government market. In this market, success comes to firms that participate in the product specification phase, gather competitive intelligence, prepare bids carefully, and produce strong communications to enhance their companies' reputations.

Business Buying Situations

Business buyers in companies, institutions, and government organizations face many decisions in the course of making a purchase. The number of decisions depends on the type of buying situation. Robinson and others distinguish three types of buying situations: the straight rebuy, the modified rebuy, and the new task.[5]

> *Straight rebuy:* The *straight rebuy* is a buying situation in which the purchasing department reorders on a routine basis (e.g., office supplies, bulk chemicals). The buyer chooses from suppliers on an "approved list." These suppliers make an effort to maintain product and service quality. They often propose automatic reordering systems to help purchasing agents save time. The "out-suppliers" attempt to offer something new or to exploit dissatisfaction with a current supplier. Out-suppliers try to get a small order and then enlarge their purchase share over time.

> *Modified rebuy:* The *modified rebuy* is a situation in which the buyer wants to modify product specifications, prices, delivery requirements, or other terms. The modified rebuy usually involves additional decision participants on both sides. The in-suppliers become nervous and have to protect the account; the out-suppliers see an opportunity to gain some business.

> *New task:* The *new task* is a buying situation in which a purchaser buys a product or service for the first time (e.g., office building, new security system). The greater the cost or risk, the larger the number of decision participants and the greater their information gathering—and therefore the longer the time to decision completion.[6]

New-task buying passes through several stages: awareness, interest, evaluation, trial, and adoption.[7] Communication tools' effectiveness varies at each stage. Mass media are most important during the initial awareness stage, salespeople have their greatest impact at the interest stage, and technical sources are the most important during the evaluation stage.

The business buyer makes the fewest decisions in the straight-rebuy situation and the most in the new-task situation. In the new-task situation, the buyer has to determine product specifications, price limits, delivery terms and times, service terms, payment terms, order quantities, acceptable suppliers, and the selected supplier. Different participants influence each decision, and the order in which these decisions are made can vary. The new-task situation is, therefore, the business marketer's greatest opportunity and challenge. For this reason, marketers should try to reach as many key buying influencers as possible and provide helpful information and assistance. Because of the complicated selling involved in new-task situations, many companies use a *missionary sales force* consisting of their best salespeople.

Systems Buying and Selling

Many business buyers prefer to buy a total solution to their problem from one seller. This practice, called *systems buying,* originated with government purchases of major weapons and communication systems. The government solicited bids from prime contractors; the winning contractor then bid out and assembled the system from subcomponents purchased from other contractors. Thus, the prime contractor was providing a "turnkey solution" that allowed the buyer to, in effect, turn one key and get the job done.

Sellers have increasingly recognized that buyers like to purchase in this way, and many have adopted systems selling as a marketing tool. Systems selling can take different forms. For example, many auto parts manufacturers now sell whole systems, such as the seating system, the braking system, or the door system. A variant on systems selling is *systems contracting,* in which a single supply source provides the buyer with all required *MRO supplies* (maintenance, repair, and operating supplies). This lowers the buyer's costs because the seller maintains the inventory, less time is spent on supplier selection, and the buyer enjoys price protection during the life of the contract. The seller benefits from lower operating costs because of steady demand and reduced paperwork.

Systems selling is a key industrial marketing strategy in bidding to build large-scale industrial projects such as dams, steel factories, and pipelines. Project engineering firms must compete on price, quality, reliability, and other attributes to win these contracts. For example, when the Indonesian government requested bids to build a cement factory near Jakarta, a U.S. firm made a proposal that included choosing the site, designing the cement factory, hiring the construction crews, assembling the materials and equipment, and turning over the finished factory to the Indonesian government. The proposal of a Japanese bidder included all of these services, plus hiring and training the factory workers, exporting the cement, and using the cement to build roads and office buildings around Jakarta. Although the Japanese proposal was more costly, it won. This is true system selling: The firm took the broadest view of its customer's needs and positioned itself as an economic development agency.

PARTICIPANTS IN THE BUSINESS BUYING PROCESS

Who does the buying of the trillions of dollars' worth of goods and services needed by business organizations? Purchasing agents are influential in straight-rebuy and modified-rebuy situations, whereas other department personnel are more influential in new-buy situations. Engineering personnel carry the most influence in selecting product components, and purchasing agents dominate in selecting suppliers.[8] These are just some of the people who may be part of the buying center.

The Buying Center

Webster and Wind call the decision-making unit of a buying organization the *buying center.* The buying center is composed of "all those individuals and groups who participate in the purchasing decision-making process, who share some common goals and the risks arising from the decisions."[9] The buying center includes organizational members who play any of seven roles in the purchase decision process:[10]

➤ *Initiators:* People who request that something be purchased, including users or others.

➤ *Users:* Those who will use the product or service; often, users initiate the buying proposal and help define product requirements.

➤ *Influencers:* People who influence the buying decision, including technical personnel. They often help define specifications and also provide information for evaluating alternatives.

➤ *Deciders:* Those who decide on product requirements or on suppliers.

➤ *Approvers:* People who authorize the proposed actions of deciders or buyers.

➤ *Buyers:* People who have formal authority to select the supplier and arrange the purchase terms, including high-level managers. Buyers may help shape product specifications, but their major role is selecting vendors and negotiating.

➤ *Gatekeepers:* People who have the power to prevent sellers or information from reaching members of the buying center; examples are purchasing agents, receptionists, and telephone operators.

There is also a trend toward team-based buying. In one survey, 87 percent of the purchasing executives at Fortune 1000 companies see more use of teams drawn from different departments and functions to make buying decisions.[11] This trend is leading to more team selling, as shown in the earlier Cutler-Hammer example.

To target their efforts properly, business marketers have to figure out: Who are the major decision participants? What decisions do they influence? What is their level of influence? What evaluation criteria do they use? When a buying center includes many participants, the business marketer will not have the time or resources to reach all of them. Small sellers concentrate on reaching the *key buying influencers.* Larger sellers go for *multilevel in-depth selling* to reach as many buying-center participants as possible. Their salespeople virtually "live" with their high-volume customers. In general, the most successful companies rely more heavily on communications to reach hidden buying influences and keep their current customers sold.[12]

Furthermore, the buying center can be highly dynamic, so business marketers need to periodically review their assumptions about who is participating. For years, Kodak sold X-ray film to hospital lab technicians, not noticing that buying decisions were increasingly being made by professional administrators. As sales declined, Kodak was finally forced to revise its market targeting strategy.

Major Influences on Business Buying

Business buyers respond to many influences when they make their decisions. When supplier offerings are similar, buyers can satisfy the purchasing requirements with any supplier, and they place more weight on the personal treatment they receive. When supplier offerings differ substantially, buyers are more accountable for their choices and pay more attention to economic factors. Business buyers respond to four main influences: environmental, organizational, interpersonal, and individual[13] (Figure 6.1); culture is also a factor.

Environmental Factors

Within the macroenvironment, business buyers pay close attention to numerous economic factors, including interest rates and levels of production, investment, and consumer spending. In a recession, business buyers reduce their investment in plant, equipment, and inventories. Business marketers can do little to stimulate total demand in recessionary periods; they can only fight harder to increase or maintain their share of demand.

Companies that fear materials shortages often buy and hold large inventories and sign long-term contracts with suppliers to ensure steady availability. In fact, DuPont, Ford, and other major companies regard long-term *supply planning* as a major responsibility of their purchasing managers.

Business buyers also actively monitor technological, political-regulatory, and competitive developments. For example, environmental concerns can cause changes in business buyer behavior. A printing firm might favor suppliers that carry recycled papers or use environmentally safe ink. One buyer claimed, "We push suppliers with technical expertise to be more socially conscious."

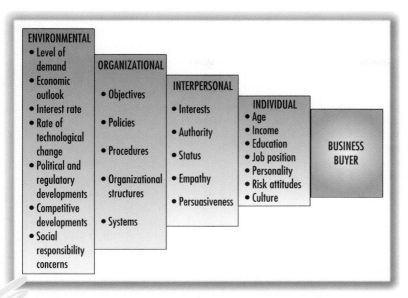

Figure 6.1   Major Influences on Business Buying Behavior

Organizational Factors

Every organization has specific purchasing objectives, policies, procedures, organizational structures, and systems. Business marketers need to be aware of the following organizational trends in purchasing:

➤ *Purchasing department upgrading.* Spurred by competitive pressures, companies are staffing their purchasing departments with MBAs who aspire to be CEOs—like Thomas Stallkamp, DaimlerChrysler's recently retired president. In his earlier role as executive vice president of procurement and supply, Stallkamp was highly successful in cost-cutting and in streamlining manufacturing processes.[14] These new, more strategically positioned "procurement departments" seek out the best value from fewer and better suppliers. At Caterpillar and other multinationals, purchasing departments have been elevated into "strategic supply departments" with responsibility for global sourcing and partnering. In response to this trend, business marketers must correspondingly upgrade their sales personnel to match the higher caliber of the business buyers.

➤ *Cross-functional roles.* In a recent survey, most purchasing professionals described their job as more strategic, technical, team-oriented, and involving more responsibility than ever before. "Purchasing is doing more cross-functional work than it did in the past," says David Duprey, a buyer for Anaren Microwave Inc., which makes microwave-signal processing devices for communication and defense. Sixty-one percent of buyers surveyed said the buying group was more involved in new-product design and development than it was 5 years ago. More than half of the buyers now participate in cross-functional teams, with suppliers well represented.[15]

➤ *Centralized purchasing.* In multidivisional companies, most purchasing is carried out by separate divisions because of their differing needs. Some companies, however, have recentralized their purchasing, identifying materials purchased by several divisions and buying them centrally to gain more purchasing clout. Individual divisions can buy from other sources if they can get a better deal, but centralized purchasing usually produces substantial savings. For the business marketer, this means dealing with fewer and higher-level buyers, and using a national account sales group to deal with large corporate buyers.

➤ *Decentralized purchasing of small-ticket items.* More companies are decentralizing selected purchasing operations by empowering employees to purchase small-ticket items such as special binders and coffee makers. This has come about through the availability of corporate purchasing cards issued by credit-card firms. Companies distribute the cards to supervisors, clerks, and secretaries; the cards incorporate codes that set credit limits and restrict usage. National Semiconductor's purchasing chief says these cards have cut processing costs from $30 an order to a few cents. "Now buyers and suppliers can spend less time on paperwork, so purchasing departments have more time for building partnerships."[16]

➤ *Internet purchasing.* By 2003, business-to-business buying on the Internet is projected to reach $1 trillion per year (compared with a projected $108 billion for consumer buying).[17] The move to Internet purchasing has dramatic and far-reaching implications. Companies are not only posting their own Web pages to sell to business buyers, they are establishing Intranets for internal communication and extranets to link with regular suppliers and distributors. So far, most businesses are using extranets to buy MRO supplies. However, a growing number, such as General Electric, are preparing to buy nearly all supplies on-line to shave transaction and personnel costs, reduce time between order and delivery, and consolidate purchasing. In fact, GE Information Services is a leader in helping GE internal business units and outside companies use the Internet to buy from and sell to other businesses; its Trading Process Network lets companies buy raw materials, components, and just about anything else with a few clicks of the mouse. Internet purchasing can help forge closer relations between partners and buyers, and it levels the playing field between large and small suppliers. At the same time, it can potentially erode supplier-buyer loyalty and open the door to possible security disasters.[18]

➤ *Long-term contracts.* Business buyers are increasingly initiating or accepting long-term contracts with reliable suppliers. For example, General Motors wants to buy from fewer suppliers who are willing to locate close to its plants and produce high-quality components. In addition, business marketers are setting up electronic data interchange (EDI) systems so their customers such as hospitals and bookstores can enter and transmit purchase orders electronically.

➤ *Purchasing-performance evaluation and buyers' professional development.* Many companies have set up incentive systems to reward purchasing managers for good buying performance, in much the same way that sales personnel receive bonuses for good selling performance. These systems are leading purchasing managers to increase their pressure on sellers for the best terms.

➤ *Lean production.* Many manufacturers have moved toward lean production, which enables them to produce a more high-quality product at lower cost, in less time, using less labor. Lean production incorporates just-in-time (JIT) production, stricter quality control, frequent and reliable supply delivery, suppliers locating closer to customers, computerized purchasing, stable production schedules made available to suppliers, and single sourcing with early supplier involvement. JIT II, the next level of customer-supplier partnerships, focuses on reducing the costs and time involved in day-to-day purchasing transactions by locating one or more supplier employees at the customer's site, in the role of buyer-materials planners. Massachusetts's Bose Corporation pioneered this arrangement with G&F Industries, its first in-plant supplier. Says Christ Labonte, a G&F manager, "It's a fresh, nontraditional agreement based on trust. After people get comfortable in their partnering, they start turning up rocks they wouldn't have turned up and revealing causes that were sacred cows."[19]

Interpersonal Factors

Buying centers usually include several participants with differing interests, authority, status, empathy, and persuasiveness. The business marketer is not likely to know what kind of group dynamics take place during the buying decision process. Therefore, successful firms strive to find out as much as possible about individual buying center participants and their interaction and train sales personnel and others from the marketing organization to be more attuned to the influence of interpersonal factors.

Individual Factors

Each buyer carries personal motivations, perceptions, and preferences, as influenced by the buyer's age, income, education, job position, personality, attitudes toward risk, and culture. Moreover, buyers definitely exhibit different buying styles. For example, some younger, highly educated buyers are expert at conducting rigorous, computerized analyses of competitive proposals before choosing a supplier. Other buyers are "toughies" from the old school and pit competitors against one another. Understanding these factors can better prepare marketers for dealing with individuals within the buying center.

Cultural Factors

Savvy marketers carefully study the culture and customs of each country or region where they want to sell their products, to better understand the cultural factors that can affect buyers and the buying organization. For example, in Germany, businesspeople prefer to be introduced by their full, correct titles, and they shake hands at both the beginning and the end of business meetings. As another example, both Korean and Japanese businesspeople observe Confucian ethics based on respect for authority and the primacy of the group over the individual.[20] Marketers that sell to firms in other nations must be aware of such cultural attitudes and practices, because they permeate business-to-business transactions.

THE PURCHASING/PROCUREMENT PROCESS

Industrial buying passes through eight stages called *buyphases,* as identified by Robinson and associates in the *buygrid* framework shown in Table 6.2.[21] In modified-rebuy or straight-rebuy situations, some of these stages are compressed or bypassed. For example, in a straight-rebuy situation, the buyer normally has a favorite supplier or a ranked list of suppliers. Thus, the supplier search and proposal solicitation stages are skipped. In the sections that follow, we examine each of the eight stages for a typical new-task buying situation.

Stage 1: Problem Recognition

The buying process begins when someone in the company recognizes a problem or need that can be met by acquiring a good or service. The recognition can be triggered by internal or external stimuli. Internally, problem recognition commonly occurs when a firm decides to develop a new product and needs new equipment and materi-

Table 6.2   Buygrid Framework: Major Stages (Buyphases) of the Industrial Buying Process in Relation to Major Buying Situations (Buyclasses)

		New Task	Buyphases Modified Rebuy	Straight Rebuy
Buyphases	1. Problem recognition	Yes	Maybe	No
	2. General need description	Yes	Maybe	No
	3. Product specification	Yes	Yes	Yes
	4. Supplier search	Yes	Maybe	No
	5. Proposal solicitation	Yes	Maybe	No
	6. Supplier selection	Yes	Maybe	No
	7. Order-routine specification	Yes	Maybe	No
	8. Performance review	Yes	Yes	Yes

Source: Adapted from Patrick J. Robinson, Charles W. Faris, and Yoram Wind, *Industrial Buying and Creative Marketing* (Boston: Allyn & Bacon, 1967), p. 14.

als, when a machine breaks down and requires new parts, when purchased material turns out to be unsatisfactory, and when a purchasing manager senses an opportunity to obtain lower prices or better quality. Externally, problem recognition can occur when a buyer gets new ideas at a trade show, sees a supplier's ad, or is contacted by a sales representative offering a better product or a lower price. For their part, business marketers can stimulate problem recognition by direct mail, telemarketing, effective Internet communications, and calling on prospects.

Stage 2: General Need Description

Once a problem has been recognized, the buyer has to determine the needed item's general characteristics and the required quantity. For standard items, this is not a very involved process. For complex items, the buyer will work with others—engineers, users, and so on—to define the needed characteristics. These may include reliability, durability, price, or other attributes. In this stage, business marketers can assist buyers by describing how their products would meet such needs.

Stage 3: Product Specification

With a general need description in hand, the buying organization can develop the item's technical specifications. Often, the company will assign a product value analysis (PVA) engineering team to the project. **Product value analysis** is an approach to cost reduction in which components are carefully studied to determine if they can be redesigned or standardized or made by cheaper methods of production.

The PVA team will examine the high-cost components in a given product, because 20 percent of the parts usually account for 80 percent of the costs of manufacturing it. The team will also identify overdesigned product components that last longer than the product itself, then decide on the optimal product characteristics. Tightly written specifications will allow the buyer to refuse components that are too expensive or that fail to meet the specified standards. Suppliers, too, can use product value analysis as a tool for positioning themselves to win an account. By getting in early and influencing buyer specifications, a supplier can significantly increase its chances of being chosen.

Stage 4: Supplier Search

The buyer now tries to identify the most appropriate suppliers, by examining trade directories, doing a computer search, phoning other firms for recommendations, scanning trade advertisements, and attending trade shows. However, these days the most likely place to look is on the Internet. This levels the playing field, because smaller suppliers have the same advantages as larger ones and can be listed in the same on-line catalogs for a nominal fee.

One of the more comprehensive, global on-line catalog libraries is being assembled by Worldwide Internet Solutions Network Inc, better known as WIZ-net (www.wiz-net.net). The firm's database includes full catalogs from more than 72,000 manufacturers, distributors, and industrial service providers around the world, containing more than 8 million product specifications. For purchasing managers, this kind of one-stop shopping can be an incredible time saver (and price saver, because it allows easier comparison shopping). And it is more convenient: WIZ-Net also offers secure e-mail so buyers can communicate directly with suppliers to ask for bids or to place orders.[22]

To get noticed during this buyphase, the supplier should get listed in major on-line catalogs or services, develop communications to reach buyers who are seeking new suppliers, and build a good reputation in the marketplace. Suppliers who lack capacity or have a poor reputation will be rejected, while those who qualify may be visited by buyer's agents, who will examine their facilities and meet their personnel. After evaluating each company, the buyer will end up with a short list of qualified suppliers.

Stage 5: Proposal Solicitation

In this stage, the buyer is ready to invite qualified suppliers to submit proposals. When the item is complex or expensive, the buyer will require a detailed written proposal from each qualified supplier. After evaluating the proposals, the buyer will invite a few suppliers to make formal presentations.

Business marketers must thus be skilled in researching, writing, and presenting proposals. Their written proposals should be marketing documents, not just technical documents. Their oral presentations should inspire confidence, positioning their company's capabilities and resources so that they stand out from the competition.

A supplier's first priority during this stage is to become qualified or, in some cases, to become certified, so it will be invited to submit proposals. Consider the hurdles that Xerox has set up for suppliers. Only suppliers that meet ISO 9000 international quality standards (see Chapter 2) can qualify for certification. These suppliers must complete the Xerox Multinational Supplier Quality Survey, participate in Xerox's Continuous Supplier Involvement process, and undergo rigorous quality training and evaluation based on the Malcolm Baldrige National Quality Award criteria. Not surprisingly, only 176 companies worldwide have become certified Xerox suppliers.[23]

Stage 6: Supplier Selection

Before selecting a supplier, the buying center will specify desired supplier attributes (such as product reliability and service reliability) and indicate their relative importance. It will then rate each supplier on these attributes to identify the most attractive one.

At this point, the buyer may attempt to negotiate with preferred suppliers for better prices and terms before making the final selection. Despite moves toward strategic sourcing, partnering, and participation in cross-functional teams, buyers still spend a large chunk of their time haggling over price, which remains a key criterion for supplier selection.[24] Marketers can counter a buyer's request for a lower price in a number of ways. They may be able to show evidence that the "life-cycle cost" of using the product is lower than that of competitors' products. They can also cite the value of the services the buyer now receives, especially where those services are superior to those offered by competitors.

Hewlett-Packard, for example, has worked hard to become a "trusted advisor" to its customers, selling specific solutions to their unique problems. Along the way, HP discovered that some companies want a partner and others simply want a product that works. Still, the company estimates that the trusted-advisor approach has contributed to 60 percent growth of its high-end computer business.[25]

As part of the supplier selection process, buying centers must decide how many suppliers to use. In the past, many companies preferred a large supplier base to ensure adequate supplies and to obtain price concessions. Out-suppliers would try to get in the door by offering an especially low price.

Increasingly, however, companies are reducing the number of suppliers. Companies such as Ford, Motorola, and AlliedSignal have cut the number of suppliers anywhere from 20 percent to 80 percent. The suppliers who remain are responsible for larger component systems, for achieving continuous quality and performance improvements, and for lowering prices annually by a given percentage.

There is even a trend toward single sourcing, using one supplier. The *Knoxville News-Sentinel* and the *New York Daily News* newspapers both rely on a single source for their newsprint. This makes it easier to control newsprint inventories and maintain paper consistency to avoid the time and expense of changing presses for different papers.[26]

Stage 7: Order-Routine Specification

After selecting suppliers, the buyer negotiates the final order, listing the technical specifications, the quantity needed, the delivery schedule, and so on. In the case of MRO items, buyers are moving toward blanket contracts rather than periodic purchase orders. A *blanket contract* establishes a long-term relationship in which the supplier promises to resupply the buyer as needed at agreed-upon prices over a specified period. Because the seller holds the stock, blanket contracts are sometimes called *stockless purchase plans.* The buyer's computer automatically sends an order to the seller when stock is needed, and the supplier arranges delivery and billing according to the blanket contract.

Blanket contracting leads to more single-source buying and ordering of more items from that single source. This system locks suppliers in tighter with the buyer and makes it difficult for out-suppliers to break in unless the buyer becomes dissatisfied with the in-supplier's prices, quality, or service.

Stage 8: Performance Review

In the final stage of the buying process, the buyer periodically reviews the performance of the chosen supplier(s). Three methods are commonly used. The buyer may contact the end users and ask for their evaluations. Or the buyer may rate the supplier on several criteria using a weighted score method. Or the buyer might aggregate the cost of poor supplier performance to come up with adjusted costs of purchase, including price. The performance review may lead the buyer to continue, modify, or end the relationship with the supplier. Therefore, to stay in the running for future purchases, suppliers should monitor their performance carefully using the same criteria applied by the product's buyers and end users. Smart suppliers also analyze the rivals who compete for the same business, as discussed in the next chapter.

EXECUTIVE SUMMARY

Organizational buying is the decision-making process by which formal organizations establish the need for purchased products and services, and then identify, evaluate, and choose among alternative brands and suppliers. The business market consists of all of the organizations that acquire goods and services used in the production of other products or services that are sold, rented, or supplied to others: profit-seeking companies, institutions, and government agencies.

Compared to consumer markets, business markets generally have fewer and larger buyers, a closer customer-supplier relationship, and more geographically concentrated buyers. Demand in the business market is derived from demand in the consumer market and fluctuates with the business cycle. Nonetheless, the total demand for many business goods and services is quite price-inelastic. Business marketers need to be aware of the role of professional purchasers and their influencers, the need for multiple sales calls, and the importance of direct purchasing, reciprocity, and leasing.

Three types of buying situations are the straight rebuy, the modified rebuy, and the new task. Systems buying is a practice in which the buyer wants to purchase a total solution to its problem from one seller. The buying center is the decision-making unit of a buying organization. It consists of initiators, users, influencers, deciders, approvers, buyers, and gatekeepers.

To influence the buying center, marketers must be aware of environmental, organizational, interpersonal, individual, and cultural factors. The buying process consists of eight stages called buyphases: (1) problem recognition, (2) general need description, (3) product specification, (4) supplier search, (5) proposal solicitation, (6) supplier selection, (7) order-routine specification, and (8) performance review. Successful marketers anticipate and provide what buyers are seeking in each buyphase, increasing the chances that they will be selected and, ultimately, build a long-term relationship with their customers.

NOTES

1. Frederick E. Webster Jr. and Yoram Wind, *Organizational Buying Behavior* (Upper Saddle River, NJ: Prentice-Hall, 1972), p. 2.
2. Robert Hiebeler, Thomas B. Kelly, and Charles Ketteman, *Best Practices: Building Your Business with Customer-focused Solutions* (New York: Arthur Andersen/Simon & Schuster, 1998), pp. 122–24.
3. Hiebeler, Kelly, and Ketteman, *Best Practices*, pp. 124–26.
4. Laura M. Litvan, "Selling to Uncle Sam: New, Easier Rules," *Nation's Business*, March 1995, pp. 46–48; Ellen Messmer, "Feds Do E-Commerce the Hard Way," *Network World*, April 13, 1998, pp. 31–32; Anna Muoio, "Fast Agency, Slow Government," *Fast Company*, December 1999, pp. 344, 346, 348.
5. Patrick J. Robinson, Charles W. Faris, and Yoram Wind, *Industrial Buying and Creative Marketing* (Boston: Allyn & Bacon, 1967).
6. See Daniel H. McQuiston, "Novelty, Complexity, and Importance as Causal Determinants of Industrial Buyer Behavior," *Journal of Marketing*, April 1989, pp. 66–79; and Peter Doyle, Arch G. Woodside, and Paul Mitchell, "Organizational Buying in New Task and Rebuy Situations," *Industrial Marketing Management*, February 1979, pp. 7–11.
7. Urban B. Ozanne and Gilbert A. Churchill, Jr., "Five Dimensions of the Industrial Adoption Process," *Journal of Marketing Research*, August 1971, pp. 322–28.

8. See Donald W. Jackson Jr., Janet E. Keith, and Richard K. Burdick, "Purchasing Agents' Perceptions of Industrial Buying Center Influence: A Situational Approach," *Journal of Marketing,* Fall 1984, pp. 75–83.

9. Webster and Wind, *Organizational Buying Behavior,* p. 6.

10. Ibid., pp. 78–80.

11. See " 'I Think You Have a Great Product, but It's Not My Decision,' " *American Salesman,* April 1994, pp. 11–13.

12. Ibid.

13. Webster and Wind, *Organizational Buying Behavior,* pp. 33–37.

14. Sara Lorge, "Purchasing Power," *Sales & Marketing Management,* June 1998, pp. 43–46; Joann Muller, "The One-Year Itch at Daimler-Chrysler," *Business Week,* November 15, 1999, p. 42.

15. Tim Minahan, "OEM Buying Survey—Part 2: Buyers Get New Roles but Keep Old Tasks," *Purchasing,* July 16, 1998, pp. 208–209.

16. Shawn Tully, "Purchasing's New Muscle," *Fortune,* February 20, 1995; Mark Fitzgerald, "Decentralizing Control of Purchasing," *Editor and Publisher,* June 18, 1994, pp. 8, 10.

17. Mohanbir Sawhney and Steven Kaplan, "Let's Get Vertical," *Business 2.0,* September 1999, p. 85.

18. Robert Yoegel, "The Evolution of B-to-B Selling on the 'Net,' " *Target Marketing,* August 1998, p. 34; Andy Reinhardt, "Extranets: Log On, Link Up, Save Big," *Business Week,* June 22, 1998, p. 134; John Evan Frook, "Buying Behemoth—By Shifting $5B in Spending to Extranets, GE Could Ignite a Development Frenzy," *InternetWeek,* August 17, 1998, p. 1; John Jesitus, "Procuring an Edge," *Industry Week,* June 23, 1997, pp. 56–62.

19. Lance Dixon, "JLG Industries Offers JIT II Advice," *Purchasing,* January 15, 1998, p. 39.

20. (Germany, Japan) Teresa C. Morrison, Wayne A. Conaway, and Joseph J. Douress, *Dun & Bradstreet's Guide to Doing Business Around the World* (New York: Prentice-Hall, 1997); (Korean) "Tips, Tricks and Pitfalls to Avoid when Doing Business in the Tough but Lucrative Korean Market," *Business America,* June 1997, p. 7.

21. Robinson, Faris, and Wind, *Industrial Buying and Creative Marketing.*

22. John H. Sheridan, "Buying Globally Made Easier," *Industry Week,* February 2, 1998, pp. 63–64.

23. See "Xerox Multinational Supplier Quality Survey," *Purchasing,* January 12, 1995, p. 112.

24. Minahan, "OEM Buying Survey—Part 2: Buyers Get New Roles but Keep Old Tasks." To see how the Internet is affecting supplier selection, see Kevin Ferguson, "Purchasing in Packs," *Business Week,* November 1, 1999, pp. EB32–38.

25. Rick Mullin, "Taking Customer Relations to the Next Level," *The Journal of Business Strategy,* January-February 1997, pp. 22–26.

26. Donna Del Moro, "Single-Source Newsprint Supply," *Editor & Publisher,* October 25, 1997, pp. 42–45.

Dealing with the Competition

In this chapter, we will address the following questions:

■ How can a company identify its primary competitors and ascertain their strategies, objectives, strengths and weaknesses, and reaction patterns?

■ How can a company design a competitive intelligence system?

■ Should a company position itself as market leader, challenger, follower, or nicher?

■ How can a company balance a customer-versus-competitor orientation?

In the two previous chapters we examined the dynamics of consumer and business markets. In this chapter, we examine the role of competition within markets and industries and explore how companies can position themselves relative to competitors.

Given the ever-changing dynamics of the global marketplace and the burgeoning Internet marketspace, understanding customers is no longer enough. Companies must now pay keen attention to all kinds of competitors. The most successful companies are those that have developed and implemented systems for gathering continuous intelligence about competitors.[1] Moreover, companies need to design competitive strategies geared toward their relative market position and maintain a careful balance of customer and competitor orientations.

COMPETITIVE MARKETS AND COMPETITORS

Today, competition is not only rife, but is growing more intense every year. Many U.S., European, and Japanese companies are setting up production in lower-cost countries and bringing cheaper goods to market. In addition, the Internet is facilitating the entry of new types of competitors, bringing rivalry in many markets and industries to a fever pitch.

Thus, it is more important than ever for companies to study competition at various levels (brand, industry, form, generic) carefully, as discussed in Chapter 1. Companies must also look at competition from the viewpoint of the market and the industry.

Competition and Market Attractiveness

In analyzing competition, Michael Porter identified five forces that determine the intrinsic, long-run profit attractiveness of a market or market segment: industry competitors, potential entrants, substitutes, buyers, and suppliers. His model is shown in Figure 7.1.

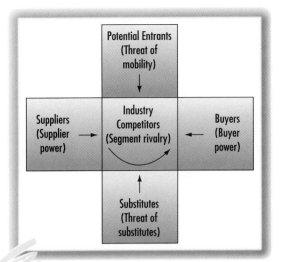

Figure 7.1   Five Forces that Determine Market Attractiveness

The competitive threats posed by these five forces are:

1. *Threat of intense segment rivalry:* A segment is unattractive if it already contains numerous, strong, or aggressive competitors. It is even more unattractive if the segment is
   stable or declining, if a great deal of plant capacity is being added, if fixed costs are
   high, if exit barriers are high, or if competitors have high stakes in staying in the segment. These conditions will lead to frequent price wars, advertising battles, and new-
   product introductions—making competition more expensive.

2. *Threat of new entrants:* A segment's attractiveness varies with the height of its entry and exit
   barriers (explained in more detail later).[2] The most attractive segment has high entry
   barriers and low exit barriers (see Figure 7.2), so few new firms can enter, while poor-per-
   forming firms can exit easily. Profit potential is high when both entry and exit barriers
   are high, but firms face more risk because poorer-performing firms stay in and fight it
   out. When entry and exit barriers are both low, firms enter and leave the industry easily,
   and the returns are stable and low. The worst case is when entry barriers are low and exit
   barriers are high: Firms can enter during good times but find it hard to leave during bad
   times. The result is chronic overcapacity and depressed earnings for all.

3. *Threat of substitute products:* A segment is unattractive when there are actual or potential substitutes for the product. Substitutes place a limit on prices and on the profits
   that a segment can earn. The company has to monitor the price trends in substitutes
   closely. If technology advances or competition increases in these substitute industries,
   prices and profits in the segment are likely to fall.

4. *Threat of buyers' growing bargaining power:* A segment is unattractive if the buyers possess
   strong or growing bargaining power, which allows them to force prices down, demand
   more quality or services, and set competitors against each other—all at the expense of
   seller profitability. Buyers' bargaining power grows when they become more concentrated or organized, when the product represents a significant fraction of the buyers'
   costs, when the product is undifferentiated, when the buyers' switching costs are low,
   when buyers are price sensitive, or when buyers can integrate upstream. To compete,
   sellers should select buyers with less power to negotiate, switch suppliers, or develop
   superior offers that strong buyers cannot refuse.

	Exit Barriers	
	Low	High
Entry Barriers Low	Low, stable returns	Low, risky returns
Entry Barriers High	High, stable returns	High, risky returns

Figure 7.2   Barriers and Profitability

5. *Threat of suppliers' growing bargaining power:* A segment is unattractive if the company's suppliers are able to raise prices or reduce quantity supplied. Suppliers tend to be powerful when they are concentrated or organized, when there are few substitutes, when the supplied product is an important input, when the costs of switching suppliers are high, and when suppliers can integrate downstream. The best defenses are to build win-win relations with suppliers or use multiple supply sources.

Identifying Competitors

It would seem a simple task for a company to identify its competitors. Coca-Cola knows that Pepsi-Cola is its major competitor, and Sony knows that Matsushita is a major competitor. But the range of a company's actual and potential competitors is actually much broader. In fact, a company is more likely to be hurt by emerging competitors or new technologies than by current competitors.

In recent years, many businesses have failed to look to the Internet for their most formidable competitors. Not long ago, Barnes & Noble and Borders bookstore chains were competing to see who could build the most megastores. While these massive bookstore chains were battling for retail dominance, Jeffrey Bezos was building an on-line empire called Amazon.com with an almost unlimited selection of books. Now both Barnes & Noble and Borders are playing catch-up in boosting traffic and sales for their own on-line stores, even as Amazon.com expands into more product categories.[3]

Such "competitor myopia"—a focus on current competitors rather than latent ones—can actually render a business extinct. Encyclopaedia Britannica, for example, was invited but refused to provide content for Microsoft's Encarta CD-ROM-based encyclopedia. When introduced, the Encarta sold for only $50, making Encyclopaedia Britannica's $1,250 set of 32 volumes look less appealing to parents. This competitive situation forced Encyclopaedia Britannica to change its business model by dismissing its home sales force and offering free access to data via the Web.[4]

The businesses with the most to fear from Internet technology are the world's middlemen, such as travel agencies, car dealers, insurance brokers, real estate brokers, stock brokers, and employee placement firms. By facilitating direct contact between buyers and sellers, the Internet is causing *disintermediation*—the displacement of traditional intermediaries. At the same time, this direct contact has opened up great opportunities for new businesses, such as Amazon.com, to forge and nurture bonds with customers. As e-commerce grows and a greater percentage of the world's consumers and businesses get wired, companies will feel even more competition in many markets. Thus, it is vital for companies to correctly identify and deal with potential as well as existing competitors.

Industry Concept of Competition

To understand industry competition, we must first define an industry. An **industry** is a group of firms that offer a product or class of products that are close substitutes for each other. Industries are classified according to number of sellers; degree of product differentiation; presence or absence of entry, mobility, and exit barriers; cost structure; degree of vertical integration; and degree of globalization.

Number of Sellers and Degree of Differentiation

The starting point for describing an industry is to specify the number of sellers and determine whether the product is homogeneous or highly differentiated. These characteristics give rise to four industry structure types:

➤ *Pure monopoly:* Only one firm provides a certain product or service in a certain country or area (for example, a gas company). An unregulated monopolist might charge a high price, do little or no advertising, and offer minimal service. If partial substitutes are available and there is some danger of competition, the monopolist might invest in more service and technology. A regulated monopolist is required to charge a lower price and provide more service as a matter of public interest.

➤ *Oligopoly:* A small number of (usually) large firms produce products that range from highly differentiated to standardized. In *pure oligopoly,* a few companies produce essentially the same commodity (such as oil), so all have difficulty charging more than the going price. If competitors match services, the only way to gain a competitive advantage is through lower costs. In *differentiated oligopoly,* a few companies offer products (such as autos) partially differentiated by quality, features, styling, or services. Each competitor may seek leadership in one of these attributes, attract customers seeking that attribute, and charge a price premium for that attribute.

➤ *Monopolistic competition:* Many competitors are able to differentiate their offers in whole or part (restaurants are a good example). Competitors focus on market segments where they can meet customer needs in a superior way and command a price premium.

➤ *Pure competition:* Many competitors offer the same product and service, so, without differentiation, all prices will be the same. No competitor will advertise unless advertising can create psychological differentiation (such as cigarettes), in which case the industry is actually monopolistically competitive.

The competitive structure of any industry can change over time. For example, the maker of the Palm Pilot handheld computerized organizer initially enjoyed a pure monopoly, because no similar products existed at that time. Soon, however, a few other companies, such as Casio and Everex, entered the industry, turning it into an oligopoly. As Handspring and additional competitors introduced their products, the industry took on a monopolistically competitive structure. When demand growth slows, however, some competitors will probably exit, returning the industry to an oligopoly dominated by Palm Pilot and a few key competitors.[5]

Entry, Mobility, and Exit Barriers

Industries differ greatly in ease of entry. It is easy to open a new restaurant but difficult to enter the aircraft industry. Major *entry barriers* include high capital requirements; economies of scale; patents and licensing requirements; scarce locations, raw materials, or distributors; and reputation requirements. Even after a firm enters an industry, it may face *mobility barriers* in trying to enter more attractive market segments.

Firms often face *exit barriers*,[6] such as legal or moral obligations to customers, creditors, and employees; government restrictions; low asset salvage value; lack of alternative opportunities; high vertical integration; and emotional barriers. Many firms stay in an industry as long as they cover their variable costs and some or all of their fixed costs; their continued presence, however, dampens profits for everyone.

Cost Structure

Each industry has a certain cost burden that shapes much of its strategic conduct. For example, steelmaking involves heavy manufacturing and raw-material costs; toy manufacturing involves heavy distribution and marketing costs. Firms will strategize to reduce these costs. The steel company with the most modern (i.e., most cost-efficient) plant will have a great advantage over other steel companies.

Degree of Vertical Integration

Many companies benefit from integrating backward or forward (*vertical integration*). For example, major oil producers carry on oil exploration, oil drilling, oil refining, chemical manufacture, and service-station operation. Vertical integration often lowers costs, and the company gains a larger share of the value-added stream. In addition, a vertically integrated firm can manage prices and costs in different parts of the value chain to earn profits where taxes are lowest. On the other hand, vertical integration may cause high costs in certain parts of the value chain and restrict a firm's strategic flexibility.

Degree of Globalization

Some industries are highly local (such as lawn care); others are global (such as oil, aircraft engines, and cameras). Companies in global industries need to compete on a global basis if they are to achieve economies of scale and keep up with the latest advances in technology.[7]

For example, five companies formerly dominated the U.S. forklift market—Clark Equipment, Caterpillar, Allis Chalmers, Hyster, and Yale. Ultimately, debt-burdened Clark sold its assets, and Caterpillar became a minor partner in a venture with Mitsubishi. Only Hyster held on to its market share. By speeding up product development, concentrating on low-end models, and moving some production to Ireland, Hyster was able to compete against international rivals Nissan, Toyota, and Komatsu. Hyster also filed an antidumping suit against Japanese models and won the case.

Market Concept of Competition

In addition to the industry approach, companies need to identify competitors using the market approach: Competitors are those that satisfy the same customer need. For example, a customer who buys word processing software really wants "writing ability"—a need that can be satisfied by pencils, pens, or typewriters. The market concept of competition opens up a broader set of actual and potential competitors that companies must identify and analyze.

COMPETITOR ANALYSIS

Once a company identifies its primary competitors, it must analyze them by ascertaining their characteristics, specifically their strategies, objectives, strengths and weaknesses, and reaction patterns.

Strategies

A group of firms that follow the same strategy in a given target market is called a *strategic group*.[8] Suppose a company wants to enter the major appliance industry. What is its strategic group? It develops the chart shown in Figure 7.3 and discovers four strategic groups based on product quality and level of vertical integration. Group A has one competitor (Maytag), group B has three (General Electric, Whirlpool, and Sears), group C has four, and group D has two. This analysis shows that the height of the entry barriers differs for each group. In addition, if the company successfully enters a group, this analysis identifies the group members that will be its key competitors. However, this is not a one-time analysis, because resourceful competitors revise their strategies over time. Smart marketers must therefore continuously monitor their competitors' strategies.

Objectives

Once a company has identified its main competitors and their strategies, it must ask: What is each competitor seeking in the marketplace? What drives each competitor's behavior? Although one initial assumption is that competitors strive to maximize profits, companies differ in the weights they put on short-term versus long-term profits. Most U.S. firms seek short-term profit maximization, largely because they must satisfy their stockholders or risk losing their confidence. In contrast, Japanese firms readily accept lower profits because they operate largely on a market-share-maximization model.

An alternative assumption is that each competitor pursues some mix of objectives: current profitability, market-share growth, cash flow, technological leadership, and service leadership. Knowing how a competitor weighs each objective will help the company anticipate its reactions. Many factors can shape a competitor's objectives, including size, history, current management, and financial situation. If the competitor is a division of a larger company, it is important to know whether the parent company is running it for growth or milking it.[9] Finally, a company must monitor its competitors' expansion plans and, as appropriate, try to establish mobility barriers to block or slow rivals' growth.

Strengths and Weaknesses

Whether competitors can carry out their strategies and reach their goals depends on their resources and capabilities. This is why marketers need to gather information on

Figure 7.3   Strategic Groups in the Major Appliance Industry

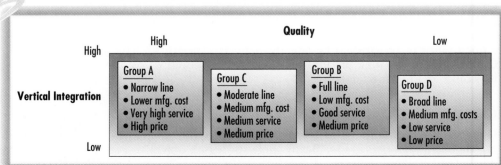

each competitor's strengths and weaknesses. According to the Arthur D. Little consulting firm, a firm will occupy one of six competitive positions in the target market:[10]

➤ *Dominant:* This firm controls the other competitors' behavior and has many strategic options.

➤ *Strong:* This firm can take independent action without endangering its long-term position and can maintain its long-term position regardless of competitors' actions.

➤ *Favorable:* This firm has an exploitable strength and a better opportunity to improve its position.

➤ *Tenable:* This firm's performance is sufficient for it to remain in business, but it exists at the sufferance of the dominant company and has less opportunity to improve its position.

➤ *Weak:* This firm has unsatisfactory performance and an opportunity for improvement; it must change or exit.

➤ *Nonviable:* This firm has unsatisfactory performance and no opportunity for improvement.

To gauge strengths and weaknesses, a company should monitor share of market, share of mind, and share of heart when analyzing each competitor (see Table 7.1). *In general, companies that make steady gains in share of mind and heart will inevitably make gains in market share and profitability.* Companies should also identify any assumptions that competitors hold that are no longer valid—and take advantage of this weakness. For example, while larger rivals such as Compaq continued to stress traditional computer distribution channels, Michael Dell boldly pioneered direct-to-customer sales. This allowed Dell Computer to charge less while delivering exactly what each customer wanted. Extending this strategy to the Internet gave Dell an even more powerful competitive edge.[11]

Reaction Patterns

Each competitor has a certain philosophy of doing business, a certain internal culture, and certain guiding beliefs. Most competitors fall into one of four categories:

➤ *The laid-back competitor:* A competitor that does not react quickly or strongly to a rival's move. On past occasions, Gillette and Heinz reacted slowly to competitive attacks. Laid-back competitors may feel that their customers are loyal; they may be

Table 7.1　Gauging a Competitor's Strengths and Weaknesses

Basis of Analysis	Description
1. Share of market	The competitor's share of the target market
2. Share of mind	The percentage of customers who name the competitor when asked to "name the first company that comes to mind in this industry"
3. Share of heart	The percentage of customers who name the competitor when asked to "name the company from whom you would prefer to buy the product"

milking the business; they may be slow in noticing the move; they may lack the funds to react. Rivals must try to assess the reasons for the behavior.

➤ *The selective competitor:* A competitor that reacts only to certain types of attacks. It might respond to price cuts, but not to advertising expenditure increases. Shell and Exxon are selective competitors, responding only to price cuts but not to promotions. Knowing what sparks a rival's reaction offers clues to the most feasible lines of attack against that competitor.

➤ *The tiger competitor:* A competitor that reacts swiftly and strongly to any assault. P&G fights back when a new detergent enters the market, as Lever Brothers found out when it introduced "ultra," more concentrated versions of its Wisk and Surf detergents. In response, P&G vastly outspent Lever to support its own brands, preventing Lever from obtaining enough shelf space to compete.

➤ *The stochastic competitor:* A competitor that exhibits no predictable reaction pattern; its actions are not predictable on the basis of its economic situation, history, or anything else. Many small businesses are stochastic competitors, competing on miscellaneous fronts when they can afford it.

Clearly, a company that understands how its competitors react will be better able to anticipate reaction patterns and develop strategies for minimizing the impact on its own performance.

THE COMPETITIVE INTELLIGENCE SYSTEM

Every company needs a competitive intelligence system to track its competitors and the competitive trends in the industry and the market. Such a system need not be computerized, although the Internet and computer databases can be very useful components. Once the system is up and running, it will provide a stream of intelligence on which to make decisions about competitive strategy.

Designing the Competitive Intelligence System

The four main steps in designing a competitive intelligence system are: setting up the system, collecting the data, evaluating and analyzing the data, then disseminating information and responding to queries.

1. *Setting up the system.* The first step calls for identifying vital types of competitive information, identifying the best information sources, and assigning someone to manage the system and its services. In smaller companies that cannot afford a formal competitive intelligence office, specific executives should be assigned to watch specific competitors. Then any manager who needs to know about a specific competitor would contact the corresponding in-house expert.[12]

2. *Collecting the data.* The data are collected on a continuous basis from the field (sales force, channels, suppliers, market research firms, trade associations), from people who do business with competitors, from observing competitors, and from published data. In addition, a vast store of data on both domestic and international firms is available via CD-ROM and on-line services. Companies can learn a great deal from Web sites maintained by competitors and by trade associations. For example, when the controller of Stone Container's specialty-packaging division checked a trade association Web site, he found that a rival had won an award for a new process using ultraviolet-resistant lacquers. The site revealed the machines' configuration and run rate, which Stone's engineers used to replicate the process.[13]

3. *Evaluating and analyzing the data.* In this step of the process, company managers check the data they have collected for validity and reliability. Then they interpret the findings and organize the results so users can conveniently find what they need.

4. *Disseminating information and responding.* Key information is sent to relevant decision makers, and managers' inquiries are answered. With a well-designed system, company managers receive timely information about competitors via phone calls, e-mails, bulletins, newsletters, and reports. Managers can also request information when they need help interpreting a competitor's sudden move, when they need to know a competitor's weaknesses and strengths, or when they want to discuss a competitor's likely response to a contemplated company move.

Selecting Competitors to Attack and to Avoid

With good competitive intelligence, managers will find it easier to evaluate their competitive situations and then formulate appropriate competitive strategies. Smart marketers start by assessing how customers view their firm and their competitors.

Customer Value Analysis

Very often, managers conduct a *customer value analysis* to reveal the company's strengths and weaknesses relative to various competitors. In this analysis, the company first asks customers what attributes and performance levels they look for in choosing a product and vendors. Next, the company asks customers to rate the importance of these different attributes and describe where they see the company's and competitors' performances on each attribute.

Then the company must examine how customers in each targeted segment rate its performance against a particular competitor on an attribute-by-attribute basis. If the company's offer exceeds the competitor's offer on all important attributes, the company can charge a higher price (thereby earning higher profits), or it can charge the same price and gain more market share. Of course, the company must periodically redo its studies of customer value and competitors' standings as the economy, technology, products, and features change.

Classes of Competitors

After the company has conducted its customer value analysis, it can focus its attack on one of the following classes of competitors: strong versus weak competitors, close versus distant competitors, or "good" versus "bad" competitors.

➤ *Strong versus weak.* Most companies aim at weak competitors, because this requires fewer resources per share point gained. Yet, in attacking weak competitors, the firm will barely improve its own capabilities. Thus, the firm should also compete with strong competitors to keep up with the best. Even strong competitors have some weaknesses, and the firm may prove to be a worthy opponent.

➤ *Close versus distant.* Most companies compete with competitors who most resemble them. For instance, Chevrolet competes with Ford, not with Jaguar. At the same time, a company should avoid trying to destroy the closest competitor. One risk is that a much larger competitor will buy out the weakened rival; another risk is that additional, stronger competitors will enter the market.

➤ *Good versus bad.* Every industry contains "good" and "bad" competitors.[14] A company should support its good competitors and attack its bad competitors. Good competitors play by the industry's rules, make realistic assumptions about the industry's growth potential, set prices in reasonable relation to costs, favor a healthy industry, limit themselves to a portion or segment of the industry, motivate others to lower costs or improve differentiation, and accept the general level of their share and profits. Bad competitors try to buy share rather than earn it, take large risks, invest in overcapacity, and upset industrial equilibrium.

DESIGNING COMPETITIVE STRATEGIES

A company can gain further insight into its competitive position by classifying its competitors and itself according to the role each plays in the target market: leader, challenger, follower, or nicher. On the basis of this classification, the company can take specific actions in line with its current and desired roles.

Market-Leader Strategies

Many industries contain one firm that is the acknowledged market leader, with the largest share of the relevant product market. This market leader usually leads the other firms in price changes, new-product introductions, distribution coverage, and promotional intensity. Some of the best-known market leaders are Microsoft (computer software), Procter & Gamble (consumer packaged goods), Caterpillar (earthmoving equipment), Coca-Cola (soft drinks), McDonald's (fast food), Gillette (razor blades), and America Online (Internet access).

Unless a dominant firm enjoys a legal monopoly, it must maintain constant vigilance to avoid missing key developments. One development might be competitive product innovations; Motorola's analog cell phones, for example, suffered when Nokia's and Ericsson's digital models took over. Or the leader might continue to spend conservatively while a challenger spends liberally, it might experience higher costs cutting into profits, or it might misjudge its competition and get left behind. Another risk is that the dominant firm might look old-fashioned against newer, peppier rivals. For example, Levi Strauss has lost ground against stylish brands like Tommy Hilfiger and newcomers like Paris Blues.[15]

Remaining number one calls for action on three fronts. First, the leader must expand total market demand. Second, it must protect its current market share through good defensive and offensive actions. Third, the firm can try to further increase its market share, even if market size remains constant.

Expanding the Total Market

The dominant firm normally gains the most when the total market expands. If Americans take more photographs, Kodak stands to gain the most because it sells most of the country's film. If Kodak can convince more Americans to buy cameras and take photos, take photos on more occasions, or take more photos on each occasion, Kodak will benefit considerably. In general, the leader should aim for new users, new uses, and more usage of its products.

➤ *New users.* Every product class can potentially attract buyers who are unaware of the product or who are resisting it because of price or lack of certain features. A company can search for new users among buyers who might use it but do not (*market-penetration strategy*), those who have never used it (*new-market segment strategy*), or those who live elsewhere (*geographical-expansion strategy*).

➤ *New uses.* Markets can be expanded through discovering and promoting new uses for the product. For example, cereal manufacturers would gain if they could promote cereal eating on occasions other than breakfast—perhaps as a snack. Sometimes customers deserve credit for discovering new uses. Arm & Hammer's baking soda had downward-drifting sales for 125 years. Then the company discovered that consumers use the product as a refrigerator deodorant. It heavily promoted this use and succeeded in getting half of all U.S. homes to place an open box of baking soda in the refrigerator. When Arm & Hammer discovered that consumers use the product to quell kitchen grease fires, it promoted that use, again with great results.

➤ *More usage.* A third strategy is to convince people to use more product per use occasion. France-based Michelin Tire, for example, wanted French car owners to drive their cars more miles per year—thus leading to more tire replacement. The company conceived the idea of rating restaurants around France. Once it began promoting the names of many of the best restaurants in the south of France, Parisians began taking weekend drives to Provence and the Riviera. Michelin also published guidebooks with maps and lists of sights along the way to encourage additional driving.

Defending Market Share

While trying to expand total market size, the dominant firm must continuously defend its current business against rival attacks. The leader is like a large elephant being attacked by a swarm of bees, some domestic and some foreign. Coca-Cola must guard against Pepsi-Cola; Gillette against Bic; Hertz against Avis; McDonald's against Burger King; General Motors against Ford; and Kodak against Fuji.

What can the market leader do to defend its terrain? The most constructive response is *continuous innovation*. The leader leads the industry in developing new product and customer services, distribution effectiveness, and cost cutting. It keeps increasing its competitive strength and value to customers. Here, the best defense is a good offense. For example, International Gaming Technology, a manufacturer of slot machines and video poker machines, has maintained 75 percent share of a mature market that has a limited number of new customers. How? By forming partnerships with both casino operators and competitive gaming manufacturers to develop innovative, new equipment. The firm spends aggressively on R&D, is dedicated to customer service, and involves customers throughout the sales process, from initial product development to final placement on the casino floor.[16]

Even when it does not launch offensives, the market leader must leave no major flanks exposed. It must keep its costs down, and its prices must reflect the value that customers see in the brand. In addition, the leader must consider what segments to defend (even at a loss) and what segments to surrender. The aim of defensive strategy is to reduce the probability of attack, divert attacks to less threatening areas, and lessen their intensity. A dominant firm can use six defense strategies, which are shown in Figure 7.4:[17]

➤ *Position defense.* The basic defense is to build an impregnable fortification around one's territory. For instance, Coca-Cola, in spite of selling nearly half the soft drinks of the world, has acquired fruit drink companies and diversified into desalinization equipment and plastics. Although defense is important, leaders under attack would be foolish to put all of their resources into only building fortifications around their current product.

➤ *Flank defense.* The market leader should also erect outposts to protect a weak front or possibly serve as an invasion base for counterattack. The success of Starbucks, for example, spawned a host of competitors. With its own sales growth slowing, and competition increasing, Starbucks is using a number of flank defenses. It is feverishly trying to push out innovative new, noncoffee-related products. It is also

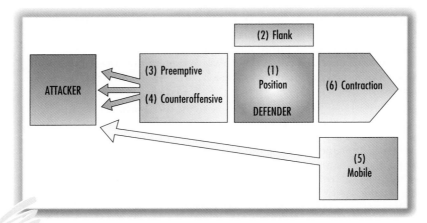

Figure 7.4   Defense Strategies

selling its coffee beans in supermarkets and is opening restaurants. The first Cafe Starbucks opened to capacity crowds, and more restaurants are planned as a way to extend traffic into the evening, because 85 percent of the company's retail store business is completed by 3 P.M.[18]

➤ *Preemptive defense.* A more aggressive maneuver is to attack *before* a rival starts its offense, which can be done in several ways. A company can hit one competitor here, another there, and keep everyone off balance. Or it can try to envelop the market, as Seiko has done with 3,000 watch models distributed worldwide.[19] Other strategies focus on sustained price attacks or sending out market signals to dissuade competitors from attacking.[20] Deep-pocketed market leaders may even entice competitors into costly attacks, as Heinz did when Hunt's attacked the ketchup market. Heinz was willing to lose money temporarily as Hunt's added new flavors, cut prices, offered inducements to retailers, and boosted ad spending to twice the level of Heinz. This strategy failed because Hunt's products did not deliver the same quality and Heinz continued to enjoy consumer preference. Hunt's finally gave up.

➤ *Counteroffensive defense.* Most market leaders, when attacked, will counterattack in the face of a competitor's price cut, promotion blitz, or product improvement. One effective counterattack is to invade the attacker's main market so it will have to defend the territory. Another approach is to use economic or political clout to deter the attacker. For example, the leader may subsidize lower prices for a vulnerable product with revenue from more profitable products, prematurely announce a forthcoming product upgrade to prevent customers from buying the competitor's product, or lobby legislators to take political action that would hurt the competition.

➤ *Mobile defense.* In mobile defense, the leader stretches its domain over new territories that can serve as future centers for defense and offense, using market broadening and market diversification. With *market broadening,* the company shifts its focus from the current product to the underlying generic need. The company gets involved in R&D across the whole range of technology associated with that need, which is how "petroleum" companies recast themselves as "energy" companies to enter oil, nuclear, hydroelectric, and other industries. *Market diversification* into unrelated industries is the other alternative. When U.S. tobacco companies like Philip Morris acknowledged the growing curbs on cigarette smoking, they moved quickly into industries such as beer, liquor, beverages, and foods.

➤ *Contraction defense.* Large companies sometimes recognize that they can no longer defend all of their territory. The best course of action then appears to be *planned contraction* (also called *strategic withdrawal*), giving up weaker territories and reassigning resources to stronger territories. This move consolidates competitive strength in the market and concentrates mass at pivotal positions. Heinz, General Mills, and Georgia-Pacific are among the companies that have used the contraction defense to significantly prune their product lines in recent years.

Expanding Market Share

Research indicates that, in many market segments, the leaders can improve their profitability by increasing their market share. Depending on the market, one share point can be worth tens of millions of dollars. A one-share-point gain in coffee is worth $48 million, and in soft drinks, $120 million! No wonder normal competition has turned into marketing warfare as companies pursue market-share expansion and leadership as their objective. General Electric, for example, decided it must be number one or two in each market or else get out; it divested its computer business and its air-conditioning business because it could not achieve leadership in these industries.

The cost of buying higher market share may far exceed its revenue value, so a company should consider three factors before pursuing increased market share. The first factor is the possibility of provoking antitrust action: Jealous competitors may cry "monopoly" if a dominant firm makes further inroads. This is what happened when software giant Microsoft had to fight a lengthy legal battle to defend against accusations of monopoly by states' attorneys general and the U.S. Justice Department.[21]

The second factor is economic cost. Profitability may fall, not rise, with further market-share gains after a certain level, driving the cost of gaining further share higher than the value. Here, a leader must recognize that "holdout" customers may dislike the company, be loyal to competitive suppliers, have unique needs, or prefer dealing with smaller suppliers. Also, the cost of legal work, public relations, and lobbying rises with market share. Pushing for higher market share is less justified when there are few scale or experience economies, unattractive market segments exist, buyers want multiple sources of supply, and exit barriers are high. Some market leaders have even increased profitability by selectively decreasing market share in weaker areas.[22]

The third factor is that companies might pursue the wrong marketing-mix strategy in their bid for higher market share and therefore fail to increase profits. Companies that win more market share by cutting price are buying, not earning, a larger share, and their profits may be lower. Each of these factors is associated with potential risks and rewards that must be weighed before a company makes its choice.

Market-Challenger Strategies

Firms that occupy second, third, and lower ranks in an industry are often called runner-up, or trailing, firms. Some, such as Colgate, Ford, Avis, and Pepsi-Cola, are quite large in their own right. These firms can adopt one of two postures. They can attack the leader and other competitors in an aggressive bid for further market share (acting like market challengers). Or they can play ball and not "rock the boat" (acting like market followers). Market challengers can use the following competitive attack strategies.

Defining the Strategic Objective and Opponent(s)

A market challenger must first define its strategic objective; most aim to increase market share. Then the challenger must decide whom to attack. Attacking the market leader is a high-risk, but potentially high-payoff, strategy if the leader is not serving the market well. Another way to attack the leader is to out-innovate it across the whole segment. Xerox wrested the copy market from 3M by developing a better copying process; later, Canon grabbed a large chunk of Xerox's market by introducing desk copiers. If the attacking company goes after the market leader, its objective might be to grab a certain share. Bic is under no illusion that it can topple Gillette in the razor market—it is simply seeking a larger share.

A second choice for the market challenger is to attack firms of its own size that are underperforming and underfinanced. These firms have aging products, charge excessive prices, or are not satisfying customers in other ways. A third choice is to attack small local and regional firms. If the attacker goes after a small local company, its aim might be to drive that competitor out of existence.

Choosing a General Attack Strategy

Given clear opponents and objectives, what attack options are available? We can distinguish among five attack strategies, as shown in Figure 7.5: frontal, flank, encirclement, bypass, and guerilla attacks.

In a pure frontal attack, the attacker matches its opponent's product, advertising, price, and distribution. The *principle of force* says that the side with the greater resources will win, unless the defender enjoys a terrain advantage. A modified frontal attack, such as undercutting an opponent's price, can work if the market leader does not retaliate and if the competitor convinces the market that its product is equal to the leader's.

A flank attack can be directed along two strategic dimensions. In a geographical attack, the challenger spots areas where the opponent is underperforming. For example, some of IBM's rivals, such as Honeywell, chose to set up strong sales branches in

Figure 7.5   Attack Strategies

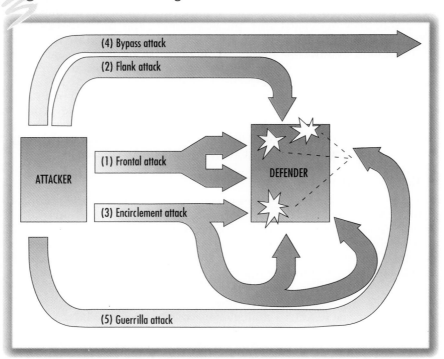

medium- and smaller-size cities that were relatively neglected by IBM. In a segmental attack, the challenger moves to serve uncovered market needs, as Miller Brewing Company did when it introduced light beer.

A flanking strategy is another name for identifying shifts in market segments that are causing gaps to develop, then rushing in to fill the gaps and develop them into strong segments. Flank attacks make excellent marketing sense and are particularly attractive to a challenger with fewer resources. Moreover, flank attacks are much more likely to be successful than frontal attacks.

The encirclement maneuver is an attempt to capture a wide slice of the enemy's territory through a "blitz"—launching a grand offensive on several fronts. Encirclement makes sense when the challenger commands superior resources and believes a swift encirclement will break the opponent's will. For example, in taking a stand against archrival Microsoft, whose software is ubiquitous, Sun Microsystems licensed its Java software for all types of consumer devices. Now Delphi Automotive Systems plans to offer a Java-based system to outfit autos with such features as voice-activated e-mail, while Motorola expects to use Java in pagers, cell phones, and much more. In short, Sun's encirclement strategy revolves around making Java the lingua franca for every imaginable digital device.[23]

The most indirect assault strategy is the bypass. It involves bypassing the enemy and attacking easier markets to broaden one's resource base. This strategy offers three lines of approach: diversifying into unrelated products, diversifying into new geographical markets, and leapfrogging into new technologies to supplant existing products. For example, PepsiCo used a bypass when it paid $3.3 billion for Tropicana as a new weapon in its war against Coca-Cola. Tropicana's 42 percent share of the orange juice market blows away Coke-owned Minute-Maid, which has only 24 percent of the market—giving Pepsi at least one way to beat Coke.[24]

Guerrilla warfare consists of waging small, intermittent attacks to harass and demoralize the opponent and eventually secure permanent footholds. The guerrilla challenger uses both conventional and unconventional means of attack, such as selective price cuts, intense promotional blitzes, and occasional legal actions. Consider the way upstart The Princeton Review used guerrilla marketing against its established rival in test preparation services, Kaplan Educational Centers. Princeton Review's ads brashly advised, "Friends don't let friends take Kaplan" while touting Princeton Review's smaller, livelier classes. Princeton's founder also posted horror stories about Kaplan on the Internet. Ultimately, this guerrilla warfare paid off: Princeton eventually became the market leader in SAT preparation.

Normally, guerrilla warfare is practiced by a smaller firm against a larger one. A guerrilla campaign can be costly, although less expensive than a frontal, encirclement, or flank attack. Still, guerrilla warfare must be backed by a stronger attack if the challenger hopes to beat the opponent.

Choosing a Specific Attack Strategy

Having chosen a broad attack strategy, the company must now develop more specific attack strategies, such as:

➤ *Price-discount:* The challenger can offer a comparable product at a lower price. This works if (1) the challenger can convince buyers that its product and service are comparable to the leader's; (2) buyers are price-sensitive; and (3) the leader refuses to cut price in spite of the competitor's attack.

➤ *Cheaper goods:* The challenger can offer an average- or low-quality product at a much lower price. Little Debbie snack cakes are lower-quality than Drake's but sell at a lower price. Firms that use this strategy, however, can be attacked by firms whose prices are even lower.

➤ *Prestige goods:* A challenger can launch a higher-quality product and charge more than the leader. Mercedes gained on Cadillac in the U.S. market by offering a higher-quality car at a higher price.

➤ *Product proliferation:* The challenger can attack the leader by offering more product variety, giving buyers more choice. Blue Mountain Arts, now owned by Excite@Home, became the leader in on-line greeting cards by offering a dizzying array of choices for virtually any occasion.[25]

➤ *Product innovation:* The challenger can pursue product innovation, the way 3M enters new markets by introducing a product improvement or breakthrough.

➤ *Improved services:* The challenger can offer new or better services to customers.

➤ *Distribution innovation:* A challenger might develop a new channel of distribution. Start-up eToys used a novel Internet-only strategy to attack Toys 'R Us in the toy retailing market.

➤ *Manufacturing cost reduction:* The challenger might achieve lower manufacturing costs through more efficient purchasing, lower labor costs, and/or more modern production equipment.

➤ *Intensive advertising promotion:* Some challengers attack by boosting advertising and promotion spending, a strategy that can work if the challenger's product or advertising message is superior.

One attack strategy is insufficient. A smart challenger recognizes that success depends on combining several strategies to improve its position over time.

Market-Follower Strategies

Why would a company choose a market-follower strategy? Theodore Levitt has argued that a strategy of product imitation might be as profitable as a strategy of product innovation.[26] The innovator bears the expense of developing the new product, getting it into distribution, and educating the market. The reward for all this work and risk is normally market leadership—even though another firm can then copy or improve on the new product. Although it probably will not overtake the leader, the follower can achieve high profits because it did not bear any of the innovation expense.

In fact, many companies prefer to follow rather than challenge the leader. This pattern is common in industries such as steel, fertilizers, and chemicals, where few opportunities exist for product differentiation and image differentiation, service quality is often comparable, and price sensitivity runs high. Short-run grabs for market share only provoke retaliation, so most firms present similar offers to buyers, usually by copying the leader; this keeps market shares highly stable.

There are four broad strategies for market followers:

➤ *Counterfeiter:* The counterfeiter duplicates the leader's product and package and sells it on the black market or through disreputable dealers. Both Apple Computer and Rolex have been plagued by counterfeiters, especially in the Far East.

➤ *Cloner:* The cloner emulates the leader's products, name, and packaging, with slight variations. For example, Ralcorp Holding sells imitations of name-brand cereals in lookalike boxes at lower prices.[27]

➤ *Imitator:* The imitator copies some things from the leader but maintains differentiation in terms of packaging, advertising, pricing, and so on. The leader does not respond as long as the imitator does not attack the leader aggressively.

➤ *Adapter:* The adapter adapts or improves the leader's products, perhaps for different markets. S&S Cycle, for example, supplies engines to firms that build Harley-like cruiser bikes. It buys a new Harley-Davidson bike every year and takes the engine apart to see what it can improve upon.[28]

Normally, a follower earns less than the leader. For example, a study of food processing companies found that only the top two firms were profitable. Thus, followership is not always a rewarding path.

Market-Nicher Strategies

An alternative to being a follower in a large market is to be a leader in a small market, or niche. Smaller firms normally avoid competing with larger firms by targeting small markets of little or no interest to the larger firms. For example, by focusing on hospital face masks, Tecnol Medical Products competes against two giants: Johnson & Johnson and 3M. Tecnol transformed this ordinary product into a lucrative line of specialty masks that shield health care workers from infection. Now the company has surpassed Johnson & Johnson and 3M to become the top mask supplier to U.S. hospitals.[29]

Yet cultivating a niche is only one facet of these companies' success. Tecnol's success can be attributed to its ability to pick its fight carefully (surgical masks are small potatoes to Johnson & Johnson and 3M), keep costs down by developing and producing products in-house, innovate constantly by launching new products every year, and acquire smaller rivals to expand its product offering.

Increasingly, even large firms are setting up business units or companies to serve niches. Through smart niching, firms with low shares of the total market can still be highly profitable. This is because the market nicher ends up knowing the target customers so well that it meets their needs better than other firms that are selling to this niche casually. As a result, the nicher can charge a substantial price over costs. The nicher achieves *high margin,* whereas the mass marketer achieves *high volume.*

The key idea in nichemanship is specialization. Table 7.2 shows the specialist roles open to nichers. However, because niches can weaken, the firm must continually create new niches, expand niches, and protect its niches. By developing strength in two or more niches, the company increases its chances for survival. In fact, firms entering a market should aim at a niche initially.

Balancing Customer and Competitor Orientations

We have stressed the importance of a company's positioning itself competitively as a market leader, challenger, follower, or nicher. Yet a company must not spend all of its time focusing on competitors. We can distinguish between two types of companies: competitor-centered and customer-centered.

A *competitor-centered company* looks at each situation in terms of what competitors are doing (increasing distribution, cutting prices, introducing new services) and then formulates competitive reactions (increasing advertising expenditures, meeting price cuts, increasing the sales-promotion budget). This kind of planning has both pluses and minuses. On the positive side, the company develops a fighter orientation, training its marketers to be alert for weaknesses in its competitors' and its own position. On the negative side, the company is too reactive. Rather than formulating and executing a consistent customer-oriented strategy, it determines its moves based on its competitors' moves rather than its own goals.

A *customer-centered company* focuses more on customer developments in formulating its strategies. Its marketers might learn through research, for example, that the

Table 7.2   Specialized Niche Roles

Niche Specialty	Description
End-user specialist	The firm specializes in serving one type of end-use customer.
Vertical-level specialist	The firm specializes at some vertical level of the production-distribution value chain.
Customer-size specialist	The firm concentrates on selling to small, medium-size, or large customers.
Specific-customer specialist	The firm limits its selling to one or a few customers.
Geographic specialist	The firm sells only in a certain locality, region, or area of the world.
Product or product-line specialist	The firm carries or produces only one product line or product.
Product-feature specialist	The firm specializes in producing a certain type of product or product feature.
Job-shop specialist	The firm customizes its products for individual customers.
Quality-price specialist	The firm operates at the low- or high-quality ends of the market.
Service specialist	The firm offers one or more services not available from competitors.
Channel specialist	The firm specializes in serving only one channel of distribution.

total market is growing at 4 percent annually, while the quality-sensitive segment is growing at 8 percent annually. They might also find that the deal-prone customer segment is growing fast, but these customers do not stay with any supplier for very long. And they might find that more customers are asking for a 24-hour hot line, which no one else offers. In response, this company could put more effort into reaching and satisfying the quality segment, avoid cutting prices, and research the possibility of installing a hot line.

Clearly, the customer-centered company is in a better position to identify new opportunities and set a strategy toward long-run profits. By monitoring customer needs, it can decide which customer groups and emerging needs are the most important to serve, given its resources and objectives. In practice, of course, successful companies monitor both customers and competitors carefully. And in monitoring customers, these companies enhance their ability to identify market segments and select target markets, as discussed in the next chapter.

EXECUTIVE SUMMARY

To prepare an effective marketing strategy, a company must study its competitors as well as its actual and potential customers. The closest competitors are those seeking to satisfy the same customers and needs and making similar offers; latent competitors are those who may offer new or other ways to satisfy the same needs. The company should identify competitors by using both industry and market-based analyses, then analyze competitors' strategies, objectives, strengths, weaknesses, and reaction patterns.

Through a competitive intelligence system, companies can continuously collect, analyze, and disseminate competitive information to provide managers with timely information about competitors so they can more easily formulate appropriate strategies. In selecting which competitors to attack and which to avoid, managers conduct a customer value analysis, which reveals the company's strengths and weaknesses relative to competitors. The aim of this analysis is to determine the benefits that customers want and how they perceive the relative value of competitors' offers.

A firm can gain further insight into its competitive position by classifying competitors and itself according to their roles in the target market: leader, challenger, follower, or nicher. To remain dominant, the market leader (who has the highest market share) looks for ways to expand total market demand, attempts to protect its current market share, and perhaps tries to increase its market share.

A market challenger attacks the market leader and other competitors in an aggressive bid for more market share. After defining their strategic objectives and opponents, challengers can choose from five types of general attack (frontal, flank, encirclement, bypass, guerrilla) and a number of more specific attack strategies. A market follower is a runner-up firm that is willing to maintain its market share and not rock the boat. A follower can play the role of counterfeiter, cloner, imitator, or adapter. A market nicher serves small market segments that are not being served by larger firms. The key to nichemanship is specialization; multiple niching is generally preferable to single niching.

As important as a competitive orientation is in today's global markets, companies should not overdo the competitive emphasis. Instead, companies should monitor both customers and competitors.

NOTES

1. See Leonard M. Fuld, *The New Competitor Intelligence: The Complete Resource for Finding, Analyzing, and Using Information About Your Competitors* (New York: John Wiley, 1995); John A. Czepiel, *Competitive Marketing Strategy* (Upper Saddle River, NJ: Prentice-Hall, 1992).
2. Michael E. Porter, *Competitive Strategy* (New York: Free Press, 1980), pp. 22–23.
3. Leslie Kaufman with Saul Hansell, "Holiday Lessons in Online Retailing," *New York Times,* January 2, 2000, sec. 3, pp. 1, 14; Heather Green, "Distribution: Retail," *Business Week,* January 10, 2000, p. 130.
4. Jerry Useem, "Withering Britannica Bets It All on the Web," *Fortune,* November 22, 1999, pp. 344, 348; Michael Krantz, "Click Till You Drop," *Time,* July 20, 1998, pp. 34–39; Michael Krauss, "The Web Is Taking Your Customers for Itself," *Marketing News,* June 8, 1998, p. 8.
5. See Amy Doan, "Palm Flop," *Forbes,* November 29, 1999, www.forbes.com.
6. See Kathryn Rudie Harrigan, "The Effect of Exit Barriers upon Strategic Flexibility," *Strategic Management Journal* 1 (1980): 165–76.
7. Porter, *Competitive Strategy,* ch. 13.
8. Ibid., ch. 7.
9. William E. Rothschild, *How to Gain (and Maintain) the Competitive Advantage* (New York: McGraw-Hill, 1989), ch. 5.
10. See Robert V. L. Wright, *A System for Managing Diversity* (Cambridge, MA: Arthur D. Little, December 1974).
11. Eric Nee, "The Geek Elite," *Fortune,* November 8, 1999, pp. 220–24.

12. For more discussion, see Leonard M. Fuld, *Monitoring the Competition* (New York: John Wiley, 1988).

13. "Spy/Counterspy," *Context,* Summer 1998, pp. 20–21.

14. Michael E. Porter, *Competitive Advantage* (New York: Free Press, 1985), ch. 6.

15. Bernhard Warner, "Levi's Internet Blues Keep Keepin' On," *The Industry Standard,* November 8, 1999, www.thestandard.com/subject/ecommerce.

16. Erika Rasmusson, "The Jackpot," *Sales & Marketing Management,* June 1998, pp. 35–41.

17. These six defense strategies, as well as the five attack strategies, are taken from Philip Kotler and Ravi Singh, "Marketing Warfare in the 1980s," *Journal of Business Strategy,* Winter 1981, pp. 30–41. For additional reading, see Gerald A. Michaelson, *Winning the Marketing War: A Field Manual for Business Leaders* (Lanham, MD: Abt Books, 1987); Al Ries and Jack Trout, *Marketing Warfare* (New York: McGraw-Hill, 1990); Jay Conrad Levinson, *Guerrilla Marketing* (Boston, MA: Houghton-Mifflin Co., 1984); and Barrie G. James, *Business Wargames* (Harmondsworth, England: Penguin Books, 1984).

18. Seanna Broder, "Reheating Starbucks," *Business Week,* September 28, 1998, p. A1.

19. "Seiko," *Hoover's Capsules,* January 2000, www.hoovers.com.

20. See Porter, *Competitive Strategy,* ch. 4.

21. Steve Hamm, "Microsoft's Future," *Business Week,* January 19, 1998, pp. 58–68; Mike McNamee, "1999: The Triumphs and the Turkeys," *Business Week,* December 27, 1999, pp. 126, 128.

22. Philip Kotler and Paul N. Bloom, "Strategies for High Market-Share Companies," *Harvard Business Review,* November–December 1975, pp. 63–72. Also see Porter, *Competitive Advantage,* pp. 221–26.

23. Robert D. Hof, "A Java in Every Pot? Sun Aims to Make It the Language of All Smart Appliances," *Business Week,* July 27, 1998, p. 71.

24. Holman W. Jenkins Jr., "Business World: On a Happier Note, Orange Juice," *Wall Street Journal,* September 23, 1998, p. A23.

25. Tom Davey, "Excite Climbs Bluemountain.com," *Redherring.com,* October 26, 1999, www.redherring.com.

26. Theodore Levitt, "Innovative Imitation," *Harvard Business Review,* September–October 1966, pp. 63 ff. Also see Steven P. Schnaars, *Managing Imitation Strategies: How Later Entrants Seize Markets from Pioneers* (New York: Free Press, 1994).

27. Greg Burns, "A Fruit Loop by Any Other Name," *Business Week,* June 26, 1995, pp. 72, 76.

28. Stuart F. Brown, "The Company that Out-Harleys Harley," *Fortune,* September 28, 1998, pp. 56–57.

29. Stephanie Anderson, "Who's Afraid of J&J and 3M?" *Business Week,* December 5, 1994, pp. 66–68.

Identifying Market Segments and Selecting Target Markets

In this chapter, we will address the following questions:

■ How and why is segmentation applied to consumer and business markets?

■ How can a company use mass customization to effectively meet the needs of individual customers?

■ What targeting strategies can a company use to select and enter the most attractive market segments?

A company cannot serve everyone in broad markets such as soft drinks (for consumers) and computers (for businesses), because the customers are too numerous and diverse in their buying requirements. This is why successful marketers look for specific market segments that they can serve more effectively. Instead of scattering their marketing efforts (a "shotgun" approach), they will be able to focus on the buyers whom they have the greatest chance of satisfying (a "rifle" approach).

The most targeted marketing strategies are built around meeting each customer's unique requirements. Such mass customization strategies are particularly well suited to Internet marketing, where leaders such as Dell can maintain an interactive dialogue with customers and create a unique bundle of goods and services specifically for their individual needs and wants.

Target marketing requires marketers to take three major steps: (1) Identify and profile distinct groups of buyers who might require separate products or marketing mixes (market segmentation); (2) select one or more market segments to enter (market targeting); and (3) establish and communicate the products' key distinctive benefits in the market (market positioning). This chapter focuses on the first two steps; the following chapter will discuss positioning strategy.

USING MARKET SEGMENTATION

Market segmentation aims to increase a company's precision marketing. In contrast, sellers that use *mass marketing* engage in the mass production, distribution, and promotion of one product for all buyers. Henry Ford epitomized this strategy when he offered the Model T Ford "in any color, as long as it is black." Coca-Cola also used mass marketing when it sold only one kind of Coke in a 6.5-ounce bottle.

The argument for mass marketing is that it creates the largest potential market, which leads to the lowest costs, which in turn can lead to lower prices or higher margins. However, many critics point to the increasing splintering of the market, which makes mass marketing more difficult. According to Regis McKenna, "[Consumers] have more ways to shop: at giant malls, specialty shops, and superstores; through mail-order catalogs, home shopping networks, and virtual stores on the Internet. And they are bombarded with messages pitched through a growing number of channels: broadcast and narrow-cast television, radio, on-line computer networks, the Internet, telephone services such as fax and telemarketing, and niche magazines and other print media."[1]

This proliferation of media and distribution channels is making it difficult to practice "one size fits all" marketing. Some observers even claim that mass marketing is dying. Therefore, to stay focused rather than scattering their marketing resources, more marketers are using market segmentation. In this approach, which falls midway between mass marketing and individual marketing, each segment's buyers are assumed to be quite similar in wants and needs, yet no two buyers are really alike. To use this technique, a company must understand both the levels and the patterns of market segmentation.

Levels of Market Segmentation

Regardless of whether they serve the consumer market or the business market—offering either goods or services—companies can apply segmentation at one of four levels: segments, niches, local areas, and individuals.

Segment Marketing

A *market segment* consists of a large identifiable group within a market, with similar wants, purchasing power, geographical location, buying attitudes, or buying habits. For example, an automaker may identify four broad segments in the car market: buyers who are primarily seeking (1) basic transportation, (2) high performance, (3) luxury, or (4) safety.

Because the needs, preferences, and behavior of segment members are similar but not identical, Anderson and Narus urge marketers to present *flexible market offerings* instead of one standard offering to all members of a segment.[2] A flexible market offering consists of the product and service elements that all segment members value, plus options (for an additional charge) that some segment members value. For example, Delta Airlines offers all economy passengers a seat, food, and soft drinks, but it charges extra for alcoholic beverages and earphones.

Segment marketing allows a firm to create a more fine-tuned product or service offering and price it appropriately for the target audience. The choice of distribution channels and communications channels becomes much easier, and the firm may find it faces fewer competitors in certain segments.

Niche Marketing

A *niche* is a more narrowly defined group, typically a small market whose needs are not being well served. Marketers usually identify niches by dividing a segment into subsegments or by defining a group seeking a distinctive mix of benefits. For example, a tobacco company might identify two subsegments of heavy smokers: those who are trying to stop smoking, and those who don't care.

In an attractive niche, customers have a distinct set of needs; they will pay a premium to the firm that best satisfies their needs; the niche is not likely to attract other competitors; the nicher gains certain economies through specialization; and the niche has size, profit, and growth potential. Whereas segments are fairly large and normally attract several competitors, niches are fairly small and may attract only one or two rivals. Still, giants such as IBM can and do lose pieces of their market to nichers: Dalgic labeled this confrontation "guerrillas against gorillas."[3]

Some larger firms have therefore turned to niche marketing. Ramada Franchises Enterprises, for example, offers lodgings in several niches: Ramada Limited for economy travelers; Ramada Inn as a mid-price, full-service hotel; Ramada Plaza for the upper-mid-price niche; Ramada Hotels for good quality, three-star service; and Ramada Renaissance hotels, offering excellent, four-star service. Many German mid-size companies are also profiting through smart niching: Tetra Food supplies 80 percent of the food for tropical fish; Hohner holds 85 percent of the world harmonica market; and Becher has 50 percent of the world's oversized umbrella market. These firms are succeeding in their chosen niches because they are dedicated to their customers, offer superior service, and innovate continuously.[4]

Now the low cost of marketing on the Internet is making it more profitable for firms—including small businesses—to serve even seemingly minuscule niches. In fact, 15 percent of all commercial Web sites with fewer than 10 employees take in more than $100,000, and 2 percent ring up more than $1 million. The recipe for Internet niching success: Choose a hard-to-find product that customers don't need to see and touch. Consider Steve Warrington's successful on-line venture selling ostriches and every product derived from them (www.ostrichesonline.com). Launched for next to nothing on the Web, Warrington's business generates annual sales of $4 million-plus. Visitors to the site can buy ostrich meat, feathers, leather jackets, videos, eggshells, and skin-care products derived from ostrich body oil.[5]

Local Marketing

Target marketing is leading to some marketing programs that are tailored to the needs and wants of local customer groups (trading areas, neighborhoods, even individual stores). Citibank, for instance, adjusts its banking services in each branch depending on neighborhood demographics; Kraft helps supermarket chains identify the cheese assortment and shelf positioning that will optimize cheese sales in low-, middle-, and high-income stores and in different ethnic neighborhoods.

Those favoring local marketing see national advertising as wasteful because it fails to address local needs. On the other hand, opponents argue that local marketing drives up manufacturing and marketing costs by reducing economies of scale. Moreover, logistical problems become magnified when companies try to meet varying local requirements, and a brand's overall image might be diluted if the product and message differ in different localities.

Individual Marketing

The ultimate level of segmentation leads to "segments of one," "customized marketing," or "one-to-one marketing."[6] For centuries, consumers were served as individuals: The tailor made the suit and the cobbler designed shoes for the individual. Much business-to-business marketing today is customized, in that a manufacturer will customize the offer, logistics, communications, and financial terms for each major account. Now technologies such as computers, databases, robotic production, intranets and extranets, e-mail, and fax communication are permitting companies to return to customized marketing, also called "mass customization."[7] *Mass customization* is the ability to prepare individually designed products and communications on a mass basis to meet each customer's requirements.

For example, Andersen Windows, a $1 billion Minnesota-based manufacturer of residential windows, turned to mass customization after additions to its product line led to fat, unwieldy catalogs and a bewildering array of choices for homeowners and contractors. Then the firm equipped 650 showrooms with an interactive computer catalog linked directly to the factory. Using this catalog, salespeople help customers customize each window, check the design for structural soundness, and generate a price quote. Andersen has also developed a "batch of one" manufacturing process in which everything is made to order, thus reducing its finished parts inventory (a major cost to the company).[8]

Joseph Pine, author of *Mass Customization*, says, "Anything you can digitize, you can customize." In fact, the Internet is bringing mass customization to an astonishing array of products. Mattel's Barbie.com site invites girls to log on and design their own Barbie Pal doll by specifying skin tone, eye color, hairdo and hair color, clothes, accessories, and name. CDuctive, a hip, New York-based company, lets customers cut their own CDs online. If a customer likes acid jazz, he can click on the category, see the various titles, listen to a brief sample of each, and then click to order a CD with his chosen tunes.[9] Technology like this is transforming marketing from "a broadcast medium to a dialog medium," allowing the customer to actively participate in the design of the product and offer.

Although individual customers are taking more initiative in designing and buying products, marketers still need to influence the process in a variety of ways. They need toll-free phone numbers and e-mail addresses to enable buyers to reach them with questions, suggestions, and complaints; they must involve customers more in the product-specification process; and they need a Web site with complete, updated information about the company's products, service guarantees, and locations.

Patterns of Market Segmentation

Market segments can be built up in many ways. One common method is to identify *preference segments*. Suppose ice cream buyers are asked how much they value sweetness and creaminess as two product attributes. Three different patterns can emerge:

➤ *Homogeneous preferences:* Figure 8.1a shows a market in which all of the consumers have roughly the same preference, so there are no natural segments. We predict that existing brands would be similar and cluster around the middle of the scale in both sweetness and creaminess.

➤ *Diffused preferences:* At the other extreme, consumer preferences may be scattered throughout the space (Figure 8.1b), indicating great variance in consumer preferences. One brand might position in the center to appeal to the most people; if several brands are in the market, they are likely to position throughout the space and show real differences to reflect consumer-preference differences.

➤ *Clustered preferences:* The market might reveal distinct preference clusters, called *natural market segments* (Figure 8.1c). The first firm in this market might position in the center to appeal to all groups, choose the largest market segment (*concentrated marketing*), or develop several brands for different segments. If the first firm has only one brand, competitors would enter and introduce brands in the other segments.

Smart marketers examine such segmentation patterns carefully to better understand the various positions they might take in a market—and the competitive implications (see Chapter 7).

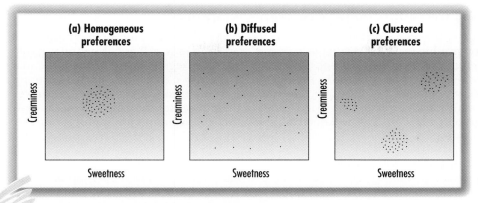

Figure 8.1   Basic Market-Preference Patterns

Market-Segmentation Procedure

Marketers use a three-step procedure for identifying market segments:

1. *Survey stage.* The researcher conducts exploratory interviews and focus groups to gain insight into customer motivations, attitudes, and behavior. Then the researcher prepares a questionnaire and collects data on attributes and their importance ratings, brand awareness and brand ratings, product-usage patterns, attitudes toward the product category, and respondents' demographics, geographics, psychographics, and mediagraphics.

2. *Analysis stage.* The researcher applies *factor analysis* to the data to remove highly correlated variables, then applies *cluster analysis* to create a specified number of maximally different segments.

3. *Profiling stage.* Each cluster is profiled in terms of its distinguishing attitudes, behavior, demographics, psychographics, and media patterns, then each segment is given a name based on its dominant characteristic. In a study of the leisure market, Andreasen and Belk found six segments:[10] passive homebody, active sports enthusiast, inner-directed self-sufficient, culture patron, active homebody, and socially active. They found that performing arts organizations could sell the most tickets by targeting culture patrons as well as socially active people.

Companies can uncover new segments by researching the hierarchy of attributes that customers consider when choosing a brand. For instance, car buyers who first decide on price are price dominant; those who first decide on car type (e.g., passenger, sport-utility) are type dominant; those who first decide on brand are brand dominant. With these segments, customers may have distinct demographics, psychographics, and mediagraphics to be analyzed and addressed through marketing programs.[11]

SEGMENTING CONSUMER AND BUSINESS MARKETS

Because of the inherent differences between consumer and business markets (discussed in Chapters 5 and 6), marketers cannot use exactly the same variables to segment both. Instead, they use one broad group of variables as the basis for consumer segmentation and another broad group for business segmentation.

Bases for Segmenting Consumer Markets

In segmenting consumer markets, marketers can apply geographic, demographic, and psychographic variables related to *consumer characteristics* as well as behavioral variables related to *consumer responses* (see Table 8.1). Once the segments are formed, the marketer sees whether different characteristics are associated with each consumer-response segment. For example, the researcher might examine whether car buyers who want "quality" versus "low price" differ in their geographic, demographic, and psychographic makeup. This will determine whether the segments are useful for marketing purposes.

Geographic Segmentation

Geographic segmentation calls for dividing the market into different geographical units such as nations, states, regions, counties, cities, or neighborhoods. The company can operate in one or a few geographic areas or operate in all but pay attention to local variations. Some marketers even segment down to a specific zip code. Consider Blockbuster, which has databases to track the video preferences of its 85 million members and buys additional demographic data about each store's local area. As a result of this segmentation, it stocks its San Francisco stores with more gay-oriented videos, reflecting the city's large gay population, while it stocks Chicago stores with more family-oriented videos. Blockbuster can even distinguish between patterns of East Dallas and South Dallas customers.[12]

Demographic Segmentation

In *demographic segmentation,* the market is divided into groups on the basis of age and the other variables in Table 8.1. One reason this is the most popular consumer segmentation method is that consumer wants, preferences, and usage rates are often associated with demographic variables. Another reason is that demographic variables are easier to measure. Even when the target market is described in nondemographic terms (say, a personality type), the link back to demographic characteristics is needed in order to estimate the size of the target market and the media that should be used to reach it efficiently.

Here is how certain demographic variables have been used to segment consumer markets:

➤ *Age and life-cycle stage.* Consumer wants and abilities change with age, as Gerber realized when it decided to expand beyond its traditional baby foods line because the market was growing more slowly due to lower birthrates, babies staying on formula longer, and children moving to solid foods sooner. The company hopes that parents who buy its baby food will go on to buy its Graduates foods for 1- to 3-year olds.[13] However, age and life cycle can be tricky variables. For example, Ford originally designed its Mustang automobile to appeal to young people who wanted an inexpensive sport car. But when Ford found that the car was being purchased by all age groups, it recognized that the target market was not the chronologically young, but the psychologically young.

➤ *Gender.* Gender segmentation has long been applied in clothing, hairstyling, cosmetics, and magazines. Occasionally other marketers notice an opportunity for gender segmentation. The Internet portal iVillage.com reaped the benefits of gender segmentation after initially trying to appeal to a broader market of baby boomers. Noticing that Parent Soup and other offerings for women were the most popular, iVillage soon evolved into the leading women's on-line community. Its home page entreats visitors to "Join our community of smart, compassionate, real women."[14]

Table 8.1   Major Segmentation Variables for Consumer Markets

Geographic	
Region	Pacific, Mountain, West North Central, West South Central, East North Central, East South Central, South Atlantic, Middle Atlantic, New England
City or metro size	Under 4,999; 5,000–19,999; 20,000–49,999; 50,000–99,999; 100,000–249,999; 250,000–499,999; 500,000–999,999; 1,000,000–3,999,999; 4,000,000 or over
Density	Urban, suburban, rural
Climate	Northern, southern

Demographic	
Age	Under 6, 6–11, 12–19, 20–34, 35–49, 50–64, 65+
Family Size	1–2, 3–4, 5+
Family life cycle	Young, single; young, married, no children; young, married, youngest child under 6; young, married, youngest child 6 or over; older, married, with children; older, married, no children under 18; older, single; other
Gender	Male, female
Income	Under $9,999; $10,000–$14,999; $15,000–$19,999; $20,000–$29,999; $30,000–$49,999; $50,000–$99,999; $100,000 and over
Occupation	Professional and technical; managers, officials, and proprietors; clerical, sales; craftspeople; forepersons; operatives; farmers; retired; students; homemakers; unemployed
Education	Grade school or less; some high school; high school graduate; some college; college graduate
Religion	Catholic, Protestant, Jewish, Muslim, Hindu, other
Race	White, Black, Asian, Hispanic
Generation	Baby boomers, Generation Xers
Nationality	North American, South American, British, French, German, Italian, Japanese
Social class	Lower lowers, upper lowers, working class, middle class, upper middles, lower uppers, upper uppers

Psychographic	
Lifestyle	Straights, swingers, longhairs
Personality	Compulsive, gregarious, authoritarian, ambitious

Behavioral	
Occasions	Regular occasion, special occasion
Benefits	Quality, service, economy, speed
User status	Nonuser, ex-user, potential user, first-time user, regular user
Usage rate	Light user, medium user, heavy user
Loyalty status	None, medium, strong, absolute
Readiness stage	Unaware, aware, informed, interested, desirous, intending to buy
Attitude toward product	Enthusiastic, positive, indifferent, negative, hostile

➤ *Income.* Income segmentation is a long-standing practice in such categories as automobiles, boats, clothing, cosmetics, and travel. However, income does not always predict the best customers for a given product. The most economical cars are not bought by the really poor, but rather by those who think of themselves as poor relative to their status aspirations; medium-price and expensive cars tend to be purchased by the overprivileged segments of each social class.

➤ *Generation.* Each generation is profoundly influenced by the times in which it grows up—the music, movies, politics, and events of that period. Some marketers target Generation Xers (those born between 1964 and 1984), while others target Baby Boomers (those born between 1946 and 1964).[15] Meredith and Schewe have proposed a more focused concept they call cohort segmentation.[16] *Cohorts* are groups of people who share experiences of major external events (such as World War II) that have deeply affected their attitudes and preferences. Because members of a cohort group feel a bond with each other for having shared these experiences, effective marketing appeals use the icons and images that are prominent in the targeted cohort group's experience.

➤ *Social class.* Social class strongly influences preference in cars, clothing, home furnishings, leisure activities, reading habits, and retailers, which is why many firms design products for specific social classes. However, the tastes of social classes can change over time. The 1980s were about greed and ostentation for the upper classes, but the 1990s were more about values and self-fulfillment. Affluent tastes now run toward more utilitarian rather than ostentatious products.[17]

Psychographic Segmentation

In *psychographic segmentation,* buyers are divided into different groups on the basis of lifestyle or personality and values. People within the same demographic group can exhibit very different psychographic profiles.

➤ *Lifestyle.* People exhibit many more lifestyles than are suggested by the seven social classes, and the goods they consume express their lifestyles. Meat seems an unlikely product for lifestyle segmentation, but one Kroger supermarket in Nashville found that segmenting self-service meat products by lifestyle, not by type of meat, had a big payoff. This store grouped meats by lifestyle, creating such sections as "Meals in Minutes" and "Kids Love This Stuff" (hot dogs, hamburger patties, and the like). By focusing on lifestyle needs, not protein categories, Kroger's encouraged habitual beef and pork buyers to consider lamb and veal as well—boosting sales and profits.[18] But lifestyle segmentation does not always work: Nestlé introduced a special brand of decaffeinated coffee for "late nighters," and it failed, presumably because people saw no need for such a specialized product.

➤ *Personality.* Marketers can endow their products with *brand personalities* that correspond to consumer personalities. Apple Computer's iMac computers, for example, have a friendly, stylish personality that appeals to buyers who do not want boring, ordinary personal computers.[19]

➤ *Values.* Core values are the belief systems that underlie consumer attitudes and behaviors. Core values go much deeper than behavior or attitude, and determine, at a basic level, people's choices and desires over the long term. Marketers who use this segmentation variable believe that by appealing to people's inner selves, it is possible to influence purchase behavior. Although values often differ from culture to culture, Roper Reports has identified six values segments stretching across 35 countries: strivers (who focus more on material and professional goals), devouts (who consider tradition and duty very important), altruists (who are interested in social issues), intimates (who value close personal relationships and family highly), fun seekers (who tend to be younger and usually male), and creatives (who are interested in education, knowledge, and technology).[20]

Behavioral Segmentation

In *behavioral segmentation,* buyers are divided into groups on the basis of their knowledge of, attitude toward, use of, or response to a product. Many marketers believe that behavioral variables—occasions, benefits, user status, usage rate, loyalty status, buyer-readiness stage, and attitude—are the best starting points for constructing market segments.

➤ *Occasions.* Buyers can be distinguished according to the occasions on which they develop a need, purchase a product, or use a product. For example, air travel is triggered by occasions related to business, vacation, or family, so an airline can specialize in one of these occasions. Thus, charter airlines serve groups of people who fly to a vacation destination. Occasion segmentation can help firms expand product usage, as the Curtis Candy Company did when it promoted trick-or-treating at Halloween and urged consumers to buy candy for the eager little callers. A company can also consider critical life events to see whether they are accompanied by certain needs. This kind of analysis has led to service providers such as marriage, employment, and bereavement counselors.

➤ *Benefits.* Buyers can be classified according to the benefits they seek. One study of travelers uncovered three benefit segments: those who travel to be with family, those who travel for adventure or education, and those who enjoy the "gambling" and "fun" aspects of travel.[21]

➤ *User status.* Markets can be segmented into nonusers, ex-users, potential users, first-time users, and regular users of a product. The company's market position also influences its focus. Market leaders (such as America Online) focus on attracting potential users, whereas smaller firms (such as Earthlink, a fast-growing Internet service provider) try to lure users away from the leader.

➤ *Usage rate.* Markets can be segmented into light, medium, and heavy product users. Heavy users are often a small percentage of the market but account for a high percentage of total consumption. Marketers usually prefer to attract one heavy user rather than several light users, and they vary their promotional efforts accordingly. Repp's Big & Tall Stores, which operates 200 stores and a catalog business, has identified 12 segments by analyzing customer response rates, average sales, and so on. Some segments get up to eight mailings a year, while some get only one to three mailings. The chain tries to steer low-volume catalog shoppers into nearby stores, and it offers infrequent customers an incentive such as 15 percent off to buy during a particular period. Repp gets a 6 percent response to these segmented mailings, far more than the typical 0.5 response rate for nonsegmented mailings.[22]

➤ *Loyalty status.* Buyers can be divided into four groups according to brand loyalty status: (1) hard-core loyals (who always buy one brand), (2) split loyals (who are loyal to two or three brands), (3) shifting loyals (who shift from one brand to another, and (4) switchers (who show no loyalty to any brand).[23] Each market consists of different numbers of these four types of buyers; thus, a *brand-loyal market* has a high percentage of hard-core loyals. Companies that sell in such a market have a hard time gaining more market share, and new competitors have a hard time breaking in. One caution: What appears to be brand loyalty may actually reflect habit, indifference, a low price, a high switching cost, or the nonavailability of other brands. For this reason, marketers must carefully interpret what is behind observed purchasing patterns.

➤ *Buyer-readiness stage.* A market consists of people in different stages of readiness to buy a product: Some are unaware of the product, some are aware, some are informed, some are interested, some desire the product, and some intend to buy. The relative numbers make a big difference in designing the marketing program.

➤ *Attitude.* Five attitude groups can be found in a market: (1) enthusiastic, (2) positive, (3) indifferent, (4) negative, and (5) hostile. So, for example, workers in a political campaign use the voter's attitude to determine how much time to spend with that voter. They may thank enthusiastic voters and remind them to vote, reinforce those who are positively disposed, try to win the votes of indifferent voters, and spend no time trying to change the attitudes of negative and hostile voters.

Multi-Attribute Segmentation (Geoclustering)

Marketers are increasingly combining several variables in an effort to identify smaller, better defined target groups. Thus, a bank may not only identify a group of wealthy retired adults, but within that group may distinguish several segments depending on current income, assets, savings, and risk preferences.

One of the most promising developments in multi-attribute segmentation is *geoclustering,* which yields richer descriptions of consumers and neighborhoods than does traditional demographics. Geoclustering can help a firm answer such questions as: Which clusters (neighborhoods or zip codes) contain our most valuable customers? How deeply have we already penetrated these segments? Which markets provide the best opportunities for growth?

Claritas Inc. has developed a geoclustering approach called PRIZM (Potential Rating Index by Zip Markets), classifying over half a million U.S. residential neighborhoods into 62 lifestyle groupings called PRIZM Clusters.[24] The groupings take into consideration 39 factors in five broad categories: (1) education and affluence, (2) family life cycle, (3) urbanization, (4) race and ethnicity, and (5) mobility, and cover specific geographic areas defined by Zip code, Zip + 4, census tract, and block group.

Each cluster has a descriptive title, such as *American Dreams* and *Rural Industria.* Within each cluster, members tend to lead similar lives, drive similar cars, have similar jobs, and read similar magazines. The American Dreams cluster, for example, is upscale and ethnic—a big-city mosaic of people likely to buy imported cars, *Elle* magazine, Mueslix cereal, tennis weekends, and designer jeans. In contrast, Rural Industria contains young families in heartland offices and factories whose lifestyle is typified by trucks, *True Story* magazine, Shake n' Bake, fishing trips, and tropical fish.[25]

Geoclustering is an especially valuable segmentation tool because it captures the increasing diversity of the American population. Moreover, it can help even smaller firms identify microsegments that are economically feasible because of lower database costs, more sophisticated software, increased data integration, and wider use of the Internet.[26]

Bases for Segmenting Business Markets

Business markets can be segmented with some variables that are employed in consumer market segmentation, such as geography, benefits sought, and usage rate. Yet business marketers can also use several other variables. Bonoma and Shapiro proposed segmenting the business market with the variables shown in Table 8.2. The demographic variables are the most important, followed by the operating variables—down to the personal characteristics of the buyer.

Table 8.2   Major Segmentation Variables for Business Markets

Demographic

1. *Industry:* Which industries should we serve?
2. *Company size:* What size companies should we serve?
3. *Location:* What geographical areas should we serve?

Operating Variables

4. *Technology:* What customer technologies should we focus on?
5. *User or nonuser status:* Should we serve heavy users, medium users, light users, or nonusers?
6. *Customer capabilities:* Should we serve customers needing many or fewer services?

Purchasing Approaches

7. *Purchasing-function organization:* Should we serve companies with highly centralized or decentralized purchasing organizations?
8. *Power structure:* Should we serve companies that are engineering dominated, financially dominated, and so on?
9. *Nature of existing relationships:* Should we serve companies with which we have strong relationships or simply go after the most desirable companies?
10. *General purchase policies:* Should we serve companies that prefer leasing? Service contracts? Systems purchases? Sealed bidding?
11. *Purchasing criteria:* Should we serve companies that are seeking quality? Service? Price?

Situational Factors

12. **Urgency:** Should we serve companies that need quick and sudden delivery or service?
13. **Specific application:** Should we focus on certain applications of our product rather than all applications?
14. **Size of order:** Should we focus on large or small orders?

Personal Characteristics

15. **Buyer–seller similarity:** Should we serve companies whose people and values are similar to ours?
16. **Attitudes toward risk:** Should we serve risk-taking or risk-avoiding customers?
17. **Loyalty:** Should we serve companies that show high loyalty to their suppliers?

Source: Adapted from Thomas V. Bonoma and Benson P. Shapiro, *Segmenting the Industrial Market* (Lexington, MA: Lexington Books, 1983).

A company should first decide which industries it wants to serve. Then, within a chosen target industry, the company can further segment by company size, possibly setting up separate operations for selling to large and small customers. Small businesses, in particular, have become a Holy Grail for business marketers, both on and off the Internet.[27] Small businesses are now responsible for 50 percent of the U.S. gross domestic product, according to the Small Business Administration—and this segment is growing even faster than the large company segment.

IBM, already successful in marketing to corporate giants, is one of many companies targeting small businesses. Within the segment of U.S. firms with 1,000 or fewer employees, IBM is further targeting the segment of minority-owned businesses. IBM's strategy is to devote some field salespeople exclusively to small and medium-size businesses, hire executives responsible for targeting subsegments, become more involved in professional associations frequented by minority small-business owners, and offer more flexible contact options such as telesales and service.[28]

Looking beyond small businesses, marketers can be more effective even within mature commodity industries if they use segmentation for better targeting. For example, Rangan, Moriarty, and Swartz found these four business segments within the steel strapping industry:[29]

1. *Programmed buyers:* Buyers who see the product as not very important to their operation. This is a very profitable segment: The buyers view the product as a routine purchase item, usually paying full price and receiving below-average service.

2. *Relationship buyers:* Buyers who regard the product as moderately important and are knowledgeable about competitive offerings. They get a small discount and a modest amount of service and prefer the vendor as long as the price is not far out of line. This is the second most profitable segment.

3. *Transaction buyers:* Buyers who see the product as very important to their operations. They are price and service sensitive and receive some discounts, but they know the competition and will switch for a better price, even at the sacrifice of some service.

4. *Bargain hunters:* Buyers who see the product as very important and demand low prices and top service. They know the alternative suppliers, bargain hard, and are ready to switch if dissatisfied. The company needs these buyers for volume purposes, but they are not very profitable.

Clearly, developing a segmentation scheme for this kind of industry will help a business marketer determine where to increase or decrease price and service, since each segment reacts differently.[30]

Effective Segmentation

Even after applying segmentation variables to a consumer or business market, marketers must realize that not all segmentations are useful. For example, table salt buyers could be divided into blond and brunette customers, but hair color is not relevant to the purchase of salt. Furthermore, if all salt buyers buy the same amount of salt each month, believe all salt is the same, and would pay only one price for salt, this market would be minimally segmentable from a marketing perspective.

To be useful, market segments must be:

➤ *Measurable:* The size, purchasing power, and characteristics of the segments can be measured.

➤ *Substantial:* The segments are large and profitable enough to serve. A segment should be the largest possible homogeneous group worth going after with a tailored marketing program.

➤ *Accessible:* The segments can be effectively reached and served.

➤ *Differentiable:* The segments are conceptually distinguishable and respond differently to different marketing mixes. If two segments respond identically to a particular offer, they do not constitute separate segments.

➤ *Actionable:* Effective programs can be formulated for attracting and serving the segments.

MARKET TARGETING STRATEGIES

Once the firm has identified its market-segment opportunities, it is ready to initiate market targeting. Here, marketers evaluate each segment to determine how many and which ones to target and enter.

Evaluating Market Segments

In evaluating different market segments, the firm must look at two factors: (1) the segment's overall attractiveness, and (2) the company's objectives and resources. First, the firm must ask whether a potential segment has the characteristics that make it generally attractive, such as size, growth, profitability, scale economies, and low risk.

Second, the firm must consider whether investing in the segment makes sense given the firm's objectives and resources. Some attractive segments could be dismissed because they do not mesh with the company's long-run objectives; some should be dismissed if the company lacks one or more of the competences needed to offer superior value.

Selecting and Entering Market Segments

Having evaluated different segments, the company can consider five patterns of target market selection, as shown in Figure 8.2.

Single-Segment Concentration

Many companies concentrate on a single segment: Volkswagen, for example, concentrates on the small-car market, while Porsche concentrates on the sports car market. Through concentrated marketing, the firm gains a thorough understanding of the segment's needs and achieves a strong market presence. Furthermore, the firm enjoys operating economies by specializing its production, distribution, and promotion; if it attains segment leadership, it can earn a high return on its investment.

However, concentrated marketing involves higher than normal risks if the segment turns sour because of changes in buying patterns or new competition. For these reasons, many companies prefer to operate in more than one segment.

Selective Specialization

Here the firm selects a number of segments, each objectively attractive and appropriate. There may be little or no synergy among the segments, but each segment

Figure 8.2   Five Patterns of Target Market Selection

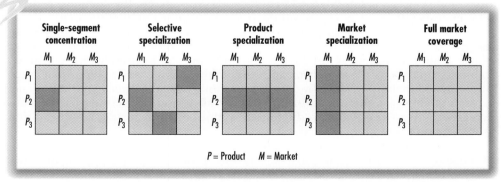

promises to be a moneymaker. This multisegment coverage strategy has the advantage of diversifying the firm's risk.

Consider a radio broadcaster that wants to appeal to both younger and older listeners using selective specialization. Emmis Communications owns New York's WRKS-RM, which describes itself as "smooth R&B [rhythm and blues] and classic soul" and appeals to older listeners, as well as WQHT-FM, which plays hip-hop (urban street music) for under-25 listeners.[31]

Product Specialization

Another approach is to specialize in making a certain product for several segments. An example would be a microscope manufacturer that sells microscopes to university laboratories, government laboratories, and commercial laboratories. The firm makes different microscopes for different customer groups but does not manufacture other instruments that laboratories might use. Through a product specialization strategy, the firm builds a strong reputation in the specific product area. The downside risk is that the product may be supplanted by an entirely new technology.

Market Specialization

With market specialization, the firm concentrates on serving many needs of a particular customer group. An example would be a firm that sells an assortment of products only to university laboratories, including microscopes, oscilloscopes, and chemical flasks. The firm gains a strong reputation in serving this customer group and becomes a channel for further products that the customer group could use. However, the downside risk is that the customer group may have its budgets cut.

Full Market Coverage

Here a firm attempts to serve all customer groups with all of the products they might need. Only very large firms can undertake a full market coverage strategy. Examples include IBM (computer market), General Motors (vehicle market), and Coca-Cola (drink market). Large firms can cover a whole market in two broad ways: through undifferentiated marketing or differentiated marketing.

In *undifferentiated marketing*, the firm ignores market-segment differences and goes after the whole market with one market offer. Focusing on a basic buyer need, it designs a product and a marketing program that will appeal to the broadest number of buyers. To reach the market, the firm uses mass distribution backed by mass advertising to create a superior product image in people's minds. The narrow product line keeps down costs of research and development, production, inventory, transportation, marketing research, advertising, and product management; the undifferentiated advertising program keeps down advertising costs. Presumably, the company can turn its lower costs into lower prices to win the price-sensitive segment of the market.

In *differentiated marketing*, the firm operates in several market segments and designs different programs for each segment. General Motors does this with its various vehicle brands and models; Intel does this with chips and programs for consumer, business, small business, networking, digital imaging, and video markets.[32] Differentiated marketing typically creates more total sales than does undifferentiated marketing. However, the need for different products and marketing programs also increases the firm's costs for product modification, manufacturing, administration, inventory, and promotion.

Because differentiated marketing leads to both higher sales and higher costs, we cannot generalize regarding this strategy's profitability. Still, companies should be cautious about oversegmenting their market. If this happens, they may want to use *coun-*

tersegmentation to broaden their customer base. Smith Kline Beecham introduced Aquafresh toothpaste to attract three benefit segments simultaneously: those seeking fresh breath, whiter teeth, and cavity protection. Next, the company moved deeper into countersegmentation by launching flavored toothpastes for children, toothpaste for people with sensitive teeth, and other toothpaste products.

Targeting Multiple Segments and Supersegments

Very often, companies start out by marketing to one segment, then expand to others. For example, Paging Network Inc.—known as PageNet—is a small developer of paging systems, and was the first to offer voice mail on pagers. To compete with Southwestern Bell and other Bell companies, it sets its prices about 20 percent below rivals' prices. Initially, PageNet used geographic segmentation to identify attractive markets in Ohio and Texas where local competitors were vulnerable to its aggressive pricing. Next, the firm developed a profile of users for paging services so it could target salespeople, messengers, and service people. PageNet also used lifestyle segmentation to target additional consumer groups, such as parents who leave their children with a sitter. Finally, PageNet began distributing its pagers through Kmart, Wal-Mart, and Home Depot, offering attractive discounts in return for the right to keep the monthly service charge revenues on any pagers sold.[33]

In targeting more than one segment, a company should examine segment interrelationships on the cost, performance, and technology side. A company that is carrying fixed costs, such as a sales force or store outlets, can generally add products to absorb and share some of these costs. Smart companies know that economies of scope can be just as important as economies of scale. Moreover, companies should look beyond isolated segments to target a *supersegment,* a set of segments that share some exploitable similarity. For example, many symphony orchestras target people with broad cultural interests, rather than only those who regularly attend concerts.

Still, a company's invasion plans can be thwarted when it confronts blocked markets. This problem calls for *megamarketing,* the strategic coordination of economic, psychological, political, and public-relations skills to gain the cooperation of a number of parties in order to enter or operate in a given market. Pepsi used megamarketing to enter India after Coca-Cola left the market. First, it worked with a local business group to gain government approval for its entry over the objections of domestic soft-drink companies and antimultinational legislators. Pepsi also offered to help India export enough agricultural products to more than cover the cost of importing soft-drink concentrate and promised economic development for some rural areas. By winning the support of these and other interest groups, Pepsi was finally able to crack the Indian market.

Ethical Choice of Market Targets

Market targeting sometimes generates public controversy.[34] The public is concerned when marketers take unfair advantage of vulnerable groups (such as children) or disadvantaged groups (such as inner-city poor people), or promote potentially harmful products. For example, the cereal industry has been criticized for marketing to children. Critics worry that high-powered appeals presented through the mouths of lovable animated characters will overwhelm children's defenses and lead them to eat too much sugared cereal or poorly balanced breakfasts.

As another example, R. J. Reynolds was criticized for plans to market Uptown, a menthol cigarette targeted toward low-income African Americans. Recently, internal documents from R. J. Reynolds and Brown & Williamson Tobacco Corporation (marketer of the Kool brand) have revealed the extent to which these companies target black youths aged 16 to 25, particularly with menthol brands.[35]

Not all attempts to target children, minorities, or other segments draw criticism. Colgate-Palmolive's Colgate Junior toothpaste has special features designed to get children to brush longer and more often. Golden Ribbon Playthings has developed a highly acclaimed and very successful black character doll named "Huggy Bean" to connect minority consumers with their African heritage. Other companies are also responding to the needs of specific segments. Black-owned ICE theaters noticed that although moviegoing by blacks has surged, there is a dearth of inner-city theaters, so it began opening theaters in Chicago and other cities. ICE partners with the black communities in which it operates, using local radio stations to promote films and featuring favorite foods at concession stands.[36]

Thus, in the choice of market targets, the issue is not who is targeted, but rather how and for what purpose. Socially responsible marketing calls for targeting and positioning (discussed in Chapter 9) that serve not only the company's interests but also the interests of those targeted.[37]

EXECUTIVE SUMMARY

Companies usually are more effective when they target their markets. Target marketing involves three activities: market segmentation, market targeting, and market positioning. Markets can be targeted at four levels: segments, niches, local areas, and individuals. Market segments are large, identifiable groups within a market, with similar wants, purchasing power, location, buying attitudes, or buying habits. A niche is a more narrowly defined group.

Many marketers localize their marketing programs for certain trading areas, neighborhoods, and even individual stores. The ultimate in segmentation is individual marketing and mass customization, a trend that is growing as more customers take the initiative in designing and buying products and brands. In addition, marketers must analyze the patterns of segmentation in a market to get a sense of their positioning alternatives and that of the competitors.

Markets are segmented in a three-step procedure of surveying, analyzing, and profiling. The major segmentation variables for consumer markets are geographic, demographic, psychographic, and behavioral, to be used singly or in combination. Business marketers can use all of these variables along with operating variables, purchasing approaches, situational factors, and personal characteristics. To be useful, market segments must be measurable, substantial, accessible, differentiable, and actionable.

Once a firm has identified its market-segment opportunities, it has to evaluate the various segments and decide how many and which ones to target. In evaluating segments, managers look at the segment's attractiveness indicators and the company's objectives and resources. In choosing which segments to target, the company can focus on a single segment, selected segments, a specific product, a specific market, or the full market; in the full market, it can use either differentiated or undifferentiated marketing. It is important for marketers to choose target markets in a socially responsible manner, by ensuring that the targeting serves the interests of the market being targeted as well as the company.

NOTES

1. Regis McKenna, "Real-Time Marketing," *Harvard Business Review,* July–August 1995, p. 87.
2. See James C. Anderson and James A. Narus, "Capturing the Value of Supplementary Services," *Harvard Business Review,* January–February 1995, pp. 75–83.

3. See Tevfik Dalgic and Maarten Leeuw, "Niche Marketing Revisited: Concept, Applications, and Some European Cases," *European Journal of Marketing* 28, no. 4 (1994): 39–55.

4. Hermann Simon, *Hidden Champions* (Boston: Harvard Business School Press, 1996).

5. Paul Davidson, "Entrepreneurs Reap Riches from Net Niches," *USA Today,* April 20, 1998, p. B3.

6. See Don Peppers and Martha Rogers, *The One to One Future: Building Relationships One Customer at a Time* (New York: Currency/Doubleday, 1993).

7. B. Joseph Pine II, *Mass Customization* (Boston: Harvard Business School Press, 1993); B. Joseph Pine II, Don Peppers, and Martha Rogers, "Do You Want to Keep Your Customers Forever?" *Harvard Business Review,* March–April 1995, pp. 103–14.

8. "Creating Greater Customer Value May Require a Lot of Changes," *Organizational Dynamics,* Summer 1998, p. 26.

9. Andy Wang, "CDuctive.com Kicks Off New MP3 Store," *E-Commerce Times,* June 2, 1999, www.ecommercetime.com; Erick Schonfeld, "The Customized, Digitized, Have-It-Your-Way Economy," *Fortune,* September 28, 1998, pp. 115–24; Jim Barlow, "Individualizing Mass Production," *Houston Chronicle,* April 13, 1997, p. e1; Sarah Schafer, "Have It Your Way," *Inc.,* November 18, 1997, pp. 56–64.

10. Alan R. Andreasen and Russell W. Belk, "Predictors of Attendance at the Performing Arts," *Journal of Consumer Research,* September 1980, pp. 112–20.

11. For a market-structure study of the hierarchy of attributes in the coffee market, see Dipak Jain, Frank M. Bass, and Yu-Min Chen, "Estimation of Latent Class Models with Heterogeneous Choice Probabilities: An Application to Market Structuring," *Journal of Marketing Research,* February 1990, pp. 94–101.

12. Kate Kane, "It's a Small World," *Working Woman,* October 1997, p. 22.

13. Leah Rickard, "Gerber Trots Out New Ads Backing Toddler Food Line," *Advertising Age,* April 11, 1994, pp. 1, 48.

14. Lisa Napoli, "A Focus on Women at iVillage.com," *New York Times,* August 3, 1998, p. D6; Linda Himelstein, "I Am Cyber-Woman. Hear Me Roar," *Business Week,* November 15, 1999, p. 40.

15. For more on generations, see Michael R. Solomon, *Consumer Behavior,* 3d ed. (Upper Saddle River, NJ: Prentice-Hall, 1996), ch. 14; and Frank Feather, *The Future Consumer* (Toronto: Warwick Publishing Co., 1994), pp. 69–75.

16. Geoffrey Meredith and Charles Schewe, "The Power of Cohorts," *American Demographics,* December 1994, pp. 22–29.

17. Andrew E. Serwer, "42,496 Secrets Bared," *Fortune,* January 24, 1994, pp. 13–14; Kenneth Labich, "Class in America," *Fortune,* February 7, 1994, pp. 114–26.

18. "Lifestyle Marketing," *Progressive Grocer,* August 1997, pp. 107–10.

19. Peter Burrows, "Can Apple Take Its Game to the Next Level?" *Business Week,* December 20, 1999, p. 52.

20. Tom Miller, "Global Segments from 'Strivers' to 'Creatives,' " *Marketing News,* July 20, 1998, p. 11.

21. Junu Bryan Kim, "Taking Comfort in Country: After Decade of '80s Excess, Marketers Tap Easy Lifestyle as Part of Ad Messages," *Advertising Age,* January 11, 1993, pp. S1–S4.

22. Jeff Gremillion, "Can Smaller Niches Bring Riches?" *Mediaweek,* October 20, 1997, pp. 50–51.

23. This classification was adapted from George H. Brown, "Brand Loyalty—Fact or Fiction?" *Advertising Age,* June 1952–January 1953, a series. See also Peter E. Rossi, R. McCulloch, and G. Allenby, "The Value of Purchase History Data in Target Marketing," *Marketing Science* 15, no. 4 (1996): 321–40.

24. Other leading suppliers of geodemographic data are ClusterPlus (by Donnelly Marketing Information Services) and C.A.C.I. International, which offers ACORN.

25. Christina Del Valle, "They Know Where You Live—and How You Buy," *Business Week,* February 7, 1994, p. 89.

26. See Michael J. Weiss, *The Clustering of America* (New York: Harper & Row, 1988).

27. Jesse Berst, "Why Small Business Is Suddenly Big Business," *ZDNet AnchorDesk,* November 29, 1999, www.anchordesk.com; Michele Marchetti, "Dell Computer," *Sales & Marketing Management,* October 1997, pp. 50–53.

28. Geoffrey Brewer, "Lou Gerstner Has His Hands Full," *Sales & Marketing Management,* May 1998, pp. 36–41.

29. V. Kasturi Rangan, Rowland T. Moriarty, and Gordon S. Swartz, "Segmenting Customers in Mature Industrial Markets," *Journal of Marketing,* October 1992, pp. 72–82.

30. For another interesting approach to segmenting the business market, see John Berrigan and Carl Finkbeiner, *Segmentation Marketing: New Methods for Capturing Business* (New York: HarperBusiness, 1992).

31. Wendy Brandes, "Advertising: Black-Oriented Radio Tunes into Narrower Segments," *Wall Street Journal,* February 13, 1995, p. B5; "Emmis Reports Record Third Quarter" Emmis, *PR Newswire,* December 21, 1999, www.prnewswire.com.

32. Tom Davey, "Intel Reorganization Reflects Changing Market," *Information Week Online,* November 25, 1999, www.informationweek.com.

33. See Norton Paley, "Cut Out for Success," *Sales & Marketing Management,* April 1994, pp. 43–44.

34. See Bart Macchiette and Roy Abhijit, "Sensitive Groups and Social Issues," *Journal of Consumer Marketing* 11, no. 4 (1994): 55–64.

35. Barry Meier, "Data on Tobacco Show a Strategy Aimed at Blacks," *New York Times,* February 6, 1998, p. A1; Gregory Freeman, "Ads Aimed at Blacks and Children Should Exact a High Price," *St. Louis Post-Dispatch,* p. B1.

36. Roger O. Crockett, "They're Lining Up for Flicks in the 'Hood,'" *Business Week,* June 8, 1998, pp. 75–76.

37. See "Selling Sin to Blacks," *Fortune,* October 21, 1991, p. 100; Martha T. Moore, "Putting on a Fresh Face," *USA Today,* January 3, 1992, pp. B1, B2; Dorothy J. Gaiter, "Black-Owned Firms Are Catching an Afrocentric Wave," *Wall Street Journal,* January 8, 1992, p. B2; and Maria Mallory, "Waking Up to a Major Market," *Business Week,* March 23, 1992, pp. 70–73.

**Part III
Making Marketing
Decisions**

Developing, Differentiating, and Positioning Products Through the Life Cycle

In this chapter, we will address the following questions:

■ What challenges does a company face in developing and introducing new products?

■ What are the main stages in developing new products, and how can they be better managed?

■ What factors affect the rate at which consumers adopt new products?

■ What marketing strategies are appropriate at each stage of the product life cycle?

■ How can a company choose and communicate an effective positioning in the market?

Every company, regardless of size, must research and create new products to maintain or build sales. Why? Customers want new products and choices, and competitors will be doing their best to supply them. Over 16,000 new products (including line extensions and new brands) arrive on grocery and drugstore shelves every year, having made their way through the new product development process from bright idea to testing to commercialization.

Not every new product catches on, of course, and those that do are adopted by customers at different rates. This is why smart marketers target early adopters and use marketing tactics that will facilitate consumer movement through the various stages in the adoption process.

Companies normally reformulate their marketing strategy several times during a product's life as economic conditions change, competitors launch new assaults, and the product passes through new stages of buyer interest and requirements. Successful companies plan marketing strategies that are appropriate to each stage in the product's life cycle and hope to extend each product's life and profitability, knowing that no product lasts forever. The key to setting one offering apart from competing offers throughout the life cycle is to select a suitable differentiation strategy and create a distinctive position in the market.

CHALLENGES IN NEW PRODUCT DEVELOPMENT

Companies that fail to develop new products (either goods or services) are putting themselves at great risk. Over time, existing products are vulnerable to changing customer needs and tastes, new technologies, shortened product life cycles, and increased competition. Yet new-product development also entails considerable risk: Texas Instruments lost $660 million before withdrawing from the home computer business; RCA lost $500 million on its videodisc players; Federal Express lost $340 million on its Zap mail service; and the British-French Concorde aircraft will never recover its investment.[1]

A company can add new products in two ways: through acquisition (buying another company, buying another firm's patent, or buying a license or franchise) or through development (using its own laboratories, hiring independent researchers, or hiring a new-product-development firm). Moreover, there is more than one category of new product.

Types of New Products

Even though thousands of products are offered for the first time each year, less than 10 percent are entirely new and innovative. Booz, Allen & Hamilton has identified six categories of new products:[2]

1.   *New-to-the-world products:* New, innovative products that create an entirely new market, such as the Palm Pilot handheld computerized organizer.

2.   *New product lines:* New products that allow a company to enter an established market for the first time, such as Fuji's brand of disks for Zip drives.

3.   *Additions to existing product lines:* New products that supplement a company's established product lines (package sizes, flavors, and so on), such as Amazon.com's auctions and e-mail greeting cards.

4.   *Improvements and revisions of existing products:* New products that provide improved performance or greater perceived value and replace existing products, such as Microsoft Office 2000.

5.   *Repositionings:* Existing products that are targeted to new markets or market segments, such as repositioning Johnson & Johnson's Baby Shampoo for adults as well as youngsters.

6.   *Cost reductions:* New products that provide similar performance at lower cost, such as Intel's Celeron chip.

The new-to-the-world category involves the greatest cost and risk because these products are new to both the company and the marketplace, so positive customer response is far from certain. That's why most new-product activities are improvements on existing products. At Sony, for example, over 80 percent of new-product activity is undertaken to modify and improve existing Sony products. Even new-product improvements are not guaranteed to succeed, however.

Why New Products Fail—and Succeed

New products are failing at a disturbing rate; by one estimate, 80 percent of recently launched products are no longer around.[3] Given the high costs—a company can spend $20 million to $50 million to develop and advertise one new product—it is a wonder that companies continue to innovate at all. Yet product failures can serve one useful purpose: Inventors, entrepreneurs, and new-product team leaders can learn valuable lessons about what *not* to do.

Some of the reasons for new-product failure are: (1) a high-level executive pushes a favorite idea through in spite of negative market research findings; (2) the idea is good, but the market size is overestimated; (3) the product is not well designed; (4) the product is incorrectly positioned, ineffectively advertised, or overpriced; (5) development costs are higher than expected; or (6) competitors fight back harder than expected.

What can a company do to develop successful new products? Cooper and Kleinschmidt found that new products with a high product advantage succeed 98 percent of the time, compared to products with a moderate advantage (58 percent success) or minimal advantage (18 percent success).[4] Madique and Zirger studied successful product launches in the electronics industry and found greater new-product success when the firm: has a better understanding of customer needs; a higher performance-to-cost ratio; a head-start in introducing the product before competitors; a higher expected contribution margin; a higher budget for promoting and launching the product; more use of cross-functional teamwork; and stronger top-management support.[5]

MANAGING NEW PRODUCTS: IDEAS TO STRATEGY

The process of developing new products spans eight stages, each with a particular set of marketing challenges and questions to answer (see Figure 9.1). If the company cannot answer "yes" to the key question at each of the first six stages, the new product will be dropped; in the final two stages, the company has the option of further development or modification rather than immediately dropping the new product. This section covers the stages from idea to strategy and analysis; the following section covers the stages from product development through market testing and commercialization.

Idea Generation

The marketing concept holds that *customer needs and wants* are the logical place to start the search for new product ideas. Hippel has shown that the highest percentage of ideas for new industrial products originates with customers.[6] Many of the best ideas come from asking customers to describe their problems with current products. For instance, in an attempt to grab a foothold in steel wool soap pads, 3M organized consumer focus groups and asked about problems with these products. The most frequent complaint was that the pads scratched expensive cookware. This finding produced the idea for the highly successful Scotch-Brite Never Scratch soap pad.[7] In addition to customers, new-product ideas can come from many sources: scientists, competitors, employees, channel members, sales reps, top management, inventors, patent attorneys, university and commercial laboratories, industrial consultants, advertising agencies, marketing research firms, and industry publications.

Idea Screening

Once the firm has collected a number of new product ideas, the next step is to screen out the weaker ideas, because product-development costs rise substantially with each successive development stage. Most companies require new-product ideas to be described on a standard form that can be reviewed by a new-product committee. The

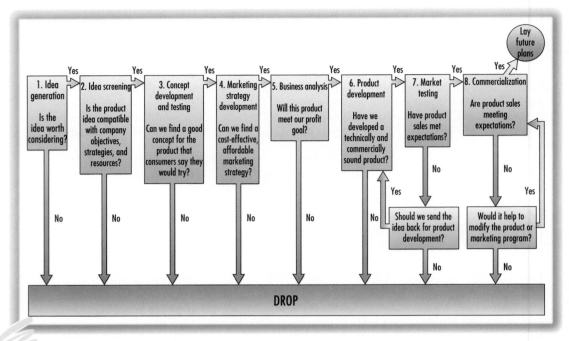

Figure 9.1   The New-Product-Development Decision Process

description states the product idea, the target market, and the competition, along with a rough estimate of the market size, product price, development time and costs, manufacturing costs, and rate of return. The new-product committee then reviews each idea against criteria such as: Does the product meet a need? Would it offer superior value? Will the new product deliver the expected sales volume, sales growth, and profit? The ideas that survive this screening move on to the concept development stage.

Concept Development

A *product idea* is a possible product the company might offer to the market. In contrast, a *product concept* is an elaborated version of the idea expressed in meaningful consumer terms. A product idea can be turned into several concepts by asking: Who will use this product? What primary benefit should this product provide? When will people consume or use this product? By answering such questions, a company can often form several product concepts, select the single most promising concept, and create a *product-positioning map* for it. Figure 9.2a shows the positioning of a product concept, a low-cost instant breakfast drink, compared to other breakfast foods already on the market.

Next, the product concept has to be turned into a *brand concept*. To transform the concept of a low-cost instant breakfast drink into a brand concept, the company must decide how much to charge and how calorific to make its drink. Figure 9.2b shows a *brand-positioning map* that reflects the positions of three instant breakfast drink brands. The gaps on this map indicate that the new brand concept would have to be distinctive in the medium-price, medium-calorie market or the high-price, high-calorie market.

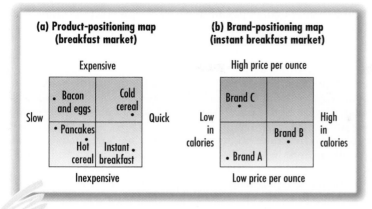

Figure 9.2   Product and Brand Positioning

Concept Testing

Concept testing involves presenting the product concept to appropriate target consumers and getting their reactions. The concepts can be presented symbolically or physically. However, the more the tested concepts resemble the final product or experience, the more dependable concept testing is. In the past, creating physical prototypes was costly and time-consuming, but computer-aided design and manufacturing programs have changed that. Today firms can design a number of prototypes via computer and then create plastic models to obtain feedback from potential consumers.[8] Companies are also using virtual reality to test product concepts.

Many companies today use *customer-driven engineering* to design new products. Customer-driven engineering attaches high importance to incorporating customer preferences in the final design. National Semiconductor uses the Internet to enhance its customer-driven engineering by tracking what customers search for on its Web site. Sometimes, says the company's Web services manager, it is more important to know when a customer did not find a product than when he did. That helps National Semiconductor shrink the time needed to identify market niches and create new products.[9]

Marketing Strategy Development

After testing and selecting a product concept for development, the new-product manager must draft a three-part preliminary marketing-strategy plan for introducing the new product into the market. The first part will describe the target market's size, structure, and behavior; the planned product positioning; and the sales, market share, and profit goals sought in the first few years. The second part will outline the planned price, distribution strategy, and marketing budget for the first year. The third part will describe the long-run sales and profit goals and marketing-mix strategy over time. This plan forms the basis for the business analysis that is conducted before management makes a final decision on the new product.

Business Analysis

In this stage, the company evaluates the proposed new product's business attractiveness by preparing sales, cost, and profit projections to determine whether these satisfy company objectives. If they do, the product concept can move to the product-development stage. Note that this cannot be a static process: As new information emerges, the business analysis must be revised and expanded accordingly.

Estimating Total Sales

First, management needs to estimate whether sales will be high enough to yield a satisfactory profit. Total estimated sales are the sum of estimated first-time sales, replacement sales, and repeat sales. For one-time purchased products, such as a retirement home, sales rise at the beginning, then peak, and later approach zero as the number of potential buyers is exhausted; if new buyers keep entering the market, the curve will not drop to zero. Infrequently purchased products—such as automobiles and industrial equipment—exhibit replacement cycles that are dictated by physical wearing out or by obsolescence due to changing styles, features, and performance; sales forecasting calls for estimating first-time sales and replacement sales separately.

For frequently purchased products, such as consumer and industrial nondurables like soap, the number of first-time buyers initially increases and then decreases as fewer buyers are left (assuming a fixed population). Repeat purchases occur soon, providing that the product satisfies some buyers. The sales curve eventually falls to a plateau representing a level of steady repeat-purchase volume; by this time, the product is no longer a new product.

Estimating Costs and Profits

After preparing the sales forecast, management should analyze expected costs and profits based on estimates prepared by the R&D, manufacturing, marketing, and finance departments. Companies can also use other financial measures to evaluate new-product proposals. The simplest is *break-even analysis,* in which management estimates how many units of the product the company will have to sell to break even with the given price and cost structure.

The most complex method of estimating profit is *risk analysis.* Here, three estimates (optimistic, pessimistic, and most likely) are obtained for each uncertain variable affecting profitability under an assumed marketing environment and marketing strategy for the planning period. The computer simulates possible outcomes and computes a rate-of-return probability distribution showing the range of possible rates of returns and their probabilities.[10]

MANAGING NEW PRODUCTS: DEVELOPMENT TO COMMERCIALIZATION

If the product concept passes the business analysis test, it moves on to be developed into a physical product. Up to now, it has existed only as a word description, drawing, or prototype. This step involves a large jump in investment that dwarfs the costs incurred in the earlier stages. If the company determines that the product idea cannot be translated into a technically and commercially feasible product, the accumulated project cost will be lost—except for any useful information gained in the process.

Product Development

The job of translating target customer requirements into a working prototype is helped by a set of methods known as *quality function deployment* (QFD). This methodology takes the list of desired *customer attributes* (CAs) generated by market research and turns them into a list of *engineering attributes* (EAs) that the engineers can use. For example, customers of a proposed truck may want a certain acceleration rate (CA). Engineers turn this into the required horsepower and other engineering equivalents (EAs). QFD allows firms to measure the trade-offs and costs of satisfying customer requirements; it also improves communication among marketing, engineering, and manufacturing.[11]

Next, the firm uses QFD to develop one or more physical versions of the product concept. The goal is to find a prototype that customers believe embodies the key attributes described in the product-concept statement, that performs safely under normal use, and that can be produced within the budget. The rise of the World Wide Web has driven more rapid prototyping and more flexible development; prototype-driven firms such as Yahoo! and Microsoft cherish quick-and-dirty tests and experiments.[12]

When the prototypes are ready, they are put through rigorous *functional tests* and *customer tests. Alpha testing* means testing the product within the firm to see how it performs in different applications. After refining the prototype further, the company moves to *beta testing*, enlisting customers to use the prototype and give feedback on their experiences. Beta testing is most useful when the potential customers are heterogeneous, the potential applications are not fully known, several decision makers are involved in purchasing the product, and opinion leadership from early adopters is sought.[13]

Consumer testing can take a variety of forms, from bringing consumers into a laboratory to giving them samples to use in their homes. In-home placement tests are common with products ranging from ice cream flavors to new appliances. For example, when DuPont developed its new synthetic carpeting, it installed free carpeting in several homes in exchange for the homeowners' willingness to report their likes and dislikes about the carpeting.

Market Testing

After management is satisfied with functional and psychological performance, the product is ready to be dressed up with a brand name and packaging, and put to a market test. The new product is now introduced into an authentic setting to learn how large the market is and how consumers and dealers react to handling, using, and repurchasing the product. For example, idealab! is in the business of launching new Internet ventures (eToys was one). Before starting CarsDirect, a Web-based car buying service, idealab! put up a live Web page and monitored on-line market reaction. In just one evening, the site sold four cars—results that hinted at the product's potential for strong market acceptance.[14]

Consumer-Goods Market Testing

In testing consumer products, the company seeks to estimate four variables: trial, first repeat purchase, adoption, and purchase frequency. The company hopes to find all of these variables at high levels. In some cases, however, it will find many consumers trying the product but few rebuying it. Or it might find high permanent adoption but low purchase frequency (as with gourmet frozen foods).

The major methods of consumer-goods market testing, from the least to the most costly, are:

➤ *Sales-wave research.* Consumers who initially try the product at no cost are reoffered the product, or a competitor's product, at slightly reduced prices, as many as three to five times (sales waves). The company notes how many customers select its product again and their reported level of satisfaction.

➤ *Simulated test marketing.* Up to 40 qualified buyers first answer questions about brand familiarity and product preferences. These buyers are invited to look at commercials or print ads, including one for the new product, then they are given money and brought into a store where they can make purchases. The company notes how many people buy the new brand and competing brands as a test of the ad's relative effectiveness against competing ads in simulating trial. Consumers are also asked why they bought or did not buy; nonbuyers receive a free sample of the new product and are reinterviewed later to determine product attitudes, usage, satisfaction, and repurchase intention.[15]

➤ *Controlled test marketing*. A research firm manages a panel of stores that will carry new products for a fee. The company with the new product specifies the number of stores and geographic locations it wants to test. The research firm delivers the product to the participating stores and controls shelf position; number of facings, displays, and point-of-purchase promotions; and pricing. Sales results can be measured through electronic scanners at the checkout. The company can also evaluate the impact of local advertising and promotions during this test.

➤ *Test markets*. When full-blown, the company chooses a few representative cities, the sales force tries to sell the trade on carrying the product and giving it good exposure, and the company unleashes a full advertising and promotion campaign in these markets. Here, marketers must decide on the number and location of test cities, length of the test, what to track, and what action to take. Today, many firms are skipping extended test marketing and relying instead on faster and more economical market-testing methods, such as smaller test areas and shorter test periods.

Business-Goods Market Testing

Business goods can also benefit from market testing. Expensive industrial goods and new technologies will normally undergo both alpha and beta testing. In addition, new business products are sometimes market-tested at trade shows. Trade shows such as the annual Toy Fair and semiannual Internet World draw a large number of buyers who view many new products in a few concentrated days. The vendor can observe how much interest buyers show in the new product, how they react to various features and terms, and how many express purchase intentions or place orders. The disadvantage of trade shows is that they reveal the product to competitors; therefore, the vendor should be ready to launch the product soon after the trade show.

Commercialization

If the company goes ahead with commercialization, it will face its largest costs to date. The company will have to contract for manufacture or build or rent a full-scale manu-facturing facility. Plant size will be a critical decision. The company may choose to build a smaller plant than called for by the sales forecast, to be on the safe side. Quaker Oats did this when it launched its 100 Percent Natural breakfast cereal. Unfortunately, demand so exceeded the company's sales forecast that for about a year it could not supply enough product to the stores. Although Quaker Oats was gratified with the response, the low forecast cost it a considerable amount of profit.

In addition to promotional decisions, other major decisions during this stage include:

➤ *When (timing)*. Marketing timing is critical. If a firm learns that a competitor is nearing the end of its development work, it can choose: *first entry* (being first to market, locking up key distributors and customers, and gaining reputational leadership; however, if the product is not thoroughly debugged, it can acquire a flawed image); *parallel entry* (launching at the same time as a rival may gain both products more attention from the market); or *late entry* (waiting until after a competitor has entered lets the competitor bear the cost of educating the market and may reveal problems to avoid).

➤ *Where (geographic strategy).* The company must decide whether to launch the new product in a single locality, a region, several regions, the national market, or the international market. Smaller companies often select one city for a blitz campaign, entering other cities one at a time; in contrast, large companies usually launch within a whole region and then move to the next region, although companies with national distribution generally launch new models nationally. Firms are increasingly rolling out new products simultaneously across the globe, which raises new challenges in coordinating activities and obtaining agreement on strategy and tactics.

➤ *To whom (target-market prospects).* Within the rollout markets, the company must target its initial distribution and promotion to the best prospect groups. Presumably, the company has already profiled the prime prospects—who would ideally be early adopters, heavy users, and opinion leaders who are able to be reached at a low cost.[16] The company should rate the various prospect groups on these characteristics and then target the best prospect group to generate strong sales as soon as possible, motivate the sales force, and attract further prospects.

➤ *How (introductory market strategy).* The company must develop an action plan for introducing the new product into the rollout markets. To coordinate the many activities involved in launching a new product, management can use network-planning techniques such as *critical path scheduling* (CPS), which uses a master chart to show the simultaneous and sequential activities that must take place to launch the product. By estimating how much time each activity takes, the planners can estimate the project's completion time. A delay in any activity on the critical path will delay the entire project.[17]

THE CONSUMER ADOPTION PROCESS

Adoption is an individual's decision to become a regular user of a product. How do potential customers learn about new products, try them, and adopt or reject them? In the past, companies used a *mass-market approach* to introduce new products, on the assumption that most people are potential buyers. Yet consumers have different levels of interest in new products and brands. The theory of innovation diffusion and consumer adoption helps marketers to identify and target *early adopters*—people who adopt products before the majority of consumers in the market.

Stages in the Adoption Process

An *innovation* refers to any good, service, or idea that is *perceived* by someone as new. The idea may have a long history, but it is an innovation to the person who sees it as new. Innovations take time to spread through the social system. Rogers defines the *innovation diffusion process* as "the spread of a new idea from its source of invention or creation to its ultimate users or adopters."[18] The consumer-adoption process focuses on the mental process through which an individual passes from first hearing about an innovation to final adoption.

Adopters of new products have been observed to move through five stages: (1) *awareness* (consumer becomes aware of the innovation but has no information about it); (2) *interest* (consumer is stimulated to seek information about the innovation); (3) *evaluation* (consumer considers whether to try the innovation); (4) *trial* (consumer tries the innovation to estimate its value; and (5) *adoption* (consumer decides to make full and regular use of the innovation).

Factors Influencing the Adoption Process

As Figure 9.3 shows, people adopt new products at different rates: Innovators are the first to adopt something new, while laggards are the last. Rogers defines a person's innovativeness as "the degree to which an individual is relatively earlier in adopting new ideas than the other members of his social system." Because people differ in their readiness to try new products, there are consumption pioneers and early adopters for each product. After a slow start, an increasing number of people adopt the innovation, the number reaches a peak, and then it diminishes as fewer nonadopters remain.

Another factor affecting adoption is *personal influence,* the effect one person has on another's attitude or purchase probability. Although personal influence is greater in some situations and for some individuals, it is more important in the evaluation stage of the adoption process than in the other stages. It generally has more influence on late adopters and is more important in risky situations, as well.

Five characteristics influence the rate of adoption of an innovation: (1) *relative advantage*—the degree to which the innovation appears superior to existing products; (2) *compatibility*—the degree to which the innovation matches the values and experiences of the individuals; (3) *complexity*—the degree to which the innovation is relatively difficult to understand or use; (4) *divisibility*—the degree to which the innovation can be tried on a limited basis; and (5) *communicability*—the degree to which the beneficial results of use are observable or describable to others. The new-product marketer has to research and consider all of these factors in designing the new product and its marketing program.[19]

Finally, organizations vary in their readiness to adopt innovations. Adoption is associated with variables in the organization's environment, the organization itself (size, profits, pressure to change), and its managers. Other forces come into play when trying to get a product adopted into organizations that receive the bulk of their funding from the government. And a controversial or innovative product can be squelched by negative public opinion.

Figure 9.3   Adopter Categorization on the Basis of Relative Time of Adoption of Innovation

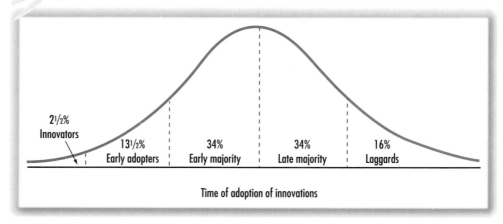

MARKETING THROUGH THE PRODUCT LIFE CYCLE

In today's highly dynamic marketing environment, a company's marketing strategy must change as the product, market, and competitors change over time. Here, we describe the concept of the product life cycle (PLC) and the changes that companies make as the product passes through each stage of the life cycle.

The Concept of the Product Life Cycle

To say that a product has a life cycle is to assert four things: (1) Products have a limited life; (2) product sales pass through distinct stages with different challenges, opportunities, and problems for the seller; (3) profits rise and fall at different stages of the product life cycle; and (4) products require different marketing, financial, manufacturing, purchasing, and human resource strategies in each stage. Most product life-cycle curves are portrayed as a bell-shape (Figure 9.4).

This PLC curve is typically divided into four stages:[20]

➤ *Introduction:* A period of slow sales growth as the product is introduced in the market. Profits are nonexistent in this stage because of the heavy expenses incurred with product introduction.

➤ *Growth:* A period of rapid market acceptance and substantial profit improvement.

➤ *Maturity:* A period of a slowdown in sales growth because the product has achieved acceptance by most potential buyers. Profits stabilize or decline because of increased competition.

➤ *Decline:* The period when sales show a downward drift and profits erode.

Table 9.1 summarizes the characteristics, objectives, and strategies associated with each stage.

Marketing Strategies: Introduction Stage

Because it takes time to roll out a new product and fill dealer pipelines, sales growth tends to be slow at this stage. Buzzell identified several causes for the slow growth:

Figure 9.4   Sales and Profit Life Cycles

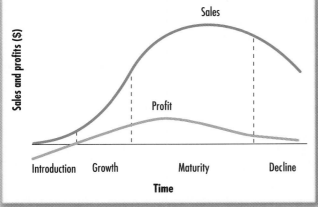

Table 9.1   Summary of Product Life Cycle Characteristics, Objectives, and Strategies

	Introduction	Growth	Maturity	Decline
Characteristics				
Sales	Low sales	Rapidly rising sales	Peak sales	Declining sales
Costs	High cost per customer	Average cost per customer	Low cost per customer	Low cost per customer
Profits	Negative	Rising profits	High profits	Declining profits
Customers	Innovators	Early adopters	Middle majority	Laggards
Competitors	Few	Growing number	Stable number beginning to decline	Declining number
Marketing Objectives				
	Create product awareness and trial	Maximize market share	Maximize profit while defending market share	Reduce expenditure and milk the brand
Strategies				
Product	Offer a basic product	Offer product extensions, service, warranty	Diversify brands and items	Phase out weak models
Price	Charge cost-plus	Price to penetrate market	Price to match or best competitors'	Cut price
Distribution	Build selective distribution	Build intensive distribution	Build more intensive distribution	Go selective: phase out unprofitable outlets
Advertising	Build product awareness among early adopters and dealers	Build awareness and interest in the mass market	Stress brand differences and benefits	Reduce to level needed to retain hard-core loyals
Sales Promotion	Use heavy sales promotion to entice trial	Reduce to take advantage of heavy consumer demand	Increase to encourage brand switching	Reduce to minimal level

Sources: Chester R. Wasson, *Dynamic Competitive and Product Life Cycles* (Austin, TX: Austin Press, 1978); John A. Weber, "Planning Corporate Growth with Inverted Product Life Cycles," *Long Range Planning,* October 1976, pp. 12–29; and Peter Doyle, "The Realities of the Product Life Cycle," *Quarterly Review of Marketing,* Summer 1976.

delays in the expansion of production capacity, technical problems ("working out the bugs"), delays in obtaining adequate distribution through retail outlets, and customer reluctance to change established behaviors.[21] Sales of expensive new products are retarded by additional factors such as product complexity and fewer buyers.

Profits are negative or low in the introduction stage because of low sales and heavy distribution and promotion expenses. Much money is needed to attract distributors. Promotional expenditures are high because of the need to (1) inform potential consumers, (2) induce product trial, and (3) secure distribution. Firms focus their selling on those buyers who are the readiest to buy, usually higher-income groups. Prices tend to be high because costs are high due to relatively low output rates, technological problems in production, and high required margins to support the heavy promotional expenditures.

Companies must decide when to enter the market with a new product. Most studies indicate that the *market pioneer* gains the most advantage. Such pioneers as Amazon.com, Cisco, Coca-Cola, eBay, Eastman Kodak, Hallmark, Microsoft, Peapod.com, and Xerox developed sustained market dominance.

However, the pioneer advantage is not inevitable. Schnaars studied 28 industries in which the imitators surpassed the innovators and found several weaknesses among the failing pioneers, including new products that were too crude, were improperly positioned, or appeared before there was strong demand; product-development costs that exhausted the innovator's resources; a lack of resources to compete against entering larger firms; and managerial incompetence or unhealthy complacency. Successful imitators thrived by offering lower prices, improving the product more continuously, or using brute market power to overtake the pioneer.[22] As one example, Apple's Newton, the first handheld personal digital assistant, failed because it could not decipher the handwriting of users consistently. In contrast, imitator Palm Pilot's smaller, more advanced product was enormously successful because it allowed users to input information with a few standardized strokes of the stylus.[23]

Still, the pioneer knows that competition will eventually enter the market and charge a lower price, which will force the pioneer to lower prices. As competition and market share stabilize, buyers will no longer pay a price premium; some competitors will withdraw at this point, and the pioneer can then build share if it chooses.[24]

Marketing Strategies: Growth Stage

The growth stage is marked by a rapid climb in sales, as DVD players are currently experiencing.[25] Early adopters like the product, and additional consumers start buying it. Attracted by the opportunities, new competitors enter with new product features and expanded distribution. Prices remain where they are or fall slightly, depending on how fast demand increases. Companies maintain or increase their promotional expenditures to meet competition and to continue to educate the market. Sales rise much faster than promotional expenditures, causing a welcome decline in the promotion-sales ratio.

Profits increase during this stage as promotion costs are spread over a larger volume and unit manufacturing costs fall faster than price declines owing to the producer learning effect. During this stage, the firm uses several strategies to sustain rapid market growth as long as possible: (1) improving product quality and adding new product features and improved styling; (2) adding new models and flanker products; (3) entering new market segments; (4) increasing distribution coverage and entering new distribution channels; (5) shifting from product-awareness advertising to product-preference advertising; and (6) lowering prices to attract the next layer of price-sensitive buyers.

Marketing Strategies: Maturity Stage

At some point, the rate of sales growth will slow, and the product will enter a stage of relative maturity. This stage normally lasts longer than the previous stages, and poses formidable challenges to marketing management. *Most products are in the maturity stage of the life cycle, and most marketing managers cope with the problem of marketing the mature product.*

Three strategies for the maturity stage are market modification, product modification, and marketing-mix modification:

➤ *Market modification.* The company might try to expand the market for its mature brand by working to expand the number of brand users. This is accomplished by (1) converting nonusers; (2) entering new market segments (as Johnson & Johnson did when promoting baby shampoo for adult use); or (3) winning competitors' customers (the way Pepsi-Cola tries to woo away Coca-Cola users). Volume can also be increased by convincing current brand users to increase their usage of the brand.

➤ *Product modification.* Managers try to stimulate sales by modifying the product's characteristics through quality improvement, feature improvement, or style improvement. *Quality improvement* aims at increasing the product's functional performance—its durability, reliability, speed, taste. New features build the company's image as an innovator and win the loyalty of market segments that value these features; this is why America Online regularly introduces new versions of its Internet software. However, feature improvements are easily imitated; unless there is a permanent gain from being first, the feature improvement might not pay off in the long run.[26]

➤ *Marketing-mix modification.* Product managers can try to stimulate sales by modifying other marketing-mix elements such as prices, distribution, advertising, sales promotion, personal selling, and services. For example, Goodyear boosted its market share from 14 to 16 percent in 1 year when it began selling tires through Wal-Mart, Sears, and Discount Tire.[27] Sales promotion has more impact at this stage because consumers have reached an equilibrium in their buying patterns, and psychological persuasion (advertising) is not as effective as financial persuasion (sales-promotion deals). However, excessive sales-promotion activity can hurt the brand's image and long-run profit performance. In addition, price reductions and many other marketing-mix changes are easily imitated. The firm may not gain as much as expected, and all firms might experience profit erosion as they step up their marketing attacks on each other.

Marketing Strategies: Decline Stage

The sales of most product forms and brands eventually decline for a number of reasons, including technological advances, shifts in consumer tastes, and increased domestic and foreign competition. All of these factors lead ultimately to overcapacity, increased price cutting, and profit erosion. As sales and profits decline, some firms withdraw from the market. Those remaining may reduce the number of products they offer. They may withdraw from smaller market segments and weaker trade channels, and they may cut their promotion budget and reduce their prices further.

In a study of company strategies in declining industries, Harrigan identified five possible decline strategies:

1. *Increasing* the firm's investment (to dominate the market or strengthen its competitive position);
2. *Maintaining* the firm's investment level until the uncertainties about the industry are resolved;
3. *Decreasing* the firm's investment level selectively, by dropping unprofitable customer groups, while simultaneously strengthening the firm's investment in lucrative niches;
4. *Harvesting* ("milking") the firm's investment to recover cash quickly; and
5. *Divesting* the business quickly by disposing of its assets as advantageously as possible.[28]

The appropriate decline strategy depends on the industry's relative attractiveness and the company's competitive strength in that industry. Procter & Gamble has, on a number of occasions, successfully restaged disappointing brands that were competing in strong markets. One example is its "not oily" hand cream called Wondra, which came packaged in an inverted bottle so the cream would flow out from the bottom. Although initial sales were high, repeat purchases were disappointing. Consumers complained that the bottom got sticky and that "not oily" suggested it would not work well. P&G carried out two restagings for this product: First, it reintroduced Wondra in an upright bottle, and later, it reformulated the ingredients so they would work better. Sales then picked up.

If the company were choosing between harvesting and divesting, its strategies would be quite different. *Harvesting* calls for gradually reducing a product's or business's costs while trying to maintain its sales. The first costs to cut are R&D costs and plant and equipment investment. The company might also reduce product quality, sales force size, marginal services, and advertising expenditures. It would try to cut these costs without letting customers, competitors, and employees know what is happening. Harvesting is an ethically ambivalent strategy, and it is also difficult to execute. Yet harvesting can substantially increase the company's current cash flow.[29]

Critique of the Product Life-Cycle Concept

The PLC concept is best used to interpret product and market dynamics. As a planning tool, this concept helps managers characterize the main marketing challenges in each stage of a product's life and develop major alternative marketing strategies. As a control tool, this concept helps the company measure product performance against similar products launched in the past. The PLC concept is less useful as a forecasting tool because sales histories exhibit diverse patterns, and the stages vary in duration.

Critics claim that life-cycle patterns are too variable in their shape and duration. They also say that marketers can seldom tell what stage the product is in: A product may appear to be mature when it is actually only in a plateau prior to another upsurge. One final criticism is that the PLC pattern is the result of marketing strategies rather than an inevitable course that sales must follow. For example, when Borden owned Eagle Brand Sweetened Condensed Milk, its marketing positioned this mature product as a key ingredient in favorite holiday recipes. When the brand was sold to Eagle Family Foods, however, the new brand manager was able to boost sales with an ad campaign educating consumers on the wider range of uses for condensed milk.[30] Savvy marketers are therefore careful when using the PLC concept to analyze their products and markets.

DIFFERENTIATION AND POSITIONING STRATEGY

Companies such as Hewlett-Packard and Priceline.com invest precious resources to develop and then shepherd their new products through the product life cycle. Yet in today's highly competitive global marketplace, a product will not survive—let alone thrive—without some distinct competitive difference that sets it apart from every rival product. This is why smart companies rely on **differentiation,** the act of designing a set of meaningful differences to distinguish the company's offering from competitors' offerings. Here we examine how a company can differentiate its market offering along five dimensions: product, services, personnel, channel, and image (Table 9.2).

Table 9.2   Differentiation Variables

Product	Services	Personnel	Channel	Image
Form	Ordering ease	Competence	Coverage	Symbols
Features	Delivery	Courtesy	Expertise	Media
Performance	Installation	Credibility	Performance	Atmosphere
Conformance	Customer training	Reliability		Events
Durability	Customer consulting	Responsiveness		
Reliability	Maintenance and repair	Communication		
Repairability	Miscellaneous			
Style				
Design				

Product Differentiation

Physical products vary in their potential for differentiation. At one extreme we find products that allow little variation: chicken, steel, aspirin. Yet even here, some differentiation is possible: Starbucks brands its coffee, and P&G offers several brands of laundry detergent, each with a separate brand identity. At the other extreme are products that are capable of high differentiation, such as automobiles and furniture. Here the seller faces an abundance of design parameters, including:[31]

➤ *Form.* Many products can be differentiated in *form*—the size, shape, or physical structure of a product. Consider the many possible forms taken by products such as aspirin. Although aspirin is essentially a commodity, it can be differentiated by dosage size, shape, coating, and action time.

➤ *Features. Features* are the characteristics that supplement the product's basic function. Marketers start by asking recent buyers about additional features that would improve satisfaction, then determining which would be profitable to add, given the potential market, cost, and price.

➤ *Performance quality. Performance quality* is the level at which the product's primary characteristics operate. The Strategic Planning Institute found a significantly positive correlation between relative product quality and return on investment. Yet there are diminishing returns to higher performance quality, so marketers must choose a level suited to the target market and rivals' performance levels.

➤ *Conformance quality.* Buyers expect products to have a high *conformance quality*, which is the degree to which all of the produced units are identical and meet the promised specifications. The problem with low conformance quality is that the product will disappoint some buyers.

➤ *Durability. Durability,* a measure of the product's expected operating life under natural or stressful conditions, is important for products such as vehicles and kitchen appliances. However, the extra price must not be excessive, and the product must not be subject to rapid technological obsolescence.

➤ *Reliability.* Buyers normally will pay a premium for high *reliability,* a measure of the probability that a product will not malfunction or fail within a specified time period. Maytag, which manufactures major home appliances, has an outstanding reputation for creating reliable appliances.

➤ *Repairability.* Buyers prefer products that are easy to repair. *Repairability* is a measure of the ease of fixing a product when it malfunctions or fails. An automobile made with standard parts that are easily replaced has high repairability. Ideal repairability would exist if users could fix the product themselves with little cost or time.

➤ *Style. Style* describes the product's look and feel to the buyer. Buyers are normally willing to pay a premium for products that are attractively styled. Aesthetics have played a key role in such brands as Absolut vodka, Apple computers, Montblanc pens, Godiva chocolate, and Harley-Davidson motorcycles.[32] Style has the advantage of creating distinctiveness that is difficult to copy; however, strong style does not always mean high performance.

➤ *Design.* As competition intensifies, *design* offers a potent way to differentiate and position a company's products and services.[33] Design is the integrating force that incorporates all of the qualities just discussed; this means the designer has to figure out how much to invest in form, feature development, performance, conformance, durability, reliability, repairability, and style. To the company, a well-designed product is one that is easy to manufacture and distribute. To the customer, a well-designed product is one that is pleasant to look at and easy to open, install, use, repair, and dispose of. The designer has to take all of these factors into account.

Services Differentiation

When the physical product cannot be differentiated easily, the key to competitive success may lie in adding valued services and improving their quality. The main service differentiators are:

➤ *Ordering ease* refers to how easy it is for the customer to place an order with the company. Baxter Healthcare has eased the ordering process by supplying hospitals with computers through which they send orders directly to Baxter; consumers can now order and receive groceries without going to the supermarket by using Web-based services such as Peapod and NetGrocer.

➤ *Delivery* refers to how well the product or service is delivered to the customer, covering speed, accuracy, and customer care. Deluxe Check Printers, Inc., has built an impressive reputation for shipping out its checks one day after receiving an order—without being late once in 18 years.

➤ *Installation* refers to the work done to make a product operational in its planned location. Buyers of heavy equipment expect good installation service. Differentiation by installation is particularly important for companies that offer complex products such as computers.

➤ *Customer training* refers to how the customer's employees are trained to use the vendor's equipment properly and efficiently. General Electric not only sells and installs expensive X-ray equipment in hospitals, but also gives extensive training to users of this equipment.

➤ *Customer consulting* refers to data, information systems, and advising services that the seller offers to buyers. For example, the Rite Aid drugstore chain's communications program, called the Vitamin Institute, provides customers with research so they can make more educated judgments and feel comfortable asking for help. On the Web, Rite Aid has teamed with drugstore.com to offer even more health-related information.[34]

➤ *Maintenance and repair* describes the service program for helping customers keep purchased products in good working order, an important consideration for many products.

Personnel Differentiation

Companies can gain a strong competitive advantage through having better-trained people. Singapore Airlines enjoys an excellent reputation in large part because of its flight attendants. The McDonald's people are courteous, the IBM people are professional, and the Disney people are upbeat. The sales forces of such companies as General Electric, Cisco, Frito-Lay, Northwestern Mutual Life, and Pfizer enjoy an excellent reputation.[35] Well-trained personnel exhibit six characteristics: competence, courtesy, credibility, reliability, responsiveness, and communication.[36]

Channel Differentiation

Companies can achieve competitive advantage through the way they design their distribution channels' coverage, expertise, and performance. Caterpillar's success in the construction-equipment industry is based partly on superior channel development. Its dealers are found in more locations, are better trained, and perform more reliably than competitors' dealers. Dell Computers has also distinguished itself by developing and managing superior direct-marketing channels using telephone and Internet sales.[37]

Image Differentiation

Buyers respond differently to company and brand images. *Identity* comprises the ways that a company aims to identify or position itself or its product, whereas *image* is the way the public perceives the company or its products. Image is affected by many factors beyond the company's control. For example, Nike's mainstream popularity turns off 12-to-24-year-olds, who prefer Airwalk and other alternative brands that convey a more extreme sports image.[38] An effective image establishes the product's character and value proposition; it conveys this character in a distinctive way; and it delivers emotional power beyond a mental image. For the image to work, it must be conveyed through every available communication vehicle and brand contact, including logos, media, and special events.

Developing and Communicating a Positioning Strategy

All products can be differentiated to some extent.[39] But not all brand differences are meaningful or worthwhile. A difference is worth establishing to the extent that it satisfies the following criteria:

➤ *Important:* The difference delivers a highly valued benefit to a sufficient number of buyers.

➤ *Distinctive:* The difference is delivered in a distinctive way.

➤ *Superior:* The difference is superior to other ways of obtaining the benefit.

➤ *Preemptive:* The difference cannot be copied easily by competitors.

➤ *Affordable:* The buyer can afford to pay for the difference.

➤ *Profitable:* The company will find it profitable to introduce the difference.

Each firm needs to develop a distinctive positioning for its market offering. **Positioning** is the act of designing the company's offering and image to occupy a distinctive place in the target market's mind. The end result of positioning is the successful creation of a market-focused value proposition, a cogent reason why the target market should buy the product.

The word *positioning* was popularized by two advertising executives, Al Ries and Jack Trout. They see positioning as a creative exercise done with an existing product:

"Positioning starts with a product. A piece of merchandise, a service, a company, an institution, or even a person. . . . But positioning is not what you do to a product. Positioning is what you do to the mind of the prospect. That is, you position the product in the mind of the prospect."

Ries and Trout argue that well-known products generally hold a distinctive position in customers' minds; Coca-Cola, for example, holds the position of world's largest soft-drink firm. To compete against this kind of position, a rival can (1) strengthen its own current position in the consumer's mind (the way 7-Up advertised itself as the Uncola), (2) grab an unoccupied position (as Snapple did with its tea-based beverages), (3) deposition or reposition the competition, or (4) promote the idea that it is in the club with the "best."[40]

How Many Differences to Promote?

Each company must decide how many differences (e.g., benefits, features) to promote. Ries and Trout favor one consistent positioning message.[41] With this approach, each brand is touted as "number one" on a particular attribute, such as "best quality," "best service," "lowest price," or "most advanced technology." If a company hammers away at one positioning and delivers on it, it will probably be best known and recalled for this strength.

Not everyone sticks to single-benefit positioning. Smith Kline Beecham promotes its Aquafresh toothpaste as offering three benefits: anticavity protection, better breath, and whiter teeth. The company's challenge is to convince consumers that the brand delivers all three. Smith Kline's solution was to create a toothpaste that squeezes out of the tube in three colors, thus visually confirming the three benefits.

Communicating the Company's Positioning

Once the company has developed a clear positioning strategy, it must communicate that positioning effectively through all facets of the marketing mix and every point of contact with customers. Suppose a service company chooses the "best-in-quality" strategy. A good example is Ritz Carlton hotels, which signals high quality by training its employees to answer calls within three rings, to answer with a genuine "smile" in their voices, and to be extremely knowledgeable about all hotel information.

On the other hand, companies risk confusing the target audience if their marketing tactics run counter to their positioning. For example, a well-known frozen-food brand lost its prestige image by putting its products on sale too often. A smart company carefully coordinates its marketing-mix activities and its offer to support its positioning. New products may be the lifeblood of a growing firm, but they must be clearly differentiated and properly positioned to be competitive. The firm also faces numerous decisions in the course of managing product lines and brands, as discussed in the next chapter.

EXECUTIVE SUMMARY

Once a company has segmented the market, chosen its target customer groups, identified their needs, and determined its desired market positioning, it is ready to develop and launch new products. Although the rate of new product failure is disturbingly high, companies can improve their chances of success by creating new products with a high product advantage. Eight stages are involved in the new-product development process: idea generation, screening, concept development and testing, marketing strategy development, business analysis, product development, market testing, and commercialization. The purpose of each stage is to determine whether the idea should be dropped or moved to the next stage.

The consumer-adoption process is the process by which customers learn about new products, try them, and adopt or reject them. The five stages in this process are awareness, interest, evaluation, trial, and adoption. This process is influenced by many factors beyond the marketer's control, including consumers' and organizations' willingness to try new products, personal influences, and the characteristics of the new product or innovation.

Because economic conditions change and competitive activity varies, companies normally reformulate their marketing strategy several times during the product life cycle. The introduction stage of this cycle is marked by slow growth and minimal profits as the new product gains distribution. If successful, the product enters a growth stage marked by rapid sales and increasing profits. The company attempts to improve the product, enter new market segments and distribution channels, and reduce prices slightly. In the maturity stage, sales growth slows and profits stabilize, causing the firm to try to modify the market, the product, or the marketing mix to renew sales growth. Finally, the product enters the decline stage, when the firm must decide whether to increase, maintain, or decrease its investment; harvest the product; or divest as advantageously as possible.

In the competitive global marketplace, the key to competitive advantage is differentiation. A market offering can be differentiated by product, services, personnel, channel, and image. A difference is worth establishing to the extent that it is important, distinctive, superior, preemptive, affordable, and profitable. Positioning is the act of designing the company's offering and image to occupy a distinctive place in the target market's mind. Many marketers advocate positioning according to a single product benefit, although double- and triple-benefit positioning can be successful if used carefully.

NOTES

1. Christopher Power, "Flops," *Business Week*, August 16, 1993, pp. 76–82.
2. *New Products Management for the 1980s* (New York: Booz, Allen & Hamilton, 1982).
3. Erika Rasmussen, "Staying Power," *Sales & Marketing Management*, August 1998, pp. 44–46.
4. Robert G. Cooper and Elko J. Kleinschmidt, *New Products: The Key Factors in Success* (Chicago: American Marketing Association, 1990).
5. Modesto A. Madique and Billie Jo Zirger, "A Study of Success and Failure in Product Innovation: The Case of the U.S. Electronics Industry," *IEEE Transactions on Engineering Management*, November 1984, pp. 192–203.
6. Eric von Hippel, "Lead Users: A Source of Novel Product Concepts," *Management Science*, July 1986, pp. 791–805. Also see his *The Sources of Innovation* (New York: Oxford University Press, 1988); and "Learning from Lead Users," in *Marketing in an Electronic Age*, ed. Robert D. Buzzell (Cambridge, MA: Harvard Business School Press, 1985), pp. 308–17.
7. Constance Gustke, "Built to Last," *Sales & Marketing Management*, August 1997, pp. 78–83.
8. "The Ultimate Widget: 3-D 'Printing' May Revolutionize Product Design and Manufacturing," *U.S. News & World Report*, July 20, 1992, p. 55.
9. Dan Deitz, "Customer-Driven Engineering," *Mechanical Engineering*, May 1996, p. 68.
10. See David B. Hertz, "Risk Analysis in Capital Investment," *Harvard Business Review*, January-February 1964, pp. 96–106.
11. See John Hauser, "House of Quality," *Harvard Business Review*, May-June 1988, pp. 63–73. Customer-driven engineering is also called "quality function deployment." See Lawrence

R. Guinta and Nancy C. Praizler, *The QFD Book: The Team Approach to Solving Problems and Satisfying Customers through Quality Function Deployment* (New York: AMACOM, 1993); V. Srinivasan, William S. Lovejoy, and David Beach, "Integrated Product Design for Marketability and Manufacturing," *Journal of Marketing Research,* February 1997, pp. 154–63.

12. See Mark Borden, "Keeping Yahoo Simple—and Fast," *Fortune,* January 10, 2000, pp. 167–68.

13. Ibid., p. 99.

14. Charles Platt, "What's the Big Idea," *Wired,* September 1999, pp. 122–32; Dave Califano, "The Future of the Internet: CarsDirect," *Worth Online,* November 1999, www.worth.com.

15. Christopher Power, "Will it Sell in Podunk? Hard to Say," *Business Week,* August 10, 1992, pp. 46–47.

16. Philip Kotler and Gerald Zaltman, "Targeting Prospects for a New Product," *Journal of Advertising Research,* February 1976, pp. 7–20.

17. For details, see Keith G. Lockyer, *Critical Path Analysis and Other Project Network Techniques* (London: Pitman, 1984). Also see Arvind Rangaswamy and Gary L. Lilien, "Software Tools for New Product Development," *Journal of Marketing Research,* February 1997, pp. 177–84.

18. The following discussion leans heavily on Everett M. Rogers, *Diffusion of Innovations* (New York: Free Press, 1962). Also see his third edition, published in 1983.

19. See Hubert Gatignon and Thomas S. Robertson, "A Propositional Inventory for New Diffusion Research," *Journal of Consumer Research,* March 1985, pp. 849–67; Vijay Mahajan, Eitan Muller, and Frank M. Bass, "Diffusion of New Products: Empirical Generalizations and Managerial Uses," *Marketing Science,* 14, no. 3, part 2 (1995): G79–G89; Fareena Sultan, John U. Farley, and Donald R. Lehmann, "Reflection on 'A Meta-Analysis of Applications of Diffusion Models,' " *Journal of Marketing Research,* May 1996, pp. 247–49; Minhi Hahn, Sehoon Park, and Andris A. Zoltners, "Analysis of New Product Diffusion Using a Four-segment Trial-repeat Model," *Marketing Science,* 13, no. 3 (1994): 224–47.

20. Some authors distinguished additional stages. Wasson suggested a stage of competitive turbulence between growth and maturity. See Chester R. Wasson, *Dynamic Competitive Strategy and Product Life Cycles* (Austin, TX: Austin Press, 1978). Maturity describes a stage of sales growth slowdown and saturation, a stage of flat sales after sales have peaked.

21. Robert D. Buzzell, "Competitive Behavior and Product Life Cycles," in *New Ideas for Successful Marketing,* eds. John S. Wright and Jack Goldstucker (Chicago: American Marketing Association, 1956), p. 51.

22. Steven P. Schnaars, *Managing Imitation Strategies* (New York: Free Press, 1994).

23. Arlyn Tobias Gajilan, "The Parents of the Pilot Try for an Encore with Handspring," *Fortune,* November 22, 1999, pp. 374[H], 374[J]; Stephanie Miles, "PalmPilot In, Newton Out," *CNET News.com,* February 27, 1998, www.news.com.

24. John B. Frey, "Pricing Over the Competitive Cycle," speech presented at the 1982 Marketing Conference, Conference Board, New York.

25. "Explosive Growth in DVD Sales," *ZDNet News,* December 9, 1999, www.zdnet.com.

26. Stephen M. Nowlis and Itamar Simmonson, "The Effect of New Product Features on Brand Choice," *Journal of Marketing Research,* February 1996, pp. 36–46.

27. Allen J. McGrath, "Growth Strategies with a '90s Twist," *Across the Board,* March 1995, pp. 43–46.

28. Kathryn Rudie Harrigan, "Strategies for Declining Industries," *Journal of Business Strategy,* Fall 1980, p. 27.

29. See Philip Kotler, "Harvesting Strategies for Weak Products," *Business Horizons,* August 1978, pp. 15–22; and Laurence P. Feldman and Albert L. Page, "Harvesting: The Misunderstood Market Exit Strategy," *Journal of Business Strategy,* Spring 1985, pp. 79–85.

30. Dana James, "Rejuvenating Mature Brands Can Be Stimulating Exercise," *Marketing News,* August 16, 1999, pp. 16–17.

31. Some of these bases are discussed in David A. Garvin, "Competing on the Eight Dimensions of Quality," *Harvard Business Review,* November-December 1987, pp. 101–9.

32. See Bernd Schmitt and Alex Simonson, *Marketing Aesthetics: The Strategic Management of Brand, Identity, and Image* (New York: Free Press, 1997).

33. See Philip Kotler, "Design: A Powerful but Neglected Strategic Tool," *Journal of Business Strategy,* Fall 1984, pp. 16–21. Also see Christopher Lorenz, *The Design Dimension* (New York: Basil Blackwell, 1986).

34. Christine Bittar, "The Rite Stuff," *Brandweek,* September 14, 1998, pp. 28–29.

35. See "The 25 Best Sales Forces," *Sales & Marketing Management,* July 1998, pp. 32–50.

36. For a similar list, see Leonard L. Berry and A. Parasuraman, *Marketing Services: Competing Through Quality* (New York: Free Press, 1991), p. 16.

37. Erin Davies, "Selling Sex and Cat Food," *Fortune,* June 9, 1997, p. 36.

38. "Four Reasons Nike's Not Cool," *Fortune,* March 30, 1998, pp. 26–27.

39. Theodore Levitt, "Marketing Success through Differentiation—of Anything," *Harvard Business Review,* January-February 1980.

40. Al Ries and Jack Trout, *Positioning: The Battle for Your Mind* (New York: Warner Books, 1982).

41. Ries and Trout, *Positioning.*

Chapter 10

Managing Product Lines and Brands

In this chapter, we will address the following questions:

■ What are the characteristics of products?
■ How can a company build and manage its product mix and product lines?
■ How can a company make better brand decisions?
■ How can packaging and labeling be used as marketing tools?

Product, as successful firms the world over are keenly aware, is a key element in the *market offering*. This holds true whether the product is a television show (offered by Arts & Entertainment Network), an Internet access service (offered by AT&T), a hamburger (offered by Wendy's), a DVD player (offered by Sony), a sweater (offered by Benetton), or a chocolate bar (offered by Nestlé). No matter where the product originates, no matter which market segment is being targeted, marketing-mix planning begins with formulating an offering to meet customers' needs or wants.

In the previous chapter, we looked at how companies develop, differentiate, and position their products throughout the life cycle. In this chapter, we examine the concept of product and product-line decisions. We also explore basic brand decisions and key packaging and labeling issues. In Chapter 11, we look at how companies design and manage services as part of a complete market offering; in Chapter 12, we examine prices. All three elements—product, services, and price—must be meshed into a competitively attractive offering if a company wants to perform well in the marketplace.

THE PRODUCT AND THE PRODUCT MIX

A **product** is anything that can be offered to a market to satisfy a want or need. Products include *physical goods, services, experiences, events, persons, places, properties, organizations, information,* and *ideas.* The customer will judge the offering by three basic elements: product features and quality, services mix and quality, and price appropriateness (Figure 10.1). As a result, marketers must carefully think through the level at which they set each product's features, benefits, and quality.

Product Levels

Marketers plan their market offering at five levels, as shown in Figure 10.2.[1] Each level adds more customer value, and together the five levels constitute a *customer value hierarchy.* The most fundamental level is the *core benefit:* the fundamental service or benefit that the customer is really buying. A hotel guest is buying "rest and sleep"; the pur-

Figure 10.1   Components of the Market Offering

chaser of a drill is buying "holes." Effective marketers therefore see themselves as providers of product *benefits,* not merely product features.

At the second level, the marketer has to turn the core benefit into a *basic product.* Thus, a hotel room includes a bed, bathroom, towels, and closet. At the third level, the marketer prepares an *expected product,* a set of attributes and conditions that buyers normally expect when they buy the product. Hotel guests expect a clean bed, fresh towels, and so on. Because most hotels can meet this minimum expectation, the traveler normally will settle for whichever hotel is most convenient or least expensive.

At the fourth level, the marketer prepares an *augmented product* that exceeds customer expectations. A hotel might include a remote-control television set, fresh flowers, and express check-in and checkout. Today's competition essentially takes place at the product-augmentation level. (In less developed countries, competition takes place mostly at the expected product level.) Product augmentation leads the mar-

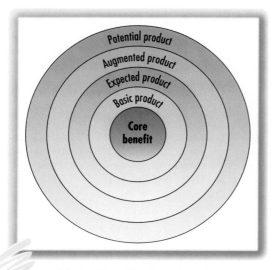

Figure 10.2   Five Product Levels

keter to look at the user's total *consumption system:* the way the user performs the tasks of getting, using, fixing, and disposing of the product.[2] As Levitt notes: "The new competition is not between what companies produce in their factories, but between what they add to their factory output in the form of packaging, services, advertising, customer advice, financing, delivery arrangements, warehousing, and other things that people value."[3]

However, product augmentation adds cost, so the marketer must determine whether customers will pay enough to cover the extra cost (of remote-control television in a hotel room, for example). Moreover, augmented benefits soon become expected benefits, which means that competitors have to search for still other features and benefits. And as companies raise the price of their augmented product, some competitors can offer a "stripped-down" version of the product at a much lower price. Thus, the hotel industry has seen the growth of fine hotels offering augmented products (Four Seasons, Ritz Carlton) as well as lower-cost lodgings offering basic products (Motel Six, Comfort Inn).

At the fifth level stands the *potential product,* which encompasses all of the possible augmentations and transformations the product might undergo in the future. Here, a company searches for entirely new ways to satisfy its customers and distinguish its offer. As one example, Marriott's TownePlace Suites all-suite hotels represent an innovative transformation of the traditional hotel product.

Product Classifications

In addition to understanding a product's position in the hierarchy, the marketer also must understand how to classify the product on the basis of three characteristics: durability, tangibility, and consumer or industrial use. Each product classification is associated with a different marketing-mix strategy.[4]

➤ *Durability and tangibility. Nondurable goods* are tangible goods that are normally consumed in one or a few uses (such as beer and soap). Because these goods are consumed quickly and purchased frequently, the appropriate strategy is to make them available in many locations, charge only a small markup, and advertise heavily to induce trial and build preference. *Durable goods* are tangible goods that normally survive many uses (such as refrigerators). These products normally require more personal selling and service, command a higher margin, and require more seller guarantees. Services are intangible, inseparable, variable, and perishable products (such as haircuts or cell phone service), so they normally require more quality control, supplier credibility, and adaptability.

➤ *Consumer-goods classification.* Classified according to consumer shopping habits, these products include: **convenience goods** that are usually purchased frequently, immediately, and with a minimum of effort, such as newspapers; **shopping goods** that the customer, in the process of selection and purchase, characteristically compares on the basis of suitability, quality, price, and style, such as furniture; **specialty goods** with unique characteristics or brand identification, such as cars, for which a sufficient number of buyers are willing to make a special purchasing effort; and **unsought goods** that consumers do not know about or do not normally think of buying, such as smoke detectors. Dealers that sell specialty goods need not be conveniently located but must communicate their locations to buyers; unsought goods require more advertising and personal sales support.

➤ *Industrial-goods classification.* **Materials** and **parts** are goods that enter the manufacturer's product completely. *Raw materials* can be either *farm products* (e.g., wheat) or *natural products* (e.g., lumber). Farm products are sold through intermediaries; natural products are generally sold through long-term supply contracts, for which price and delivery reliability are key purchase factors. *Manufactured materials* and *parts* fall into two categories: component materials (iron) and component parts (small motors); again, price and supplier reliability are important considerations. **Capital items** are long-lasting goods that facilitate developing or managing the finished product. They include two groups: installations (such as factories) and equipment (such as trucks and computers), both sold through personal selling. **Supplies** and **business services** are short-lasting goods and services that facilitate developing or managing the finished product.

Product Mix

A **product mix** (also called **product assortment**) is the set of all products and items that a particular marketer offers for sale. At Kodak, the product mix consists of two strong product lines: information products and image products. At NEC (Japan), the product mix consists of communication products and computer products.

The product mix of an individual company can be described in terms of width, length, depth, and consistency. The *width* refers to how many different product lines the company carries. The *length* refers to the total number of items in the mix. The *depth* of a product mix refers to how many variants of each product are offered. The *consistency* of the product mix refers to how closely related the various product lines are in end use, production requirements, distribution channels, or some other way.

These four product-mix dimensions permit the company to expand its business by (1) adding new product lines, thus widening its product mix; (2) lengthening each product line; (3) deepening the product mix by adding more variants; and (4) pursuing more product-line consistency.

PRODUCT-LINE DECISIONS

Especially in large companies such as Kodak and NEC, the product mix consists of a variety of product lines. In offering a product line, the company normally develops a basic platform and modules that can then be expanded to meet different customer requirements. As one example, many home builders show a model home to which additional features can be added, enabling the builders to offer variety while lowering their production costs. Regardless of the type of products being offered, successful marketers do not make product-line decisions without rigorous analysis.

Product-Line Analysis

To support decisions about which items to build, maintain, harvest, or divest, product-line managers need to analyze the sales and profits as well as the market profile of each item:

➤ *Sales and profits.* The manager must calculate the percentage contribution of each item to total sales and profits. A high concentration of sales in a few items means line vulnerability. On the other hand, the firm may consider eliminating items that deliver a low percentage of sales and profits—unless these exhibit strong growth potential.

➤ *Market profile.* The manager must review how the line is positioned against competitors' lines. A useful tool here is a product map showing which competitive products compete against the company's products on specific features or benefits. This helps management identify different market segments and determine how well the firm is positioned to serve the needs of each.

After performing these two analyses, the product-line manager is ready to consider decisions on product-line length, line modernization, line featuring, and line pruning.

Product-Line Length

Companies seeking high market share and market growth will carry longer lines; companies emphasizing high profitability will carry shorter lines of carefully chosen items. *Line stretching* occurs when a firm lengthens its product line.

With a downmarket stretch, a firm introduces a lower price line. However, moving downmarket can be risky, as Kodak found out. It introduced Kodak Funtime film to counter lower-priced brands, but the price was not low enough to match the lower-priced competitive products. When regular customers started buying Funtime—cannibalizing the core brand—Kodak withdrew Funtime.

With an upmarket stretch, a company enters the high end of the market for more growth, higher margins, or to position itself as a full-line manufacturer. All of the leading Japanese automakers have launched an upscale automobile: Toyota launched Lexus; Nissan launched Infinity; and Honda launched Acura. (Note that these marketers invented entirely new names rather than using their own names.)

Companies that serve the middle market can stretch their product lines in both directions, as the Marriott Hotel group did. Alongside its medium-price hotels, it added the Marriott Marquis to serve the upper end of the market, the Courtyard to serve a lower segment, and Fairfield Inns to serve the low-to-moderate segment.[5] The major risk of this two-way stretch is that some travelers will trade down after finding the lower-price hotels have most of what they want. But it is still better for Marriott to capture customers who move downward than to lose them to competitors.

A product line can also be lengthened by adding more items within the present range. There are several motives for *line filling:* reaching for incremental profits, trying to satisfy dealers who complain about lost sales because of missing items in the line, trying to utilize excess capacity, trying to be the leading full-line company, and trying to plug holes to keep out competitors.

Line Featuring and Line Pruning

The product-line manager typically selects one or a few items in the line to feature; this is a way of attracting customers, lending prestige, or achieving other goals. If one end of its line is selling well and the other end is selling poorly, the company may use featuring to boost demand for the slower sellers, especially if those items are produced in a factory that is idled by lack of demand. In addition, managers must periodically review the entire product line for pruning, identifying weak items through sales and cost analysis. They may also prune when the company is short of production capacity or demand is slow.

BRAND DECISIONS

Branding is a major issue in product strategy. On the one hand, developing a branded product requires a huge long-term investment, especially for advertising, promotion, and packaging. However, it need not entail actual production: Many brand-oriented companies such as Sarah Lee subcontract manufacturing to other companies. On the other hand, manufacturers eventually learn that market power comes from building their own brands. The Japanese firms Sony and Toyota, for example, have spent liberally to build their brand names globally. Even when companies can no longer afford to manufacture their products in their homelands, strong brand names continue to command customer loyalty.

What Is a Brand?

Perhaps the most distinctive skill of professional marketers is their ability to create, maintain, protect, and enhance brands.

The American Marketing Association defines a **brand** as a name, term, sign, symbol, or design, or a combination of these, intended to identify the goods or services of one seller or group of sellers and to differentiate them from those of competitors.

In essence, a brand identifies the seller or maker. Whether it is a name, trademark, logo, or another symbol, a brand is essentially a seller's promise to deliver a specific set of features, benefits, and services consistently to the buyers. The best brands convey a warranty of quality. But a brand is an even more complex symbol.[6] It can convey up to six levels of meaning, as shown in Table 10.1.

The branding challenge is to develop a deep set of positive associations for the brand. Marketers must decide at which level(s) to anchor the brand's identity. One mistake would be to promote only attributes. First, buyers are not as interested in attributes as they are in benefits. Second, competitors can easily copy attributes. Third, today's attributes may become less desirable tomorrow. Ultimately, a brand's most enduring meanings are its values, culture, and personality, which define the brand's essence. Smart firms therefore craft strategies that do not dilute the brand values and personality built up over the years.

Table 10.1   Levels of Brand Meaning

Meaning	Description	Example
Attributes	A brand brings to mind certain attributes.	Mercedes suggests expensive, well-built, durable, high-prestige vehicles.
Benefits	Attributes must be translated into functional and emotional benefits.	The attribute "durable" could translate into the functional benefit "I won't have to buy another car for several years."
Values	The brand says something about the producer's values.	Mercedes stands for high performance, safety, and prestige.
Culture	The brand may represent a certain culture.	Mercedes represents German culture: organized, efficient, high quality.
Personality	The brand can project a certain personality.	Mercedes may suggest a non-nonsense boss (person) or a reigning lion (animal).
User	The brand suggests the kind of customer who buys or uses the product.	Mercedes vehicles are more likely to be bought by 55-year-old top managers than by 20-year-old store clerks.

Brand Equity

Brands vary in the amount of power and value they have in the marketplace. At one extreme are brands that are not known by most buyers. Then there are brands for which buyers have a fairly high degree of *brand awareness*. Beyond this are brands with a high degree of *brand acceptability*. Next are brands that enjoy a high degree of *brand preference*. Finally there are brands that command a high degree of *brand loyalty*. Aaker distinguished five levels of customer attitude toward a brand:

1. Customer will change brands, especially for price reasons. No brand loyalty.
2. Customer is satisfied. No reason to change the brand.
3. Customer is satisfied and would incur costs by changing brand.
4. Customer values the brand and sees it as a friend.
5. Customer is devoted to the brand.

Brand equity is highly related to how many customers are in classes 3, 4, or 5. It is also related, according to Aaker, to the degree of brand-name recognition, perceived brand quality, strong mental and emotional associations, and other assets such as patents, trademarks, and channel relationships.[7] High brand equity allows a company to enjoy reduced marketing costs because of high brand awareness and loyalty, gives a company more leverage in bargaining with distributors and retailers, permits the firm to charge more because the brand has higher perceived quality, allows the firm to more easily launch extensions because the brand has high credibility, and offers some defense against price competition.

Some analysts see brands as outlasting a company's specific products and facilities, so brands become the company's major enduring asset. Yet every powerful brand really represents a set of loyal customers. Therefore, the fundamental asset underlying brand equity is *customer equity*. This suggests that the proper focus of marketing planning is that of extending *loyal customer lifetime value,* with brand management serving as a major marketing tool.

Unfortunately, some companies have mismanaged their greatest asset—their brands. This is what befell the popular Snapple brand almost as soon as Quaker Oats bought the beverage marketer for $1.7 billion in 1994. Snapple had become a hit through powerful grassroots marketing and distribution through small outlets and convenience stores. Analysts said that because Quaker did not understand the brand's appeal, it made the mistake of changing the ads and the distribution. Snapple lost so much money and market share that in 1997, Quaker finally sold the company for $300 million to Triarc, which has since revived the floundering brand.[8]

Branding Challenges

Branding poses several challenges to the marketer (see Figure 10.3). The first is whether or not to brand, the second is how to handle brand sponsorship, the third is choosing a brand name, the fourth is deciding on brand strategy, and the fifth is whether to reposition a brand later on.

To Brand or Not to Brand?

The first decision is whether the company should develop a brand name for its product. Branding is such a strong force today that hardly anything goes unbranded,

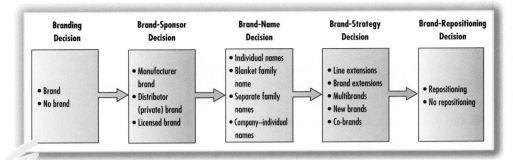

Figure 10.3   An Overview of Branding Decisions

including salt, oranges, nuts and bolts, and a growing number of fresh food products such as chicken and turkey.

In some cases, there has been a return to "no branding" of certain staple consumer goods and pharmaceuticals. *Generics* are unbranded, plainly packaged, less expensive versions of common products such as spaghetti or paper towels. They offer standard or lower quality at a price that may be as much as 20 percent to 40 percent lower than nationally advertised brands and 10 percent to 20 percent lower than retailer private-label brands. The lower price is made possible by lower-quality ingredients, lower-cost labeling and packaging, and minimal advertising.

Sellers brand their products, despite the costs, because they gain a number of advantages: The brand makes it easier for the seller to process orders; the seller's brand name and trademark legally protect unique product features; branding allows sellers to attract loyal, profitable customers and offers some protection from competition; branding helps the seller segment markets by offering different brands with different features for different benefit-seeking segments; and strong brands help build the corporate image, easing the way for new brands and wider acceptance by distributors and customers.

Distributors and retailers want brands because they make the product easier to handle, indicate certain quality standards, strengthen buyer preferences, and make it easier to identify suppliers. For their part, customers find that brand names help them distinguish quality differences and shop more efficiently.

Brand-Sponsor Decision

A manufacturer has several options with respect to brand sponsorship. The product may be launched as a *manufacturer brand* (sometimes called a national brand), a *distributor brand* (also called reseller, store, house, or private brand), or a *licensed brand name*. Another alternative is for the manufacturer to produce some output under its own name and some under reseller labels. Kellogg, John Deere, and IBM sell virtually all of their output under their own brand names, whereas Whirlpool produces both under its own name and under distributors' names (Sears Kenmore appliances).

Although manufacturers' brands dominate, large retailers and wholesalers have been developing their own brands by contracting production from willing manufacturers. Sears has created several names—Diehard batteries, Craftsman tools, Kenmore appliances—that command brand preference and even brand loyalty. Retailers such as The Body Shop and Gap sell mostly own-brand merchandise. Sainsbury, Britain's largest food chain, sells 50 percent store-label goods, and its operating margins are six times those of U.S. retailers (U.S. supermarkets average 19.7 percent private-brand sales).

Why do middlemen sponsor their own brands? First, these brands are more profitable, since they are produced at a low cost by manufacturers with excess capacity. Other costs, such as research and development, advertising, sales promotion, and physical distribution, are also much lower. This means that the private brander can charge a lower price and yet make a higher profit margin. Second, retailers develop exclusive store brands to differentiate themselves from competitors.

In years past, consumers viewed the brands in a category arranged in a brand ladder, with their favorite brand at the top and remaining brands in descending order of preference. There are now signs that this ladder is being replaced with a consumer perception of brand parity—that many brands are equivalent.[9] Instead of a strongly preferred brand, consumers buy from a set of acceptable brands, choosing whichever is on sale that day.

Today's consumers are also more price sensitive, because a steady barrage of coupons and price specials has trained them to buy on price. In fact, over time, companies have reduced advertising to 30 percent of their total promotion budget, weakening brand equity. Moreover, the endless stream of brand extensions and line extensions has blurred brand identity and led to a confusing amount of product proliferation. Further, consumers see little difference in quality among brands now that competing manufacturers and retailers are copying and duplicating the qualities of the best brands.

Of course, one of the factors that is changing the entire branding landscape is the Internet. While some "born digital" companies like America Online (AOL) and Amazon.com have used the Internet to gain brand recognition seemingly overnight, other companies have poured millions of dollars into on-line advertising with little effect on brand awareness or preference. For some low-price, low-involvement products, such as soap, the Internet offers little potential as a commerce vehicle. Still, the packaged-goods powerhouses are trying different approaches to Web marketing. Procter & Gamble, for example, has put much of its on-line marketing budget behind brands like Always panty liners, Tampax tampons, and Pampers diapers, which have narrow target audiences with more personal subject matter. With this strategy, the company has turned Pampers.com into Pampers Parenting Institute, reaching out to customers by addressing various issues of concern to new or expectant parents.[10]

All companies that have powerful brand awareness on the Web have sites that help customers do something—whether it's configuring a computer system on-line at Dell.com or offering customization options for services at Yahoo.com. Yet some of the biggest superstars of e-commerce conduct most of their branding efforts off-line: Cisco advertises in business publications, while Dell advertises in tech trade magazines and on television.[11]

AOL, like many high-tech companies, has been adept at achieving solid brand recognition through less conventional marketing approaches. Today, over half of all U.S. households are familiar with AOL brand. That's because AOL has blanketed the country for years with free software and free trial offers. The company has also cut deals to put its product in some unlikely places: inside Rice Chex cereal boxes, United Airlines in-flight meals, and Omaha Steaks packages, to name a few. AOL's marketers believe that novices need to try the service to appreciate its benefits. Then, once consumers start using AOL, the company reasons that the user-friendly program will lure them to subscribe. Also on AOL's side is sheer inertia, which prevents many people from switching to another Internet service provider.[12]

Brand-Name Decision

Manufacturers and service companies who brand their products must choose which brand names to use. Four strategies are available, as shown in Table 10.2.

Table 10.2   Brand-Name Strategies

Strategy	Examples	Rationale
Individual names	General Mills (Bisquick, Gold Medal, Betty Crocker)	The firm does not tie its reputation to the product's; if the product fails or seems low quality, the company's name or image is not hurt.
Blanket family names	Campbell's, Heinz, General Electric	The firm spends less on development because there is no need for "name" research or heavy ad spending to create brand-name recognition; also, product sales are likely to be strong if the manufacturer's name is good.
Separate family names for all products	Sears (Kenmore for appliances, Craftsman for tools); Bank One (Bank One for the physical branches, WingspanBank.com for the Internet-based bank)	Where a firm offers quite different products, separate family names are more appropriate than one blanket family name.
Company trade name with individual product names	Kellogg (Kellogg's Rice Krispies, Kellogg's Raisin Bran)	The company name legitimizes while the individual name individualizes each product.

Once a company decides on its brand-name strategy, it must choose a specific brand name. The company could choose the name of a person (Honda, Estée Lauder), location (American Airlines, Kentucky Fried Chicken), quality (Safeway, Duracell), lifestyle (Weight Watchers, Healthy Choice), or an artificial name (Exxon, eBay). Among the desirable qualities for a brand name are the following:[13]

➤ *It should suggest something about the product's benefits.* Examples: Beauty-rest, Priceline.com

➤ *It should suggest product qualities.* Examples: Spic and Span, Jiffy Lube

➤ *It should be easy to pronounce, recognize, and remember.* Examples: Tide, Amazon.com

➤ *It should be distinctive.* Examples: Kodak, Yahoo!

➤ *It should not carry poor meanings in other countries and languages.* Example: Nova is a poor name for a car to be sold in Spanish-speaking countries because it means "doesn't go."

Many firms strive to build a unique brand name that eventually will become intimately identified with the product category. Examples are Frigidaire, Kleenex, Kitty Litter, Levis, Jell-O, Popsicle, Scotch Tape, Xerox, and Fiberglas. In 1994, Federal Express officially shortened its marketing identity to FedEx, a term that has become a synonym for "to ship overnight." Yet identifying a brand name with a product category may threaten the company's exclusive rights to that name. For example, cellophane

and shredded wheat are now in the public domain and are available for any manufacturer to use.

Given the rapid growth of the global marketplace, successful companies and e-
businesses are careful to choose brand names that are meaningful worldwide and pro-
nounceable in other languages. One thing Compaq liked about the name Presario for
its line of home computers is that it conjures up similar meanings in various Latin-
influenced languages. In French, Spanish, Latin, or Portuguese, Presario has the
same, or similar, association that it does in English: It suggests an "Impresario," the
magical master of the whirl and fantasy of a stage production.

Brand Strategy Decision

A company has five choices when it comes to brand strategy. The company can introduce *line extensions* (existing brand name extended to new sizes or flavors in the existing product category), *brand extensions* (brand names extended to new-product categories), *multibrands* (new brand names introduced in the same product category), *new
brands* (new brand name for a new category product), and *co-brands* (brands bearing
two or more well-known brand names).

Line Extensions   Line extensions introduce additional items in the same product category under the same brand name, such as new flavors, forms, colors, added ingredients, and package sizes. Dannon introduced several Dannon yogurt line extensions,
including fat-free "light" yogurt and dessert flavors such as "mint chocolate cream
pie." The vast majority of new products are actually line extensions.

Line extension involves risks and has provoked heated debate among marketing
professionals.[14] On the downside, extensions may lead to the brand name losing its
specific meaning; Ries and Trout call this the "line-extension trap."[15] A consumer asking for a Coke in the past would receive a 6.5-ounce bottle. Today the seller will have
to ask: New, Classic, or Cherry Coke? Regular or diet? With or without caffeine? Bottle
or can? Sometimes the original brand identity is so strong that its line extensions serve
only to confuse and do not sell enough to cover development and promotion costs.
For example, A-1 poultry sauce flopped because people identify A-1 with beef.

However, the success of a new line extension sometimes hurts other items in the
line. Although Fig Newton's cousins Cranberry Newtons, Blueberry Newtons, and
Apple Newtons all sell well for Nabisco, the original Fig Newton now seems like just
another flavor. A line extension works best when it takes sales away from rivals, not
when it deflates or cannibalizes the company's other items.

On the upside, line extensions have a much higher chance of survival than do
brand-new products. In fact, some marketing executives defend line extensions as the
best way to build a business. Kimberly-Clark's Kleenex unit has had great success with
line extensions. "We try to get facial tissue in every room of the home," says one
Kimberly-Clark executive. "If it is there, it will get used." This philosophy led to 20 vari-
eties of Kleenex facial tissues, including a line packaged for children.

Brand Extensions A company may use its existing brand name to launch new products in other categories. Autobytel.com, a pioneer of Internet-based car sales, used
brand extensions to introduce automotive financing, insurance, and car repairs on its
Web site. A recent trend in corporate brand-building is corporations licensing their
names to manufacturers of a wide range of products—from bedding to shoes. Harley-
Davidson, for example, uses licensing to reach audiences that are not part of its core
market, with branded armchairs for women and branded a Barbie doll for the future
generation of Harley purchasers.[16]

Brand-extension strategy offers many of the same advantages as line extensions—but it also involves risks. One risk is that the new product might disappoint buyers and damage their respect for the company's other products. Another is that the brand name may be inappropriate to the new product—consider Bic perfume, a classic failure because buyers did not associate the Bic brand with fragrance products. A third risk is *brand dilution,* which occurs when consumers no longer associate a brand with a specific product or highly similar products.

Multibrands A company will often introduce additional brands in the same product category. Sometimes the firm is trying to establish different features or appeal to different buying motives. Multibranding also enables the company to lock up more distributor shelf space and to protect its major brand by setting up *flanker brands.* For example, Seiko uses one brand for higher-priced watches (Seiko Lasalle) and another for lower-priced watches (Pulsar) to protect its flanks. Ideally, a company's brands within a category should cannibalize the competitors' brands and not each other. At the very least, net profits from multibrands should be larger despite some cannibalism.[17]

New Brands When a company launches products in a new category, it may find that none of its current brand names are appropriate. If Timex decides to make toothbrushes, it is not likely to call them Timex toothbrushes. Yet establishing a new brand name in the U.S. marketplace for a mass-consumer-packaged good can cost anywhere from $50 million to $100 million, making this an extremely critical decision.

Co-brands A rising phenomenon is the emergence of *co-branding* (also called *dual branding*), in which two or more well-known brands are combined in an offer. Each brand sponsor expects that the other brand name will strengthen preference or purchase intention. In the case of co-packaged products, each brand hopes it might be reaching a new audience by associating with the other brand.

Co-branding takes a variety of forms. One is *ingredient co-branding,* as when Volvo advertises that it uses Michelin tires or Betty Crocker's brownie mix includes Hershey's chocolate syrup. Another form is *same-company co-branding,* as when General Mills advertises Trix and Yoplait yogurt. Still another form is *joint venture co-branding,* as in the case of General Electric and Hitachi lightbulbs in Japan and the MSNBC Web site from Microsoft and NBC. Finally, there is *multiple-sponsor co-branding,* as in the case of Taligent, a technological alliance of Apple, IBM, and Motorola.[18]

Many manufacturers make components—motors, computer chips, carpet fibers—that enter into final branded products, and whose individual identity normally gets lost. These manufacturers hope their brand will be featured as part of the final product. Intel's consumer-directed brand campaign convinced many people to buy only PCs with "Intel Inside." As a result, many PC manufacturers buy chips from Intel at a premium price rather than buying equivalent chips from other suppliers.

Brand Repositioning

However well a brand is currently positioned, the company may have to reposition it later when facing new competitors or changing customer preferences. Consider 7-Up, which was one of several soft drinks bought primarily by older people who wanted a bland, lemon-flavored drink. Research indicated that although a majority of soft-drink consumers preferred a cola, they did not prefer it all of the time, and many other consumers were noncola drinkers. 7-Up sought leadership in the noncola market by calling itself the Uncola and positioning itself as a youthful and refreshing drink, the one to reach for instead of a cola. Thus, 7-Up successfully established itself as the alternative to colas, not just another soft drink.

PACKAGING AND LABELING

Most physical products have to be packaged and labeled. Some packages—such as the Coke bottle—are world famous. Many marketers have called packaging a fifth P, along with price, product, place, and promotion; however, packaging and labeling are usually treated as an element of product strategy.

Packaging

Packaging includes the activities of designing and producing the container for a product. The container is called the *package,* and it might include up to three levels of material. Old Spice aftershave lotion is in a bottle *(primary package)* that is in a cardboard box *(secondary package)* that is in a corrugated box *(shipping package)* containing six dozen boxes of Old Spice.

The following factors have contributed to packaging's growing use as a potent marketing tool:

➤ *Self-service:* The typical supermarket shopper passes by some 300 items per minute. Given that 53 percent of all purchases are made on impulse, an effective package attracts attention, describes features, creates confidence, and makes a favorable impression.

➤ *Consumer affluence:* Rising consumer affluence means consumers are willing to pay a little more for the convenience, appearance, dependability, and prestige of better packages.

➤ *Company and brand image:* Packages contribute to instant recognition of the company or brand. Campbell Soup estimates that the average shopper sees its red and white can 76 times a year, the equivalent of $26 million worth of advertising.

➤ *Innovation opportunity:* Innovative packaging can bring benefits to consumers and profits to producers. Toothpaste pump dispensers, for example, have captured 12 percent of the toothpaste market because they are more convenient and less messy.

Developing an effective package for a new product requires several decisions. The first task is to establish the *packaging concept,* defining what the package should basically *be* or *do* for the particular product. Then decisions must be made on additional elements—size, shape, materials, color, text, and brand mark, plus the use of any "tamperproof" devices. All packaging elements must be in harmony and, in turn, must harmonize with the product's pricing, advertising, and other marketing elements. Next come engineering tests to ensure that the package stands up under normal conditions; visual tests, to ensure that the script is legible and the colors harmonious; dealer tests, to ensure that dealers find the packages attractive and easy to handle; and, finally, consumer tests, to ensure favorable response.

Tetra Pak, a major Swedish multinational, provides an example of the power of innovative packaging and customer orientation. The firm invented an "aseptic" package that enables milk, fruit juice, and other perishable liquid foods to be distributed without refrigeration. This allows dairies to distribute milk over a wider area without investing in refrigerated trucks and facilities. Supermarkets can carry Tetra Pak packaged products on ordinary shelves, which saves expensive refrigerator space. The firm's motto is "the package should save more than it costs."

Labeling

Every physical product must carry a label, which may be a simple tag attached to the product or an elaborately designed graphic that is part of the package. Labels perform several functions. First, the label *identifies* the product or brand—for instance, the name Sunkist stamped on oranges. The label might also *grade* the product, the way canned peaches are grade labeled A, B, and C. The label might *describe* the product: who made it, where it was made, when it was made, what it contains, how it is to be used, and how to use it safely. Finally, the label might *promote* the product through attractive graphics.

Labels eventually become outmoded and need freshening up. The label on Ivory soap has been redone 18 times since the 1890s, with gradual changes in the size and design of the letters. The label on Orange Crush soft drink was substantially changed when competitors' labels began to picture fresh fruits, thereby pulling in more sales. In response, Orange Crush developed a label with new symbols to suggest freshness and with much stronger and deeper colors.

Legal concerns about labels and packaging stretch back to the early 1900s and continue today. The Food and Drug Administration (FDA) recently took action against the potentially misleading use of such descriptions as "light," "high fiber," and "low fat." Meanwhile, consumerists are lobbying for additional labeling laws to require *open dating* (to describe product freshness), *unit pricing* (to state the product cost in standard measurement units), *grade labeling* (to rate the quality level), and *percentage labeling* (to show the percentage of each important ingredient).

Some tangible products that incorporate packaging and labels also involve some service component, such as delivery or installation. Therefore, marketers must be skillful not only in managing product lines and brands, but also in designing and managing services—the subject of the next chapter.

EXECUTIVE SUMMARY

Planning the product portion of a market offering calls for coordinated decisions on the product mix, product lines, brands, and packaging and labeling. The marketer needs to think through the five levels of the product: core benefit (the fundamental benefit or service the customer is really buying), basic product, expected product (a set of attributes that buyers expect), augmented product (additional services and benefits that distinguish the company's offer from the competition), and potential product (all of the augmentations and transformations the product might ultimately undergo).

Products can be classified in several ways. In terms of durability and reliability, products can be nondurable goods, durable goods, or services. In the consumer-goods category are convenience goods, shopping goods, specialty goods, and unsought goods. In the industrial-goods category are materials and parts, capital items, and supplies and business services.

A product mix is the set of all products and items offered for sale by the marketer. This mix can be classified according to width, length, depth, and consistency, providing four dimensions for developing the company's marketing strategy. To support product decisions, product-line managers first analyze each product's sales, profits, and market profile. Managers can then change their product-line strategy by line stretching or line filling, by featuring certain products, and by pruning to eliminate some products.

Branding is a major product-strategy issue. High brand equity translates into high brand-name recognition, high perceived brand quality, strong mental associations, and other important assets. In creating brand strategy, firms must decide whether or not to brand; whether to produce manufacturer brands, or distributor or private brands; which brand name to use, and whether to use line extensions, brand extensions, multibrands, new brands, or co-brands. The best brand names suggest something about the product's benefits; suggest product qualities; are easy to pronounce, recognize, and remember; are distinctive; and do not carry negative meanings or connotations in other countries or languages.

Many physical products have to be packaged and labeled. Well-designed packages create convenience value for customers and promotional value for producers. Marketers start by developing a packaging concept and then testing it functionally and psychologically to make sure it achieves its desired objectives and is compatible with public policy and environmental concerns. Physical products also require labeling for identification and possible grading, description, and product promotion.

NOTES

1. This discussion is adapted from Theodore Levitt, "Marketing Success through Differentiation—of Anything," *Harvard Business Review,* January-February 1980, pp. 83–91. The first level, core benefit, has been added to Levitt's discussion.
2. See Harper W. Boyd Jr. and Sidney Levy, "New Dimensions in Consumer Analysis," *Harvard Business Review,* November–December 1963, pp. 129–40.
3. Theodore Levitt, *The Marketing Mode* (New York: McGraw-Hill, 1969), p. 2.
4. For some definitions, see *Dictionary of Marketing Terms,* ed. Peter D. Bennett (Chicago: American Marketing Association, 1995). Also see Patrick E. Murphy and Ben M. Enis, "Classifying Products Strategically," *Journal of Marketing,* July 1986, pp. 24–42.
5. "Fairfield Inn by Marriott to be Positioned in Lower-Moderate Lodging Segment," *PR Newswire,* January 19, 2000.
6. See Jean-Noel Kapferer, *Strategic Brand Management: New Approaches to Creating and Evaluating Brand Equity* (London: Kogan Page, 1992), pp. 38 ff; Jennifer L. Aaker, "Dimensions of Brand Personality," *Journal of Marketing Research,* August 1997, pp. 347–56.
7. David A. Aaker, *Building Strong Brands* (New York: Free Press, 1995). Also see Kevin Lane Keller, *Strategic Brand Management: Building, Measuring, and Managing Brand Equity* (Upper Saddle River, NJ: Prentice-Hall, 1998).
8. Margaret Webb Pressler, "The Power of Branding," *Washington Post,* July 27, 1997, p. H1; "Triarc Reports Strong Second Quarter 1999 Results With Adjusted EBITDA Up 12 Percent," Triarc news release, August 19, 1999, www.triarc.com.
9. See Paul S. Richardson, Alan S. Dick, and Arun K. Jain, "Extrinsic and Intrinsic Cue Effects on Perceptions of Store Brand Quality," *Journal of Marketing,* October 1994, pp. 28–36.
10. Saul Hensell, "Selling Soap Without the Soap Operas, Mass Marketers Seek Ways to Build Brands on the Web," *New York Times,* August 24, 1998, p. D1.
11. Jeffrey O'Brien, "Web Advertising and the Branding Mission," *Upside,* September 1998, pp. 90–94; Ellen Neuborne, "Branding on the Net," *Business Week,* November 9, 1998, pp. 76–86.
12. Patricia Nakache, "Secrets of the New Brand Builders," *Fortune,* June 22, 1998, pp. 167–70; John Ellis, "Digital Matters: 'People Need a Haven from the Web That's on the Web,' " *Fast Company,* January-February 2000, pp. 242–46.

13. See Kim Robertson, "Strategically Desirable Brand Name Characteristics," *Journal of Consumer Marketing,* Fall 1989, pp. 61–70.
14. Robert McMath, "Product Proliferation," *Adweek (Eastern Ed.) Superbrands 1995 Supplement,* 1995, pp. 34–40; John A. Quelch and David Kenny, "Extend Profits, Not Product Lines," *Harvard Business Review,* September–October 1994, pp. 153–60; and Bruce G. S. Hardle, Leonard M. Lodish, James V. Kilmer, David R. Beatty, et al., "The Logic of Product-Line Extensions," *Harvard Business Review,* November–December 1994, pp. 53–62.
15. Al Ries and Jack Trout, *Positioning: The Battle for Your Mind* (New York: McGraw-Hill, 1981).
16. Constance L. Hays, "No More Brand X: Licensing of Names Adds to Image and Profit," *New York Times,* June 12, 1998.
17. See Mark B. Taylor, "Cannibalism in Multibrand Firms," *Journal of Business Strategy,* Spring 1986, pp. 69–75.
18. Bernard L. Simonin and Julie A. Ruth, "Is a Company Known by the Company It Keeps? Assessing the Spillover Effects of Brand Alliances on Consumer Brand Attitudes," *Journal of Marketing Research,* February 1998, pp. 30–42.

Chapter 11
Designing and Managing Services

In this chapter, we will address the following questions:

- How are services defined and classified?
- How can service firms improve their competitive differentiation, service quality, and productivity?
- How can goods-producing companies improve their customer support services?

Marketing theory and practice developed initially in connection with physical products such as toothpaste, cars, and steel. Yet one of the major megatrends of recent years has been the phenomenal growth of services. In the United States, service jobs now account for 79 percent of all jobs and 74 percent of gross domestic product. According to the Bureau of Labor Statistics, service occupations will be responsible for all net job growth through the year 2005.[1] These numbers have led to a growing interest in the special challenges and opportunities of services marketing.[2]

More and more market offerings now contain a service component, both to meet the needs of the targeted customer segment and to create a distinctive differentiation for competitive reasons. Many manufactured goods are supported by services such as *warranties* (formal statements of expected product performance) or *guarantees* (assurances that the product can be returned if its performance is unsatisfactory). By judiciously offering one or more service features, a smart marketer can enhance its image while adding value that, in turn, attracts loyal customers and builds long-term profits.

THE NATURE OF SERVICES

Service industries are quite varied. The *government sector,* with its courts, employment services, hospitals, loan agencies, military services, police and fire departments, post office, regulatory agencies, and schools, is in the service business. The *private nonprofit sector,* with its museums, charities, churches, colleges, foundations, and hospitals, is in the service business. A good part of the *business sector,* with its airlines, banks, hotels, insurance companies, Internet service providers, law firms, management consulting firms, medical practices, motion-picture companies, plumbing-repair companies, real estate firms, and Web-based services, is in the service business. Many workers in the *manufacturing sector,* such as computer operators, accountants, and legal staff, are really service providers. In fact, they make up a "service factory" that provides services to the "goods factory."

A **service** is any act or performance that one party can offer to another that is essentially intangible and does not result in the ownership of anything. Its production may or may not be tied to a physical product.

Services such as banking and other financial services are a mainstay of the Internet. E*Trade, for example, the second-largest U.S. on-line broker, allows customers to quickly buy and sell stocks, bonds, and mutual funds at a low cost through its Web site. E*Trade's nearly 2 million accountholders can also use the Web site to locate research about stocks and bonds, plan their portfolios, and get checking accounts and loans through the firm's Telebanc subsidiary. Even noncustomers can access the site's free financial news, tax and investment tips, and money-related chat rooms.[3]

Many manufacturers and distributors also use a service strategy to differentiate themselves. Acme Construction Supply in Portland, Oregon, has invested more than $135,000 in its Night Owl delivery service: Acme personnel deposit orders into lockboxes at construction sites during the nighttime hours, so materials are available first thing in the morning. Says the company's regional team leader, "People that are very, very price sensitive don't do business here. But people who see the overall value we provide do. And it's very intimidating to our competition. They have to walk around our delivery boxes every day to make their sales calls."[4]

Categories of Service Mix

As the previous examples show, services are often part of a company's total offering in the marketplace. Five categories of an offering's service mix can be distinguished:

1. *Pure tangible good:* The offering is a tangible good such as soap; no services accompany the product.

2. *Tangible good with accompanying services:* The offering consists of a tangible good accompanied by one or more services. General Motors, for example, offers repairs, maintenance, warranty fulfillment, and other services along with its cars and trucks.

3. *Hybrid:* The offering consists of equal parts of goods and services. For example, people patronize restaurants for both food and service.

4. *Major service with accompanying minor goods and services:* The offering consists of a major service along with additional services or supporting goods. For example, airline passengers are buying transportation service, but they get food and drinks, as well.

5. *Pure service:* The offering consists primarily of a service; examples include baby-sitting and psychotherapy.

An increasing number of companies that are known for their tangible goods offerings are now looking to boost profits from services. Consider General Electric, which built its business on the production of goods such as refrigerators and light bulbs. These days, its fastest-growing unit is GE Capital, which consists of 28 businesses ranging from credit cards to truck leasing to insurance. Germany's Siemens is moving in the same direction by setting up a financial services division as a profit center.[5]

Characteristics of Services and Their Marketing Implications

Services have four major characteristics that greatly affect the design of marketing programs: intangibility, inseparability, variability, and perishability.

Intangibility

Services are intangible. Unlike physical products, they cannot be seen, tasted, felt, heard, or smelled before they are bought. The person who is getting a face lift cannot see the exact results before the purchase, just as the patient in the psychiatrist's office cannot know the exact outcome before treatment.

To reduce uncertainty, buyers will look for signs or evidence of the service quality. They will draw inferences about quality from the place, people, equipment, communication material, symbols, and price that they see. Therefore, the service provider's task is to "manage the evidence," to "tangibilize the intangible."[6] Whereas product marketers are challenged to add abstract ideas, service marketers are challenged to add physical evidence and imagery to abstract offers. This is why Allstate uses the slogan "You're in good *hands* with Allstate."

In general, service marketers must be able to transform intangible services into concrete benefits. Consider Dun & Bradstreet, a $2 billion firm with a database of 11 million U.S. firms that businesses can access to check the creditworthiness of their commercial customers. D&B's senior VP of marketing says, "If we're calling on a bank's credit manager, we'll research the bank's portfolio of customers, and using the information in our database, score them based on their creditworthiness and stability and say, 'You have X% of customers in the high-risk category and X% in low-risk.'"[7] This translates D&B's intangible services into tangible benefits for banking customers.

Inseparability

Services are typically produced and consumed simultaneously, unlike physical goods, which are manufactured, put into inventory, distributed through resellers, and consumed later. If a person renders the service, then the provider is part of the service. Because the client is also present as the service is produced, provider-client interaction is a special feature of services marketing—both provider and client affect the outcome.

Often, buyers of services have strong provider preferences. Several strategies exist for getting around this limitation. One is higher pricing in line with the provider's limited time. Another is having the provider work with larger groups or work faster. A third alternative is to train more service providers and build up client confidence, as H&R Block has done with its national network of trained tax consultants.

Variability

Because services depend on who provides them and when and where they are provided, they are highly variable. Knowing this, service firms can take three steps toward quality control. The first is recruiting the right service employees and providing them with excellent training. This is crucial regardless of whether employees are highly skilled professionals or low-skilled workers.

For example, the California-based Horn Group handles public relations for high-powered Silicon Valley software makers and technology consultants. Founder Sabrina Horn invests heavily in training her employees and in building morale and enthusiasm. She has developed education programs that include lunchtime seminars on everything from how to write a press release to how to manage an account. Employees also receive tuition reimbursement for continuing education.[8]

The second step is standardizing the service-performance process throughout the organization. Companies can do this by preparing a flowchart that depicts every service event and process. Using this flowchart, management can identify potential fail points and then plan improvements. The third step—taken by Priceline.com and many other service firms—is monitoring customer satisfaction through suggestion and complaint systems, customer surveys, and comparison shopping.

Table 11.1 Strategies for Improving the Match between Demand and Supply

Demand-Side Strategies	Supply-Side Strategies
Use *differential pricing* to shift demand from peak to off-peak periods; movie theaters and car rental firms do this by lowering prices during off-peak periods.	*Hire part-time employees* to meet peak demand; restaurants, stores, and Web-based businesses often bring in temporary staffers to help out during holidays and other peak periods.
Cultivate nonpeak demand to build sales during off-peak periods; hotels do this with their weekend minivacation packages.	*Introduce peak-time efficiency routines* to keep productivity high during periods of high demand; paramedics often assist physicians during busy periods.
Develop complementary services to provide alternatives for customers during peak periods; many banks do this by providing drop-off boxes for deposits and payments.	*Increase consumer participation* to speed transactions; this is one reason why supermarkets are experimenting with self-service checkouts where shoppers scan and bag their own groceries.
Install reservation systems to better manage demand levels; airlines, hotels, and physicians employ such systems extensively.	*Plan facilities for future expansion* to increase supply; an amusement park can buy surrounding land for later development as demand increases.
	Share services with other providers to help manage demand; hospitals can do this by sharing medical-equipment purchases and scheduling.

Source: Adapted from W. Earl Sasser, "Match Supply and Demand in Service Industries," *Harvard Business Review,* November-December 1976, pp. 133–40.

Perishability

Services cannot be stored; once an airplane takes off or a movie starts, any unsold seats cannot be held for future sale. Perishability is not a problem when demand for a service is steady, but fluctuating demand can cause problems. For example, public-transportation companies have to own much more equipment because of higher rush-hour demand, just as Charles Schwab must have sufficient server capacity to handle its brokerage customers' on-line trading during peak stock market periods.

Service providers can deal with perishability challenges in a number of ways. Table 11.1 shows some strategies proposed by Sasser for better matching demand and supply in a service business.[9]

MARKETING STRATEGIES FOR SERVICE FIRMS

In addition to the traditional four Ps of marketing, service providers must pay attention to three more Ps suggested by Booms and Bitner for services marketing: people, physical evidence, and process.[10] Because most services are provided by *people,* the selection, training, and motivation of employees can make a huge difference in customer satisfaction. Ideally, service employees should exhibit competence, a caring attitude, responsiveness, initiative, problem-solving ability, and goodwill.

Companies should also try to demonstrate their service quality through *physical evidence* and presentation. Thus, a hotel such as the Four Seasons will develop a look and observable style of handling customers that embodies its intended customer value proposition (in this case, luxury accommodations). Finally, service companies can choose among different *processes* to deliver their service. For instance, McDonald's outlets offer self-service, while Olive Garden restaurants offer table service.

A service encounter is affected by both visible and invisible elements (see Figure 11.1). Consider a customer visiting a bank to get a loan (service X). The customer sees other customers waiting for this and other services. The customer also sees a physical environment (the building, interior, equipment, and furniture) as well as bank personnel. Not visible to the customer is a whole "backroom" production process and organization system that supports the visible business. Thus, the service outcome, and whether or not people will be satisfied and ultimately remain loyal to a service provider, are influenced by a host of variables.[11]

In view of this complexity, Gronroos has argued that service marketing requires not only external marketing, but also internal and interactive marketing (Figure 11.2).[12] *External marketing* describes the normal work to prepare, price, distribute, and promote the service to customers. *Internal marketing* describes the work to train and motivate employees to serve customers well. Berry has argued that the most important contribution the marketing department can make is to be "exceptionally clever in getting everyone else in the organization to practice marketing."[13]

Interactive marketing describes the employees' skill in serving the client. Because the client judges service not only by its *technical quality* (e.g., Was the surgery successful?) but also by its *functional quality* (e.g., Did the surgeon show concern and inspire

Figure 11.1   Elements in a Service Encounter

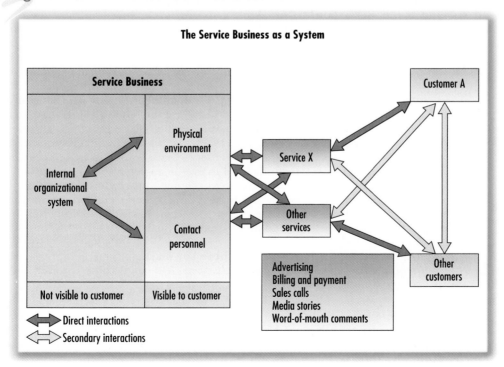

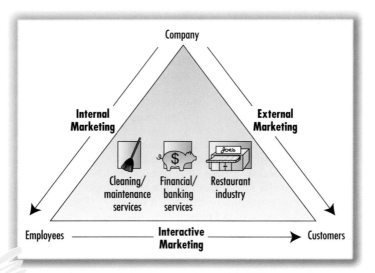

Figure 11.2   Three Types of Marketing in Service Industries

confidence?),[14] service providers must deliver services that are "high touch" as well as "high tech."[15]

Consider how Charles Schwab, the nation's largest discount brokerage house, uses the Web to create an innovative combination of high-tech and high-touch services. One of the first major brokerage firms to provide on-line trading, Schwab now provides millions of investors with Web-based financial and company information, account data, and detailed research. By offering high-tech services, Schwab has taken on the role of on-line investment adviser. Nonetheless, the on-line trading service does not entirely replace the personal service offered by Schwab in its local branches or via the telephone.[16]

In some cases, customers cannot judge the technical quality of a service even after they have received it, as shown in Figure 11.3.[17] At the left are goods that are high in *search qualities*—characteristics the buyer can evaluate before purchase. In the middle are goods and services that are high in *experience qualities*—characteristics the buyer can evaluate after purchase. At the right are services that are high in *credence qualities*—characteristics the buyer normally finds hard to evaluate even after consumption.[18]

Because services are generally high in experience and credence qualities, there is more risk in their purchase. As a result, service buyers tend to rely more on word of mouth than on advertising when selecting a provider. Second, they rely heavily on price, personnel, and physical cues to judge quality. Third, they are highly loyal to service providers who satisfy them.

Given these issues, service firms face three key marketing tasks: increasing *competitive differentiation, service quality,* and *productivity.* Although these interact, we will examine each separately.

Managing Differentiation

Service marketers frequently complain about the difficulty of differentiating their services on more than price alone. Price is a major marketing focus in service industries such as communications, transportation, and energy, which have experienced intense

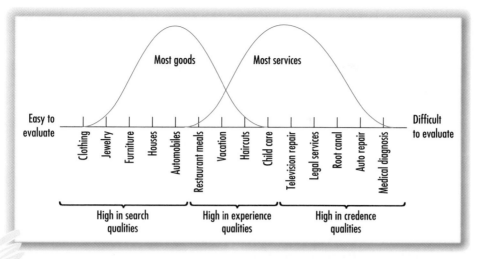

Figure 11.3   Continuum of Evaluation for Different Types of Products

price competition since deregulation. In a deregulated environment, the continued expansion of budget-priced airlines like Southwest Airlines indicated that many fliers care more about travel costs than service. Similarly, the success of E*Trade and other discount Web-based brokerages showed that many customers had little loyalty to more established brokerages when they could save money by trading on-line. To the extent that customers view a service as fairly homogeneous, they care less about the provider than the price.

The alternative to price competition in services marketing is to develop a differentiated offer, delivery, or image.

➤ *Offer.* The service offering can include innovative features. The customer expects the *primary service package;* to this *secondary service features* can be added. Marriott, for example, offers hotel rooms (primary service package) with connections for computers, fax machines, and e-mail (secondary service features). Although most service innovations are easily copied, the company that regularly introduces new features will gain a succession of temporary competitive advantages and earn a reputation for innovation. Amazon.com has continually expanded its offering to include auctions, e-mail greeting cards, and other services, reinforcing the firm's reputation as an Internet pioneer and retaining loyal customers.

➤ *Delivery.* A service company can hire and train better people to deliver its service (Home Depot, Nordstrom). It can develop a more attractive physical environment in which to deliver the service (Borders Books and Music stores, Cineplex Odeon movie theaters). Or it can design a superior delivery process (McDonald's, eBay). Delivery thus enhances the firm's differentiation.

➤ *Image.* Service companies can also differentiate their image through symbols and branding. Prudential uses the Rock of Gibralter as its corporate symbol to signify strength and stability. Differentiation through branding is a specialty of the charge-card division of American Express. Worldwide, a record 41.5 million people "can't leave home without it." Yet, now the company needs to reinvent itself: Credit cards like Visa and MasterCard have eaten into Amex's turf, and customers are flocking to no-fee credit cards with frequent-flier miles and other benefits. Fighting back, Amex has launched a walletful of new products, including the "Blue Card," aimed at upscale 25- to 35-year-olds. And the firm has carefully retained all of the positive things its brand stands for, such as good service, prestige, and value, making them relevant to the young, hip, affluent consumer.[19]

Managing Service Quality

Another way for a service firm to succeed is by delivering consistently higher-quality service than that of its competitors and by exceeding customers' expectations. These expectations are formed by the firm's past experiences, word of mouth, and advertising. After receiving the service, customers compare the perceived service with the expected service. If the perceived service falls below the expected service, customers lose interest in the provider. If the perceived service meets or exceeds their expectations, they are apt to use the provider again.

Parasuraman, Zeithaml, and Berry formulated a service-quality model that highlights the main requirements for delivering high service quality.[20] The model, shown in Figure 11.4, identifies five gaps that cause unsuccessful service delivery:

Figure 11.4   Service-Quality Model

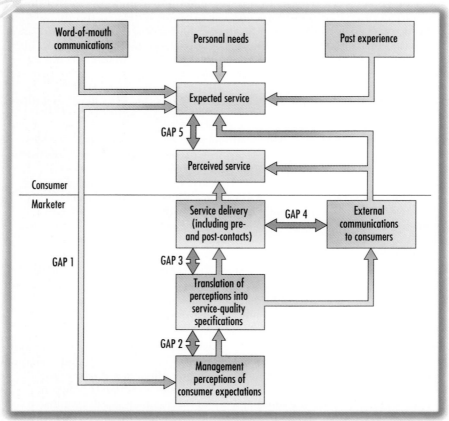

1. *Gap between consumer expectation and management perception:* Management does not always perceive correctly what customers want. Hospital administrators may think that patients want better food, but patients may be more concerned with nurse responsiveness.

2. *Gap between management perception and service-quality specification:* Management might correctly perceive the customers' wants but not set a specified performance standard. Hospital administrators may tell the nurses to give "fast" service without specifying it quantitatively.

3. *Gap between service-quality specifications and service delivery:* Service personnel might be poorly trained, or incapable or unwilling to meet the standard. Or they may be held to conflicting standards, such as taking time to listen to customers and serving them fast.

4. *Gap between service delivery and external communications:* Customer expectations are affected by statements made by company representatives and ads. If a hospital brochure shows an attractive, modern room, but the patient finds an older, unappealing room, external communications will have distorted the customer's expectations.

5. *Gap between perceived service and expected service:* This gap occurs when the consumer misperceives the service quality. The physician may keep visiting the patient to show care, but the patient may interpret this as an indication that something really is wrong.

In addressing these gaps and pursuing service quality, well-managed service companies share the following common practices: a strategic concept, a history of top-management commitment to quality, high standards, systems for monitoring service performance and customer complaints, and an emphasis on employee satisfaction.

Strategic Concept
Top service companies are "customer obsessed." These firms have a clear sense of their target customers and their needs, and they have developed a distinctive strategy for satisfying these needs. Cleveland-based Progressive Insurance, for example, knows its customers want to get their auto accident claims processed and paid as quickly as possible. Thus, its service strategy focuses on expediting claims handling. The company now has a fleet of claims adjusters ready to rush to the scene of any auto accident in their territory. There, the adjusters record all of the information they need and often settle claims on the spot.[21]

Top-Management Commitment
Market-leading companies such as Marriott, Disney, and McDonald's have thorough commitments to service quality. Every month, their management looks not only at financial performance but also at service performance. Top-management commitment can be demonstrated in various ways. Founder Sam Walton of Wal-Mart required the following employee pledge: "I solemnly swear and declare that every customer that comes within 10 feet of me, I will smile, look them in the eye, and greet them, so help me Sam." To reinforce its corporate-wide commitment to service quality, L.L. Bean's management has tacked up a "What is a Customer?" poster in every office (see Chapter 2).

High Standards
The best service providers set high service-quality standards. Swissair, for example, aims at having 96 percent or more of its passengers rate its service as good or superior. Citibank aims to answer phone calls within 10 seconds and customer letters within 2 days. Still, service standards must be set appropriately high. A 98 percent accuracy standard may sound good, but it would result in FedEx losing 64,000 packages a day, 10 misspelled words on each page, 400,000 misfilled prescriptions daily, and unsafe

drinking water 8 days a year. Companies can be distinguished between those offering "merely good" service and those offering "breakthrough" service aiming at 100 percent defect-free service.[22]

Monitoring Systems

Top firms regularly audit service performance, both their own and their competitors'. They use a number of measurement devices: comparison shopping, ghost shopping, customer surveys, suggestion and complaint forms, service-audit teams, and letters to the president. General Electric sends out 700,000 response cards a year asking households to rate its service people's performance; Citibank checks continuously on measures of ART (accuracy, responsiveness, and timeliness). RedEnvelope Gifts Online, an on-line retailer specializing in upscale gifts, analyzes how many of its orders were correctly filled, how many were shipped on time, and how many orders were returned by customers.[23]

When designing customer feedback mechanisms, service marketers need to ask the right questions, as United Parcel Service (UPS) discovered. UPS always assumed that on-time delivery was its customers' paramount concern, and based its definition of quality on the results of time-and-motion studies. To get packages to customers faster, UPS would factor in such details as how long it took elevators to open and how long it took people to answer their doorbells. Accordingly, UPS's surveys included questions about whether customers were pleased with delivery time and whether they thought the company could be any speedier. Yet, when the company began asking broader questions about service improvements, it discovered that what customers wanted most was more face-to-face contact with drivers. If drivers were less hurried and would answer questions, customers might get practical advice on shipping. UPS has now taken service a step further, allowing customers to track their UPS shipments and deliveries through its Web site (www.ups.com), where customers can also order shipping supplies and request parcel pick-up.[24]

Satisfying Customer Complaints

Studies of customer dissatisfaction show that although customers are dissatisfied with their purchases about 25 percent of the time, only about 5 percent complain. The other 95 percent either feel that complaining is not worth the effort, or that they don't know how or to whom to complain. Of the 5 percent who complain, only about half report a satisfactory problem resolution. Yet the need to resolve a customer problem in a satisfactory manner is critical. On average, a satisfied customer tells three people about a good product experience, but the average dissatisfied customer gripes to 11 people. If each of them tells still other people, the number of people exposed to bad word of mouth may grow exponentially.

Toys 'R' Us found this out recently when it failed to deliver toys ordered through its Web site (www.toysrus.com) in time for Christmas. Even though the retailer offered $100 gift certificates to make up for the inconvenience, so many customers were outraged by the delivery problems that the situation made national news and led to a class-action lawsuit.[25]

Nonetheless, customers whose complaints are satisfactorily resolved often become more company-loyal than customers who were never dissatisfied. About 34 percent of customers who register major complaints will buy again from the company if their complaint is resolved, and this number rises to 52 percent for minor complaints. If the complaint is resolved quickly, between 52 percent (major complaints) and 95 percent (minor complaints) will buy again from the company.[26]

Tax and Brown have found that companies that encourage disappointed customers to complain—and also empower employees to remedy the situation on the spot—achieve higher revenues and greater profits than companies that do not have a systematic approach for addressing service failures.[27] They also found that companies that are effective at resolving complaints:

➤ Develop hiring criteria and training programs that take into account employees' service-recovery role.

➤ Develop guidelines for service recovery that focus on achieving fairness and customer satisfaction.

➤ Remove barriers that make it difficult for customers to complain, while developing effective response systems. Pizza Hut prints its toll-free number on all pizza boxes. When a customer complains, Pizza Hut sends voice mail to the store manager, who must call the customer within 48 hours and resolve the complaint.

➤ Maintain customer and product databases that let the company analyze types and sources of complaints and adjust its policies accordingly.

Satisfying Both Employees and Customers

Excellently managed service companies believe that employee relations will affect customer relations. In these firms, management carries out internal marketing and provides employee support and rewards for good performance. In addition, management regularly audits employee job satisfaction. Rosenbluth and Peters, in *The Customer Comes Second,* go so far as to say that the company's employees, not the company's customers, have to be made number one if the company hopes to truly satisfy its customers.[28]

The Safeway supermarket chain found this out when it instituted a customer-friendly policy that actually caused stress for many of its employees. Its Superior Service program mandates employee friendliness toward customers, with rules such as: Make eye contact with all customers, smile, and greet each customer. To ensure compliance, the store employs "mystery shoppers" who secretly grade workers. Those who are graded "poor" are sent to a training program to learn how to be friendlier. Although surveys show that customers are pleased with the program, many employees have admitted being stressed out and several have quit over the plan. Disgruntled workers complain that they must override their own instincts in favor of the corporate friendliness formula. For instance, employees are required to greet harried customers whose body language tells workers that they want to be left alone. The program has set off a spirited debate on the Internet over false-versus-real friendliness. At one Internet discussion group titled "Forced Smiles at Safeway," opinion ran 2-to-1 against the program.[29]

Managing Productivity

Service firms are under great pressure to keep costs down and increase productivity. There are seven approaches to improving service productivity:

1. Have service providers work more skillfully. Top service companies such as Starbucks go out of their way to hire and foster more skillful workers through better selection and training.

2. Increase the quantity of service by surrendering some quality. Doctors working for some HMOs have moved toward handling more patients and giving less time to each patient.

3. Industrialize the service by adding equipment and standardizing production. Levitt recommended that companies adopt a "manufacturing attitude" toward producing services as represented by McDonald's assembly-line approach to fast-food retailing, culminating in the "technological hamburger."[30]

4. Reduce or make obsolete the need for a service by inventing a product solution, the way carpet-cleaning services offer stain-removing products for consumers to use on their own.

5. Design a more effective service. For example, hiring paralegal workers reduces the need for more expensive legal professionals.

6. Present customers with incentives to substitute their own labor for company labor. Customers of iPrint (www.iprint.com) save at least 25 percent by designing, inputting, and proofreading the content of their printing jobs before submitting their orders through iPrint's Web site.[31]

7. Use technology to give better customer service and make service workers more productive. Companies, such as Cisco Systems, that use their Web sites to empower customers can lessen workloads, capture valuable customer data, and increase the value of their businesses. Cisco's on-line Knowledge Base of Frequently Asked Questions (FAQs) allows customers to quickly find answers to questions without talking to any employees. As a result, Cisco cut the number of customer calls by 70 percent or 50,000 calls a month, saving $10 million a month.[32]

MANAGING PRODUCT SUPPORT SERVICES

Although service industries are an important part of the economy, a growing number of product-based industries are also offering a service bundle. Manufacturers of equipment such as small appliances, computers, tractors, and airplanes generally have to provide product support services. In fact, product support service is becoming a major battleground for competitive advantage. Some equipment companies, such as Caterpillar Tractor and John Deere, make over 50 percent of their profits from these services. In the global marketplace, companies that make a good product but provide poor local service support are seriously disadvantaged. This is why Subaru contracted to use the Australian Volkswagen dealer network to provide parts and service when it began selling its autos in that market.

To design the best service support program, a manufacturer must identify and prioritize the services its customers value most. In general, customers worry about three things:[33]

➤ *Reliability and failure frequency.* Customers buy with an expectation of reliability. A farmer may tolerate a combine that breaks down once a year, but not more often. Similarly, eBay's on-line auction customers are concerned when the Web site is unavailable or experiencing problems.

➤ *Downtime duration.* The longer the downtime, the higher the cost, which is why customers count on the seller's ability to fix the product (laptop, minivan) quickly or at least provide a loaner.[34]

➤ *Out-of-pocket costs of maintenance and repair.* Customers are concerned with the amount they will have to spend on regular maintenance and repair costs (such as replacement batteries for laptops).

A buyer considers all of these factors when choosing a vendor. As part of the decision process, the buyer tries to estimate the *life-cycle cost,* which is the product's purchase cost plus the discounted cost of maintenance and repair less the discounted salvage value. Smart companies therefore consider the costs and the options for diffusing customer worries when designing presale and postsale support services.

Presale Service Strategy

Before any sale can be made, the marketer has to design an appealing and competitive service offer that will attract customers. In the case of expensive equipment, such as medical equipment, manufacturers offer *facilitating services* such as installation, repairs, and financing. They may also add *value-augmenting services*. Look at Herman Miller, a leading office-furniture company that works hard to understand and then deliver what its business customers value. Along with quality products, the company offers: (1) 5-year product warranties; (2) quality audits after installation; (3) guaranteed move-in dates; (4) trade-in allowances on furniture systems products; and (5) easy on-line ordering.

A manufacturer can offer and charge for enhanced product support services in different ways. One specialty organic chemical company provides a standard offering plus a basic level of services. If the customer wants additional services, it can pay extra or increase its annual purchases to a higher level, in which case additional services would be included. In a variation on this, Baxter Healthcare offers strategic customers bonus points (called "Baxter dollars") in proportion to how much they buy. They can use the bonus points to trade for different additional services. As another alternative, companies such as Compaq and IBM sell add-on service contracts in various lengths so customers can choose the service level they want beyond the basic service package.

Postsale Service Strategy

In providing postsale service, most companies progress through a series of stages. Manufacturers usually start out by running their own parts and service department, because they want to stay close to their products and learn about any problems right away. They also find it expensive and time-consuming to train others. Often, they discover that they can make good money running the parts-and-service business—and, if they are the only supplier of certain parts, they can charge a premium price. In fact, many equipment manufacturers price their equipment low and compensate by charging high prices for parts and service. This explains why competitors sometimes manufacture the same or similar parts and sell them to customers or intermediaries for less.

Over time, manufacturers—especially those who expand into international markets—switch more maintenance and repair services to authorized distributors and dealers. These intermediaries are closer to customers, operate in more locations, and can offer quicker service. Manufacturers still make a profit on the parts but leave the servicing profit to their intermediaries. Still later, independent service firms emerge. Over 40 percent of auto-service work is now done outside franchised automobile dealerships, by independent garages and chains such as Midas Muffler and Sears. Independent service organizations have sprung up to service computers, telecommunications products, and other items, typically offering lower price or faster service than offered by the manufacturer or authorized intermediaries.

Ultimately, some large business customers may prefer to handle their own maintenance and repair services. A company with several hundred personal computers, printers, and related equipment might find it cheaper to have its own service personnel on site. These companies typically press the manufacturer for a lower product price because they are providing their own services.

Major Trends in Customer Service

Service remains a critical component for product marketers in today's dynamic, interconnected global marketplace. Lele has noted the following major trends in the customer service area:[35]

1. Equipment manufacturers are building more reliable and more easily fixable equipment. One reason is the shift from electromechanical equipment to electronic equipment, which has fewer breakdowns and is more repairable. Companies are adding modularity and disposability to facilitate self-servicing by customers.

2. Customers are becoming more sophisticated about buying product support services and are pressing for "services unbundling." They want separate prices for each service element and the right to select just the elements they want.

3. Customers increasingly dislike having to deal with a multitude of service providers that handle different types of equipment. In response, some third-party service organizations have begun servicing a greater range of equipment.[36]

4. *Service contracts* (also called *extended warranties*), in which sellers agree to provide free maintenance and repair services for a specified period of time at a specified contract price, may diminish in importance. Some new car warranties now cover 100,000 miles before servicing. The increase in disposable or never-fail equipment makes customers less inclined to pay from 2 percent to 10 percent of the purchase price every year for a service.

5. Customer service choices are increasing rapidly, and this is holding down prices and profits on service. Equipment manufacturers increasingly have to figure out how to make money on their equipment independent of service contracts.

Add to these trends the now commonplace use of the Internet to deliver service, advice, and maintenance or repair information at any hour to any customer at any location—and it is clear that the most successful companies will be those that marry high-tech capabilities with customizable, high-touch customer service. Such top-quality customer service comes at a price, of course; pricing strategies and programs for goods and services will be discussed in the next chapter.

EXECUTIVE SUMMARY

A service is any act or performance that one party offers to another that is essentially intangible and does not result in the ownership of anything. Its production may or may not be tied to a tangible product. As the United States has moved increasingly toward a service economy, marketers have become more interested in the special challenges involved in marketing services.

Services are intangible, inseparable, variable, and perishable. Each characteristic poses challenges and requires certain strategies. Marketers must find ways to give tangibility to intangibles, to increase the productivity of service providers, to increase and standardize the quality of the service provided, and to match the supply of services during peak and nonpeak periods with market demand.

Service marketing strategy covers three additional Ps: people, physical evidence, and process. Successful services marketing calls not only for external marketing, but also for internal marketing to motivate employees and interactive marketing to emphasize both "high-tech" and "high-touch" elements.

Because services are generally high in experience and credence qualities, there is more risk in their purchase. The service organization therefore faces three tasks in marketing: (1) It must differentiate its offer, delivery, or image; (2) it must manage service quality in order to meet or exceed customers' expectations; and (3) it must manage worker productivity by getting its employees to work more skillfully, increasing the quantity of service by surrendering some quality, industrializing the service, inventing new product solutions, designing more effective services, presenting customers with incentives to substitute their own labor for company labor, or using technology to save time and money.

Even product-based companies must provide support services for their customers. To provide the best support, a manufacturer must identify and prioritize the services that customers value most. The service mix includes both presale services (such as facilitating services and value-augmenting services) and postsale services (customer service departments, repair and maintenance services).

NOTES

1. Ronald Henkoff, "Service Is Everybody's Business," *Fortune,* June 27, 1994, pp. 48–60.
2. See G. Lynn Shostack, "Breaking Free from Product Marketing," *Journal of Marketing,* April 1977, pp. 73–80; Leonard L. Berry, "Services Marketing Is Different," *Business,* May-June 1980, pp. 24–30; Eric Langeard, John E. G. Bateson, Christopher H. Lovelock, and Pierre Eiglier, *Services Marketing: New Insights from Consumers and Managers* (Cambridge, MA: Marketing Science Institute, 1981); Karl Albrecht and Ron Zemke, *Service America! Doing Business in the New Economy* (Homewood, IL: Dow Jones-Irwin, 1986); Karl Albrecht, *At America's Service* (Homewood, IL: Dow Jones-Irwin, 1988); Benjamin Scheider and David E. Bowen, *Winning the Service Game* (Boston: Harvard Business School Press, 1995); and Leonard L. Berry, *Discovering the Soul of Service* (New York: Free Press, 1999).
3. Sam Zuckerman, "E-Trade Loses $5.2 Million Despite Late Business Surge," *San Francisco Chronicle,* January 20, 2000, www.sfgate.com.
4. John R. Johnson, "Service at a Price," *Industrial Distribution,* May 1998, pp. 91–94.
5. Reed Abelson, "Hints of Change at GE Capital as Financial Companies Lose Favor," *New York Times,* October 2, 1998, p. D1; Laura Covill, "Siemens the Financial Engineer," *Euromoney,* August 1998, pp. 65–66.
6. See Theodore Levitt, "Marketing Intangible Products and Product Intangibles," *Harvard Business Review,* May-June 1981, pp. 94–102; and Berry, "Services Marketing Is Different."
7. Geoffrey Brewer, "Selling an Intangible," *Sales & Marketing Management,* January 1998, pp. 52–58.
8. Ibid.
9. See W. Earl Sasser, "Match Supply and Demand in Service Industries," *Harvard Business Review,* November-December 1976, pp. 133–40.
10. See B. H. Booms and M. J. Bitner, "Marketing Strategies and Organizational Structures for Service Firms," in *Marketing of Services,* eds. J. Donnelly and W. R. George (Chicago: American Marketing Association, 1981), pp. 47–51.
11. Keaveney has identified more than 800 critical behaviors of service firms that cause customers to switch services. These behaviors fit into eight categories ranging from price, inconvenience, and core service failure to service encounter failure, failed employee response to service failures, and ethical problems. See Susan M. Keaveney, "Customer Switching Behavior in Service Industries: An Exploratory Study," *Journal of Marketing,* April 1995, pp. 71–82. See also Michael D. Hartline and O. C. Ferrell, "The Management of Customer-Contact Service Employees: An Empirical Investigation," *Journal of Marketing,* October 1996, pp. 52–70; Lois A. Mohr, Mary Jo Bitner, and Bernard H. Booms, "Critical Service Encounters: The Employee's Viewpoint," *Journal of Marketing,* October 1994, pp. 95–106; Linda L. Price, Eric J. Arnould, and Patrick Tierney, "Going to Extremes: Managing Service Encounters and Assessing Provider Performance," *Journal of Marketing,* April 1995, pp. 83–97.
12. Christian Gronroos, "A Service Quality Model and Its Marketing Implications," *European Journal of Marketing* 18, no. 4 (1984): 36–44. Gronroos's model is one of the most thoughtful contributions to service-marketing strategy.
13. Leonard Berry, "Big Ideas in Services Marketing," *Journal of Consumer Marketing,* Spring 1986, pp. 47–51. See also Walter E. Greene, Gary D. Walls, and Larry J. Schrest, "Internal Marketing: The Key to External Marketing Success," *Journal of Services Marketing* 8, no. 4

(1994): 5–13; John R. Hauser, Duncan I. Simester, and Birger Wernerfelt, "Internal Customers and Internal Suppliers," *Journal of Marketing Research*, August 1996, pp. 268–80.

14. Gronroos, "A Service Quality Model," pp. 38–39.

15. See Philip Kotler and Paul N. Bloom, *Marketing Professional Services* (Upper Saddle River, NJ: Prentice-Hall, 1984).

16. Laurie J. Flynn, "Eating Your Young," *Context*, Summer 1998, pp. 45–47; Louise Lee, "Can Schwab Hang On to Its Heavy Hitters?" *Business Week*, January 31, 2000, p. 46; see also Mark Schwanhausser, "Schwab Evolves in the Web Era," *Chicago Tribune*, October 12, 1998, Business Section, p. 10; and John Evan Frook, "Web Proves It's Good for Business," *Internet Week*, December 21, 1998, p. 15.

17. See Valarie A. Zeithaml, "How Consumer Evaluation Processes Differ between Goods and Services," in Donnelly and George, eds., *Marketing of Services*, pp. 186–90.

18. Amy Ostrom and Dawn Iacobucci, "Consumer Trade-offs and the Evaluation of Services," *Journal of Marketing*, January 1995, pp. 17–28.

19. Suzanne Bidlake, "John Crewe, American Express Blue Card," *Advertising Age International*, December 14, 1998, p. 10; Sue Beenstock, "Blue Blooded," *Marketing*, June 4, 1998, p. 14; Pamela Sherrid, "A New Class Act at AMEX," *U.S. News & World Report*, June 23, 1997, pp. 39–40.

20. A. Parasuraman, Valarie A. Zeithaml, and Leonard L. Berry, "A Conceptual Model of Service Quality and Its Implications for Future Research," *Journal of Marketing*, Fall 1985, pp. 41–50. See also Susan J. Devlin and H. K. Dong, "Service Quality from the Customers' Perspective," *Marketing Research: A Magazine of Management & Applications*, Winter 1994, pp. 4–13; William Boulding, Ajay Kalra, and Richard Staelin, "A Dynamic Process Model of Service Quality: From Expectations to Behavioral Intentions," *Journal of Marketing Research*, February 1993, pp. 7–27.

21. Ian C. MacMillan and Rita Gunther McGrath, "Discovering New Points of Differentiation," *Harvard Business Review*, July-August 1997, pp. 133–45.

22. See James L. Heskett, W. Earl Sasser, Jr., and Christopher W. L. Hart, *Service Breakthroughs* (New York: Free Press, 1990).

23. Dan Brekke, "The Future Is Now—or Never," *New York Times Magazine*, January 23, 2000, pp. 30–33.

24. David Greising, "Quality: How to Make It Pay," *Business Week*, August 8, 1994, pp. 54–59.

25. "Hagens Berman Announces Class Action Lawsuit Against Toysrus.com; Class Action Calls Toysrus.com 'The E-Grinch Who Stole Christmas,'" *Business Wire*, January 12, 2000; Wendy Zellner, "Shop Till the Ball Drops," *Business Week*, January 10, 2000, pp. 42–44.

26. See John Goodman, Technical Assistance Research Program (TARP), *U.S. Office of Consumer Affairs Study on Complaint Handling in America*, 1986; Albrecht and Zemke, *Service America!;* Berry and Parasuraman, *Marketing Services;* Roland T. Rust, Bala Subramanian, and Mark Wells, "Making Complaints a Management Tool," *Marketing Management* 1, no. 3 (1992): 41–45; Stephen S. Tax, Stephen W. Brown, and Murali Chandrashekaran, "Customer Evaluations of Service Complaint Experiences: Implications for Relationship Marketing," *Journal of Marketing*, April 1998, pp. 60–76.

27. Stephen S. Tax and Stephen W. Brown, "Recovering and Learning from Service Failure," *Sloan Management Review*, Fall 1998, pp. 75–88.

28. See Hal F. Rosenbluth and Diane McFerrin Peters, *The Customer Comes Second* (New York: William Morrow, 1992).

29. Kirstin Downey Grimsley, "Service with a Forced Smile; Safeway's Courtesy Campaign Also Elicits Some Frowns," *Washington Post*, October 18, 1998, p. A1.

Designing Pricing Strategies and Programs

In this chapter, we will address the following questions:

■ How should a company price a new good or service?

■ How should the price be adapted to meet varying circumstances and opportunities?

■ When should the company initiate a price change, and how should it respond to competitive price changes?

All for-profit organizations and many nonprofit organizations set prices on their goods or services. Whether the price is called *rent* (for an apartment), *tuition* (for education), *fare* (for travel), or *interest* (for borrowed money), the concept is the same. Throughout most of history, prices were set by negotiation between buyers and sellers. Setting one price for all buyers arose with the development of large-scale retailing at the end of the nineteenth century, when Woolworth's and other stores followed a "strictly one-price policy" because they carried so many items and had so many employees.

Now, 100 years later, technology is taking us back to an era of negotiated pricing. The Internet, corporate networks, and wireless setups are linking people, machines, and companies around the globe, connecting sellers and buyers as never before. Web sites like Compare.Net and PriceScan.com allow buyers to compare products and prices quickly and easily. On-line auction sites like eBay.com and Onsale.com make it easy for buyers and sellers to negotiate prices on thousands of items. At the same time, new technologies are allowing sellers to collect detailed data about customers' buying habits, preferences—even spending limits—so they can tailor their products and prices.[1]

In the entire marketing mix, price is the one element that produces revenue; the others produce costs. Price is also one of the most flexible elements: It can be changed quickly, unlike product features and channel commitments. Although price competition is a major problem facing companies, many do not handle pricing well. The most common mistakes are these: Pricing is too cost-oriented; price is not revised often enough to capitalize on market changes; price is set independent of the rest of the marketing mix rather than as an intrinsic element of market-positioning strategy; and price is not varied enough for different product items, market segments, and purchase occasions.

Figure 12.1   Nine Price-Quality Strategies

		Price		
		High	Medium	Low
Product Quality	High	1. Premium strategy	2. High-value strategy	3. Super-value strategy
	Medium	4. Overcharging strategy	5. Medium-value strategy	6. Good-value strategy
	Low	7. Rip-off strategy	8. False economy strategy	9. Economy strategy

SETTING THE PRICE

A firm must set a price for the first time when it develops a new product, introduces its regular product into a new distribution channel or geographical area, and enters bids on new contract work. Price is also a key element used to support a product's quality positioning, as described in Chapter 9. Because a firm, in developing its strategy, must decide where to position its product on price and quality, there can be competition between price-quality segments (see Figure 12.1).

In setting a product's price, marketers follow a six-step procedure: (1) selecting the pricing objective; (2) determining demand; (3) estimating costs; (4) analyzing competitors' costs, prices, and offers; (5) selecting a pricing method; and (6) selecting the final price (see Figure 12.2).

Step 1: Selecting the Pricing Objective

A company can pursue any of five major objectives through pricing:

➤ *Survival.* This is a short-term objective that is appropriate only for companies that are plagued with overcapacity, intense competition, or changing consumer wants. As long as prices cover variable costs and some fixed costs, the company will be able to remain in business.

➤ *Maximum current profit.* To maximize current profits, companies estimate the demand and costs associated with alternative prices and then choose the price that produces maximum current profit, cash flow, or return on investment. However, by emphasizing current profits, the company may sacrifice long-run performance by

Figure 12.2   Setting Pricing Policy

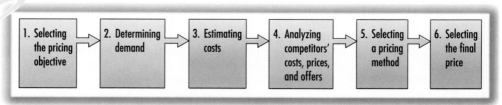

ignoring the effects of other marketing-mix variables, competitors' reactions, and legal restraints on price.

➤ *Maximum market share.* Firms such as Texas Instruments choose this objective because they believe that higher sales volume will lead to lower unit costs and higher long-run profit. With this *market-penetration pricing,* the firms set the lowest price, assuming the market is price sensitive. This is appropriate when (1) the market is highly price sensitive, so a low price stimulates market growth; (2) production and distribution costs fall with accumulated production experience; and (3) a low price discourages competition.

➤ *Maximum market skimming.* Many companies favor setting high prices to "skim" the market. This objective makes sense under the following conditions: (1) A sufficient number of buyers have a high current demand; (2) the unit costs of producing a small volume are not so high that they cancel the advantage of charging what the traffic will bear; (3) the high initial price does not attract more competitors to the market; and (4) the high price communicates the image of a superior product.

➤ *Product-quality leadership.* Companies such as Maytag that aim to be product-quality leaders will offer premium products at premium prices. Because they offer top quality plus innovative features that deliver wanted benefits, these firms can charge more. Maytag can charge $800 for its European-style washers—double what most other washers cost—because, as its ads point out, the appliances use less water and electricity and prolong the life of clothing by being less abrasive. Here, Maytag's strategy is to encourage buyers to trade up to new models before their existing appliances wear out.[2]

Nonprofit and public organizations may adopt other pricing objectives. A university aims for partial cost recovery, knowing that it must rely on private gifts and public grants to cover the remaining costs, while a nonprofit theater company prices its productions to fill the maximum number of seats. As another example, a social services agency may set prices geared to the varying incomes of clients.

Step 2: Determining Demand

Each price will lead to a different level of demand and, therefore, will have a different impact on a company's marketing objectives. The relationship between alternative prices and the resulting current demand is captured in a *demand curve.* Normally, demand and price are inversely related: The higher the price, the lower the demand. In the case of prestige goods, however, the demand curve sometimes slopes upward because some consumers take the higher price to signify a better product. Still, if the price is too high, the level of demand may fall.

Price Sensitivity

The demand curve shows the market's probable purchase quantity at alternative prices, summing the reactions of many individuals who have different price sensitivities. The first step in estimating demand is to understand what affects price sensitivity. Nagle says there is less price sensitivity when:

➤ The product is more distinctive,

➤ Buyers are less aware of substitutes,

➤ Buyers cannot easily compare the quality of substitutes,

➤ The expenditure is a lower part of buyer's total income,

➤ The expenditure is small compared to the total cost of the end product,

➤ Part of the cost is borne by another party,

➤ The product is used in conjunction with assets previously bought,

➤ The product is assumed to have more quality, prestige, or exclusiveness, and

➤ Buyers cannot store the product.[3]

A number of forces, such as deregulation and instant price comparisons that are available over the Internet, have turned products into commodities in the eyes of consumers and increased their price sensitivity. More than ever, companies need to understand the price sensitivity of their target market and the trade-offs that people are willing to make between price and product characteristics. Even in the energy marketplace, where you would think that a kilowatt is a kilowatt is a kilowatt, some utility companies are buying power, branding it, marketing it, and providing unique services to customers.

Vermont-based GreenMountain.com for example, is working hard to differentiate its energy products. Through extensive marketing research, the energy firm uncovered a large market of prospects who not only were concerned with the environment, but also were willing to pay more to protect it. Because GreenMountain.com is a "green" power provider—a large percentage of its power is hydroelectric—customers can help ease the environmental burden by purchasing its power. This differentiation helps the firm compete against "cheaper" brands that focus on price-sensitive consumers.[4]

Estimating Demand Curves

Companies can use one of three basic methods to estimate their demand curves. The first involves statistically analyzing past prices, quantities sold, and other factors to estimate their relationships. However, building a model and fitting the data with the proper techniques calls for considerable skill.

The second approach is to conduct price experiments, as when Bennett and Wilkinson systematically varied the prices of several products sold in a discount store and observed the results.[5] An alternative here is to charge different prices in similar territories to see how sales are affected.

The third approach is to ask buyers to state how many units they would buy at different proposed prices.[6] One problem with this method is that buyers might understate their purchase intentions at higher prices to discourage the company from setting higher prices.

In measuring the price-demand relationship, the marketer must control for various factors that will influence demand, such as competitive response. Also, if the company changes other marketing-mix factors besides price, the effect of the price change itself will be hard to isolate.[7]

Price Elasticity of Demand

Marketers need to know how responsive, or elastic, demand would be to a change in price. If demand hardly changes with a small change in price, we say the demand is *inelastic*. If demand changes considerably, demand is *elastic*.

Demand is likely to be less elastic when (1) there are few or no substitutes or competitors; (2) buyers do not readily notice the higher price; (3) buyers are slow to change their buying habits and search for lower prices; and (4) buyers think the higher prices are justified by quality differences, normal inflation, and so on. If demand is elastic, sellers will consider lowering the price to produce more total revenue. This makes sense as long as the costs of producing and selling more units do not increase disproportionately.[8]

Price elasticity depends on the magnitude and direction of the contemplated price change. It may be negligible with a small price change and substantial with a large price change; it may differ for a price cut versus a price increase. Finally, long-run price elasticity may differ from short-run elasticity. Buyers may continue to buy from their current supplier after a price increase because they do not notice the increase, or the increase is small, or they are distracted by other concerns, or they find that choosing a new supplier takes time. But they may eventually switch suppliers. The distinction between short-run and long-run elasticity means that sellers will not know the total effect of a price change until time passes.

Step 3: Estimating Costs

While demand sets a ceiling on the price the company can charge for its product, costs set the floor. Every company should charge a price that covers its cost of producing, distributing, and selling the product and provides a fair return for its effort and risk.

Types of Costs and Levels of Production

A company's costs take two forms—fixed and variable. *Fixed costs* (also known as *overhead*) are costs that do not vary with production or sales revenue, such as payments for rent, heat, interest, salaries, and other bills that must be paid regardless of output.

In contrast, *variable costs* vary directly with the level of production. For example, each calculator produced by Texas Instruments (TI) involves a cost of plastic, micro-processing chips, packaging, and the like. These costs tend to be constant per unit produced, but they are called variable because their total varies with the number of units produced.

Total costs consist of the sum of the fixed and variable costs for any given level of production. *Average cost* is the cost per unit at that level of production; it is equal to total costs divided by production. Management wants to charge a price that will at least cover the total production costs at a given level of production.

To price intelligently, management needs to know how its costs vary with different levels of production. A firm's cost per unit is high if only a few units are produced every day, but as production increases, fixed costs are spread over a higher level of production results in each unit, bringing the average cost down. At some point, however, higher production will lead to higher average cost because the plant becomes inefficient (due to problems such as machines breaking down more often). By calculating costs for different-sized plants, a company can identify the optimal plant size and production level to achieve economies of scale and bring down the average cost.

Accumulated Production

Suppose TI runs a plant that produces 3,000 calculators per day. As TI gains experience producing calculators, its methods improve. Workers learn shortcuts, materials flow more smoothly, and procurement costs fall. The result, as Figure 12.3 shows, is that average cost falls with accumulated production experience. Thus, the average cost of producing the first 100,000 hand calculators is $10 per calculator. When the company has produced the first 200,000 calculators, the average cost has fallen to $9. After its accumulated production experience doubles again to 400,000, the average cost is $8. This decline in the average cost with accumulated production experience is called the *experience curve* or *learning curve*.

Now suppose TI competes against two other firms (A and B) in this industry. TI is the lowest-cost producer at $8, having produced 400,000 units in the past. If all three firms sell the calculator for $10, TI makes $2 profit per unit, A makes $1 per unit, and B breaks even. The smart move for TI would be to lower its price to $9 to drive B out of

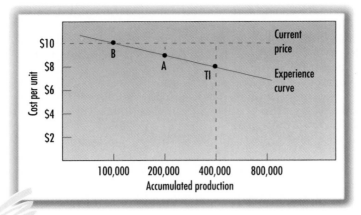

Figure 12.3   The Experience Curve

the market; even A will consider leaving. Then TI will pick up the business that would have gone to B (and possibly A). Furthermore, price-sensitive customers will enter the market at the lower price. As production increases beyond 400,000 units, TI's costs will drop even more, restoring its profits even at a price of $9. TI has used this aggressive pricing strategy repeatedly to gain market share and drive others out of the industry.

Experience-curve pricing is risky because aggressive pricing may give the product a cheap image. This strategy also assumes that the competitors are weak and not willing to fight. Finally, the strategy may lead the firm into building more plants to meet demand while a competitor innovates a lower-cost technology and enjoys lower costs, leaving the leader stuck with old technology.

Differentiated Marketing Offers

Today's companies try to adapt their offers and terms to different buyers. Thus, a manufacturer will negotiate different terms with different retail chains, meaning the costs and profits will differ with each chain. To estimate the real profitability of dealing with different retailers, the manufacturer needs to use *activity-based cost (ABC) accounting* instead of *standard cost accounting.*[9]

ABC accounting tries to identify the real costs associated with serving different customers. Both the variable costs and the overhead costs must be tagged back to each customer. Companies that fail to measure their costs correctly are not measuring their profit correctly, and they are likely to misallocate their marketing effort. Identifying the true costs arising in a customer relationship also enables a company to explain its charges better to the customer.

Target Costing

We have seen that costs change with production scale and experience. They can also change as a result of a concentrated effort by the company's designers, engineers, and purchasing agents to reduce them. Many Japanese firms use a method called *target costing.*[10] First, they use market research to establish a new product's desired functions, then they determine the price at which the product will sell given its appeal and competitors' prices. They deduct the desired profit margin from this price, and this leaves the target cost they must achieve.

Next, the firms examine each cost element—design, engineering, manufacturing, sales—and break them down into further components, looking for ways to reengineer components, eliminate functions, and bring down supplier costs. The objective is to bring the final cost projections into the target cost range. If they cannot succeed, they may decide against developing the product because it could not sell for the target price and make the target profit. When they can succeed, profits are likely to follow.

Step 4: Analyzing Competitors' Costs, Prices, and Offers

Within the range of possible prices determined by market demand and company costs, the firm must take into account its competitors' costs, prices, and possible price reactions. If the firm's offer is similar to a major competitor's offer, then the firm will have to price close to the competitor or lose sales. If the firm's offer is inferior, it will not be able to charge more than the competitor charges. If the firm's offer is superior, it can charge more than does the competitor—remembering, however, that competitors might change their prices in response at any time.

Step 5: Selecting a Pricing Method

The three Cs—the customers' demand schedule, the cost function, and competitors' prices—are major considerations in setting price (see Figure 12.4). First, costs set a floor to the price. Second, competitors' prices and the price of substitutes provide an orienting point. Third, customers' assessment of unique product features establishes the ceiling price. Companies must therefore select a pricing method that includes one or more of these considerations. We will examine six price-setting methods: markup pricing, target-return pricing, perceived-value pricing, value pricing, going-rate pricing, and sealed-bid pricing.

Markup Pricing

The most elementary pricing method is to add a standard markup to the product's cost. Construction companies do this when they submit job bids by estimating the total project cost and adding a standard markup for profit. Similarly, lawyers and accountants typically price by adding a standard markup on their time and costs.

Suppose a toaster manufacturer has the following costs and sales expectations:

Variable cost per unit	$ 10
Fixed cost	300,000
Expected unit sales	50,000

Figure 12.4   The Three Cs Model for Price Setting

The manufacturer's unit cost is given by:

$$\text{Unit cost} = \text{variable cost} + \frac{\text{fixed costs}}{\text{unit sales}} = \$10 + \frac{\$300,000}{50,000} = \$16$$

If the manufacturer wants to earn a 20 percent markup on sales, its markup price is given by:

$$\text{Markup price} = \frac{\text{unit cost}}{(1 - \text{desired return on sales})} = \frac{\$16}{1 - 0.2} = \$20$$

Here, the manufacturer charges dealers $20 per toaster and makes a profit of $4 per unit. If the dealers want to earn 50 percent on their selling price, they will mark up the toaster to $40. This is equivalent to a cost markup of 100 percent.

Does the use of standard markups make logical sense? Generally, no. Any pricing method that ignores current demand, perceived value, and competition is not likely to lead to the optimal price. Markup pricing works only if the marked-up price actually brings in the expected level of sales.

Companies that introduce a new product often price it high, hoping to recover their costs as rapidly as possible. But a high-markup strategy could be fatal if a competitor is pricing low. This happened to Philips, the Dutch electronics manufacturer, in pricing its videodisc players. Philips wanted to make a profit on each videodisc player. Meanwhile, Japanese competitors priced low and succeeded in building their market share rapidly, which in turn pushed down their costs substantially.

Markup pricing remains popular for a number of reasons. First, sellers can determine costs much more easily than they can estimate demand. By tying the price to cost, sellers simplify the pricing task. Second, when all firms in the industry use this pricing method, prices tend to be similar, which minimizes price competition. Third, many people feel that cost-plus pricing is fairer to both buyers and sellers: Sellers do not take advantage of buyers when demand becomes acute, and sellers earn a fair return on investment.

Target-Return Pricing

In *target-return pricing,* the firm determines the price that would yield its target rate of return on investment (ROI). Target pricing is used by many firms, including General Motors, which prices its automobiles to achieve a 15–20 percent ROI.

Suppose the toaster manufacturer in the previous example has invested $1 million and wants to earn a 20 percent return on its invested capital. The target-return price is given by the following formula:

$$\text{Target-return price} = \frac{\text{unit cost} + \text{desired return} \times \text{invested capital}}{\text{unit sales}}$$

$$= \$16 + \frac{.20 \times \$1,000,000}{50,000} = \$20$$

The manufacturer will realize this 20 percent ROI provided its costs and estimated sales turn out to be accurate. But what if sales do not reach 50,000 units? The manufacturer can prepare a *break-even chart* to learn what would happen at other sales levels (Figure 12.5). Note that fixed costs remain the same regardless of sales volume, while variable costs, which are not shown in the figure, rise with volume. Total costs equal the sum of fixed costs and variable costs; the total revenue curve rises with each unit sold.

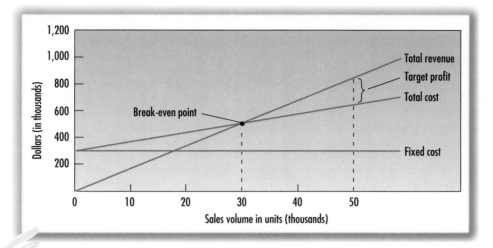

Figure 12.5   Break-Even Chart

According to this break-even chart, the total revenue and total cost curves cross at 30,000 units. This is the *break-even volume*. It can be verified by the following formula:

$$\text{Break-even volume} = \frac{\text{fixed cost}}{\text{price} - \text{variable cost}} = \frac{\$300,000}{\$20-10} = 30,000$$

If the manufacturer sells 50,000 units at $20, it earns a $200,000 profit on its $1 million investment. But much depends on price elasticity and competitors' prices, two elements that are ignored by target-return pricing. In practice, the manufacturer needs to consider different prices and estimate their probable impacts on sales volume and profits. The manufacturer should also search for ways to lower its fixed or variable costs, because lower costs will decrease its required break-even volume.

Perceived-Value Pricing

An increasing number of companies base price on customers' *perceived value*. They see the buyers' perceptions of value, not the seller's cost, as the key to pricing. Then they use the other marketing-mix elements, such as advertising, to build up perceived value in buyers' minds.[11]

For example, when DuPont developed a new synthetic fiber for carpets, it demonstrated to carpet manufacturers that they could afford to pay DuPont as much as $1.40 per pound for the new fiber and still make their target profit. DuPont calls the $1.40 the *value-in-use price*. But pricing the new material at $1.40 per pound would leave the carpet manufacturers indifferent. So DuPont set the price lower than $1.40 to induce carpet manufacturers to adopt the new fiber. In this situation, DuPont used its manufacturing cost only to judge whether there was enough profit to go ahead with the new product.

The key to perceived-value pricing is to determine the market's perception of the offer's value accurately. Sellers with an inflated view of their offer's value will overprice their product, while sellers with an underestimated view will charge less than they could. Market research is therefore needed to establish the market's perception of value as a guide to effective pricing.[12]

Value Pricing

Value pricing is a method in which the company charges a fairly low price for a high-quality offering. Value pricing says that the price should represent a high-value offer to consumers. This is a major trend in the computer industry, which has shifted from charging top dollar for cutting-edge computers to offering basic computers at lower prices. For instance, Monorail Computer started selling PCs in 1996 for as little as $999 to woo price-sensitive buyers. Compaq and others quickly followed suit. More recently, eMachines began selling its PCs for less than $500 without a monitor, targeting the 55 percent of computerless households with annual incomes of $25,000 to $30,000.[13]

Value pricing is not a matter of simply setting lower prices on one's products compared to those of competitors. It is a matter of reengineering the company's operations to become a low-cost producer without sacrificing quality, and lowering prices significantly to attract a large number of value-conscious customers. An important type of value pricing is *everyday low pricing (EDLP)*, which takes place at the retail level. Retailers such as Wal-Mart and Amazon.com use EDLP pricing, posting a constant, everyday low price with few or no temporary price discounts. These constant prices eliminate week-to-week price uncertainty and can be contrasted to the "high-low" pricing of promotion-oriented competitors. In *high-low pricing*, the retailer charges higher prices on an everyday basis but then runs frequent promotions in which prices are temporarily lowered below the EDLP level.[14]

Retailers adopt EDLP for a number of reasons, the most important of which is that constant sales and promotions are costly and erode consumer confidence in the credibility of everyday prices. Consumers also have less time and patience for such time-honored traditions as watching for specials and clipping coupons. Yet promotions are an excellent way to create excitement and draw shoppers. For this reason, EDLP is not a guarantee of success. As supermarkets face heightened competition from store rivals and alternative channels, many are drawing shoppers using a combination of high-low and EDLP strategies, with increased advertising and promotions.[15]

Going-Rate Pricing

In *going-rate pricing*, the firm bases its price largely on competitors' prices. The firm might charge the same, more, or less than its major competitor(s) charges. In oligopolistic industries that sell a commodity such as steel, paper, or fertilizer, firms normally charge the same price. The smaller firms "follow the leader," changing their prices when the market leader's prices change rather than when their own demand or costs change. Some firms may charge a slight premium or slight discount, but they typically preserve the amount of difference. When costs are difficult to measure or competitive response is uncertain, firms feel that the going price represents a good solution, since it seems to reflect the industry's collective wisdom as to the price that will yield a fair return and not jeopardize industrial harmony.

Sealed-Bid Pricing

Competitive-oriented pricing is common when firms submit sealed bids for jobs. In bidding, each firm bases its price on expectations of how competitors will price rather than on a rigid relationship to the firm's own costs or demand. Sealed-bid pricing involves two opposite pulls. The firm wants to win the contract—which means submitting the lowest price—yet it cannot set its price below cost.

To solve this dilemma, the company would estimate the profit and the probability of winning with each price bid. By multiplying the profit by the probability of winning the bid on the basis of that price, the company can calculate the expected profit for each bid. For a firm that makes many bids, this method is a way of playing the odds to achieve maximum profits in the long run. However, firms that bid only occasionally or that badly want to win certain contracts will not find it advantageous to use the expected-profit criterion.

Step 6: Selecting the Final Price

The previous pricing methods narrow the range from which the company selects its final price. In selecting that price, the company must consider additional factors: psychological pricing, the influence of other marketing-mix elements on price, company pricing policies, and the impact of price on other parties.

Psychological Pricing

Many consumers use price as an indicator of quality. Image pricing is especially effective with ego-sensitive products such as perfumes and expensive cars. A $100 bottle of perfume might contain $10 worth of scent, but gift givers pay $100 to communicate their high regard for the receiver. Similarly, price and quality perceptions of cars interact:[16] Higher-priced cars are perceived to possess high quality; higher-quality cars are likewise perceived to be higher priced than they actually are. In general, when information about true quality is unavailable, price acts as a signal of quality.

When looking at a particular product, buyers carry in their minds a *reference price* formed by noticing current prices, past prices, or the buying context. Sellers often manipulate these reference prices. For example, a seller can situate its product among expensive products to imply that it belongs in the same class. Reference-price thinking is also created by stating a high manufacturer's suggested price, by indicating that the product was priced much higher originally, or by pointing to a rival's high price.[17]

Often sellers set prices that end in an odd number, believing that customers who see a television priced at $299 instead of $300 will perceive the price as being in the $200 range rather than the $300 range. Another explanation is that odd endings convey the notion of a discount or bargain, which is why both toysrus.com and etoys.com set prices ending in 99. But if a company wants a high-price image instead of a low-price image, it should avoid the odd-ending tactic.

The Influence of Other Marketing-Mix Elements

The final price must take into account the brand's quality and advertising relative to competition. When Farris and Reibstein examined the relationships among relative price, relative quality, and relative advertising for 227 consumer businesses, they found that brands with average relative quality but high relative advertising budgets were able to charge premium prices. Consumers apparently were willing to pay higher prices for known products than for unknown products. They also found that brands with high relative quality and high relative advertising obtained the highest prices, while brands with low quality and advertising charged the lowest prices. Finally, the positive relationship between high prices and high advertising held most strongly in the later stages of the product life cycle for market leaders.[18] Smart marketers therefore ensure that their prices fit with other marketing-mix elements.

Company Pricing Policies

The price must be consistent with company pricing policies. To accomplish this, many firms set up a pricing department to develop policies and establish or approve decisions. The aim is to ensure that the salespeople quote prices that are reasonable to customers and profitable to the company.

Impact of Price on Other Parties

Management must also consider the reactions of other parties to the contemplated price. How will distributors and dealers feel about it? Will the sales force be willing to sell at that price? How will competitors react? Will suppliers raise their prices when they see the company's price? Will the government intervene and prevent this price from being charged?

In the last case, marketers need to know the laws regulating pricing. U.S. legislation outlaws price-fixing, so sellers must set prices without talking to competitors. Many federal, state, and local laws also protect consumers against deceptive pricing practices. For example, it is illegal for a company to set artificially high "regular" prices, then announce a "sale" at prices close to previous everyday prices.

ADAPTING THE PRICE

Companies usually do not set a single price, but rather a pricing structure that reflects variations in geographical demand and costs, market-segment requirements, purchase timing, order levels, delivery frequency, guarantees, service contracts, and other factors. As a result of discounts, allowances, and promotional support, a company rarely realizes the same profit from each unit of a product that it sells. Here we will examine several price-adaptation strategies: geographical pricing, price discounts and allowances, promotional pricing, discriminatory pricing, and product-mix pricing.

Geographical Pricing

In geographical pricing, the company decides how to price its products to different customers in different locations and countries. For example, should the company charge distant customers more to cover higher shipping costs, or set a lower price to win additional business? Another issue is how to get paid. This is particularly critical when foreign buyers lack sufficient hard currency to pay for their purchases. Many buyers want to offer other items in payment in a practice known as *countertrade,* which accounts for 15–25 percent of world trade and takes several forms:[19]

➤ *Barter:* The direct exchange of goods, with no money and no third party involved. For example, Eminence S.A., a major clothing maker in France, bartered $25 million worth of U.S.-produced underwear and sportswear to customers in eastern Europe in exchange for transportation, magazine advertising space, and other goods and services.

➤ *Compensation deal:* The seller is paid partly in cash and partly in products. A British aircraft manufacturer used this approach to sell planes to Brazil for 70 percent cash and the rest in coffee.

➤ *Buyback arrangement:* The seller sells a plant, equipment, or technology to another country and agrees to accept as partial payment products manufactured with the supplied equipment. As one example, a U.S. chemical firm built a plant for an Indian company and accepted partial payment in cash and the remainder in chemicals manufactured at the plant.

➤ *Offset:* The seller receives full payment in cash but agrees to spend a substantial amount of that money in that country within a stated time period. For example, PepsiCo sells its cola syrup to Russia for rubles and agrees to buy Russian vodka at a certain rate for sale in the United States.

Price Discounts and Allowances

Most companies will adjust their list price and give discounts and allowances for early payment, volume purchases, and off-season buying, as shown in Table 12.1. However, companies must do this carefully or they will find that their profits are much less than planned.[20]

Table 12.1   Price Discounts and Allowances

Cash Discounts:	A *cash discount* is a price reduction to buyers who pay their bills promptly. A typical example is "2/10, net 20," which means that payment is due within 30 days and that the buyer can deduct 2 percent by paying the bill within 10 days. Such discounts are customary in many industries.
Quantity Discounts:	A *quantity discount* is a price reduction to those buyers who buy large volumes. A typical example is "$10 per unit for less than 100 units; $9 per unit for 100 or more units." Quantity discounts must be offered equally to all customers and must not exceed the cost savings to the seller associated with selling large quantities. They can be offered on a noncumulative basis (on each order placed) or a cumulative basis (on the number of units ordered over a given period).
Functional Discounts:	*Functional discounts* (also called *trade discounts*) are offered by a manufacturer to trade-channel members if they will perform certain functions, such as selling, storing, and record keeping. Manufacturers may offer different functional discounts to different trade channels but must offer the same functional discounts within each channel.
Seasonal Discounts:	A *seasonal discount* is a price reduction to buyers who buy merchandise or services out of season. Ski manufacturers will offer seasonal discounts to retailers in the spring and summer to encourage early ordering. Hotels, motels, and airlines will offer seasonal discounts in slow selling periods.
Allowances:	*Allowances* are extra payments designed to gain reseller participation in special programs. *Trade-in allowances* are price reductions granted for turning in an old item when buying a new one. Trade-in allowances are most common in durable-goods categories. *Promotional allowances* are payments or price reductions to reward dealers for participating in advertising and sales support programs.

Promotional Pricing

Companies can use any of seven promotional pricing techniques to stimulate early purchase (see Table 12.2). However, smart marketers recognize that promotional-pricing strategies are often a zero-sum game. If they work, competitors copy them and they lose their effectiveness. If they do not work, they waste company money that could have been put into longer impact marketing tools, such as building up product quality and service or strengthening product image through advertising.

Table 12.2   Promotional Pricing Techniques

Technique	Description	Example
Loss-leader pricing	Stores drop the price on well-known brands to stimulate additional store traffic.	Kmart cuts the price of selected toys to attract shoppers before Christmas.
Special-event pricing	Sellers establish special prices in certain seasons to draw in more customers.	Staples offers special prices on stationery items during a back-to-school sale.
Cash rebates	Manufacturers offer cash rebates to encourage purchase of their products within a specified period; this helps clear inventories without cutting the stated price.	Mazda advertises cash rebates on the purchase of selected previous-year models to clear these vehicles out of dealer inventory.
Low-interest financing	Instead of cutting its price, the company can offer customers low-interest financing.	Ford offers low- or no-interest financing to encourage the purchase of selected vehicles.
Longer payment terms	Sellers stretch loans over longer periods and thus lower the monthly payments that customers pay.	Auto companies and mortgage banks use this approach because consumers are more concerned with affordable payments than with the interest rate.
Warranties and service contracts	Companies can promote sales by adding a free or low-cost warranty or service contract.	Real estate brokers offer special warranties on selected homes to expedite sales.
Psychological discounting	Used legitimately, this involves offering the item at substantial savings from the normal price.	A jewelry store lowers the price of a diamond ring and advertises "Was $359, now $299."

Discriminatory Pricing

Companies often adjust their basic price to accommodate differences in customers, products, locations, and so on. *Discriminatory pricing* occurs when a company sells a product or service at two or more prices that do not reflect a proportional difference in costs. Discriminatory pricing takes several forms:

➤ *Customer-segment pricing:* Different customer groups pay different prices for the same good or service. For example, museums often charge a lower admission fee to students and senior citizens.

➤ *Product-form pricing:* Different versions of the product are priced differently but not proportionately to their respective costs. Evian, for instance, prices a 48-ounce bottle of its mineral water at $2, while its 1.7 ounce moisturizer spray sells for $6.

➤ *Image pricing:* Some companies price the same product at two different levels based on image differences. For instance, a perfume manufacturer can put its perfume in one bottle with a certain name and image priced at $10 an ounce; the same perfume in another bottle with a different name and image could be priced at $30 an ounce.

➤ *Location pricing:* The same product is priced differently at different locations even though the costs are the same; for example, theaters often vary seat prices according to audience preferences for different locations.

➤ *Time pricing:* Prices are varied by season, day, or hour. Public utilities use time pricing, varying energy rates to commercial users by time of day and weekend versus weekday. A special form of time pricing is *yield pricing,* which is often used by airlines to fill as many seats as possible.

Price discrimination works when (1) the market is segmentable and the segments show different intensities of demand; (2) members in the lower-price segment cannot resell the product to the higher-price segment; (3) competitors cannot undersell the firm in the higher-price segment; (4) the cost of segmenting and policing the market does not exceed the extra revenue derived from price discrimination; (5) the practice does not breed customer resentment and ill will; and (6) the particular form of price discrimination is not illegal (practices such as *predatory pricing*—selling below cost with the intention of destroying competition—are against the law).[21]

Today's Internet technology helps sellers discriminate between buyers as well as helping buyers discriminate between sellers. For example, Personify software allows companies to examine the "clickstream" of an on-line shopper, looking at the way that individual navigates through a Web site. Based on that behavior, the software can instantaneously target shoppers for specific products and prices. At the same time, Web sites such as MySimon are giving buyers instant price comparisons on specific products, while Web sites such as Priceline.com allow buyers to name their own price for airline tickets, long-distance phone service, hotel rooms, mortgages, groceries, and other goods and services—including an electronic yard sale for personal items.[22] These and other Internet innovations clearly signal the return to fluid pricing rather than the fixed pricing approach that came into acceptance a century ago.

Product-Mix Pricing

Price-setting logic must be modified when the product is part of a product mix. In this case, the firm searches for a set of prices that maximizes profits on the total mix. Pricing a product line is difficult because the various products have demand and cost interrelationships and are subject to different degrees of competition. We can distinguish six situations involving product-mix pricing:

➤ *Product-line pricing.* Many sellers use well-established price points (such as $200, $350, and $500 for suits) to distinguish the products in their line. The seller's task is to establish perceived-quality differences that justify the price differences.

➤ *Optional-feature pricing.* Automakers and many other firms offer optional products, features, and services along with their main product. Pricing these options is a sticky problem because companies must decide which items to include in the standard price and which to offer as options.

➤ *Captive-product pricing.* Some products require the use of ancillary, or *captive,* products. In the razor industry, manufacturers often price their razors low and set high markups on their blades. However, there is a danger in pricing the captive product too high in the *aftermarket* (the market for ancillary supplies to the main product). Caterpillar, for example, makes high profits in the aftermarket by pricing its parts and service high. This practice has given rise to "pirates," who counterfeit the parts and sell them to "shady tree" mechanics who install them, sometimes without passing on the cost savings to customers. Meanwhile, Caterpillar loses sales.[23]

➤ *Two-part pricing,* which is practiced by many service firms, consists of a fixed fee plus a variable usage fee. As an example, telephone users pay a minimum monthly fee plus charges for calls beyond a certain area. The challenge is how much to charge for the basic service and how much for the variable usage. The fixed fee should be low enough to induce purchase; the profit can then be made on the usage fees.

➤ *By-product pricing.* The production of certain goods—meats, chemicals, and so on— often results in by-products, which can be priced according to their value to customers. Any income earned on the by-products will make it easier for the company to charge less for the main product if competition forces it to do so. Sometimes companies do not realize how valuable their by-products are. Until Zoo-Doo Compost Company came along, many zoos did not realize that one of their by-products—their occupants' manure—could be an excellent source of additional revenue.[24]

➤ *Product-bundling pricing.* Sellers often bundle their products and features at a set price. An auto manufacturer, for instance, might offer an option package at less than the cost of buying all of the options separately. Because customers may not have planned to buy all of the components, the savings on the price bundle must be substantial enough to induce them to buy the bundle.[25]

INITIATING AND RESPONDING TO PRICE CHANGES

After setting initial prices and creating a pricing structure for their products, firms may need to cut or raise prices in certain situations. Here we will examine the challenges of initiating price cuts, initiating price increases, reacting to price changes, and responding to competitors' price changes. For an overview of strategic pricing options involving marketing-mix variables, see Table 12.3.

Initiating Price Cuts

Several circumstances might lead a firm to cut prices. One is *excess plant capacity:* If the firm needs additional business but cannot generate it through increased sales effort or other measures, it may initiate a price cut. In doing so, however, the company risks triggering a price war. Another circumstance is a *declining market share,* which may prompt the firm to cut prices as a way of regaining share. In addition, companies sometimes initiate price cuts in a *drive to dominate the market through lower costs.* Either the company starts with lower costs than those of its competitors or it initiates price cuts in the hope of gaining market share and lower costs.

When considering price-cutting, marketers need to be aware of three possible traps: (1) Customers may assume that lower-priced products have lower quality; (2) a low price buys market share but not market loyalty because the same customers will shift to any lower-price firm; and (3) higher-priced competitors may cut their prices and still have longer staying power because of deeper cash reserves.

Initiating Price Increases

A successful price increase can raise profits considerably. For example, if the company's profit margin is 3 percent of sales, a 1 percent price increase will increase profits by 33 percent if sales volume does not drop. In many cases, firms increase prices just to maintain profits in the face of *cost inflation.* This occurs when rising costs— unmatched by productivity gains—squeeze profit margins, leading firms to regularly increase prices. In fact, companies often raise their prices by more than the cost increase in anticipation of further inflation or government price controls in a practice called *anticipatory pricing.*

Table 12.3   Marketing-Mix Alternatives

Strategic Options	Reasoning	Consequences
1. Maintain price and perceived quality. Engage in selective customer pruning.	Firm has higher customer loyalty. It is willing to lose poorer customers to competitors.	Smaller market share. Lowered profitability.
2. Raise price and perceived quality.	Raise price to cover rising costs. Improve quality to justify higher prices.	Smaller market share. Maintained profitability.
3. Maintain price and raise perceived quality.	It is cheaper to maintain price and raise perceived quality.	Smaller market share. Short-term decline in profitability. Long-term increase in profitability.
4. Cut price partly and raise perceived quality.	Must give customers some price reduction but stress higher value of offer.	Maintained market share. Short-term decline in profitability. Long-term maintained profitability.
5. Cut price fully and maintain perceived quality.	Discipline and discourage price competition.	Maintained market share. Short-term decline in profitability.
6. Cut price fully and reduce perceived quality.	Discipline and discourage price competition and maintain profit margin.	Maintained market share. Maintained margin. Reduced long-term profitability.
7. Maintain price and reduce perceived quality.	Cut marketing expense to combat rising.	Smaller market share. Maintained margin. Reduced long-term profitability.
8. Introduce an economy model.	Give the market what it wants.	Some cannibalization but higher total volume.

Another factor leading to price increases is *overdemand*. When a company cannot supply all of its customers, it can use one of the following pricing techniques:

➤ With *delayed quotation pricing*, the company does not set a final price until the product is finished or delivered. This is prevalent in industries with long production lead times.

➤ With *escalator clauses*, the company requires the customer to pay today's price and all or part of any inflation increase that occurs before delivery, based on some specified price index. Such clauses are found in many contracts involving industrial projects of long duration.

➤ With *unbundling*, the company maintains its price but removes or prices separately one or more elements that were part of the former offer, such as free delivery or installation.

➤ With *reduction of discounts*, the company no longer offers its normal cash and quantity discounts.

Instead of raising prices, companies can respond to higher costs or overdemand in other ways, as shown in Table 12.3.

Reactions to Price Changes

Any price change can provoke a response from the firm's stakeholders. Savvy marketers pay close attention to customers' reactions, because customers often question the motivation behind price changes.[26] Customers are most price sensitive to products that cost a lot or are bought frequently; they hardly notice higher prices on low-cost items that they buy infrequently. Some buyers are less concerned with price than with the total costs of obtaining, operating, and servicing the product over its lifetime. So a seller can charge more and maintain sales if customers are convinced that total lifetime costs are lower.

Competitors are most likely to react to a price change when there are few firms offering the product, the product is homogeneous, and buyers are highly informed. Anticipating competitive reaction is complicated because each rival may have different interpretations of a company's price cut: One may think the company is trying to steal the market, while another may believe that the company wants the entire industry to reduce prices to stimulate total demand. Still, a firm will be unable to interpret competitors' price changes or other marketing-mix adjustments unless it continuously monitors and analyzes its rivals' activities, as was discussed in Chapter 7.

Responding to Competitors' Price Changes

How should a firm respond to a price cut that is initiated by a competitor? In markets characterized by high product homogeneity, the firm should search for ways to enhance its augmented product, but if it cannot find any, it will have to meet the price reduction. If the competitor raises its price in a homogeneous product market, the other firms might not match it, unless the price increase will benefit the industry as a whole. By not matching it, the leader will have to rescind the increase.

In nonhomogeneous product markets, a firm has more latitude to consider the following issues: (1) Why did the competitor change the price? Is it to steal the market, to utilize excess capacity, to meet changing cost conditions, or to lead an industrywide price change? (2) Does the competitor plan to make the price change temporary or permanent? (3) What will happen to the company's market share and profits if it does not respond? Are other companies going to respond? (4) What are the competitor's and other firms' responses likely to be to each possible reaction?

Market leaders often face aggressive price cutting by smaller competitors trying to build market share, the way Amazon.com has attacked Barnes and Noble. The brand leader can respond by:

➤ *Maintaining price and profit margin*, believing that (1) it would lose too much profit if it reduced its price, (2) it would not lose much market share, and (3) it could regain market share when necessary. However, the risk is that the attacker may get more confident, the leader's sales force may get demoralized, and the leader can lose more share than expected. Then the leader may panic, lower price to regain share, and find that regaining market share is more difficult and costly than expected.

➤ *Maintaining price while adding value* to its product, services, and communications. This may be less expensive than cutting price and operating at a lower margin.

➤ *Reducing price* to match the competitor's price, because (1) its costs fall with volume, (2) it would lose market share in a price-sensitive market, and (3) it would be hard to rebuild market share once it is lost, even though this will cut short-term profits.

➤ *Increasing price and improving quality* by introducing a new product to bracket the attacking brand.

➤ *Launching a low-price fighter line* or creating a separate lower-price brand to combat competition. Miller Beer, for example, launched a lower-priced beer brand called Red Dog.

The best response varies with the situation. Successful firms consider the product's stage in the life cycle, its importance in the company's portfolio, the competitor's intentions and resources, the market's price and quality sensitivity, the behavior of costs with volume, and the company's alternative opportunities.

EXECUTIVE SUMMARY

Price is the only one of the four Ps that produces revenue. In setting prices, a company follows a six-step procedure: (1) Select the pricing objective, (2) determine demand, (3) estimate costs, (4) analyze competitors' costs, prices, and offers, (5) select a pricing method, and (6) select the final price.

Companies do not usually set a single price, but rather a pricing structure that reflects variations in geographical demand and costs, market-segment requirements, purchase timing, order levels, and other factors. Several price-adaptation strategies are available: (1) geographical pricing; (2) price discounts and allowances; (3) promotional pricing; (4) discriminatory pricing, in which the company sells a product at different prices to different market segments; and (5) product-mix pricing, which includes setting prices for product lines, optional features, captive products, two-part items, by-products, and product bundles.

After developing pricing strategies, firms often face situations in which they need to change prices by initiating price cuts or price increases. In these situations, companies need to consider how stakeholders will react to price changes. In addition, marketers must develop strategies for responding to competitors' price changes. The firm's strategy often depends on whether it is producing homogeneous or nonhomogeneous products. Market leaders who are attacked by lower-priced competitors can choose to maintain price, raise the perceived quality of their product, reduce price, increase price and improve quality, or launch a low-price fighter line.

NOTES

1. Amy E. Cortese, "Good-Bye to Fixed Pricing?" *Business Week,* May 4, 1998, pp. 71–84.
2. Steve Gelsi, "Spin-Cycle Doctor," *Brandweek,* March 10, 1997, pp. 38–40; Tim Stevens, "From Reliable to 'Wow,'" *Industry Week,* June 22, 1998, pp. 22-26.
3. Thomas T. Nagle and Reed K. Holden, *The Strategy and Tactics of Pricing,* 2d ed. (Upper Saddle River, NJ: Prentice-Hall, 1995), ch. 4. This is an excellent reference book for making pricing decisions.
4. Kevin J. Clancy, "At What Profit Price?" *Brandweek,* June 23, 1997, pp. 24–28; "GreenMountain.com Begins Supplying Cleaner Electricity to Pennsylvania State Government," *PR Newswire,* January 4, 2000.
5. See Sidney Bennett and J. B. Wilkinson, "Price-Quantity Relationships and Price Elasticity Under In-Store Experimentation," *Journal of Business Research,* January 1974, pp. 30–34.
6. John R. Nevin, "Laboratory Experiments for Estimating Consumer Demand—A Validation Study," *Journal of Marketing Research,* August 1974, pp. 261–68; and Jonathan Weiner, "Forecasting Demand: Consumer Electronics Marketer Uses a Conjoint Approach to Configure Its New Product and Set the Right Price," *Marketing Research: A Magazine of Management & Applications,* Summer 1994, pp. 6–11.

7. An excellent summary of the various methods for estimating price sensitivity and demand can be found in Nagle and Holden, *The Strategy and Tactics of Pricing*, ch. 13.

8. For summary of elasticity studies, see Dominique M. Hanssens, Leonard J. Parsons, and Randall L. Schultz, *Market Response Models: Econometric and Time Series Analysis* (Boston: Kluwer Academic Publishers, 1990), pp. 187–91.

9. See Robin Cooper and Robert S. Kaplan, "Profit Priorities from Activity-Based Costing," *Harvard Business Review,* May-June 1991, pp. 130–35. For more on ABC, see ch. 24.

10. See "Japan's Smart Secret Weapon," *Fortune,* August 12, 1991, p. 75.

11. Tung-Zong Chang and Albert R. Wildt, "Price, Product Information, and Purchase Intention: An Empirical Study," *Journal of the Academy of Marketing Science,* Winter 1994, pp. 16–27. See also G. Dean Kortge and Patrick A. Okonkwo, "Perceived Value Approach to Pricing," *Industrial Marketing Management,* May 1993, pp. 133–40.

12. For an empirical study of nine methods used by companies to assess customer value, see James C. Anderson, Dipak C. Jain, and Pradeep K. Chintagunta, "Customer Value Assessment in Business Markets: A State-of-Practice Study," *Journal of Business-to-Business Marketing* 1, no. 1 (1993): 3–29.

13. Roger Crockett, "PC Makers Race to the Bottom," *Business Week,* October 12, 1998, p. 48; Patricia Fusco, "Emachines, FreePC to Merge," *InternetNews.com,* November 30, 1999, www.internetnews.com.

14. Stephen J. Hoch, Xavier Dreze, and Mary J. Purk, "EDLP, Hi-Lo, and Margin Arithmetic," *Journal of Marketing,* October 1994, pp. 16–27; Rajiv Lal and R. Rao, "Supermarket Competition: The Case of Everyday Low Pricing," *Marketing Science* 16, no. 1 (1997); 60–80.

15. Becky Bull, "No Consensus on Pricing," *Progressive Grocer,* November 1998, pp. 87–90.

16. Gary M. Erickson and Johny K. Johansson, "The Role of Price in Multi-Attribute Product-Evaluations," *Journal of Consumer Research,* September 1985, pp. 195–99.

17. K. N. Rajendran and Gerard J. Tellis, "Contextual and Temporal Components of Reference Price," *Journal of Marketing,* January 1994, pp. 22–34.

18. Paul W. Farris and David J. Reibstein, "How Prices, Expenditures, and Profits Are Linked," *Harvard Business Review,* November–December 1979, pp. 173–84. See also Makoto Abe, "Price and Advertising Strategy of a National Brand Against Its Private-Label Clone: A Signaling Game Approach," *Journal of Business Research,* July 1995, pp. 241–50.

19. See Michael Rowe, *Countertrade* (London: Euromoney Books, 1989); P. N. Agarwala, *Countertrade: A Global Perspective* (New Delhi: Vikas Publishing House, 1991); and Christopher M. Korth, ed., *International Countertrade* (New York: Quorum Books, 1987).

20. See Michael V. Marn and Robert L. Rosiello, "Managing Price, Gaining Profit," *Harvard Business Review,* September–October 1992, pp. 84–94. See also Gerard J. Tellis, "Tackling the Retailer Decision Maze: Which Brands to Discount, How Much, When, and Why?" *Marketing Science* 14, no. 3, pt. 2 (1995); 271–99.

21. For more information on specific types of price discrimination that are illegal, see Henry R. Cheeseman, *Contemporary Business Law* (Upper Saddle River, NJ: Prentice-Hall, 2000).

22. Clint Boulton, "Priceline Unleashes Long Distance Service," *E-Commerce News,* November 8, 1999, www.internetnews.com; "What Am I Bid for These Old LPs?" *Business Week,* January 10, 2000, p. 57.

23. See Robert E. Weigand, "Buy In–Follow On Strategies for Profit," *Sloan Management Review,* Spring 1991, pp. 29–37.

24. Susan Krafft, "Love, Love Me Doo," *American Demographics,* June 1994, pp. 15–16.

25. See Gerald J. Tellis, "Beyond the Many Faces of Price: An Integration of Pricing Strategies," *Journal of Marketing,* October 1986, p. 155. This excellent article also analyzes and illustrates other pricing strategies.

26. For an excellent review, see Kent B. Monroe, "Buyers' Subjective Perceptions of Price," *Journal of Marketing Research,* February 1973, pp. 70–80.

C h a p t e r   1 3

Selecting and Managing Marketing Channels

In this chapter, we will address the following questions:

- What work is performed by marketing channels?
- What decisions do companies face in designing, managing, evaluating, and modifying their channels?
- What trends are taking place in channel dynamics?
- How can channel conflict be managed?

Decisions about marketing channels, which help producers deliver goods and services to their target markets, are among the most critical facing management—because the channels that are chosen intimately affect all of the other marketing decisions. For example, the company's pricing depends on whether it uses a direct Web presence, discount merchants, or high-quality boutiques. Also, the firm's sales force and advertising decisions depend on how much training and motivation its dealers need.

Another reason why these decisions are so critical is that they involve relatively long-term commitments to other firms. When an automaker signs up independent dealers to sell its vehicles, the automaker cannot simply buy them out the next day and replace them with company-owned outlets. As Corey observed, "A distribution system . . . is a key external resource. Normally it takes years to build, and it is not easily changed. It ranks in importance with key internal resources such as manufacturing, research, engineering, and field sales personnel and facilities. It represents a significant corporate commitment to large numbers of independent companies whose business is distribution—and to the particular markets they serve. It represents, as well, a commitment to a set of policies and practices that constitute the basic fabric on which is woven an extensive set of long-term relationships."[1]

Technology is, of course, having a profound effect on channel decisions and management. In an era when buyers and sellers alike seek speedier sales transactions, marketing-channel technologies (including automated inventory and storage systems) and the Internet are adding value by expediting the flow of physical goods, ownership, payment, information, and promotion. In this chapter, we explore the selection and management of marketing channels from the viewpoint of producers of goods and services; in Chapter 14, we examine marketing-channel issues from the perspective of the retailers, wholesalers, and physical-distribution agencies that serve as channel intermediaries.

WHAT WORK IS PERFORMED BY MARKETING CHANNELS?

Most producers do not sell their goods directly to the final users. Between them stands a set of intermediaries that perform a variety of functions. These intermediaries constitute a marketing channel (also called a trade channel or distribution channel).

Marketing channels are sets of interdependent organizations involved in the process of making a product or service available for use or consumption.[2] Why would a producer delegate some of the selling job to intermediaries? Although delegation means relinquishing some control over how and to whom the products are sold, producers gain several advantages by using channel intermediaries:

> ➤ Many producers lack the financial resources to carry out direct marketing. For example, General Motors sells its cars through more than 8,100 dealer outlets in North America alone. Even General Motors would be hard-pressed to raise the cash to buy out its dealers.

> ➤ Direct marketing simply is not feasible for some products. The William Wrigley Jr. Company would not find it practical to establish retail gum shops or sell gum by mail order. It would have to sell gum along with many other small products, and would end up in the drugstore and grocery store business. Wrigley finds it easier to work through a network of privately owned distribution organizations.

> ➤ Producers who do establish their own channels can often earn a greater return by increasing their investment in their main business. If a company earns a 20 percent rate of return on manufacturing and only a 10 percent return on retailing, it does not make sense to undertake its own retailing.

Intermediaries normally achieve superior efficiency in making goods widely available and accessible to target markets. Through their contacts, experience, specialization, and scale of operation, these specialists usually offer the firm more than it can achieve on its own. According to Stern and El-Ansary, "Intermediaries smooth the flow of goods and services. . . . This procedure is necessary in order to bridge the discrepancy between the assortment of goods and services generated by the producer and the assortment demanded by the consumer. The discrepancy results from the fact that manufacturers typically produce a large quantity of a limited variety of goods, whereas consumers usually desire only a limited quantity of a wide variety of goods."[3]

As shown in Figure 13.1, working through a distributor as intermediary cuts the number of contacts that manufacturers must have with customers. Part (a) shows three producers, each using direct marketing to reach three customers, for a total of nine contacts. Part (b) shows the three producers working through one distributor, who contacts the three customers, for a total of only six contacts. Clearly, working through a distributor is more efficient in such situations.

Channel Functions and Flows

A marketing channel performs the work of moving goods from producers to consumers, overcoming the time, place, and possession gaps that separate goods and ser-

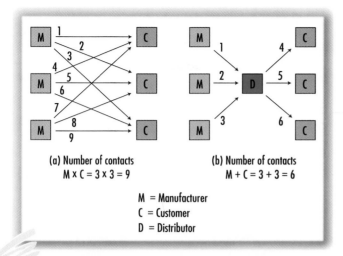

(a) Number of contacts
M x C = 3 x 3 = 9

(b) Number of contacts
M + C = 3 + 3 = 6

M = Manufacturer
C = Customer
D = Distributor

Figure 13.1   How a Distributor Effects Economy of Effort

vices from those who need or want them. Members of the marketing channel perform a number of key functions:

➤ They gather information about potential and current customers, competitors, and other actors and forces in the marketing environment.

➤ They develop and disseminate persuasive communications to stimulate purchasing.

➤ They reach agreement on price and other terms so that transfer of ownership or possession can be effected.

➤ They place orders with manufacturers.

➤ They acquire the funds to finance inventories at different levels in the marketing channel.

➤ They assume risks connected with carrying out channel work.

➤ They provide for the successive storage and movement of physical products.

➤ They provide for buyers' payment of their bills through banks and other financial institutions.

➤ They oversee actual transfer of ownership from one organization or person to another.

Some functions (physical, title, promotion) constitute a *forward flow* of activity from the company to the customer; other functions (ordering and payment) constitute a *backward flow* from customers to the company. Still others (information, negotiation, finance, and risk taking) occur in both directions. Five flows are illustrated in Figure 13.2 for the marketing of forklift trucks. If these flows were superimposed in one diagram, the tremendous complexity of even simple marketing channels would be apparent.

The question is not *whether* these channel functions need to be performed—they must be—but rather *who* is to perform them. All channel functions have three things in common: They use up scarce resources; they can often be performed better through specialization; and they can be shifted among channel members. If a manu-

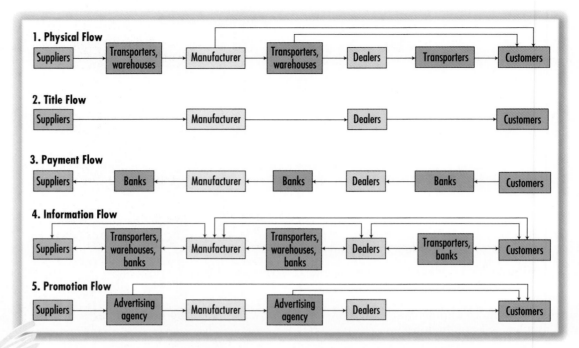

Figure 13.2   Five Marketing Flows in the Marketing Channel for Forklift Trucks

facturer shifts some functions to intermediaries, its costs and prices go down, but the intermediaries will charge more to cover their increased responsibilities. Still, if the intermediaries are more efficient than the manufacturer, the prices to consumers should be lower. If consumers perform some functions themselves, they should enjoy still lower prices. In general, changes in channel institutions tend to reflect the discovery of more efficient ways to combine or separate the economic functions that provide assortments of products to target customers.

Channel Levels

The producer and the final customer are part of every channel. We will use the number of intermediary levels to designate the length of a channel. Figure 13.3a illustrates several consumer-goods marketing channels of different lengths, while Figure 13.3b illustrates industrial marketing channels.

A *zero-level channel* (also called a *direct-marketing channel*) consists of a manufacturer selling directly to the final customer through Internet selling, door-to-door sales, home parties, mail order, telemarketing, TV selling, manufacturer-owned stores, and other methods. A *one-level channel* contains one selling intermediary, such as a retailer. A *two-level channel* contains two intermediaries; a *three-level channel* contains three intermediaries. From the producer's point of view, obtaining information about end users and exercising control becomes more difficult as the number of channel levels increases.

Channels normally describe a forward movement of products. One can also talk about *backward channels,* which recycle trash and old or obsolete products no longer used by customers. Several intermediaries play a role in backward channels, including

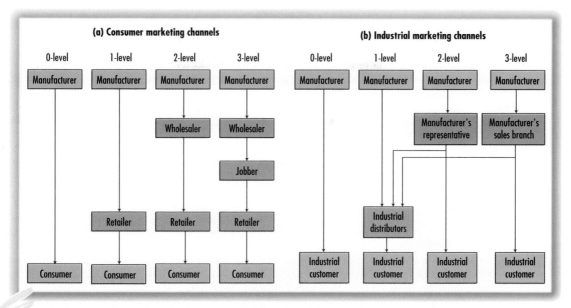

Figure 13.3   Consumer and Industrial Marketing Channels

manufacturers' redemption centers, community groups, traditional intermediaries such as soft-drink intermediaries, trash-collection specialists, recycling centers, trash-recycling brokers, and central-processing warehousing.[4]

Service Sector Channels

The concept of marketing channels is not limited to the distribution of physical goods. Producers of services and ideas also face the problem of making their output available and accessible to target populations. For instance, schools develop "educational-dissemination systems" and hospitals develop "health-delivery systems." These institutions must determine agencies and locations for reaching a population that is spread out over an area. Similarly, many states face the problem of locating branch campuses to serve a burgeoning and increasingly well-educated population, just as cities must find ways of creating and locating playgrounds children.[5]

As Internet technology advances, service industries such as banking, travel, and securities trading are putting more emphasis on this fast-growing channel. Consider the decisions faced by Merrill Lynch, a full-service, full-price brokerage firm that traditionally sold stocks and bonds through its 17,000 commissioned brokers. After watching discount broker Charles Schwab grab an early—and sizable—head start in on-line securities trading, Merrill Lynch fought back by launching its Merrill Lynch Direct Web site (www.mldirect.ml.com). This site allows the firm's customers to access financial data and trade securities without their brokers, at fees well below the firm's standard commission rates. In embracing this channel, Merrill Lynch is seeking to retain customers who want to trade electronically; at the same time, the firm needs to use its Internet presence to bring in new customers without cannibalizing transactions that otherwise would have been handled by its brokers at full commission.[6]

CHANNEL-DESIGN DECISIONS

A new firm typically starts as a local operation selling in a limited market through existing intermediaries. The problem at this point is not deciding on the best channels, but convincing the available intermediaries to handle the firm's line. If the firm is successful, it might enter new markets and select different channels in response to the opportunities and conditions in the different markets.

In designing the firm's channel system, management must carefully analyze customer needs, establish channel objectives, and identify and evaluate the major channel alternatives.

Analyzing Customers' Desired Service Output Levels

Because the point of a marketing channel is to make a product available to customers, the marketer must understand what its target customers actually want. Channels produce five service outputs:

1. *Lot size:* The number of units the channel permits a typical customer to purchase on one occasion. In buying cars for its fleet, Hertz prefers a channel from which it can buy a large lot size; a household wants a channel that permits buying a lot size of one.

2. *Waiting time:* The average time customers of that channel wait for receipt of the goods. Customers normally prefer fast delivery channels.

3. *Spatial convenience:* The degree to which the marketing channel makes it easy for customers to purchase the product. Chevrolet, for example, offers greater spatial convenience than Cadillac, because there are more Chevrolet dealers.

4. *Product variety:* The assortment breadth provided by the channel. Normally, customers prefer a greater assortment, which increases the chance of finding what they need. Relentless expansion of product variety is the special edge that has helped Amazon.com maintain its lead in Internet retailing.

5. *Service backup:* The add-on services (credit, delivery, installation, repairs) provided by the channel. The greater the service backup, the greater the work provided by the channel.[7]

Smart marketers recognize that providing greater service outputs means increased channel costs and higher prices for customers, just as a lower level means lower costs and prices. The success of discount stores and Web sites indicates that many consumers will accept lower outputs if they can save money.

Establishing Objectives and Constraints

Once it understands what customers want, the company is ready to establish channel objectives related to the targeted service output levels. According to Bucklin, under competitive conditions, channel institutions should arrange their functional tasks to minimize total channel costs with respect to desired levels of service outputs.[8] Producers can usually identify several market segments that desire differing service output levels. Thus, effective planning means determining which market segments to serve and the best channels to use in each case.

Channel objectives vary with product characteristics. For instance, perishable products such as Ben & Jerry's ice cream require more direct channels, whereas bulkier products such as Owens Corning Fiber Glass insulation require channels that minimize the shipping distance and the amount of handling in the movement from producer to consumer. In contrast, nonstandardized products, such as custom-built machinery, typically are sold directly by company sales representatives.

Channel design must also take into account the limitations and constraints of working with different types of intermediaries. As one example, reps that carry more than one firm's product line can contact customers at a low cost per customer because the total cost is shared by several clients, but the selling effort per customer will be less intense than if each company's reps did the selling. In addition, channel design can be constrained by such factors as competitors' channels, the marketing environment, and country-by-country legal regulations and restrictions. U.S. law looks unfavorably upon channel arrangements that tend to substantially lessen competition or create a monopoly.

Identifying Major Channel Alternatives

After a firm has examined its customers' desired service outputs and has set channel objectives, the next step is to identify channel alternatives. These are described by (1) the types of available intermediaries, (2) the number of intermediaries needed, and (3) the terms and responsibilities of each channel member.

Types of Intermediaries

Intermediaries known as *merchants*—such as wholesalers and retailers—buy, take title to, and resell the merchandise. *Agents*—brokers, manufacturers' representatives and sales agents—search for customers and may negotiate on the producer's behalf but do not take title to the goods. *Facilitators*—transportation companies, independent warehouses, banks, and advertising agencies—assist in the distribution process but neither take title to goods nor negotiate purchases or sales. The most successful companies search for innovative marketing channels. The Conn Organ Company, for example, sells organs through merchants such as department and discount stores, drawing more attention than it ever enjoyed in small music stores. Similarly, Ohio-based Provident Bank reaches new mortgage customers by selling through the lendingtree.com Web site, which acts as a facilitator.

Number of Intermediaries

In deciding how many intermediaries to use, successful companies use one of three strategies:

➤ *Exclusive distribution* means severely limiting the number of intermediaries. Firms such as automakers use this approach when they want to maintain control over the service level and service outputs offered by the resellers. Often it involves exclusive dealing arrangements, in which the resellers agree not to carry competing brands.

➤ *Selective distribution* involves the use of more than a few but less than all of the intermediaries who are willing to carry a particular product. In this way, the producer avoids dissipating its efforts over too many outlets, and it gains adequate market coverage with more control and less cost than intensive distribution. Nike, for example, sells its athletic shoes and apparel through seven types of outlets: (1) specialized sports stores, which carry a special line of athletic shoes; (2) general sporting goods stores, which carry a broad range of styles; (3) department stores, which carry only the newest styles; (4) mass-merchandise stores, which focus on discounted styles; (5) Niketown stores, which feature the complete line; (6) factory outlet stores, which stock mostly seconds and closeouts, and (7) the popular Fogdog Sports site (www.fogdog.com), its exclusive Web retailer.[9]

➤ *Intensive distribution* consists of the manufacturer placing the goods or services in as many outlets as possible. This strategy is generally used for items such as tobacco products, soap, snack foods, and gum, products for which the consumer requires a great deal of location convenience.

Terms and Responsibilities of Channel Members

The producer must also determine the rights and responsibilities of participating members when considering channel alternatives. From an ethical perspective, each channel member must be treated respectfully and given the opportunity to be profitable.[10] Other key rights and responsibilities include:

➤ *Price policy.* The producer establishes a price list and a schedule of discounts and allowances that intermediaries see as equitable and sufficient.

➤ *Conditions of sale.* The producer sets payment terms and guarantees for each sale. Most producers grant cash discounts to distributors for early payment; they may also offer guarantees against defective merchandise or price declines.

➤ *Territorial rights.* The producer defines the distributors' territories and the terms under which it will enfranchise other distributors. Distributors normally expect to receive full credit for all sales in their territory, whether or not they did the selling.

➤ *Mutual services and responsibilities.* The producer must carefully lay out each party's duties, especially in franchised and exclusive-agency channels. McDonald's provides franchisees with a building, promotional support, a record-keeping system, training, and technical assistance. In turn, its franchisees are expected to satisfy company standards regarding physical facilities, cooperate with new promotional programs, and buy supplies from specified vendors.

Evaluating the Major Alternatives

Once the company has identified its major channel alternatives, it must evaluate each alternative against appropriate economic, control, and adaptive criteria.

➤ *Economic criteria.* Each channel alternative will produce a different level of sales and costs, so producers must estimate the fixed and variable costs of selling different volumes through each channel. For example, in comparing a company sales force to a manufacturer's sales agency, the producer would estimate the variable cost of commissions paid to representatives and the fixed cost of rent payments for a sales office. By comparing its costs at different sales levels, the company can determine which alternative appears to be the most profitable.

➤ *Control criteria.* Producers must consider how much channel control they require, since they will have less control over members they do not own, such as outside sales agencies. In seeking to maximize profits, outside agents may concentrate on customers who buy the most, but not necessarily of the producer's goods. Furthermore, agents might not master the details of every product they carry.

➤ *Adaptive criteria.* To develop a channel, the members must make some mutual commitments for a specified period of time. Yet these commitments invariably lead to a decrease in the producer's ability to respond to a changing marketplace. In a volatile or uncertain environment, smart producers seek out channel structures and policies that provide high adaptability.

CHANNEL-MANAGEMENT DECISIONS

After a company has chosen a channel alternative, it must select, train, motivate, and evaluate the individual intermediaries. Then, because neither the marketing environment nor the product life cycle remains static, the company must be ready to modify these channel arrangements over time.

Selecting Channel Members

During the selection process, producers should determine what characteristics distinguish the better intermediaries. They will want to evaluate number of years in business, other lines carried, growth and profit record, solvency, cooperativeness, and reputation. If the intermediaries are sales agents, producers will want to evaluate the number and character of other lines carried and the size and quality of the sales force. If the intermediaries are store or Internet retailers that want exclusive distribution, the producer will want to evaluate locations, brand strength, future growth potential, and type of clientele.

Selection of channel participants is actually a two-way process: Just as producers select their channel members, the intermediaries also select their producer partners. Yet producers vary in their ability to attract qualified intermediaries. Toyota was able to attract many new dealers when it first introduced its Lexus line, but Polaroid initially had to sell through mass-merchandising outlets when photographic-equipment stores would not carry its cameras.

Selection can be a lengthy process. Consider the experience of Japan's Epson Corporation. A leading manufacturer of computer printers, Epson decided to add computers to its product line but chose to recruit new distributors rather than sell through its existing distributors. The firm hired a recruiting firm to find candidates who (1) had distribution experience with major appliances, (2) were willing and able to set up their own distributorships, (3) would accept Epson's financial arrangements, and (4) would handle only Epson equipment, although they could stock other companies' software. After the recruiting firm went to great effort to find qualified candidates, Epson terminated its existing distributors and began selling through the new channel members. Despite this time-consuming, detailed selection process, Epson never succeeded as a computer manufacturer.[11]

Training Channel Members

Companies need to plan and implement careful training programs for their distributors and dealers because the intermediaries will be viewed as the company by end users. Microsoft, for example, requires third-party service engineers who work with its software applications to complete a number of courses and take certification exams. Those who pass are formally recognized as Microsoft Certified Professionals, and they can use this designation to promote business.

As another example, Ford Motor Company beams training programs and technical information via its satellite-based Fordstar Network to more than 6,000 dealer sites. Service engineers at each dealership sit at a conference table and view a monitor on which an instructor explains procedures such as repairing onboard electronics and then answers questions. Such training initiatives keep employees updated on the latest product specifications and service requirements.

Motivating Channel Members

The most successful firms view their channel members in the same way they view their end users. This means determining their intermediaries' needs and then tailoring the channel positioning to provide superior value to these intermediaries. To improve intermediaries' performance, the company should provide training, market research, and other capability-building programs. And the company must constantly reinforce that its intermediaries are partners in the joint effort to satisfy customers.

More sophisticated companies go beyond merely gaining intermediaries' cooperation and instead try to forge a long-term *partnership* with distributors. The manufacturer communicates clearly what it wants from its distributors in the way of market coverage, inventory levels, marketing development, account solicitation, technical advice and services, and marketing information. The manufacturer then seeks distributor agreement with these policies and may introduce a compensation plan or other rewards for adhering to the policies. For example, Dayco Corporation, a maker of engineered plastics and rubber products, strengthens channel partnerships by running an annual week-long retreat with 20 distributors' executives and 20 Dayco executives.

Still, too many manufacturers think of their distributors and dealers as customers rather than as working partners. Up to now, we have treated manufacturers and distributors as separate organizations. But many manufacturers are distributors of related products made by other manufacturers, and some distributors also own or contract for the manufacture of in-house brands. JCPenney sells national brands of jeans by manufacturers such as Levi Strauss in addition to a line of jeans under the Original Arizona Jeans company private label. This situation, which is common in the jeans industry and in many others, complicates the process of selecting and motivating channel members.

Evaluating Channel Members

Producers must periodically evaluate intermediaries' performance against such standards as sales-quota attainment, average inventory levels, customer delivery time, treatment of damaged and lost goods, and cooperation in promotional and training programs.

A producer will occasionally discover that it is paying too much to particular intermediaries for what they are actually doing. As one example, a manufacturer that was compensating a distributor for holding inventories found that the inventories were actually held in a public warehouse at the manufacturer's expense. Producers should therefore set up functional discounts in which they pay specified amounts for the trade channel's performance of each agreed-upon service. Underperformers need to be counseled, retrained, remotivated, or terminated.

Modifying Channel Arrangements

Channel arrangements must be reviewed periodically and modified when distribution is not working as planned, consumer buying patterns change, the market expands, new competition arises, innovative distribution channels emerge, or the product moves into later stages in the product life cycle.

Rarely will a marketing channel remain effective over the entire product life cycle. Early buyers might be willing to pay for high value-added channels, but later buyers will switch to lower-cost channels. This was the pattern for many products, including small office copiers, which were first sold by manufacturers' direct sales forces, later through office-equipment dealers, still later through mass merchandisers, and now by mail-order firms and Internet marketers.

Miland Lele developed the grid in Figure 13.4 to show how marketing channels have changed for PCs and designer apparel at different stages in the product life cycle. As the grid indicates, new products in the introductory stage of the life cycle enter the market through specialist channels that attract early adopters. As interest grows, higher-volume channels appear (dedicated chains, department stores), offering some services, but not as many as the previous channels. In the maturity stage, where growth is slowing, some competitors move their product into lower-cost channels (mass merchandisers). In decline, even lower-cost channels emerge (mail-order, discount Web sites, off-price discounters).[12]

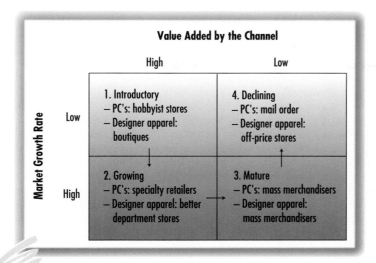

Figure 13.4   Channel Value Added and Market Growth Rate

Adding or dropping an individual channel member requires an incremental analysis to determine what the firm's profits would look like with and without this intermediary. Sometimes a producer considers dropping all intermediaries whose sales are below a certain amount. For example, Navistar noted at one time that 5 percent of its dealers sold fewer than three or four trucks a year. It cost the company more to service these dealers than their sales were worth. But dropping these dealers could have system-wide repercussions. The unit costs of producing trucks would be higher because the overhead would be spread over fewer trucks, some employees and equipment would be idled, some business in these markets would go to competitors, and other dealers might become insecure. All of these factors have to be taken into account when changing channel arrangements.

The most difficult decision involves revising the overall channel strategy.[13] Distribution channels can become outmoded over time, as a gap arises between the existing distribution system and the ideal system that would satisfy target customers' (and producers') requirements. Examples abound: Avon's door-to-door system for selling cosmetics had to be modified as more women entered the workforce, and IBM's exclusive reliance on a field sales force had to be modified with the introduction of low-priced personal computers. Dell Computer started out selling PCs by mail to consumers and businesses, briefly added retail stores as part of an expansion strategy, then cut out store distribution in favor of the Internet (www.dell.com), a direct channel where customers could more easily order customized PCs.[14]

CHANNEL DYNAMICS

In the ever-changing marketing environment, distribution channels do not stand still. New wholesaling and retailing institutions emerge, and new channel systems evolve. We look next at the recent growth of vertical, horizontal, and multichannel marketing systems and see how these systems cooperate, conflict, and compete.

Vertical Marketing Systems

One of the most significant recent channel developments is the rise of vertical marketing systems. A *conventional marketing channel* comprises an independent producer, wholesaler(s), and retailer(s). Each is a separate business seeking to maximize its own profits, even if this goal reduces profit for the system as a whole. No channel member has complete or substantial control over other members.

A *vertical marketing system* (VMS), by contrast, comprises the producer, wholesaler(s), and retailer(s) acting as a unified system. One channel member, the *channel captain,* owns the others or franchises them or has so much power that they all cooperate. The channel captain can be the producer, the wholesaler, or the retailer. VMSs arose as a result of strong channel members' attempts to control channel behavior and eliminate the conflict that results when independent channel members pursue their own objectives. They achieve economies through size, bargaining power, and elimination of duplicated services. VMSs have become the dominant mode of distribution in the U.S. consumer marketplace, serving between 70 percent and 80 percent of the total market. There are three types of VMS: corporate, administered, and contractual.

➤ A *corporate VMS* combines successive stages of production and distribution under single ownership. Vertical integration is favored by companies that desire a high level of control over their channels. For example, Sears obtains over 50 percent of the goods it sells from companies that it partly or wholly owns; Sherwin-Williams makes paint but also owns and operates 2,000 retail outlets.

➤ An *administered VMS* coordinates successive stages of production and distribution through the size and power of one of the members. Manufacturers of a dominant brand are able to secure strong trade cooperation and support from resellers. Thus Kodak, Gillette, Procter & Gamble, and Campbell Soup are able to command high levels of cooperation from their resellers in connection with displays, shelf space, promotions, and price policies.

➤ A *contractual VMS* consists of independent firms at different levels of production and distribution integrating their programs on a contractual basis to obtain more economies or sales impact than they could achieve alone. Johnston and Lawrence call them "value-adding partnerships" (VAPs).[15] Contractual VMSs are of three types:

1. *Wholesaler-sponsored voluntary chains* organize groups of independent retailers to better compete with large chain organizations. Wholesalers such as Drug Guild work with participating retailers (for Drug Guild, independent pharmacies) to standardize their selling practices and achieve buying economies so the group can compete effectively with chain organizations.

2. *Retailer cooperatives* arise when the stores take the initiative and organize a new business entity to carry on wholesaling and possibly some production. Members of retail cooperates such as ServiStar concentrate their purchases through the retailer co-op and plan their advertising jointly; profits are passed back to members in proportion to their purchases.

3. *Franchise organizations* are created when a channel member called a *franchisor* links several successive stages in the production-distribution process. Franchises include *manufacturer-sponsored retailer franchises* (the way Ford licenses dealers to sell its cars); *manufacturer-sponsored wholesaler franchises* (the way Coca-Cola licenses bottlers—who are wholesalers—to buy its syrup concentrate and then bottle and sell it to retailers); and *service-firm-sponsored retailer franchises* (the way Hertz licenses participating auto-rental businesses).

Horizontal Marketing Systems

Another channel development is the *horizontal marketing system,* in which two or more unrelated companies put together resources or programs to exploit an emerging marketing opportunity. Each company lacks the capital, know-how, production, or marketing resources to venture alone, or it is afraid of the risk. The companies might work with each other on a temporary or permanent basis or create a joint venture company. Adler calls this *symbiotic marketing.*[16]

Consider the long-standing agreement between Sara Lee Intimates and Wal-Mart, which has enabled the partners to grow their business from an initial $134 million account to a $1 billion partnership over 10 years. Both firms have merchandise, operations, MIS, and marketing managers devoted solely to this agreement. They meet regularly to iron out problems and make plans, requiring the sharing of marketing information, inventory levels, sales history, price changes, and other proprietary information.[17]

Multichannel Marketing Systems

In the past, many companies sold to a single market through a single channel. Today, with the proliferation of customer segments and channel possibilities, more companies have adopted multichannel marketing. *Multichannel marketing* occurs when a single firm uses two or more marketing channels to reach one or more customer segments.

As one example, the Parker-Hannifin Corporation (PHC) sells pneumatic drills to the lumber, fishing, and aircraft industries. Instead of selling through one industrial distributor, PHC has established three separate channels—forestry equipment distributors, marine distributors, and industrial distributors. There appears to be little conflict because each type of distributor sells to a separate target segment.

By adding more channels, companies can gain three important benefits. The first is increased market coverage—companies often add a channel to reach a customer segment that its current channels cannot reach. The second is lower channel cost—companies may add a new channel to lower the cost of selling to an existing customer group (selling by phone rather than personally visiting small customers). The third is more customized selling—companies may add a channel whose selling features fit customer requirements better (adding a technical sales force to sell more complex equipment).

However, new channels typically introduce conflict and control problems. First, different channels may end up competing for the same customers. Second, as the new channels become more independent, the company may have difficulty maintaining cooperation among all of the members. Consider the dilemma faced by insurance firms that sell home, auto, and life insurance policies through agents. On the one hand, shopping for insurance via Web sites such as Quotesmith.com and ebix.com can save customers both time and money while giving insurers access to more prospects. On the other hand, using Internet intermediaries could potentially alienate the 1.8 million U.S. insurance agents who now sell the bulk of the policies—and make their living from commissions that can range as high as 20 percent. While Geico and other insurers that sell directly to customers are moving quickly to open Internet channels, firms with established agent networks are moving more cautiously. Their dilemma is summed up by a spokesperson for the St. Paul Companies, who says: "We must work to build business on-line in a way that does not disenfranchise our agents and brokers."[18]

Conflict, Cooperation, and Competition

No matter how well channels are designed and managed, there will be some conflict, if for no other reason than the interests of independent business entities do not always coincide. Here we examine three questions: What types of conflict arise in channels? What causes channel conflict? What can be done to resolve conflict situations?

Types of Conflict and Competition

Vertical channel conflict means conflict between different levels within the same channel. As one example, General Motors has come into conflict with its dealers in trying to enforce policies on service, pricing, and advertising. As another example, Coca-Cola came into conflict with its bottlers who agreed also to bottle Dr. Pepper.

Vertical channel conflict is currently raging in consumer packaged goods, where power has shifted from producers to retailers. Even as manufacturers continue to pump out thousands of new products, retailers seeking maximum productivity from their limited shelf space are able to collect *slotting fees* from manufacturers for stocking new products, *display fees* to cover space costs, *fines* for late deliveries and incomplete orders, and *exit fees* to cover the cost of returning goods to producers. Trying to regain power from retailers, manufacturers are expanding into alternative channels, putting more emphasis on market-leading brands, and developing stronger links with important retailers through value-added distribution systems and programs that benefit all members of the channel.

Horizontal channel conflict involves conflict between members at the same level within the channel. Horizontal channel conflict erupted, for instance, when some Pizza Inn franchisees complained about other Pizza Inn franchisees cheating on ingredients, maintaining poor service, and hurting the overall Pizza Inn image.

Multichannel conflict exists when the manufacturer has established two or more channels that sell to the same market. For instance, when Goodyear began selling its tires through Sears, Wal-Mart, and Discount Tire, the move angered its independent dealers. Goodyear eventually placated them by offering exclusive tire models that would not be sold in other retail outlets.

Causes of Channel Conflict

Why does channel conflict erupt? One major cause is *goal incompatibility*. For example, the manufacturer may want to achieve rapid market penetration through a low-price policy. The dealers, in contrast, may prefer to work with high margins for short-run profitability. Sometimes conflict arises from *unclear roles and rights*. This is what happened when IBM started selling PCs to large accounts through its own sales force while its licensed dealers were also trying to sell to large accounts. Territory boundaries and credit for sales often produce conflict in such situations.

By adding new channels, a company faces the possibility of channel conflict, as the earlier insurance example indicated. Conflict can also stem from *differences in perception,* as when the producer is optimistic about the short-term economic outlook and wants dealers to carry more inventory, while its dealers are more pessimistic about future prospects.

At times, conflict can arise because of the intermediaries' *great dependence* on the manufacturer. The fortunes of exclusive dealers, such as auto dealers, are intimately affected by the manufacturer's product and pricing decisions. This creates a high potential for conflict.

Managing Channel Conflict

Some channel conflict can be constructive and can lead to more dynamic adaptation in a changing environment. Too much conflict can be dysfunctional, however, so the challenge is not to eliminate conflict but to manage it better. There are several mechanisms for effective conflict management:[19]

➤ *Adoption of superordinate goals.* Channel members come to an agreement on the fundamental goal they are jointly seeking, whether it is survival, market share, high quality, or customer satisfaction. They usually do this when the channel faces an outside threat, such as a more efficient competing channel, an adverse piece of legislation, or a shift in consumer desires.

➤ *Exchange persons between channel levels.* General Motors executives might work for a short time in some dealerships, and some dealers might work in GM's dealer policy department, as a way of helping participants appreciate each other's viewpoint.

➤ *Cooptation.* Cooptation is an effort by one organization to win the support of the leaders of another organization by including them in advisory councils, boards of directors, trade associations, and the like. As long as the initiating organization treats the leaders seriously and listens to their opinions, cooptation can reduce conflict.

➤ *Diplomacy, mediation, arbitration for chronic or acute conflict. Diplomacy* takes place when each side sends a person or group to meet with its counterpart to resolve the conflict. *Mediation* means having a skilled, neutral third party reconcile the two parties' interests. *Arbitration* occurs when the two parties agree to present their arguments to an arbitrator and accept the arbitration decision.

Legal and Ethical Issues in Channel Relations

For the most part, companies are legally free to develop whatever channel arrangements suit them. In fact, the law seeks to prevent companies from using exclusionary tactics that might keep competitors from using a channel. Here we briefly consider the legality of certain practices, including exclusive dealing, exclusive territories, tying agreements, and dealers' rights.

➤ *Exclusive dealing.* A strategy in which the seller allows only certain outlets to carry its products is called *exclusive distribution,* and when the seller requires that these dealers not handle competitors' products, this is called *exclusive dealing.* Both parties benefit from exclusive arrangements: The seller obtains more loyal and dependable outlets, and the dealers obtain a steady source of supply of special products and stronger seller support. Exclusive arrangements are legal as long as (1) they do not substantially lessen competition or tend to create a monopoly, and (2) both parties have voluntarily entered into the agreement.

➤ *Exclusive territories.* Exclusive dealing often includes exclusive territorial agreements. The producer may agree not to sell to other dealers in a given area, or the dealer may agree to sell only in its own territory. The first practice increases dealer enthusiasm and commitment and is perfectly legal—a seller has no legal obligation to sell through more outlets than it wishes. The second practice, whereby the producer tries to keep a dealer from selling outside its territory, is a major legal issue.

➤ *Tying agreements.* The producer of a strong brand sometimes sells it to dealers only if they will take some or all of the rest of the line. This practice is called *full-line forcing.* Such tying agreements are not necessarily illegal, but they do violate U.S. law if they tend to lessen competition substantially.

➤ *Dealers' rights.* Producers are free to select their dealers, but their right to terminate dealers is somewhat restricted. In general, sellers can drop dealers "for cause." But they cannot drop dealers if, for example, the dealers refuse to cooperate in a doubtful legal arrangement, such as exclusive dealing or tying agreements.

The next chapter examines the marketing strategies and challenges of retailers and wholesalers as channel members.

EXECUTIVE SUMMARY

Most producers do not sell their goods directly to final users. Between producers and final users stands one or more marketing channels, a set of marketing intermediaries performing a variety of functions. Companies use intermediaries when they lack the financial resources to carry out direct marketing, when direct marketing is not feasible, and when they can earn more by going through intermediaries. The use of intermediaries largely boils down to their superior efficiency in making goods widely available and accessible to target markets. The most important functions performed by intermediaries are gathering information, handling promotion, handling negotiation, placing orders, arranging financing, taking risks, and facilitating physical possession, payment, and title.

Manufacturers have many alternatives for reaching a market. They can sell direct through a zero-level channel or use one-, two-, or three-level channels. Deciding which type(s) of channel to use calls for analyzing customer needs, establishing channel objectives, and identifying and evaluating the major alternatives. The company must also determine whether to distribute its product exclusively, selectively, or intensively, and it must clearly spell out the terms and responsibilities of each channel member.

Effective channel management calls for selecting intermediaries, then training and motivating them. The goal is to build a long-term partnership that will be profitable for all channel members. Individual members must be evaluated periodically against preestablished standards, and overall channel arrangements may need to be modified over time. Three of the most important trends in channel dynamics are the growth of vertical marketing systems, horizontal marketing systems, and multichannel marketing systems.

All marketing channels have the potential for conflict and competition resulting from such sources as goal incompatibility, poorly defined roles and rights, perceptual differences, and interdependent relationships. Companies can manage conflict by striving for superordinate goals, exchanging people among two or more channel levels, coopting the support of leaders in different parts of the channel, and through diplomacy, mediation, or arbitration to resolve chronic or acute conflict.

Channel arrangements are up to the company, but there are certain legal and ethical issues to be considered with regard to practices such as exclusive dealing or territories, tying agreements, and dealers' rights.

NOTES

1. E. Raymond Corey, *Industrial Marketing: Cases and Concepts,* 4th ed. (Upper Saddle River, NJ: Prentice-Hall, 1991), ch. 5.
2. Louis W. Stern and Adel I. El-Ansary, *Marketing Channels,* 5th ed. (Upper Saddle River, NJ: Prentice-Hall, 1996).
3. Stern and El-Ansary, *Marketing Channels,* pp. 5–6.
4. For additional information on backward channels, see Marianne Jahre, "Household Waste Collection as a Reverse Channel—A Theoretical Perspective," *International Journal of Physical Distribution and Logistics* 25, no. 2 (1995): 39–55; and Terrance L. Pohlen and M. Theodore Farris II, "Reverse Logistics in Plastics Recycling," *International Journal of Physical Distribution and Logistics* 22, no. 7 (1992): 35–37.

5. Ronald Abler, John S. Adams, and Peter Gould, *Spatial Organizations: The Geographer's View of the World* (Upper Saddle River, NJ: Prentice-Hall, 1971), pp. 531–32.

6. Leah Nathans Spiro, "Merrill's Battle," *Business Week,* November 15, 1999, pp. 256–66; "Merrill 4Q Earnings Surge," *CNNfn,* January 25, 2000, www.cnnfn.com.

7. Louis O. Bucklin, *Competition and Evolution in the Distributive Trades* (Upper Saddle River, NJ: Prentice-Hall, 1972). Also see Stern and El-Ansary, *Marketing Channels.*

8. Louis P. Bucklin, *A Theory of Distribution Channel Structure* (Berkeley: Institute of Business and Economic Research, University of California, 1966).

9. "Fogdog Takes Lead in Holiday Etailing," *Business Journal of San Jose,* January 4, 2000, www.amcity.com; Mark Hyman, "Fogdog Is Eager to Fetch," *Business Week,* November 29, 1999, p. 173; Will Anderson, "Vendor Irate at Jersey Decision, *Atlanta Journal and Constitution,* October 7, 1996, p. R1; William McCall, "Nike Posts $72M Loss," *The Associated Press,* December 12, 1998; Philana Patterson, "Athletic Shoe Industry Hurt When Buyers Drag Feet," *Star Tribune,* December 26, 1997, p. 7B.

10. For more on relationship marketing and the governance of marketing channels, see Jan B. Heide, "Interorganizational Governance in Marketing Channels," *Journal of Marketing,* January 1994, pp. 71–85.

11. Arthur Bragg, "Undercover Recruiting: Epson America's Sly Distributor Switch," *Sales and Marketing Management,* March 11, 1985, pp. 45–49.

12. Miland M. Lele, *Creating Strategic Leverage* (New York: John Wiley, 1992), pp. 249–51. This fact struck the manufacturer of the MicroFridge, a combination minirefrigerator and microwave oven.

13. For an excellent report on this issue, see Howard Sutton, *Rethinking the Company's Selling and Distribution Channels,* research report no. 885, Conference Board, 1986, 26 pp.

14. Thomas J. Neff and James M. Citrin, *Lessons from the Top* (New York: Currency Doubleday, 1999), p. 90; "Focus: Dell Warns Q4 Results to Fall Short, Again," *Reuters,* January 26, 2000, www.hoovers.com.

15. Russell Johnston and Paul R. Lawrence, "Beyond Vertical Integration—The Rise of the Value-Adding Partnership," *Harvard Business Review,* July–August 1988, pp. 94–101. See also Judy A. Siguaw, Penny M. Simpson, and Thomas L. Baker, "Effects of Supplier Market Orientation on Distributor Market Orientation and the Channel Relationship: The Distribution Perspective," *Journal of Marketing,* July 1998, pp. 99–111; Narakesari Narayandas and Manohar U. Kalwani, "Long-Term Manufacturer–Supplier Relationships: Do They Pay Off for Supplier Firms?" *Journal of Marketing,* January 1995, pp. 1–16.

16. Lee Adler, "Symbiotic Marketing," *Harvard Business Review,* November–December 1966, pp. 59–71; and P. "Rajan" Varadarajan and Daniel Rajaratnam, "Symbiotic Marketing Revisited," *Journal of Marketing,* January 1986, pp. 7–17.

17. Robin Lewis, "Partner or Perish," *WWD Infotracs: Strategic Alliances,* February 24, 1997, p. 4.

18. Diane Brady, "Insurers Step Gingerly Into Cyberspace," *Business Week,* November 22, 1999, pp. 160, 162.

19. This section draws on Stern and El-Ansary, *Marketing Channels,* ch. 6.

Managing Retailing, Wholesaling, and Market Logistics

In this chapter, we will address the following questions:

■ What major types of organizations occupy this sector?
■ What marketing decisions do organizations in this sector make?
■ What are the major trends in this sector?

In the previous chapter, we examined marketing intermediaries from the viewpoint of manufacturers and service providers who want to build and manage marketing channels. In this chapter, we view these intermediaries—retailers, wholesalers, and logistical organizations—as requiring and forging their own marketing strategies.

Retailing is, in fact, one of the main industries propelling the growth of e-commerce. Amazon.com and eToys.com are just two of the emerging breed of "retailers" that are building relationships with on-line shoppers by offering a vast product selection at low prices with fast delivery. Despite the explosive expansion of Internet retailing, traditional bricks-and-mortar stores retain their appeal for shoppers who want to examine the merchandise in person before they buy. Wholesaling and market logistics are also being transformed by the Internet, leading to a higher degree of sophistication and more targeted, value-added offerings.

Over the years, the balance of power has shifted from producers to intermediaries; now some intermediaries, such as Wal-Mart, tend to dominate the producers who deal with them. Many have gained a competitive advantage through strategic planning, advanced information systems, and sophisticated marketing tools, measuring performance more on a return-on-investment basis than on a profit-margin basis. Like smart marketers everywhere, they segment their markets carefully, hone their targeting and positioning, and aggressively pursue market expansion and diversification strategies.

RETAILING

Retailing includes all of the activities involved in selling goods or services directly to final consumers for personal, nonbusiness use. A **retailer** or **retail store** is any business enterprise whose sales volume comes primarily from retailing. Any organization that sells to final consumers—whether a manufacturer, wholesaler, or retailer—is engaged in retailing. It does not matter how the goods or services are sold (by person, mail, telephone, vending machine, or Internet) or where they are sold (in a store, on the street, or in the consumer's home).

Types of Retailers

Retailers exhibit great variety, and new forms keep emerging. There are now store retailers, nonstore retailers, and retail organizations; the most important types of retail stores are described in Table 14.1.

Like products, retail-store types pass through stages of growth and decline that can be described as the *retail life cycle*.[1] A type emerges, enjoys a period of accelerated growth, reaches maturity, and then declines. Older retail forms took many years to reach maturity; newer retail forms reach maturity much more quickly. Department stores took 80 years to reach maturity, whereas warehouse retail outlets reached maturity in 10 years; now Internet retailers are approaching maturity in even less time.[2]

One reason that new store types emerge to challenge old store types is offered by the *wheel-of-retailing* hypothesis.[3] According to this theory, conventional retail-store types typically increase their services and raise their prices to cover the cost. These higher costs provide an opportunity for new store forms to emerge, offering lower prices and less service.

New store types emerge to meet widely different consumer preferences for service levels and specific services. Retailers can position themselves as offering one of four levels of service:

1. *Self-service:* Self-service is the cornerstone of all discount operations, allowing customers to save money by carrying out their own locate-compare-select process.

2. *Self-selection:* Customers find their own goods—although they can ask for assistance— and they then complete the transaction by paying a salesperson for the item.

3. *Limited service:* These retailers carry more shopping goods, and customers need more information and assistance. The stores also offer services (such as credit and merchandise-return privileges).

4. *Full service:* Salespeople are ready to assist in every phase of the locate-compare-select process. The high staffing cost, along with the higher proportion of specialty goods and slower-moving items plus more services, result in high-cost retailing.

By combining these different service levels with different assortment breadths, we can distinguish four broad positioning strategies:

1. *Bloomingdale's:* Stores with a broad product assortment and high value added; they pay close attention to store design, product quality, service, and image, and they enjoy a high profit margin.

2. *Tiffany:* Stores with a narrow product assortment and high value added; they cultivate an exclusive image and tend to operate on a high margin and low volume.

3. *Sunglass Hut:* Stores with a narrow line and low value added; such stores keep costs and prices low by designing similar stores and centralizing buying, merchandising, advertising, and distribution.

Table 14.1   Major Store Retailer Types

Specialty Store: Narrow product line with a deep assortment, such as apparel stores, sporting-goods stores, furniture stores, florists, and bookstores. A clothing store would be a single-line store, a men's clothing store would be a limited-line store, and a men's custom-shirt would be a superspecialty store. Example: The Body Shop.

Department Store: Several product lines—typically clothing, home furnishings, and household goods—with each line operated as a separate department managed by specialist buyers or merchandisers. Example: Sears.

Supermarket: Relatively large, low-cost, low-margin, high-volume, self-service operation designed to serve total needs for foods and household products. Supermarkets earn an operating profit of only about 1 percent on sales and 10 percent on net worth. Example: Kroger.

Convenience Store: Relatively small store located near residential area, open long hours 7 days a week, and carrying a limited line of high-turnover convenience products at slightly higher prices. Example: 7-Eleven.

Discount Store: Standard merchandise sold at lower prices with lower margins and higher volumes. Example: All-purpose: Kmart; Specialty: Circuit City.

Off-Price Retailer: Merchandise bought at less than regular wholesale prices and sold at less than retail: often leftover goods, overruns, and irregulars obtained at reduced prices from manufacturers or other retailers. These include *factory outlets* owned and operated by manufacturers (example: Mikasa); *independent off-price retailers* owned and run by entrepreneurs or by divisions of larger retail corporations (example: T.J. Maxx); *warehouse* (or *wholesale*) *clubs* selling limited selection of brand-name groceries, appliances, clothing, other goods at deep discounts to consumers who pay membership fees (example: BJ's Wholesale Club).

Superstore: Averages 35,000 square feet of selling space traditionally aimed at meeting consumers' total needs for routinely purchased food and nonfood items; usually includes services such as laundry, dry cleaning, shoe repair, check cashing, and bill paying. "Category killers" carry a deep assortment in a particular category and a knowledgeable staff (example: Petsmart). Superstores include *combination stores* that merchandise food, drugs, and prescriptions in an average 55,000 square feet of selling space (example: Jewel stores) and *hypermarkets* with up to 220,000 square feet of space combining supermarket, discount, and warehouse retailing (example: Carrefour, based in France).

Catalog Showroom: Broad selection of high-markup, fast-moving, brand-name goods at discount prices. Customers order goods from a catalog in the showroom, then pick these goods up at a merchandise pickup area in the store. Example: Service Merchandise.

4. *Wal-Mart:* Stores with a broad line and low value added; they focus on keeping prices low to create an image of being a place for good buys. Here, high volumes make up for low margins.

Although the overwhelming majority of goods and services is sold through stores, nonstore retailing—especially on-line retailing—has been growing much faster than store retailing. Nonstore retailing falls into four major categories: (1) direct selling, a $9 billion industry with over 600 companies (such as Avon) selling door-to-door or at home; (2) direct marketing, with roots in direct-mail and catalog marketing (Lands' End) and encompassing telemarketing (1-800-FLOWERS), television direct-response marketing (Home Shopping Network), and on-line shopping (Autobytel.com, www.autobytel.com); (3) automatic vending, used for many items including cigarettes, soft drinks, candy, and newspapers; and (4) buying service, a storeless retailer serving a specific clientele—usually employees of large organizations—who are entitled to buy from retailers that have agreed to provide discounts in return for membership.

Many stores remain independently owned, but an increasing number these days are part of some form of corporate retailing (see Table 14.2). Such organizations achieve economies of scale and have greater purchasing power, wider brand recognition, and better trained employees.

Retailer Marketing Decisions

Competition among retailers is more intense than ever, especially now that retailers are drawing an ever-larger share of the shopping dollar. Retailers are therefore anxious to find new marketing strategies to attract and hold customers. In the past they held customers by offering convenient location, special or unique assortments of goods, greater or better services, and store credit cards. All of this has changed. Today, national brands such as Calvin Klein and Levi Strauss are found in most department stores, in their own shops, in merchandise outlets, and in off-price discount stores; the result is that store assortments have grown more alike.

Service differentiation also has eroded. Many department stores have trimmed services while many discounters have increased services. For their part, customers have become smarter shoppers. They do not want to pay more for identical brands, especially when service differences have diminished. Nor do they need credit from a particular store, because bank credit cards are almost universally accepted.

Effective differentiation in this pressured retail environment therefore requires savvy marketing decisions about target market, product assortment and procurement, services and store atmosphere, price, promotion, and place.

Table 14.2   Major Types of Retail Organizations

Corporate Chain Store: Two or more outlets commonly owned and controlled, employing central buying and merchandising, and selling similar lines of merchandise. Such stores buy in large quantities at lower prices, and hire corporate specialists to deal with pricing, promotion, merchandising, inventory control, and sales forecasting. Example: Tower Records.

Voluntary Chain: A wholesaler-sponsored group of independent retailers engaged in bulk buying and common merchandising. Example: Independent Grocers Alliance (IGA).

Retailer Cooperative: Independent retailers who set up a central buying organization and conduct joint promotion efforts. Example: Ace Hardware.

Consumer Cooperative: A retail firm owned by its customers. In consumer coops, residents contribute money to open their own store, vote on policies, elect managers, and receive patronage dividends.

Franchise Organization: Contractual association between a franchiser (manufacturer, wholesaler, service organization) and franchisees (independent businesspeople who buy the right to own and operate one or more units). Example: Jiffy Lube.

Merchandising Conglomerate: A free-form corporation that combines several diversified retailing lines and forms under central ownership, along with some integration of distribution and management. Example: Allied Domeq PLC operates Dunkin' Donuts and Baskin-Robbins.

Target Market

A retailer's most important decision concerns the target market. Until the target market is defined and profiled, the retailer cannot make consistent decisions on product assortment, store decor, advertising messages and media, price, and service levels.

Some retailers have defined their target markets quite well. Consider The Limited, founded by Leslie Wexner as a single store targeted to young fashion-conscious women. All aspects of the store—clothing assortment, fixtures, music, colors, personnel—were orchestrated to match the target consumer. Although Wexner continued to open more stores, a decade later his original customers were no longer in the "young" group. To catch the new "youngs," he started the Limited Express; to retain both groups, he also started or acquired targeted chains such as Lane Bryant, Victoria's Secret, Lerner's, and Bath and Body Works. Today, The Limited operates 5,400 stores in the United States plus global catalog operations and several store-specific Web sites, ringing up over $9 billion in sales.[4]

The best retailers conduct periodic marketing research to ensure that they are reaching and satisfying their target customers. At the same time, they keep their positioning somewhat flexible, especially if they are managing outlets in locations with different socioeconomic patterns.

Product Assortment and Procurement

The retailer's *product assortment* must match the target market's shopping expectations. Here, the retailer has to decide on product-assortment *breadth* and *depth*. Thus, a restaurant can offer a narrow and shallow assortment (small lunch counters), a narrow and deep assortment (delicatessen), a broad and shallow assortment (cafeteria), or a broad and deep assortment (large restaurant).

The real challenge begins after defining the store's product assortment, when the retailer must develop a product-differentiation strategy. Some possibilities are to feature exclusive national brands that are not available at competing retailers (Saks uses this strategy); to feature mostly private branded merchandise (Gap uses this strategy); to feature the latest or newest merchandise first (The Sharper Image uses this strategy); or to offer customizing services (Harrod's of London uses this strategy).[5]

A growing number of stores are using *direct product profitability* (DPP) to measure a product's handling costs (receiving, moving to storage, paperwork, selecting, checking, loading, and space cost) from the time it reaches the warehouse until a customer buys it in the store. Resellers who have adopted DPP learn to their surprise that the gross margin on a product often has little relation to the direct product profit. Some high-volume products may have such high handling costs that they are less profitable and deserve less shelf space than some low-volume products.

Services and Store Atmosphere

The services mix is one of the key tools for differentiating one store from another. Options include:

➤ *Prepurchase services* such as telephone and mail orders, advertising, window and interior display, fitting rooms, shopping hours, fashion shows, and trade-ins.

➤ *Postpurchase services* such as shipping and delivery, gift wrapping, adjustments and returns, alterations and tailoring, installations, and engraving.

➤ *Ancillary services* such as general information, check cashing, parking, restaurants, repairs, interior decorating, credit, rest rooms, and baby-attendant service.

Atmosphere is another differentiation tool in the store's arsenal. Every store has a physical layout that makes it hard or easy to move around, as well as a "look." The store must embody a planned atmosphere that suits the target market and draws consumers toward purchase. Supermarkets, for instance, have found that varying the tempo of music affects the average time spent in the store and the average expenditures. Some fine department stores vaporize perfume fragrances in certain departments.

Restaurants are also presenting "packaged environments."[6] Casual dining restaurants with distinct menu and decor elements, such as Olive Garden, T.G.I. Friday's, and Outback Steakhouse, have grown into a $37 billion business. However, some "theme restaurants" such as Planet Hollywood have fallen on hard times. The message seems to be that a trendy atmosphere is not enough: Customers want good food, good prices, and updated menu offerings in a casual, family atmosphere.[7]

Price Decision

Pricing is a key positioning factor and must be decided in relation to the target market, the mix of products and services, and the competition. All retailers would like to achieve both high volumes and high gross margins, but the two usually do not go together. Most retailers fall into the *high-markup, lower-volume* group (fine specialty stores) or the *low-markup, higher-volume* group (mass merchandisers and discount stores and retailers).

Many retailers periodically put low prices on some items to serve as traffic builders or loss leaders, run occasional storewide sales, and plan markdowns on slower-moving merchandise. For example, shoe retailers expect to sell 50 percent of their shoes at the normal markup, 25 percent at a 40 percent markup, and the remaining 25 percent at cost.

Still, some retailers have abandoned high-low "sales pricing" in favor of everyday low pricing (see Chapter 12). Feather cites a study showing that supermarket chains practicing everyday low pricing are often more profitable than those practicing sales pricing.[8] Clearly, pricing is a key marketing decision that affects every retailer's bottom line.

Promotion Decision

Store retailers can use a wide range of promotion tools to generate traffic and purchases: advertising, special sales, money-saving coupons, frequent shopper rewards, in-store sampling, and in-store couponing. On-line retailers can use some of the same promotional tools; to launch its toy department, for example, Amazon.com (www.amazon.com) e-mailed $10-off coupons to customers in its database.

Each retailer must use promotion tools that support and reinforce its image positioning. Fine stores place tasteful ads in magazines such as *Vogue* and carefully train salespeople to greet customers, interpret their needs, and handle complaints. In contrast, off-price retailers arrange their merchandise to promote the idea of bargains and large savings, while conserving on service and sales assistance.

Place Decision

Retailers say that the three keys to success are "location, location, and location," because customers usually choose the most convenient place to shop. In general, stores have five major location choices, as shown in Table 14.3. Given the relationship between high traffic and high rents, successful retailers support decisions about the most advantageous locations using such assessment methods as traffic counts, surveys of shoppers' habits, and analysis of competitive locations.[9] Several software models for site location have also been formulated.[10]

Trends in Retailing

Retailing is a highly dynamic business. Some of the main developments that retailers and manufacturers need to take into account as they plan their competitive strategies are:

Table 14.3 Location Options for Retailers

Location	Description
General business district	"Downtown," the oldest and most heavily trafficked city area; rents are normally high but a renaissance is bringing shoppers back to many cities.
Regional shopping center	Large suburban mall containing 40–200 stores and, generally, one or more anchor stores such as JCPenney; draws customers from 5–20 mile radius; offers generous parking, one-stop shopping and other facilities; the most successful malls charge high rents and may get a share of stores' sales.
Community shopping center	Smaller mall with one anchor store and 20–40 smaller stores.
Strip mall (shopping strip)	A cluster of stores, usually housed in one long building.
Location within a larger store or operation	Concession space rented by McDonald's and other retailers inside the unit of a larger retailer or an operation such as an airport.

➤ *New retail forms and combinations continually emerge.* Bank branches have opened in supermarkets; gas stations include food stores that make more profit than the gas operation; bookstores feature coffee shops. Even old retail forms are reappearing: Peddler's carts are now in three-fourths of all major U.S. malls, selling everything from casual wear to crystal jewelry to condoms. With a low start-up cost and low rents, pushcarts help budding entrepreneurs test their retailing dreams without a major investment; they also help malls bring in more mom-and-pop retailers, showcase seasonal merchandise, and find permanent tenants.[11]

➤ *New retail forms have a shorter life span.* They are rapidly copied and quickly lose their novelty—which is why producers need to review and update their channel arrangements regularly.

➤ *The electronic age has significantly increased the growth of nonstore retailing.* Consumers now receive sales offers via mail, e-mail, television, and telephone—and they can respond immediately by calling a toll-free number or visiting a Web site.

➤ *Competition is increasingly intertype, or between different types of retailers.* Discount stores, department stores, and Web sites are all competing for the same consumers. The competition between chain superstores and smaller, independent stores has become particularly heated; the arrival of a superstore has forced some nearby independents out of business. Yet many independent retailers thrive by knowing their customers better and providing them with more personal service.

➤ *Today's retailers are moving toward one of two poles, operating either as mass merchandisers or as specialty retailers.* Superpower retailers are emerging, using superior information systems, volume buying power, and sophisticated logistical systems to offer strong price savings, good service, and immense product choices.[12] In the process, they are crowding out smaller manufacturers, which become dependent on one large retailer and are therefore extremely vulnerable, as well as smaller retailers that lack the budget and the buying power to compete. Many retailers are even telling manufacturers what to make, how to price and promote, and when and how to ship. Manufacturers have little choice: They stand to lose 10–30 percent of the market if they refuse.

➤ *One-stop shopping has shifted to supercenters.* Department stores like Sears used to be prized for their shopping convenience. Gradually, department stores gave way to malls. Now supercenters combining grocery items with a huge selection of nonfood merchandise—such as those operated by Wal-Mart—present an alternative format for one-stop shopping.

➤ *Marketing channels are increasingly becoming professionally managed and programmed.* Retail organizations are increasingly designing and launching new store formats targeted to different lifestyle groups. And instead of sticking to one format, they are moving into a mix of retail formats.

➤ *Technology is a critical competitive tool.* Computers are integral to retailing today, helping to produce better forecasts, control inventory costs, order from suppliers electronically, communicate with outlets, and sell to customers. Technology is also raising productivity through checkout scanning systems, electronic funds transfer, and sophisticated merchandise-handling systems.

➤ *Retailers with unique formats and strong brand positioning are increasingly moving into other countries.*[13] Many U.S. retailers, such as McDonald's, The Limited, Gap, and Wal-Mart, have gone global to boost profits. This trend is spreading through Europe and Asia, as well, with retailers such as Britain's Marks and Spencer department stores, Italy's Benetton clothing stores, France's Carrefour hypermarkets, and Sweden's IKEA furniture stores opening outlets around the world.[14]

➤ *There has been a marked rise in establishments that provide a place for people to congregate.* Such outlets include coffeehouses, tea shops, juice bars, bookshops, and brew pubs. Denver's two Tattered Cover bookstores bring people together at more than 250 events annually, from folk dancing to women's meetings. Brew pubs such as New York's Zip City Brewing and Seattle's Trolleyman Pub offer tastings and a place to pass the time. Riding this wave, Starbucks, with $1.7 billion in worldwide sales through more than 2,200 outlets, is opening new outlets at the rate of 600 per year.[15]

WHOLESALING

Wholesaling includes all of the activities involved in selling goods or services to those who buy for resale or business use. Wholesaling excludes manufacturers and farmers (because they are engaged primarily in production) and retailers.

Wholesalers (also called *distributors*) differ from retailers in a number of ways. First, wholesalers pay less attention to promotion, atmosphere, and location because they are dealing with business customers rather than final consumers. Second, wholesale transactions are usually larger than retail transactions, and wholesalers usually cover a larger trade area than retailers. Third, the government deals with wholesalers and retailers differently regarding legal regulations and taxes.

Why don't manufacturers sell directly to retailers or final consumers rather than through wholesalers? The main reason is efficiency: Wholesalers are often better at handling one or more of these functions:

➤ *Selling and promoting:* Wholesalers provide a sales force that helps manufacturers reach many small business customers at a relatively low cost.

➤ *Buying and assortment building:* Wholesalers are able to select items and build the assortments their customers need, saving their customers considerable work.

➤ *Bulk breaking:* Wholesalers can achieve savings for their customers through buying in large lots and breaking the bulk into smaller units.

➤ *Warehousing:* Wholesalers frequently hold inventories, thereby reducing the inventory costs and risks to suppliers and customers.

➤ *Transportation:* Wholesalers can often provide quicker delivery because they are closer to buyers.

➤ *Financing:* Wholesalers often finance customers by granting credit, and they finance suppliers by ordering early and paying bills on time.

➤ *Risk bearing:* Some wholesalers absorb part of the risk by taking title and bearing the cost of theft, damage, spoilage, and obsolescence.

➤ *Market information:* Wholesalers usually supply information to suppliers and customers regarding competitors' activities, new products, price developments, and so on.

➤ *Management services and counseling:* Wholesalers often help retailers train their sales clerks, suggest improvements to store layouts and displays, and help set up accounting and inventory-control systems. They may also help industrial customers with training and technical services.

The Growth and Types of Wholesaling

Wholesalers, like retailers, vary in type and function. Some take title to the products they handle, while others do not; some perform multiple functions, while others are more specialized. The major types of wholesalers are shown in Table 14.4.

Although the Internet is starting to change the industry, wholesaling has been growing at a healthy rate in the United States. One reason for this is the establishment of larger factories located far from buyers; another is the increasing need for adapting products to the needs of intermediate and final users in terms of quantities, packages, and specific features. Consider how McKesson meets the needs of its diverse customer base. As the largest distributor of pharmaceuticals in the United States and Canada, McKesson stocks and manages medical supplies and drugs for hospitals, doctors, nursing homes, and pharmacies. It provides participating pharmacies with software applications so orders can be transmitted quickly to McKesson and filled immediately with the proper products in the proper quantities. The system also reorders replenishment stock automatically for McKesson from drug manufacturers.[16] McKesson thus maintains its niche by performing valuable functions for its customers.

Wholesaler Marketing Decisions

Wholesaler-distributors have faced mounting pressures in recent years from new sources of competition, demanding customers, new technologies, and more direct-buying programs by large industrial, institutional, and retail buyers. In expanding its electronics offerings, Amazon.com, for example, has decided to buy certain products from Hewlett-Packard directly rather than through wholesalers.[17]

In response to these pressures, the industry has been working to increase asset productivity by better managing inventories and receivables. Industry members have also had to revisit their strategic decisions on target markets, product assortment and services, price, promotion, and place.

Target Market

In defining their target markets, wholesalers can choose a target group of customers by size (e.g., only large retailers), type of customer (e.g., convenience food stores only), need for service (e.g., customers who need credit), or other suitable criteria. Then, within the target group, they can identify the most profitable customers and

Table 14.4   Major Wholesaler Types

Merchant Wholesalers: Independently owned businesses that take title to the merchandise they handle. Called jobbers, distributors, or mill supply houses, these are either full service or limited service.

Full-Service Wholesalers: Carry stock, maintain a sales force, offer credit, make deliveries, and provide management assistance. *Wholesale merchants* sell primarily to retailers and provide a full range of services; *industrial distributors* sell to manufacturers only and provide several services—carrying stock, offering credit, and providing delivery.

Limited-Service Wholesalers: Offer fewer services to suppliers and customers. *Cash-and-carry* wholesalers have a limited line of fast-moving goods and sell to small retailers for cash. *Truck wholesalers* primarily sell and deliver a limited line of semiperishable merchandise to supermarkets, small groceries, hospitals and others. *Drop shippers* operate in bulk industries, such as coal; upon receiving an order, they select a manufacturer, who ships the merchandise directly to the customer, with the drop shipper retaining title and assuming the risk until delivery is complete. *Rack jobbers* serve grocery and drug retailers—mostly in nonfood items—and retain title to goods, billing retailers only for goods sold to consumers; their delivery people set up displays, price goods, keep them fresh, and keep inventory records. *Producers' cooperatives* assemble farm produce to sell in local markets, distributing profits to members at the end of the year. *Mail-order wholesalers* have no sales staff; instead, they send catalogs to retail, industrial, and institutional customers and fill orders by mail or another transportation method.

Brokers and Agents: Do not take title to goods, and perform only a few functions—mainly facilitating buying and selling—for which they earn a commission of 2–6 percent of the selling price. They generally specialize by product line or customer type.

Brokers: Chief function is bringing buyers and sellers together and assisting in negotiation. They are paid by the party who hired them and do not carry inventory, finance goods, or assume risk. The most familiar examples are food brokers, real estate brokers, and insurance brokers.

Agents: Represent either buyers or sellers on a more permanent basis. *Manufacturers' agents* represent two or more manufacturers of complementary lines, following a written agreement covering pricing policy, territories, order-handling procedure, delivery service and warranties, and commissions. *Selling agents* have contractual authority to sell a manufacturer's entire output in such product areas as textiles and industrial machinery. *Purchasing agents* have a long-term relationship with buyers and make purchases for them, often receiving, inspecting, warehousing, and shipping merchandise to buyers. *Commission merchants,* used most often in agricultural marketing, take physical possession of products and negotiate sales.

Manufacturers' and Retailers' Branches and Offices: Wholesaling operations conducted by sellers or buyers themselves rather than through independent wholesalers. Sales branches and offices are set up by manufacturers to improve inventory control, selling, and promotion. *Sales branches,* which carry inventory, are found in lumber and other industries. *Sales offices,* which do not carry inventory, are most prominent in dry-goods industries. *Purchasing offices* operate similarly to brokers but are part of the buyer's organization; many retailers set up purchasing offices in major market centers.

Miscellaneous Wholesalers: Specialized types of wholesalers, including agricultural assemblers, which buy the agricultural output of many farms; petroleum bulk plants and terminals, which consolidate the petroleum output of many wells; and auction companies, which auction cars and other items to dealers and other businesses.

proceed to build relationships using such value-added offers as automatic replenishment systems or training and consultation services. At the same time, wholesalers can discourage less-profitable customers by requiring larger orders or adding surcharges to smaller ones.

Product Assortment and Services

The wholesalers' "product" is their assortment. Wholesalers are under great pressure to carry a full line and maintain sufficient stock for immediate delivery, yet the costs of carrying huge inventories can kill profits. This is why successful wholesalers constantly reexamine how many lines to offer and then carry only the more profitable ones. They also identify the services that count most in building strong customer relationships and determine which should be dropped or charged for. The key is to find a distinct mix of services valued by their customers.

Price Decision

Wholesalers usually mark up the cost of goods by a conventional percentage, say 20 percent, to cover their expenses. Expenses may run 17 percent of the gross margin, leaving a profit margin of approximately 3 percent. In grocery wholesaling, the average profit margin is often less than 2 percent. Today, many wholesalers are experimenting with new pricing approaches: Some are trying to cut margin on selected lines in order to win important new customers; others are asking suppliers for a special price break that can be turned into an opportunity to increase the supplier's sales.

Promotion Decision

In general, wholesalers rely on their sales force to achieve promotional objectives. Yet most wholesalers see selling as a single salesperson talking to a single customer instead of a team effort to sell and service major accounts. Wholesalers would benefit from adopting some of the image-building techniques used by retailers. They need to develop an overall promotion strategy involving trade advertising, sales promotion, and publicity and make greater use of supplier promotion materials and programs.

Place Decision

Progressive wholesalers have been taking advantage of place decisions by improving materials-handling procedures and costs by developing automated warehouses and improving their supply capabilities through advanced information systems. For example, W. W. Grainger, Inc. is one of the largest business-to-business distributors of equipment, components, and supplies in the United States and Canada, offering more than 200,000 products through 520 branches. It maintains one national, two regional, and six zone distribution centers to guarantee product availability and quick service, linking the distribution centers by satellite network to slash customer-response time and boost sales. Grainger also expanded its reach by offering 24-hour-a-day ordering through its Web site (www.grainger.com).[18]

Trends in Wholesaling

For a while, wholesalers seemed to be headed for a significant decline as large manufacturers, and retailers such as Wal-Mart, moved aggressively into direct buying. Yet savvy wholesalers have rallied to the challenge, adapting their services to meet their suppliers' and target customers' changing needs as a way of adding value to the channel. They have also reduced their operating costs by investing in materials-handling technology and information systems, including Internet, intranet, and extranet technology.

After interviewing leading industrial distributors, Narus and Anderson identified four ways that wholesalers can strengthen relationships with manufacturers: (1) Seek a clear agreement with their manufacturers about their expected functions in the marketing channel; (2) gain insight into manufacturers' requirements by visiting plants and attending conventions and trade shows; (3) fulfill commitments by meeting volume targets, paying promptly, and providing feedback of customer information to manufacturers; and (4) offer value-added services to help suppliers.[19]

Wholesaling still faces considerable challenges. The industry remains vulnerable to fierce resistance to price increases and the winnowing out of suppliers based on cost and quality. And the trend toward vertical integration, in which manufacturers try to control or own their intermediaries, is still strong.

MARKET LOGISTICS

The process of getting goods to customers has traditionally been called *physical distribution*. Physical distribution starts at the factory, where managers choose warehouses and transportation carriers that will deliver products to final destinations in the desired time or at the lowest cost.

Recently, physical distribution has been expanded into the broader concept of supply chain management. *Supply chain management* starts earlier than physical distribution, covering attempts to procure the right inputs (raw materials, components, and equipment), convert them efficiently into finished products, and dispatch them to the final destinations. An even broader perspective calls for studying how the company's suppliers obtain their inputs all the way back to the raw materials. The supply chain perspective can help a company identify superior suppliers and distributors and help them improve productivity, which ultimately brings down the company's costs.

Unfortunately, the supply chain view sees markets only as destination points. The company would be more effective by first considering its target market's requirements and then designing the supply chain backward from that point. This is the view of **market logistics,** which involves planning, implementing, and controlling the physical flows of materials and final goods from points of origin to points of use to meet customer requirements at a profit.

Market logistics leads to an examination of the *demand chain*. Here is demand-chain thinking in action: At one time, German consumers purchased individual bottles of soft drinks. They said, however, that they would be willing to buy a six-pack. Retailers also favored this approach because the bottles could be loaded faster on the shelves, and more bottles would be purchased per occasion. At this point, a soft-drink manufacturer designed six-packs to fit on store shelves, which led to the design of cases and pallets that could bring six-packs efficiently to the store's receiving rooms. Working backward, factory operations were redesigned to produce the new six-packs. Once the six-packs hit the market, the soft-drink maker's market share rose substantially.

The market logistics task calls for *integrated logistics systems* (ILS), involving materials management, material flow systems, and physical distribution, abetted by information technology (IT). Third-party suppliers, such as FedEx Logistics Services or Ryder Integrated Logistics, often participate in designing or managing these systems. For example, Volvo, working with FedEx, set up a warehouse in Memphis with a complete stock of truck parts. A dealer who needs a part in an emergency calls a toll-free number; FedEx ships the part for same-day delivery to the airport, the dealership, or the repair site.

Market logistics links several activities, starting with sales forecasting, which helps the company schedule distribution, production, and inventory levels. In turn, production plans indicate the materials that the purchasing department must order. These materials arrive through inbound transportation, enter the receiving area, and are stored in raw-material inventory and later converted into finished goods. Finished-goods inventory is the link between customer orders and manufacturing activity. Customers' orders draw down the finished-goods inventory level, and manufacturing activity builds it up. Finished goods flow off the assembly line and pass through packaging, in-plant warehousing, shipping-room processing, outbound transportation, field warehousing, and customer delivery and servicing.

Management has become concerned about the total cost of market logistics, which can amount to 30–40 percent of the product's cost. The grocery industry alone thinks it can decrease its annual operating costs by 10 percent, or $30 billion, by revamping market logistics. A typical box of breakfast cereal spends 104 days chugging through a labyrinth of intermediaries to reach the supermarket.[20] With such inefficiencies, it is no wonder that experts call market logistics "the last frontier for cost economies." Lower logistics costs will permit lower prices, yield higher profit margins, or both. But although the cost of market logistics can be high, a well-planned program can be a potent marketing tool, bringing in additional customers and boosting profits through better service, faster cycle time, or lower prices.

Consider Supervalu, a Minnesota-based wholesaler-retailer of dry groceries. The firm has been experimenting with "cross-docking," in which products are moved from the supplier's truck through the distribution center and directly onto a store-bound truck. Attracted by the promise of savings on time and labor, Supervalu is cross-docking high-volume products such as paper products, and some milk and bread; about 12 percent of dry groceries are now cross-docked. In its high-tech distribution center in Anniston, Alabama, Supervalu is already benefiting from operating efficiencies and reduced costs.[21]

On the other hand, companies can lose customers when they fail to supply goods on time. Kodak found this out when it launched a national ad campaign for a new instant camera before it had delivered enough stock to the stores. Customers who could not find the camera bought Polaroid cameras instead.

Market-Logistics Objectives

Many companies state their market-logistics objective as "getting the right goods to the right places at the right time for the least cost." Unfortunately, this objective provides little practical guidance. No market-logistics system can simultaneously maximize customer service and minimize distribution cost. Maximum customer service implies large inventories, premium transportation, and multiple warehouses, all of which raise market-logistics costs.

Given that market-logistics activities involve strong trade-offs, decisions must be made on a total system basis. The starting point is to study what customers require and what competitors offer. Customers are interested in on-time delivery, supplier willingness to meet emergency needs, careful handling of merchandise, and supplier willingness to take back defective goods and resupply them quickly.

The company must then research the relative importance of these service outputs. For example, service-repair time is very important to buyers of copying equipment. Knowing this, Xerox developed a service-delivery standard that "can put a disabled machine anywhere in the continental United States back into operation within 3 hours after receiving the service request." It then designed a service division of personnel, parts, and locations to deliver on this promise.

The company must also consider competitors' service standards, seeking to match or exceed those levels. Still, the objective is to maximize profits, not sales, which means looking at the costs of providing higher service levels. Some companies offer less service and charge a lower price; others offer more service and charge a premium price. In the end, the company must establish some service promise to the market. One appliance manufacturer set these service standards: to deliver at least 95 percent of the dealer's orders within 7 days of order receipt, to fill the dealer's orders with 99 percent accuracy, to answer dealer inquiries on order status within 3 hours, and to ensure that damage to merchandise in transit does not exceed 1 percent.

The company must then design a system that will minimize the cost of achieving its set objectives. Each possible market-logistics system will lead to the following cost:

$$M = T + FW + VW + S$$

where

M = total market-logistics cost of proposed system;

T = total freight cost of proposed system;

FW = total fixed warehouse cost of proposed system;

VW = total variable warehouse costs (including inventory) of proposed system; and

S = total cost of lost sales due to average delivery delay under proposed system.

Choosing a market-logistics system calls for examining the total cost (M) associated with different proposed systems and selecting the system that minimizes it. If it is hard to measure S, the company should aim to minimize $T + FW + VW$ for a target level of customer service.

Market-Logistics Decisions

Companies must make four major decisions with regard to market logistics: (1) How should orders be handled? (order processing); (2) Where should stocks be located? (warehousing); (3) How much stock should be held? (inventory); and (4) How should goods be shipped? (transportation).

Order Processing

Most companies want to shorten the *order-to-remittance cycle*—the elapsed time between an order's receipt, delivery, and payment. This cycle involves many steps, including order transmission by the salesperson, order entry and customer credit check, inventory and production scheduling, order and invoice shipment, and receipt of payment. The longer this cycle takes, the lower the customer's satisfaction and the lower the company's profits. But companies are making great progress.

Consider the benefits of retailer Dayton-Hudson's Global Merchandising System, a supply chain information system with sophisticated applications such as forecasting, ordering, and trend analysis. When Target, a Dayton-Hudson store, orders a certain number of sweatshirts from a supplier such as Sara Lee Branded Apparel, it may specify only style. As the delivery date nears, Target analyzes trends for colors and sizes. Based on those forecasts, Sara Lee makes trial lots, and Target starts to sell them. If customers buy more navy sweatshirts, Target adjusts its order. Result: Both Sara Lee and Target have fewer goods in inventory and fewer markdowns.[22]

Warehousing

Every manufacturer has to store finished goods until they are sold because production and consumption cycles rarely match. The storage function helps to smooth discrepancies between production and quantities desired by the market. Two warehousing options are *storage warehouses,* which hold goods for moderate-to long periods, and *distribution warehouses,* which receive goods from company plants and suppliers and move them out as soon as possible. Having more stocking locations means that goods can be delivered to customers more quickly, but it also means higher warehousing costs, which is why many firms are reassessing their warehousing arrangements. When National Semiconductor closed six storage warehouses and set up a central distribution warehouse in Singapore, it was able to cut its standard delivery time by 47 percent, cut distribution costs by 2.5 percent, and boost sales by 34 percent.[23]

Newer automated warehouses are equipped with advanced materials-handling systems under the control of a central computer. The computer reads store orders and directs lift trucks and electric hoists to gather goods according to bar codes, move them to loading docks, and issue invoices. Automated warehouses save money by reducing worker injuries, labor costs, pilferage, and breakage while improving inventory control. For instance, when Helene Curtis replaced its six antiquated warehouses with a new $32 million facility, it cut its distribution costs by 40 percent.[24]

Inventory

Inventory levels represent a major market-logistics decision. Salespeople would like to have enough stock to fill all customer orders immediately, but this is not cost effective. *Inventory cost increases at an increasing rate as the customer service level approaches 100 percent.* To make an informed decision, management needs to determine how much sales and profits would increase as a result of carrying larger inventories and promising faster order fulfillment times.

Crafting an inventory strategy means knowing when to order and how much to order. As inventory draws down, management must know at what stock level to place a new order. This stock level is called the *order (reorder) point.* An order point of 20 means reordering when the stock falls to 20 units. The order point should balance the risks of stockout against the costs of overstock.

The other decision is how much to order. The larger the quantity ordered, the less frequently an order has to be placed. Here, the company is balancing order-processing costs against inventory-carrying costs. *Order-processing costs* for a manufacturer consist of *setup costs* and *running costs* (operating costs when production is running). If setup costs are low, the manufacturer can produce the item often, and the average cost per item is stable and equal to the running costs. If setup costs are high, however, the manufacturer can cut the average cost per unit by producing a long run and carrying more inventory.

Order-processing costs must be compared with *inventory-carrying costs.* The larger the average stock carried, the higher the inventory-carrying costs, including storage charges, cost of capital, taxes and insurance, and depreciation and obsolescence. This means that marketing managers who want their companies to carry larger inventories need to show that the larger inventories would produce incremental gross profit that exceeds the incremental inventory-carrying costs.

The optimal order quantity can be determined by analyzing the sum of order-processing costs and inventory-carrying costs at different order levels. As shown in Figure 14.1, the order-processing cost per unit decreases with the number of units ordered because the order costs are spread over more units. Inventory-carrying charges per unit increase with the number of units ordered because each unit remains longer in inventory. The two cost curves are summed vertically into a total-cost curve. The lowest point on the total-cost curve is projected down on the horizontal axis to find the optimal order quantity $Q*$.[25]

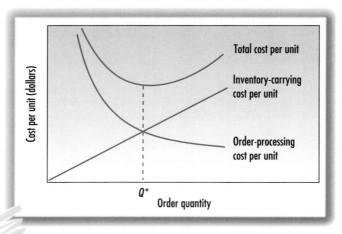

Figure 14.1   Determining Optimal Order Quantity

Just-in-time production methods have changed inventory-planning practices. With just-in-time production, supplies arrive at the factory when they are needed. If the suppliers are dependable, then the manufacturer can carry much lower levels of inventory and still meet customer-order-fulfillment standards. Tesco, the large British supermarket chain, has set up an innovative JIT market logistics system. Tesco's management reduced costly backroom storage space by arranging twice-a-day delivery of replenishment stock. And instead of using three trucks to deliver frozen goods, refrigerated goods, and regular goods, it designed new trucks with three compartments to carry all of these goods in one trip.

Transportation

Transportation choices will affect product pricing, on-time delivery performance, and the condition of the goods when they arrive, all of which influence customer satisfaction. In shipping goods to its warehouses, dealers, and customers, the company can choose among five transportation modes (rail, air, truck, waterway, and pipeline), using such criteria as speed, frequency, dependability, capability, availability, traceability, and cost. For speed, air and truck are the prime contenders; if the goal is low cost, then it is waterway and pipeline.

Shippers are increasingly combining two or more transportation modes, thanks to containerization. *Containerization* consists of putting the goods in boxes or trailers that are easy to transfer between two transportation modes. *Piggyback* describes the use of rail and trucks; *fishyback,* water and trucks; *trainship,* water and rail; and *airtruck,* air and trucks. Each coordinated mode offers specific advantages. For example, piggyback is cheaper than trucking alone, yet provides flexibility and convenience.

In deciding on transportation modes, shippers have three broad choices. If the shipper owns its own truck or air fleet, the shipper becomes a *private carrier.* A *contract carrier* is an independent organization that sells transportation services to others on a contract basis. A *common carrier* provides services between predetermined points on a schedule, and is available to all shippers at standard rates.

Transportation and all other market-logistics strategies must ultimately be derived from business strategies, rather than solely cost considerations. The most successful companies plan for electronic links among all the participants and set their logistics goals to match or exceed competitors' service standards. For some, superior market logistics has become a valuable focus for ad campaigns and other elements of integrated marketing communications, which are explored in Chapter 15.

EXECUTIVE SUMMARY

Retailing includes all of the activities involved in selling goods or services directly to final consumers for personal, nonbusiness use. Retailers include store retailing, nonstore retailing, and retail organizations. Like products, retail-store types pass through stages of growth and decline. The major types of retail stores are specialty stores, department stores, supermarkets, convenience stores, discount stores, off-price retailers, superstores, and catalog showrooms.

Although the overwhelming majority of goods and services is sold through stores, nonstore retailing (including Internet retailing) has been growing much faster than store retailing. The major types of nonstore retailing are direct selling, direct marketing, automatic vending, and buying services. An increasing number of retailers are part of corporate retailing and achieve many economies of scale, such as greater purchasing power, wider brand recognition, and better trained employees.

Both retailers and wholesalers must make decisions about target markets, product assortment and procurement, services and store atmosphere, price, promotion, and place, taking into account the major trends in the industry. Wholesaling includes all of the activities involved in selling goods or services to those who buy for resale or business use. Manufacturers use wholesalers because wholesalers can perform certain functions better and more cost effectively than the manufacturer can, such as selling and promoting, buying and assortment building, bulk breaking, warehousing, transportation, financing, risk bearing, dissemination of market information, and training and consulting.

Types of wholesalers include merchant wholesalers; full-service and limited-service wholesalers; brokers; agents; manufacturers' and retailers' sales branches, sales offices, and purchasing offices; and miscellaneous wholesalers such as agricultural assemblers. The most successful wholesalers adapt their services to meet suppliers' and target customers' needs, adding value to the channel.

Producers of physical products and services must make decisions about and set objectives for market logistics—the best way to store and move goods and services to market destinations. Logistics decisions cover order processing, warehousing, inventory, and transportation. Although the cost of market logistics can be high, a well-planned market-logistics program can be a potent tool in competitive marketing. The ultimate goal of market logistics is to meet customers' requirements in an efficient and profitable way.

NOTES

1. William R. Davidson, Albert D. Bates, and Stephen J. Bass, "Retail Life Cycle," *Harvard Business Review* (November-December 1976), pp. 89–96.
2. See Jeffrey Davis, "Chasing Retail's Tail," *Business 2.0,* January 2000, p. 172.
3. Stanley C. Hollander, "The Wheel of Retailing," *Journal of Marketing,* July 1960, pp. 37–42.
4. Hoover's Company Capsules, 1999.
5. Laurence H. Wortzel, "Retailing Strategies for Today's Marketplace," *Journal of Business Strategy,* Spring 1987, pp. 45–56.

6. For more discussion, see Philip Kotler, "Atmospherics as a Marketing Tool," *Journal of Retailing*, Winter 1973-1974, pp. 48–64; and Mary Jo Bitner, "Servicescapes: The Impact of Physical Surroundings on Customers and Employees," *Journal of Marketing*, April 1992, pp. 57–71. Also see B. Joseph Pine II and James H. Gilmore, *The Experience Economy* (Boston: Harvard Business School Press, 1999).

7. Shannon Stevens, "The Return of Red Lobster," *American Demographics*, October 1998; Chelsea J. Carter, "Theme Restaurants Face Trouble," *Associated Press*, December 17, 1998; "Planet Hollywood Announces Approval of Reorganization Plan," *PR Newswire*, January 25, 2000, www.hoovers.com.

8. Frank Feather, *The Future Consumer* (Toronto: Warwick Publishing, 1994), p. 171. Also see Stephen J. Hoch, Xavier Dreeze, and Mary E. Purk, "EDLP, Hi-Lo, and Margin Arithmetic," *Journal of Marketing*, October 1994, pp. 1–15.

9. R. L. Davies and D. S. Rogers, eds., *Store Location and Store Assessment Research* (New York: John Wiley, 1984).

10. See Sara L. McLafferty, *Location Strategies for Retail and Service Firms* (Lexington, MA: Lexington Books, 1987).

11. Diana Shaman, "Carts and Kiosks Draw Small Retailers to Malls," *New York Times*, January 16, 2000, sec. 11, p. 11.

12. Jay L. Johnson, "Supercenters: An Evolving Saga," *Discount Merchandiser*, April 1995, pp. 26–30.

13. For further discussion of retail trends, see Louis W. Stern and Adel I. El-Ansary, *Marketing Channels*, 5th ed. (Upper Saddle River, NJ: Prentice-Hall, 1996).

14. Shelley Donald Coolidge, "Facing Saturated Home Markets, Retailers Look to Rest of World," *Christian Science Monitor*, February 14, 1994, p. 7; Carla Rapoport with Justin Martin, "Retailers Go Global," *Fortune*, February 20, 1995, pp. 102–108; Amy Feldman, "Wal-Mart: How Big Can It Get?" *Money*, December 1999, pp. 158–164; Kerry Capell and Heidi Dawley, "Wal-Mart's Not-So-Secret British Weapon," *Business Week*, January 24, 2000, p. 132.

15. Patrick Harrington, "27% Rise in Profit Perks Up Starbucks," *Seattle Times*, November 19, 1999, www.seattletimes.com/news/business/html98/sbux_19991119.html.

16. Hoover's Company Profiles, 1999, and company Web site.

17. Roy R. Reynolds, "Hewlett-Packard, Amazon.com Form Web, Retail Pact," *Dow Jones Newswires*, November 30, 1999.

18. Hoover's Company Profiles, 1999, and company Web site; Susan E. Fisher, "W. W. Grainger Procures Success on the Web," *Info World*, December 10, 1999, www.infoworld.com.

19. James A. Narus and James C. Anderson, "Contributing as a Distributor to Partnerships with Manufacturers," *Business Horizons*, September–October 1987. Also see James D. Hlavecek and Tommy J. McCuistion, "Industrial Distributors—When, Who, and How," *Harvard Business Review*, March-April 1983, pp. 96–101.

20. Ronald Henkoff, "Delivering the Goods," *Fortune*, November 28, 1994, pp. 64–78.

21. Susan Reda, "Crossdocking: Can Supermarkets Catch Up?" *Stores*, February, 1998.

22. Tom Stein and Jeff Sweat, "Killer Supply Chains: Six Companies Are Using Supply Chains to Transform the Way They Do Business," *Information Week*, November 11, 1998, p. 36.

23. Henkoff, "Delivering the Goods," pp. 64–78.

24. Rita Koselka, "Distribution Revolution," *Forbes*, May 25, 1992, pp. 54–62.

25. The optimal order quantity is given by the formula $Q^* = 2DS/IC$, where D = annual demand, S = cost to place one order, and I = annual carrying cost per unit. Known as the economic-order quantity formula, it assumes a constant ordering cost, a constant cost of carrying an additional unit in inventory, a known demand, and no quantity discounts. For further reading on this subject, see Richard J. Tersine, *Principles of Inventory and Materials Management*, 4th ed. (Upper Saddle River, NJ: Prentice-Hall, 1994).

Chapter 15

Designing and Managing Integrated Marketing Communications

In this chapter, we will address the following questions:

■ What are the major steps in developing effective marketing communications?

■ What steps are involved in developing an advertising program?

■ What explains the growing use of sales promotion, and how are sales-promotion decisions made?

■ How can companies exploit the marketing potential of public relations and publicity?

M odern marketing calls for more than developing a good product, pricing it attractively, and making it accessible. Companies must also communicate with present and potential stakeholders as well as the general public. For most companies, the question is not whether to communicate but rather what to say, to whom, and how often.

The marketing communications mix consists of advertising, sales promotion, public relations and publicity, personal selling, and direct marketing, although savvy marketers know that communication goes beyond these five methods. The product's styling and price, the package's shape and color, the salesperson's manner and dress, the place's decor—all communicate something to buyers. In fact, every brand contact delivers an impression that can affect a customer's view of the company. Therefore, the entire marketing mix must be integrated to deliver a consistent message and strategic positioning.

In this chapter we first explore effective marketing communications and the communications mix, and then look more closely at advertising, sales promotion, and public relations. In Chapter 16 we discuss the sales force and personal selling; and in Chapter 17 we examine direct and on-line marketing.

DEVELOPING EFFECTIVE MARKETING COMMUNICATIONS

Today there is a new view of communications as an interactive dialogue between the company and its customers that takes place during the preselling, selling, consuming, and postconsuming stages. Successful companies are asking not only "How can we reach our customers?" but, in a break from the past, are also asking "How can our customers reach us?" Now sellers use a variety of communication platforms to stay in touch with customers, as shown in Table 15.1. Increasingly, it is the newer technologies, such as the Internet, that have encouraged more firms to move from mass communication to more targeted communication and one-to-one dialogue with customers and other stakeholders.

There are eight steps to follow in developing an effective marketing communications program: (1) identify the target audience, (2) determine the communication objectives, (3) design the message, (4) select the communication channels, (5) establish the total communications budget, (6) decide on the communications mix, (7) measure the communications' results, and (8) manage the integrated marketing communication process.

Step 1: Identifying the Target Audience

The first step is to identify a clear target audience: potential buyers of the company's products, current users, deciders, or influencers; individuals, groups, particular publics, or the general public. The target audience is a critical influence on the communicator's decisions about what to say, how to say it, when to say it, where to say it, and to whom to say it.

Table 15.1   Common Communication Platforms

Advertising	Sales Promotion	Public Relations	Personal Selling	Direct Marketing
Print, broadcast, on-line ads	Contests, games, sweepstakes, lotteries	Press kits	Sales presentations	Catalogs
Packaging	Premiums, gifts	Video news releases	Sales meetings	Mailings
Motion pictures	Sampling	Speeches	Incentive programs	Telemarketing
Brochures, booklets	Fairs, trade shows	Seminars	Fairs and trade shows	Electronic shopping
Directories	Demonstrations	Annual reports		TV shopping
Billboards, posters	Coupons	Charitable donations		Fax mail
Display signs	Rebates	Sponsorships		E-mail
Point-of-purchase displays	Low-interest financing	Publications		Voice mail
Audiovisual material	Trade-in allowances	Community relations		
Symbols and logos	Continuity programs	Lobbying		
Videotapes	Tie-ins	Identity media		
Web sites and banners		Special events		

Further analysis helps the company assess the audience's current image of the company, its products, and its competitors. **Image** is the set of beliefs, ideas, and impressions that a person holds regarding an object. People's attitudes and actions toward an object such as a product or service are highly conditioned by that object's image. In assessing image, marketers research the audience's familiarity with the product, then they ask respondents who know the product how they feel about it.

If most respondents have unfavorable feelings toward the product, the organization needs to overcome a negative image problem, which requires great patience because images persist long after the organization has changed. Once people have a certain image, they perceive what is consistent with that image. It will take highly disconfirming information to raise doubts and open their minds—but it can be done. Wolverine World Wide of Rockford, Michigan, discovered this when its Hush Puppies brand of casual shoes lost its fashionable image. Then a fashion designer used Hush Puppies dyed in bright colors, changing the product's image from stodgy to avant garde. Once the "new" Hush Puppies were in demand, sales skyrocketed from less than 30,000 to millions of pairs sold in just 2 years.[1]

Step 2: Determining the Communication Objectives

Knowing the target audience and its perceptions, the marketing communicator can now decide on the desired audience response, seeking a *cognitive, affective,* or *behavioral* response. That is, the marketer might want to put something into the consumer's mind, change an attitude, or get the consumer to act. The four best-known models of consumer-response stages are presented in Figure 15.1.

Figure 15.1   Response Hierarchy Models

Stages	Models			
	AIDA Model[a]	Hierarchy-of-Effects Model[b]	Innovation-Adoption Model[c]	Communications Model[d]
Cognitive stage	Attention ↓	Awareness ↓ Knowledge ↓	Awareness ↓	Exposure ↓ Reception ↓ Cognitive response ↓
Affective stage	Interest ↓ Desire ↓	Liking ↓ Preference ↓ Conviction ↓	Interest ↓ Evaluation ↓	Attitude ↓ Intention ↓
Behavior stage	Action	Purchase	Trial ↓ Adoption	Behavior

All of these models assume that the buyer passes through a cognitive, affective, and behavioral stage, in that order. This "learn-feel-do" sequence is appropriate when the audience has high involvement with a product category that is perceived to have high differentiation, as in purchasing an automobile. An alternative sequence, "do-feel-learn," is relevant when the audience has high involvement but perceives little or no differentiation within the product category, as in purchasing aluminum siding. A third sequence, "learn-do-feel," is relevant when the audience has low involvement and perceives little differentiation within the product category, as in purchasing salt. By choosing the right sequence, the marketer can do a better job of planning communications.[2]

Step 3: Designing the Message

Having defined the desired response, the communicator moves to developing an effective message. Ideally, the message should gain *attention*, hold *interest*, arouse *desire*, and elicit *action* (*AIDA model*—see the first column of Figure 15.1). In practice, few messages take the target audience all the way from awareness through purchase, but the AIDA framework suggests the desirable qualities of any communication. Formulating the message will require solving four problems: what to say (message content), how to say it logically (message structure), how to say it symbolically (message format), and who should say it (message source).

Message Content

In determining message content, management searches for an appeal, theme, idea, or unique selling proposition. There are three types of appeals:

➤ *Rational appeals* engage self-interest by claiming the product will produce certain benefits such as value or performance. It is widely believed that industrial buyers are most responsive to rational appeals because they are knowledgeable about the product, trained to recognize value, and accountable to others for their choices. Consumers, when they buy certain big-ticket items, also tend to gather information and estimate benefits.

➤ *Emotional appeals* attempt to stir up negative or positive emotions that will motivate purchase. Marketers search for the right *emotional selling proposition*. Even when the product is similar to the competitions' product, it may have unique associations that can be promoted (examples are Harley-Davidson and Rolex). Communicators also work with negative appeals such as fear, guilt, and shame to get people to do things (brush their teeth) or stop doing things (smoking). In addition, positive emotional appeals such as humor, love, pride, and joy are often part of the message content.

➤ *Moral appeals* are directed to the audience's sense of what is right and proper. These are often used to exhort people to support social causes. An example is the appeal "Silence = Death," which is the slogan of Act-Up, the AIDS Coalition to Unleash Power.

Multinational companies wrestle with a number of challenges in developing message content for global campaigns. First, they must decide whether the product is appropriate for a country. Second, they must make sure the targeted market segment is both legal and customary. Third, they must decide if the style of the ad is acceptable or customary in all of the countries. And fourth, they must decide whether ads should be created at headquarters or locally. FedEx, the package express carrier, has chosen to create ads at its U.S. headquarters. Long known for its humorous ads, the company recently created a campaign that ran in 20 countries with only minor changes, instead of being customized or created in each local area. This campaign helped FedEx deliver the message that "we've become a global company."[3]

Message Structure

Message effectiveness depends on structure as well as content. For example, a communicator may think that one-sided presentations that praise a product would be more effective than two-sided arguments that also mention shortcomings. Yet two-sided messages may be more appropriate, especially when some negative association must be overcome. In this spirit, Heinz ran the message "Heinz Ketchup is slow good" and Listerine ran the message "Listerine tastes bad twice a day."[4] Two-sided messages are more effective with more educated audiences and those who are initially opposed.[5]

The order in which arguments are presented is also an important part of message structure.[6] In the case of a one-sided message, presenting the strongest argument first has the advantage of establishing attention and interest. This is important in newspapers and other media where the audience often does not attend to the whole message. With a captive audience, however, a climactic presentation might be more effective. In the case of a two-sided message, if the audience is initially opposed, the communicator might start with the other side's argument and conclude with the strongest argument.[7]

Message Format

The communicator must develop a strong message format. In a print ad, the communicator has to decide on headline, copy, illustration, and color. For radio, the communicator has to choose words, voice qualities, and vocalizations. If the message is to be carried on television or in person, all of these elements plus body language (nonverbal clues) have to be planned. If the message is carried by the product or its packaging, the communicator has to pay attention to color, texture, scent, size, and shape. Web-based messages have the flexibility to combine aspects of print, radio, and television messages with a variety of special effects and interactive features to attract, retain, and reinforce audience interest.

Message Source

Messages delivered by attractive or popular sources achieve higher attention and recall, which is why advertisers often use celebrities as spokespeople. In particular, messages delivered by highly credible sources are more persuasive, so pharmaceutical companies have doctors testify about product benefits because doctors have high credibility.

Three factors that underly source credibility are expertise, trustworthiness, and likability.[8] *Expertise* is the specialized knowledge the communicator possesses to back the claim. *Trustworthiness* is related to how objective and honest the source is perceived to be. Friends are trusted more than strangers or salespeople, and people who are not paid to endorse a product are seen as more trustworthy than people who are paid.[9] *Likability* describes the source's attractiveness; qualities like candor, humor, and naturalness make a source more likable. The most credible source would score high on all three factors.

Step 4: Selecting Communication Channels

Now that the message has been designed, the communicator must select efficient communication channels to carry it. For example, pharmaceutical salespeople can rarely wrest more than 10 minutes' time from a busy physician. Because personal selling is expensive, the industry has added multiple channels: ads in medical journals, direct mail (including audio and videotapes), sampling, telemarketing, Web sites, conferences and teleconferences, and more. All of these channels are used in the hope of building physician preference for particular branded drug products. In general, firms can use two types of communication channels: personal and nonpersonal.

Personal Communication Channels

Personal communication channels involve two or more persons communicating directly with each other face to face, person to audience, over the telephone, or through e-mail. These channels derive their effectiveness through the opportunities for individualizing the presentation and feedback. Amazon.com, for example, invites on-line customers to sign up for e-mailed reviews and recommendations from experts in their choice of book, music, toy, and home improvement subjects.

Companies can take several steps to stimulate personal influence channels to work on their behalf:

➤ *Identify influential individuals and companies and devote extra effort to them:*[10] In industrial selling, the entire industry might follow the market leader in adopting innovations.

➤ *Create opinion leaders by supplying certain people with the product on attractive terms:* A new tennis racket might be offered initially to members of high school tennis teams at a special low price.

➤ *Work through community influentials such as local disk jockeys and heads of civic organizations:* When Ford introduced the Thunderbird, it sent invitations to executives offering a free car to drive for the day; 10 percent of the respondents indicated that they would become buyers, and 84 percent said they would recommend the car to a friend.

➤ *Use influential or believable people in testimonial advertising:* This is why sports equipment and apparel companies hire top athletes such as Tiger Woods as spokespeople.

➤ *Develop advertising that has high "conversation value":* Ads with high conversation value often have a slogan that becomes part of the national vernacular, such as Nike's "Just do it."

➤ *Develop word-of-mouth referral channels to build business:* Professionals such as accountants will often encourage clients to recommend their services.

➤ *Establish an electronic forum:* Toyota owners who use Internet services such as America Online can hold on-line discussions to share experiences.

Nonpersonal Communication Channels

Nonpersonal channels include media, atmospheres, and events. *Media* consist of print media (newspapers, magazines, direct mail), broadcast media (radio, television), electronic media (audiotape, videotape, CD-ROM, DVD, Web page), and display media (billboards, signs, posters). Most nonpersonal messages come through paid media.

Atmospheres are "packaged environments" that create or reinforce the buyer's leanings toward product purchase. Law offices are decorated with fine rugs and furniture to communicate "stability" and "success;"[11] Coca-Cola's Web (www.cocacola.com) site is colorful and animated to reinforce the brand's upbeat image.

Events are occurrences designed to communicate particular messages to target audiences. Tokyo's Mitsukoshi Department Store, for example, arranges special cultural events and arts exhibits in the flagship store to maintain a sophisticated, cultured image in the minds of upscale shoppers.

Although personal communication is often more effective, nonpersonal channels affect personal attitudes and behavior through a two-step flow-of-communication process. Ideas often flow from radio, television, print, and Internet sources to *opinion leaders* and from these to the less media-involved population groups. This two-step flow has several implications. First, the influence of nonpersonal channels on public opinion is mediated by opinion leaders, people whose opinions are sought or who carry their opinions to others. Second, the two-step flow shows that people interact primarily within their own social group and acquire ideas from opinion leaders in their group. Third, two-step communication suggests that marketers using nonpersonal channels should direct messages specifically to opinion leaders and let them carry the message to others. This is why many software makers give opinion leaders a preview of new programs before they are sold to the general public.

Step 5: Establishing the Marketing Communications Budget

Industries and companies vary considerably in how much they spend on promotion; expenditures might amount to 30–50 percent of sales in the cosmetics industry but only 5–10 percent in the industrial-equipment industry, with variations from company to company. How do companies decide on the promotion budget? Here are four common methods:

➤ *Affordable method.* Many companies set the promotion budget at what management thinks the firm can afford. However, this method ignores the role of promotion as an investment and the immediate impact of promotion on sales volume; it also leads to an uncertain annual budget, making long-range planning difficult.

➤ *Percentage-of-sales method.* Many firms set promotion expenditures at a specified percentage of sales (either current or anticipated) or of the sales price. Supporters say this method links promotion expenditures to the movement of corporate sales over the business cycle; encourages management to consider the interrelationship of promotion cost, selling price, and unit profit; and encourages stability when competing firms spend approximately the same percentage. On the other hand, this method views sales as the determiner of promotion rather than as the result, and it provides no logical basis for choosing the specific percentage.

➤ *Competitive-parity method.* Some companies set their promotion budget to achieve share-of-voice parity with competitors. Although proponents say that competitors' expenditures represent the collective wisdom of the industry and that maintaining competitive parity prevents promotion wars, neither argument is valid. There are no grounds for believing that competitors know better what should be spent on promotion. Company reputations, resources, opportunities, and objectives differ so much that promotion budgets are hardly a guide. Furthermore, there is no evidence that competitive parity discourages promotional wars.

➤ *Objective-and-task method.* Here, marketers develop promotion budgets by defining specific objectives, determining the tasks that must be performed to achieve these objectives, and estimating the costs of performing these tasks. The sum of these costs is the proposed promotion budget. This method has the advantage of requiring management to spell out assumptions about the relationship among dollars spent, exposure levels, trial rates, and regular usage.

Step 6: Developing and Managing the Marketing Communications Mix

Having established a communications budget, companies must decide how to allocate it over the five promotional tools. Companies differ considerably in their allocations, even within the same industry. Avon concentrates its promotional funds on personal selling, whereas Cover Girl spends heavily on advertising. Still, because companies are always searching for more efficiency by substituting one promotional tool for another, they must be careful to coordinate all of their marketing functions.

Promotional Tools

Each promotional tool has its own unique characteristics and costs.[12]

➤ *Advertising.* Advertising can be used to build up a long-term image for a product (Coca-Cola ads) or trigger quick sales (a Sears ad for a weekend sale). Advertising can reach geographically dispersed buyers efficiently. Certain forms of advertising (TV advertising) typically require a large budget, whereas other forms (newspaper advertising) can be done on a small budget. We discuss advertising in more detail later in this chapter.

➤ *Sales promotion.* Although sales-promotion tools—coupons, contests, premiums, and the like—are highly diverse, they offer three distinctive benefits: (1) *communication* (they gain attention and usually provide information that may lead the consumer to the product); (2) *incentive* (they incorporate some concession or inducement that gives value to the consumer); and (3) *invitation* (they include a distinct invitation to engage in the transaction now). Sales promotion can be used for short-run effects such as dramatizing product offers and boosting sales. Later in this chapter we discuss sales promotion in more detail.

➤ *Public relations and publicity.* The appeal of public relations and publicity is based on three distinctive qualities: (1) *high credibility* (news stories and features are more authentic and credible than ads); (2) *ability to catch buyers off guard* (reach prospects who prefer to avoid salespeople and advertisements); and (3) *dramatization* (the potential for dramatizing a company or product). This underused technique is examined later in this chapter.

➤ *Personal selling.* Personal selling has three distinctive qualities: (1) *personal confrontation* (it involves an immediate and interactive relationship between two or more persons); (2) *cultivation* (it permits all kinds of relationships to spring up, ranging from a matter-of-fact selling relationship to a deep personal friendship); and (3) *response* (it makes the buyer feel under some obligation for having listened to the sales talk).

➤ *Direct marketing.* All forms of direct marketing—direct mail, telemarketing, Internet marketing—share four distinctive characteristics: They are (1) *nonpublic* (the message is normally addressed to a specific person); (2) *customized* (the message can be prepared to appeal to the addressed individual); (3) *up-to-date* (a message can be prepared very quickly); and (4) *interactive* (the message can be changed depending on the person's response).

Factors in Setting the Marketing Communications Mix

Companies must consider several factors in developing their promotion mix:

➤ *Type of product market.* As Figure 15.2 shows, promotional allocations vary between consumer and business markets. Although advertising is used less than sales calls in business markets, it still plays a significant role in building awareness and comprehension, serving as an efficient reminder of the product, generating leads, legitimizing the company and products, and reassuring customers about their purchases. Personal selling can also make a strong contribution in consumer-goods marketing by helping to persuade dealers to take more stock and display more of the product, build dealer enthusiasm, sign up more dealers, and grow sales at existing accounts.

➤ *Push-versus-pull strategy.* A *push strategy* involves the manufacturer using sales force and trade promotion to induce intermediaries to carry, promote, and sell the product to end users. This is especially appropriate where there is low brand loyalty

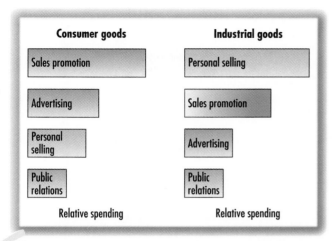

Figure 15.2   Relative Spending on Promotional Tools in Consumer versus Business Markets

in a category; brand choice is made in the store; the product is an impulse item; and product benefits are well understood. A *pull strategy* involves the manufacturer using advertising and consumer promotion to induce consumers to ask intermediaries for the product, thus inducing the intermediaries to order it. This is especially appropriate when there is high brand loyalty and high involvement in the category; people perceive differences between brands; and people choose the brand before they go to the store.

➤ *Buyer-readiness stage.* Promotional tools vary in cost effectiveness at different stages of buyer readiness, as shown in Figure 15.3. Advertising and publicity play the most important roles in the awareness-building stage. Customer comprehension is affected primarily by advertising and personal selling, while customer conviction is influenced mostly by personal selling. Closing the sale is influenced mostly by personal selling and sales promotion. Reordering is also affected mostly by personal selling and sales promotion, and somewhat by reminder advertising.

➤ *Product-life cycle stage.* Promotional tools also vary in cost effectiveness at different stages of the product life cycle. Advertising and publicity are most cost effective in the introduction stage; then all the tools can be toned down in the growth stage because demand is building word of mouth. Sales promotion, advertising, and personal selling grow more important in the maturity stage. In the decline stage, sales promotion continues strong, advertising and publicity are reduced, and salespeople give the product only minimal attention.

➤ *Company market rank.* Market leaders derive more benefit from advertising than from sales promotion. Conversely, smaller competitors gain more by using sales promotion in their marketing communications mix.

Step 7: Measuring Results

After implementing the promotional plan, the communicator must measure its impact. Members of the target audience are asked whether they recognize or recall the message, how many times they saw it, what points they recall, how they felt about the message, and their previous and current attitudes toward the product

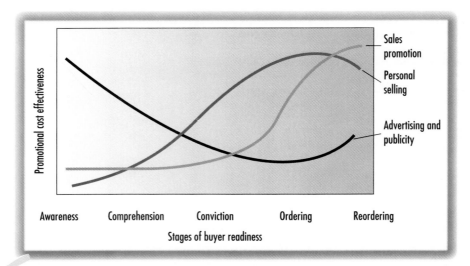

Figure 15.3 Cost Effectiveness of Different Promotional Tools at Different Buyer-Readiness Stages

and company. The communicator should also collect behavioral measures of audience response, such as how many people bought the product, liked it, and talked to others about it.

Suppose that 80 percent of the targeted customers are aware of the brand, 60 percent have tried it, and only 20 percent who have tried it are satisfied. This indicates that the communications program is effective in creating awareness, but the product fails to meet consumer expectations. However, if 40 percent of the targeted customers are aware of the brand and only 30 percent have tried it—but 80 percent of those who have tried it are satisfied—the communications program needs to be strengthened to take advantage of the brand's power.

Step 8: Managing the Integrated Marketing Communications Process

Given the fragmenting of mass markets into minimarkets, the proliferation of new types of media, and the growing sophistication of consumers, companies need to use a wider range of communication tools, messages, and audiences. To do this most effectively, companies must embrace integrated marketing communications. As defined by the American Association of Advertising Agencies, *integrated marketing communications (IMC)* is a concept of marketing communications planning that recognizes the added value of a comprehensive plan that evaluates the strategic roles of a variety of communications disciplines—for example, general advertising, direct response, sales promotion and public relations—and combines these disciplines to provide clarity, consistency, and maximum communications' impact through the seamless integration of discrete messages.

Warner-Lambert, maker of Benadryl, has creatively used IMC to promote its antihistamine drug. The company used advertising and public relations to increase brand awareness among allergy sufferers and to promote a toll-free number that provided people with the pollen count in their area. People who called the number more than once received free product samples, coupons, and materials describing the product's benefits. These people also received a newsletter with advice about coping with allergies.[13]

Savvy firms know that IMC produces stronger message consistency and greater sales impact; it also gives someone responsibility to unify the company's various brand images and messages. Properly implemented, IMC will improve the company's ability to reach the right customers with the right messages at the right time and in the right place.[14]

DEVELOPING AND MANAGING THE ADVERTISING CAMPAIGN

Advertising is any paid form of nonpersonal presentation and promotion of ideas, goods, or services by an identified sponsor.[15] Advertisers include not only business firms but also museums, charitable organizations, and government agencies that direct messages to target publics. Ads are a cost-effective way to disseminate messages, whether to build brand preference for Intel computer chips or to educate people about the dangers of drugs.

In developing an advertising program, successful firms start by identifying the target market and buyer motives. Then they can make five critical decisions, known as the five Ms: *Mission:* What are the advertising objectives? *Money:* How much can be spent? *Message:* What message should be sent? *Media:* What media should be used? *Measurement:* How should the results be evaluated? These decisions are summarized in Figure 15.4 and described in the following sections.

Figure 15.4   The Five Ms of Advertising

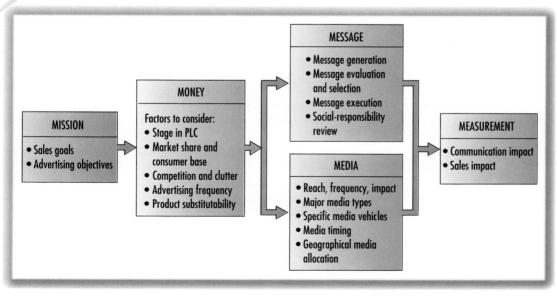

Setting the Advertising Objectives

Advertising objectives can be classified according to whether their aim is to inform, persuade, or remind.

➤ *Informative advertising* figures heavily in the pioneering stage of a product category, where the objective is to build primary demand. Thus, DVD makers initially had to inform consumers of the benefits of this technology.

➤ *Persuasive advertising* becomes important in the competitive stage, where the objective is to build selective demand for a particular brand. For example, Chivas Regal attempts to persuade consumers that it delivers more taste and status than other brands of Scotch whiskey. Some persuasive advertising is *comparative advertising*, which explicitly compares two or more brands.[16]

➤ *Reminder advertising* is important with mature products. Coca-Cola ads are primarily intended to remind people to purchase Coca-Cola. A related form of advertising is *reinforcement advertising*, which seeks to assure current purchasers that they have made the right choice. Automobile ads often depict satisfied customers enjoying special features of their new car.

The advertising objective should emerge from a thorough analysis of the current marketing situation. If the product class is mature, the company is the market leader, and brand usage is low, the proper objective should be to stimulate more usage. If the product class is new, the company is not the market leader, but the brand is superior to the leader, then the proper objective is to convince the market of the brand's superiority.

Deciding on the Advertising Budget

Management should consider these five factors when setting the advertising budget:[17]

1. *Product life cycle stage:* New products typically receive large budgets to build awareness and to gain consumer trial. Established brands usually are supported with lower budgets as a ratio to sales.

2. *Market share and consumer base:* High-market-share brands usually require less advertising expenditure as a percentage of sales to maintain their share. To build share by increasing market size requires larger advertising expenditures. On a cost-per-impression basis, it is less expensive to reach consumers of a widely used brand than to reach consumers of low-share brands.

3. *Competition and clutter:* In a market with a large number of competitors and high advertising spending, a brand must advertise more heavily to be heard. Even simple clutter from advertisements that are not directly competitive to the brand creates a need for heavier advertising.

4. *Advertising frequency:* The number of repetitions needed to put across the brand's message to consumers has an important impact on the advertising budget.

5. *Product substitutability:* Brands in a commodity class (cigarettes, beer, soft drinks) require heavy advertising to establish a differential image. Advertising is also important when a brand offers unique benefits or features.

Choosing the Advertising Message

Advertising campaigns vary in their creativity. In the late 1990s, Taco Bell launched a clever television campaign featuring a chihuahua saying, "Yo Quiero Taco Bell," meaning "I want some Taco Bell." The campaign struck a chord with the chain's 18- to 35-year-old customers and spawned an impressive array of chihuahua merchandise such as T-shirts, magnets, and talking dolls. Taco Bell's sales shot up 4.3 percent in the campaign's first year; the firm now spends $200 million a year on advertising and is keeping the chihuahua in its ad campaigns.[18]

In developing a creative strategy, advertisers follow four steps: message generation, message evaluation and selection, message execution, and social responsibility review.

Message Generation

The product's "benefit" message should be decided as part of developing the product concept. Yet there is usually latitude for a number of possible messages. Over time, the marketer might want to change the message, especially if customers seek new or different benefits from the product.

Creative people use several methods to generate possible advertising appeals. Many creative people proceed *inductively* by talking to consumers, dealers, experts, and competitors, while others use a *deductive* framework. Regardless of the process, how many alternative ad themes should the advertiser create before choosing? The more ads that are created, the higher the probability of finding an excellent one. Yet this is a balancing act, because the more time spent on creating alternative ads, the higher the costs, even with the use of computerized tools to create rough versions of ads.

Message Evaluation and Selection

A good ad normally focuses on one core selling proposition. Twedt suggested that messages be rated on *desirability, exclusiveness,* and *believability.*[19] When the March of Dimes searched for an advertising theme to raise money for its fight against birth defects, managers brainstormed several messages. They asked a group of young parents to rate each for interest, distinctiveness, and believability, assigning up to 100 points for each. For example, "Seven hundred children are born each day with a birth defect" scored 70, 62, and 80 on interest, distinctiveness, and believability, whereas "Your next baby could be born with a birth defect" scored 58, 51, and 70. The first message outperformed the second on all accounts.[20] Smart advertisers conduct market research to determine which appeal works best with their audiences.

Message Execution

The message's impact depends not only upon what is said but also on how it is said. Some ads aim for *rational positioning* and others for *emotional positioning.* U.S. ads typically present an explicit feature or benefit with a rational appeal, such as "gets clothes cleaner," while Japanese ads tend to be less direct and appeal more to the emotions.

Message execution can be decisive for highly similar products, such as detergents, cigarettes, coffee, and vodka. Consider vodka. Although it is generally viewed as a commodity product, the amount of brand preference and loyalty in the vodka market is astonishing. Most of it is based on selling an image. The Swedish brand Absolut became the largest selling imported vodka in the United States by mounting a well-integrated targeting, packaging, and advertising strategy geared toward sophisticated, upwardly mobile, affluent drinkers. The distinctively shaped bottle, suggestive of Swedish austerity, has become an icon—and is used as the centerpiece of every ad, accompanied by puns such as "Absolut Magic." The firm also runs short stories about the brand written by distinguished authors in ads designed to appeal to readers of such magazines as *The New Yorker.*[21]

In preparing an ad campaign, the advertiser usually prepares a *copy strategy statement* describing the objective, content, support, and tone of the desired ad. Creative specialists must also find a cohesive blend of *style, tone, words,* and *format* for executing the message. Any message can be presented in a number of execution styles: slice of life, lifestyle, fantasy, mood or image, musical, personality symbol, technical expertise, scientific evidence, and testimonial. For example, testimonial advertising is used by Rogaine extra-strength for men, which promises to grow back more hair than does its predecessor. Rogaine television ads feature noted sports figures such as Utah Jazz basketball star Karl Malone delivering testimonials; in the ads, Malone says he got good results after using the product for 5 months.[22]

The actual words in an ad must be memorable and attention-getting to make an impression on the audience. The following ad themes (column on left) would have had much less impact without the creative phrasing (column on right):

Theme	Creative Copy
Milk is good for you.	Got milk? (Milk industry)
Our technology can help you do almost anything.	Where do you want to go today? (Microsoft)
No hard sell, just a good car.	Drivers wanted (Volkswagen)
You set the price instead of paying the regular price.	Name your own price. (Priceline.com)

Format elements such as ad size, color, and illustration will affect an ad's impact as well as its cost. Yet a minor rearrangement of mechanical elements can improve attention-getting power. Larger-size ads gain more attention, though not necessarily by as much as their difference in cost. Four-color illustrations increase ad effectiveness as well as ad cost. Still, by carefully planning the relative dominance of different elements, companies can achieve better message delivery.

Social Responsibility Review

Advertisers and their agencies must be sure their "creative" advertising does not overstep social and legal norms. Most marketers work hard to communicate openly and honestly with consumers. Still, abuses occur, and public policymakers have developed a substantial body of laws and regulations to govern advertising. Under U.S. law, for example, companies must avoid false or deceptive advertising. Also, sellers are legally obligated to avoid bait-and-switch advertising that attracts buyers under false pretenses.[23] And, to be socially responsible, advertisers must be careful not to offend ethnic groups, racial minorities, or special-interest groups. For instance, a commercial for Black Flag insecticide was altered after a veterans group protested the playing of Taps over dead bugs.[24]

Some companies have begun building ad campaigns on a platform of social responsibility. Look at Ethical Funds, a Canadian mutual fund firm that will not invest in corporations that are involved in the production of military weapons, tobacco, nuclear power, and those with unfair employment practices, poor environmental records, or companies that support reactionary political regimes. One Ethical Funds ad shows scenes of child labor and people dying from cancer, presumably caused by smoking, then asks, "Do you know where your money goes?" Ethical Funds has grown from $100 million in assets to more than $2 billion over the last decade.[25]

Developing Media Strategies

After choosing the message, the next task is to choose media to carry it. The steps here are deciding on desired reach, frequency, and impact; choosing among major media types; selecting specific media vehicles; deciding on media timing; and deciding on geographical media allocation.

Deciding on Reach, Frequency, and Impact

Media selection involves finding the most cost-effective media to deliver the desired number of exposures to the target audience. What do we mean by the desired number of exposures? Presumably, the advertiser is seeking a certain response from the target audience—for example, a certain level of product trial. The rate of product trial will depend, among other things, on the level of audience brand awareness. The effect of exposures on audience awareness depends on the exposures' reach, frequency, and impact:

➤ *Reach (R):* The number of different persons or households that are exposed to a particular media schedule at least once during a specified time period.

➤ *Frequency (F):* The number of times within the specified time period that an average person or household is exposed to the message.

➤ *Impact (I):* The qualitative value of an exposure through a given medium (thus a food ad in *Good Housekeeping* would have a higher impact than the same ad in the *Police Gazette*).

Although audience awareness will be greater with higher reach, frequency, and impact, there are important trade-offs among these elements. It is the media planner's job to figure out, within a given budget, the most cost-effective combination of reach, frequency, and impact. Reach is most important when launching new products, flanker brands, extensions of well-known brands, or infrequently purchased brands, or when going after an undefined target market. Frequency is most important where there are strong competitors, a complex story to tell, high consumer resistance, or a frequent-purchase cycle.[26]

Many advertisers believe that a target audience needs a large number of exposures for the advertising to work. Too few repetitions can be a waste because they will hardly be noticed. Others doubt the value of high ad frequency. They believe that after people see the same ad a few times, they either act on it, get irritated by it, or stop noticing it. Krugman asserted that three exposures to an advertisement might be enough.[27] Another factor arguing for repetition is that of forgetting. The higher the forgetting rate associated with a brand, product category, or message, the higher the warranted level of repetition. But repetition is not enough. Ads wear out and viewers tune out, so advertisers need fresh executions of the message. For example, Duracell can choose from more than 40 different versions of its basic ad.

Selecting Media and Vehicles

The media planner has to know the capacity of the major media types to deliver reach, frequency, and impact. The costs, advantages, and limitations of the major media are profiled in Table 15.2.

Media planners choose among these media categories by considering the following variables:

➤ *Target-audience media habits:* For example, radio, television, and the Internet are effective media for reaching teenagers.

➤ *Product:* Media types have different potentials for demonstration, visualization, explanation, believability, and color.

➤ *Message:* A message announcing a major sale tomorrow will require radio, TV, or newspaper. A message containing a great deal of technical data might require specialized magazines or mailings.

➤ *Cost:* Television is very expensive, whereas newspaper advertising is relatively inexpensive. What counts is the cost-per-thousand exposures.

Table 15.2   Profiles of Major Media Types

Medium	Advantages	Limitations
Newspapers	Flexibility; timeliness; good local market coverage; broad acceptance; high believability	Short life; poor reproduction quality; small "pass-along" audience
Television	Combines sight, sound, and motion; appealing to the senses; high attention; high reach	High absolute cost; high clutter; fleeting exposure; less audience selectivity
Direct mail	Audience selectivity; flexibility; no ad competition within the same medium; personalization	Relatively high cost; "junk mail" image
Radio	Mass use; high geographic and demographic selectivity; low cost	Audio presentation only; lower attention than television; nonstandardized rate structures; fleeting exposure
Magazines	High geographic and demographic selectivity; credibility and prestige; high-quality reproduction; long life; good pass-along readership	Long ad purchase lead time; some waste circulation; no guarantee of position
Outdoor	Flexibility; high repeat exposure; low cost; low competition	Limited audience selectivity; creative limitations
Yellow Pages	Excellent local coverage; high believability; wide reach; low cost	High competition; long ad purchase lead time; creative limitations
Newsletters	Very high selectivity; full control; interactive opportunities; relative low costs	Costs could run away
Brochures	Flexibility; full control; can dramatize messages	Overproduction could lead to runaway costs
Telephone	Many users; opportunity to give a personal touch	Relative high cost unless volunteers are used
Internet	High selectivity; interactive possibilities; relatively low cost	Relatively new media with a low number of users in some countries

Rust and Oliver see the proliferation of newer media such as the World Wide Web hastening the death of traditional mass-media advertising as we know it. They also see a greater amount of direct producer-consumer interaction, with benefits to both parties. Producers gain more information about their customers and can customize products and messages better; customers gain greater control because they can choose whether to receive an advertising message.[28]

Although Web-based advertising is growing rapidly, many companies are reluctant to spend heavily on banner ads and hotlinks because they have no reliable way of knowing who sees or clicks on these ads. The Internet is not simply another medium; it is a profoundly different experience where on-line consumers can pull what they want out of cyberspace and leave the rest behind. Therefore, advertisers have to be creative enough to make these consumers want to pull in their cybermessages.

Given all of these media choices, the media planner must first decide on how to allocate the budget to the major media types. Then the media planner searches for the most cost-effective media vehicles within each chosen media type—relying on media measurement services for estimates of audience size, composition, and media cost.

Audiences can be measured according to: (1) *circulation*, the number of physical units carrying the advertising; (2) *audience*, the number of people exposed to the vehicle (with pass-on readership, a print vehicle will have a larger audience than its circulation figures suggest); (3) *effective audience*, the number of people with target audience characteristics exposed to the vehicle; and (4) *effective ad-exposed audience*, the number of people with target audience characteristics who actually saw the ad.

Knowing the audience size, media planners can calculate the cost-per-thousand persons reached by a vehicle. If an ad in *Newsweek* costs $100,000 and *Newsweek's* estimated readership is 3 million people, the cost of exposing the ad to 1,000 persons is approximately $33. The same ad in *Business Week* may cost $30,000 but reach only 775,000 persons—at a cost per thousand of nearly $39. The media planner then ranks each magazine by cost per thousand and favors magazines with the lowest cost per thousand for reaching target consumers. The magazines themselves often put together a "reader profile" for their advertisers, summarizing the characteristics of the magazine's readers with respect to age, income, residence, marital status, and leisure activities, to help media planners better target their audiences.

Deciding on Media Timing

In choosing media, the advertiser faces a macroscheduling problem and a microscheduling problem. The macroscheduling problem involves scheduling the advertising in relation to seasons and the business cycle. Suppose 70 percent of a product's sales occur between June and September. The firm can vary its advertising expenditures to follow the seasonal pattern, to oppose the seasonal pattern, or to be constant throughout the year. Most firms pursue a seasonal policy, although advertising in the off-season may boost sales and consumption without hurting seasonal consumption.

The microscheduling problem calls for allocating advertising expenditures within a short period to obtain maximum impact. Over a given period, advertising messages can be concentrated ("burst" advertising), dispersed continuously, or dispersed intermittently. The advertiser must also decide whether to leave ad messages level, increase them, decrease them, or alternate them in the schedule.

In launching a new product, the advertiser can choose among ad continuity, concentration, flighting, and pulsing. *Continuity* is achieved by scheduling exposures evenly throughout a given period. Generally, advertisers use continuous advertising in expanding market situations, with frequently purchased items, and in tightly defined buyer categories. *Concentration* calls for spending all of the advertising dollars in a single period. This makes sense for products with one selling season or holiday. *Flighting* calls for advertising for some period, followed by a hiatus with no advertising, followed by a second period of advertising activity. It is used when funding is limited, the purchase cycle is relatively infrequent, and with seasonal items. *Pulsing* is continuous advertising at low-weight levels reinforced periodically by waves of heavier activity.[29]

Those who favor pulsing feel that the audience will learn the message more thoroughly, and money can be saved. This was Anheuser-Busch's experience. Its research indicated that Budweiser could substantially reduce advertising in a particular market and experience no adverse sales effect for at least a year and a half. Then the company could introduce a 6-month burst of advertising and restore the previous growth rate. This analysis led Budweiser to adopt a pulsing advertising strategy.

Deciding on Geographical Allocation

In allocating media geographically, the company should consider area differences in market size, advertising response, media efficiency, competition, and profit margins. The company makes "national buys" when it places ads on national TV or radio networks or in nationally circulated publications. It makes "spot buys" when it buys TV or radio time in just a few markets or in regional editions of national publications. The company makes "local buys" when it uses local advertising media. Despite its efficiency, however, national (and international) advertising may fail to adequately address differing local situations, such as market-to-market variations in share and competitive standing.

Evaluating Advertising Effectiveness

Good planning and control of advertising depend on measures of advertising effectiveness. Yet the amount of fundamental research on advertising effectiveness is appallingly small. Advertisers should try to measure the communication effect of an ad—that is, its potential effect on awareness, knowledge, or preference—as well as the ad's sales effect:

> ➤ *Communication-effect research* seeks to determine whether an ad is communicating effectively. Called *copy testing,* it can be done before an ad is placed (pretesting) and after it is placed (posttesting). Advertisers also need to posttest the overall impact of a completed campaign.

> ➤ *Sales-effect research* is complex because sales are influenced by many factors beyond advertising, such as product features, price, and availability, as well as competitors' actions. The sales impact is easiest to measure in direct-marketing situations and hardest to measure in brand or corporate-image-building advertising. One approach is shown in Figure 15.5: A company's share of advertising expenditures produces a share of voice that earns a share of consumers' minds and hearts and ultimately a share of market. Peckham studied the relationship between share of voice and share of market for several consumer products over a number of years and found a 1-to-1 ratio for established products and a 1.5–2.0 to 1.0 ratio for new products.[30]

SALES-PROMOTION STRATEGIES

Sales promotion, a key ingredient in many marketing campaigns, consists of a diverse collection of incentive tools, mostly short term, designed to stimulate trial, or quicker or greater purchase, of particular products or services by consumers or the trade.[31] Whereas advertising offers a *reason* to buy, sales promotion offers an *incentive* to buy. Sales promotion includes tools for *consumer promotion* (samples, coupons, cash refund offers, prices off, premiums, prizes, patronage rewards, free trials, warranties, tie-in promotions, cross-promotions, point-of-purchase displays, and demonstrations); *trade*

Figure 15.5   Formula for Measuring Sales Impact of Advertising

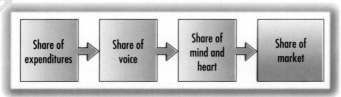

promotion (prices off, advertising and display allowances, and free goods), and *business- and sales force promotion* (trade shows and conventions, contests for sales reps, and specialty advertising).

In years past, the advertising-to-sales-promotion ratio was about 60:40. Today, in many consumer-packaged-goods companies, sales promotion accounts for 65–75 percent of the overall promotional budget. Several factors have contributed to this trend, particularly in consumer markets.[32] Internal factors include the following: Promotion is now more accepted by top management as an effective sales tool, more product managers are qualified to use sales-promotion tools, and product managers are under greater pressure to increase current sales. External factors include: The number of brands has increased, competitors use promotions frequently, many brands are seen as being similar, consumers are more price-oriented, the trade demands more deals from manufacturers, and advertising efficiency has declined because of rising costs, media clutter, and legal restraints.

In general, sales promotion seems most effective when used together with advertising. In one study, a price promotion alone produced only a 15 percent increase in sales volume. When combined with feature advertising, sales volume increased 19 percent; when combined with feature advertising and a point-of-purchase display, sales volume increased 24 percent.[33]

Purpose of Sales Promotion

Sales-promotion tools can be used to achieve a variety of objectives. Sellers use incentive-type promotions to attract new triers, to reward loyal customers, and to increase the repurchase rates of occasional users. New triers are of three types— users of another brand in the same category, users in other categories, and frequent brand switchers. Sales promotions often attract the brand switchers, because users of other brands and categories do not always notice or act on a promotion. Brand switchers are primarily looking for low price, good value, or premiums, so sales promotions are unlikely to turn them into loyal users. Sales promotions used in markets of high brand similarity produce a high sales response in the short run but little permanent gain in market share. In markets of high brand dissimilarity, however, sales promotions can alter market shares permanently.

One challenge is to balance short- and long-term objectives when combining advertising and sales promotion. Advertising typically acts to build long-term brand loyalty, but the question of whether or not sales promotion weakens brand loyalty over time is subject to different interpretations. Sales promotion, with its incessant prices off, coupons, deals, and premiums, may devalue the product offering in the buyers' minds. Therefore, companies need to distinguish between *price promotions* (which focus only on price) and *added-value promotions* (intended to enhance brand image).

Here's how Toro, a major manufacturer of lawn mowers and snowblowers, used an added-value promotion to sell its snowblowers in early September: Knowing that most people would wait to buy until the first snow, Toro offered to include Toro Snow Insurance, promising a rebate of $50 to each September buyer if it did not snow before January. This sales promotion did not hurt, and may have helped, Toro's brand image.

When a brand is price promoted too often, the consumer begins to buy it mainly when it goes on sale. So there is risk in putting a well-known brand leader on promotion over 30 percent of the time.[34] Kellogg, Kraft, and other market leaders are trying to return to "pull" marketing by increasing their advertising. They blame the heavy use of sales promotion for decreasing brand loyalty, increasing consumer price sensitivity, brand-quality-image dilution, and a focus on short-run marketing planning.

Farris and Quelch, however, counter that sales promotion enables manufacturers to adjust to short-term variations in supply and demand, test high list prices, sell more than they would ordinarily sell at the list price, adapt programs to different consumer segments, induce consumers to try new products, and lead to more varied retail formats. On the consumer side, sales promotion raises awareness of prices and helps consumers feel satisfied as smart shoppers.[35]

Major Decisions in Sales Promotion

In using sales promotion, a company must establish its objectives, select the tools, develop the program, pretest the program, implement and control it, and evaluate the results.

➤ *Establishing objectives.* Sales-promotion objectives are derived from broader promotion objectives, which are derived from more basic marketing objectives that are developed for the product. The specific objectives for sales promotion vary with the target market. For consumers, objectives include encouraging purchase of larger-size units, building trial among nonusers, and attracting switchers away from competitors' brands. For retailers, objectives include persuading retailers to carry new items and higher levels of inventory, encouraging off-season buying, offsetting competitive promotions, building brand loyalty, and gaining entry into new retail outlets. For the sales force, objectives include encouraging support of a new product or model, encouraging more prospecting, and stimulating off-season sales.[36]

➤ *Selecting consumer-promotion tools.* The main consumer-promotion tools are summarized in Table 15.3. We can distinguish between manufacturer promotions and retailer promotions. The former is illustrated by the auto industry's frequent use of rebates and gifts to motivate test-drives and purchases; the latter includes price cuts, retailer coupons, and retailer contests or premiums. We can also distinguish between sales-promotion tools that are "consumer-franchise building," which reinforce the consumer's brand understanding, and those that are not. The former imparts a selling message along with the deal, as in the case of coupons that include a selling message. Sales-promotion tools that are not consumer-franchise building include price-off packs, premiums that are unrelated to a product, contests and sweepstakes, consumer refund offers, and trade allowances.

➤ *Selecting trade-promotion tools.* Manufacturers can use a number of trade-promotion tools, as shown in Table 15.4, to (1) persuade an intermediary to carry the product, (2) persuade an intermediary to carry more units, (3) induce retailers to promote the brand by featuring, display, and price reduction, and (4) stimulate retailers and their salespeople to push the product. The growing power of large retailers has increased their ability to demand trade promotion at the expense of consumer promotion and advertising, so manufacturers often spend more on trade promotion than they would like.[37]

➤ *Selecting business- and sales force promotion tools.* Companies spend billions of dollars on business- and sales force promotion tools, shown in Table 15.5, to gather business leads, impress and reward customers, and motivate the sales force to greater effort. Companies typically develop budgets for each business-promotion tool that remain fairly constant from year to year.

➤ *Developing the program.* In deciding to use a particular incentive, marketers have to consider: (1) the *size* of the incentive (a certain minimum is necessary if the promotion is to succeed; a higher level will produce more sales response but at a diminishing rate); (2) the *conditions* for participation (whether to offer the incentive to everyone or

Table 15.3   Major Consumer-Promotion Tools

> **Samples:** Offer of a free amount of a product or service.
>
> **Coupons:** Certificates offering a stated saving on the purchase of a specific product.
>
> **Cash Refund Offers (rebates):** Provide a price reduction after purchase: Consumer sends a specified "proof of purchase" to the manufacturer who "refunds" part of the purchase price by mail.
>
> **Price Packs (cents-off deals):** Promoted on the package or label, these offer savings off the product's regular price.
>
> **Premiums (gifts):** Merchandise offered at low or no cost as an incentive to buy a particular product.
>
> **Prizes (contests, sweepstakes, games):** *Prizes* offer consumers the chance to win cash, trips, or merchandise as a result of purchasing something. A *contest* calls for consumers to submit an entry to be examined by judges who will select the best entries. A *sweepstakes* asks consumers to submit their names for a drawing. A *game* presents consumers with something every time they buy—bingo numbers, missing letters—that might help them win a prize.
>
> **Patronage Awards:** Values in cash or points given to reward patronage of a certain seller.
>
> **Free Trials:** Inviting prospects to try the product free in the hope that they will buy the product.
>
> **Product Warranties:** Explicit or implicit promises by sellers that the product will perform as specified or that the seller will fix it or refund the customer's money during a specified period.
>
> **Tie-in Promotions:** Two or more brands or companies team up on coupons, refunds, and contests to increase pulling power.
>
> **Cross-Promotions:** Using one brand to advertise another noncompeting brand.
>
> **Point-of-Purchase (POP) Displays and Demonstrations:** Displays and demonstrations that take place at the point of purchase or sale.

to select groups); (3) the *duration* (if the period is too short, many prospects will not be able to take advantage of it—but if it runs too long, it loses some of its "act now" force); (4) the *distribution vehicle* (each distribution method involves a different level of reach, cost, and impact); (5) the *timing* (annually, one-time, or some other dates—which must be communicated and coordinated with other departments); and (6) the *total sales-promotion budget* (including administrative costs and incentive costs).

➤ *Pretesting the program.* Although most sales-promotion programs are designed on the basis of experience, savvy marketers use pretests to determine if the tools are appropriate, the incentive size is optimal, and the presentation method is efficient. Strang maintains that promotions usually can be tested quickly and inexpensively and that large companies should test alternative strategies in selected market areas with each national promotion.[38]

➤ *Implementing and evaluating the program.* Implementation planning must cover *lead time* (the time needed to prepare the program before the launch) and *sell-in time* (which begins with the launch and ends when approximately 95 percent of the deal merchandise is in the hands of consumers). After implementation, manufacturers can measure sales-promotion effectiveness using sales data, consumer surveys, and experiments (see Chapter 4 for more details on research techniques).

Table 15.4   Major Trade-Promotion Tools

Price-Off (off-invoice or off-list): A straight discount off the list price on each case purchased during a stated time period. The offer encourages dealers to buy a quantity or carry a new item that they might not ordinarily buy. The dealers can use the buying allowance for immediate profit, advertising, or price reductions.

Allowance: An amount offered in return for the retailer's agreeing to feature the manufacturer's products in some way. An *advertising allowance* compensates retailers for advertising the manufacturer's product. A *display allowance* compensates them for carrying a special product display.

Free Goods: Offers of extra cases of merchandise to intermediaries who buy a certain quantity or who feature a certain flavor or size. Manufacturers might offer push money or free specialty advertising items to retailers that carry the company's name.

Source. For more information, see Betty Spethman, "Trade Promotion Redefined," *Brandweek,* March 13, 1995, pp. 25–32.

Table 15.5   Major Business and Sales Force Promotion Tools

Trade Shows and Conventions: Industry associations organize annual trade shows and conventions where firms selling products and services to this industry buy space and set up booths and displays to demonstrate their products. Participating vendors expect several benefits, including generating new sales leads, maintaining customer contacts, introducing new products, meeting new customers, selling more to present customers, and educating customers with publications, videos, and other audiovisual materials.

Sales Contests: A *sales contest* aims at inducing the sales force or dealers to increase sales over a stated period, with prizes going to those who succeed. Incentives work best when they are tied to measurable and achievable sales objectives (such as finding new accounts or reviving old accounts) for which employees feel they have an equal chance.

Specialty Advertising: Specialty advertising consists of useful, low-cost items (such as calendars) bearing the company's name and address, and sometimes an advertising message, that salespeople give to prospects and customers.

PUBLIC RELATIONS STRATEGIES

Not only must the company relate constructively to customers, suppliers, and dealers, but it must also relate to a large number of interested publics. A **public** is any group that has an actual or potential interest in or impact on a company's ability to achieve its objectives. **Public relations (PR)** involves a variety of programs that are designed to promote or protect a company's image or its individual products.

The wise company takes concrete steps to manage successful relations with its key publics. PR departments typically perform five functions: (1) *press relations* (presenting news and information about the organization in the most positive light); (2) *product publicity* (publicizing specific products); (3) *corporate communication* (promoting understanding of the organization through internal and external communications); (4) *lobbying* (dealing with legislators and government officials to promote or defeat legislation and regulation); and (5) *counseling* (advising management about public issues and company positions and image—and advising in the event of a mishap).[39]

Marketing Public Relations

Many companies are turning to *marketing public relations (MPR)* to directly support corporate or product promotion and image making. Thus MPR, like financial PR and community PR, serves a special constituency, namely the marketing department.[40] MPR plays an important role in:

➤ *Assisting in the launch of new products:* The amazing success of toys such as the Pokemon line owes a great deal to clever publicity.

➤ *Assisting in repositioning a mature product:* New York City had extremely bad press in the 1970s until the "I Love New York" campaign began.

➤ *Building interest in a product category:* Companies and trade associations use MPR to rebuild declining interest in commodities such as eggs and expand consumption of products such as pork.

➤ *Influencing specific target groups:* McDonald's sponsors special neighborhood events in Latino and African American communities to build goodwill.

➤ *Defending products that have encountered public problems:* Johnson & Johnson's masterly use of MPR was a major factor in saving Tylenol from extinction following two incidents in which poison-tainted Tylenol capsules were found.

➤ *Building the corporate image in a way that reflects favorably on its products:* Richard Branson's outrageous publicity stunts have created a bold, upstart image for his U.K.-based Virgin Group.

As the power of mass advertising weakens, marketing managers are turning to MPR to cost-effectively build awareness and brand knowledge and to reach local communities and specific audiences. The company does not pay for the space or time obtained in the media; it pays only for a staff to develop and circulate the stories and manage certain events. A story picked up by the news media could be worth millions of dollars in equivalent advertising—and would be more credible than advertising.

Major Decisions in Marketing PR

In considering when and how to use MPR, management must follow the same process as it does for advertising and sales promotion: Establish the marketing objectives, choose the messages and vehicles, implement the plan carefully, and evaluate the results. The main tools of MPR are described in Table 15.6.[41]

➤ *Establishing the marketing objectives.* These may include: Build awareness of a product, service, person, organization, or an idea; add credibility by communicating a message in an editorial context; boost sales force and dealer enthusiasm; and hold down promotion costs while gaining share of mind. Management needs to set specific objectives for each MPR campaign so the results can be evaluated. PR expert Thomas L. Harris suggests PR and direct-response marketing work together to build marketplace excitement before media advertising breaks, build a core customer base, build a one-to-one relationship with consumers, turn satisfied customers into advocates, and influence opinion leaders and influencers.[42]

➤ *Choosing messages and vehicles.* The MPR expert must identify or develop interesting stories to tell about the product. If there are few stories, the expert should propose

Table 15.6   Major Tools in Marketing PR

Publications: Companies rely extensively on published materials to reach and influence target markets, including annual reports, brochures, articles, printed and on-line newsletters and magazines, and audiovisual materials.

Events: Companies can draw attention to new products or other company activities by arranging special events like news conferences, on-line chats, seminars, exhibits, contests and competitions, and sport and cultural sponsorships that will reach the target publics.

News: One of the major tasks of PR professionals is to find or create favorable news about the company, its products, and its people. The next step—getting the media to accept press releases and attend press conferences—calls for marketing and interpersonal skills.

Speeches: Speeches are another tool for creating product and company publicity and building the company's image.

Public-Service Activities: Companies can build goodwill by contributing money and time to good causes.

Identity Media: To attract attention and spark recognition, the firm's visual identity is carried by its logos, stationery, brochures, signs, business forms, business cards, Web site, buildings, uniforms, and dress codes.

newsworthy events to sponsor as a way of stimulating media coverage. For example, when Anheuser-Busch sponsored a Black World Championship Rodeo in Brooklyn, the event attracted more than 5,000 spectators.

➤ *Implementing and evaluating the plan.* PR implementation must be handled with care. A great story is easy to place, but other stories might not get past busy editors. One of the chief assets of publicists is their personal relationship with media editors. MPR's contribution to the bottom line is difficult to measure because it is used along with other promotional tools. The easiest measure is the number of *exposures* obtained in the media, including the audience size and the cost of that space and time if purchased at advertising rates. Other measures include changes in *product awareness, comprehension,* or *attitude* resulting from the MPR campaign (after allowing for the effect of other promotional tools). The most satisfactory measure, however, is sales-and-profit impact, allowing the company to determine its return on MPR investment.

EXECUTIVE SUMMARY

Modern marketing calls for more than developing a good product, pricing it attractively, and making it accessible to target customers. Companies must also communicate with present and potential stakeholders, and with the general public. The marketing communications mix consists of five major modes of communication: advertising, sales promotion, public relations and publicity, personal selling, and direct marketing.

Developing effective marketing communications involves eight steps: (1) Identify the target audience, (2) determine the communication objectives, (3) design the message, (4) select the communication channels, (5) establish the total communications budget, (6) decide on the communications mix, (7) measure the communications' results, and (8) manage the integrated marketing communication process.

Managing the communications process calls for integrated marketing communications (IMC), a concept that recognizes the added value of a comprehensive plan that evaluates the strategic roles of a variety of communications disciplines and combines these disciplines to provide clarity, consistency, and maximum communications' impact through the seamless integration of discrete messages.

Advertising is any paid form of nonpersonal presentation and promotion of ideas, goods, or services by an identified sponsor. Developing an advertising program involves setting objectives, setting a budget, choosing the advertising message, determining how the message will be generated, evaluating and selecting messages, executing the message, developing media strategies by establishing the ad's desired reach, frequency, and impact and then choosing the media that will deliver the desired results, and evaluating the communication and sales effects of the advertising.

Sales promotion consists of a diverse collection of incentive tools, mostly short term, that are designed to stimulate trial or quicker or greater purchase of particular goods or services by consumers or the trade. Sales promotion includes tools for consumer promotion, trade promotion, and business- and sales force promotion. In using sales promotion, as in using advertising, a company must set its objectives, select the tools, develop the program, pretest the program, implement and control it, and evaluate the results. Although the use of sales promotion is growing—and the technique tends to increase sales and market share in the short run—it is not generally considered a long-term brand-building technique.

A public is any group that has an actual or potential interest in or impact on a company's ability to achieve its objectives. Public relations (PR) involves a variety of programs designed to promote or protect a company's image or its individual products. Marketing public relations (MPR) is often used to support corporate or product promotion and image-building. MPR can affect public awareness at a fraction of the cost of advertising, and is often much more credible. The main tools of PR are publications, events, news, speeches, public-service activities, and identity media.

In considering when and how to use MPR, management must establish the marketing objectives, choose the PR messages and vehicles, implement the plan carefully, and evaluate the results. Results are usually evaluated in terms of number of exposures and cost savings; awareness, comprehension, or attitude changes; and sales-and-profit contribution.

NOTES

1. John Bigness, "Back to Brand New Life," *Chicago Tribune,* October 4, 1998; Chris Reidy, "Putting on the Dog to be Arnold's Job," *Boston Globe,* August 28, 1998.
2. See Michael L. Ray, *Advertising and Communications Management* (Upper Saddle River, NJ: Prentice-Hall, 1982).
3. "FedEx Will Quit Joking Around Overseas," *Los Angeles Times,* January 21, 1997, p. B20.
4. See Ayn E. Crowley and Wayne D. Hoyer, "An Integrative Framework for Understanding Two-Sided Persuasion," *Journal of Consumer Research,* March 1994, pp. 561–74.
5. See C. I. Hovland, A. A. Lumsdaine, and F. D. Sheffield, *Experiments on Mass Communication,* vol. 3 (Princeton, NJ: Princeton University Press, 1948), ch. 8; and Crowley and Hoyer, "An Integrative Framework." For an alternative viewpoint, see George E. Belch, "The Effects of Message Modality on One- and Two-Sided Advertising Messages," in *Advances in Consumer Research,* eds. Richard P. Bagozzi and Alice M. Tybout (Ann Arbor, MI: Association for Consumer Research, 1983), pp. 21–26.
6. Curtis P. Haugtvedt and Duane T. Wegener, "Message Order Effects in Persuasion: An Attitude Strength Perspective," *Journal of Consumer Research,* June 1994, pp. 205–18; H. Rao Unnava, Robert E. Burnkrant, and Sunil Erevelles, "Effects of Presentation Order and

Communication Modality on Recall and Attitude," *Journal of Consumer Research,* December 1994, pp. 481–90.

7. See Brian Sternthal and C. Samuel Craig, *Consumer Behavior: An Information Processing Perspective* (Upper Saddle River, NJ: Prentice-Hall, 1982), pp. 282–84.

8. Herbert C. Kelman and Carl I. Hovland, "Reinstatement of the Communication in Delayed Measurement of Opinion Change," *Journal of Abnormal and Social Psychology* 48 (1953): 327–35.

9. David J. Moore, John C. Mowen, and Richard Reardon, "Multiple Sources in Advertising Appeals: When Product Endorsers Are Paid by the Advertising Sponsor," *Journal of the Academy of Marketing Science,* Summer 1994, pp. 234–43.

10. Michael Cafferky has identified four kinds of people that companies try to reach to stimulate word-of-mouth referrals: opinion leaders, marketing mavens, influentials, and product enthusiasts. For more, see *Let Your Customers Do the Talking* (Chicago: Dearborn Financial Publishing, 1995), pp. 30–33.

11. See Philip Kotler, "Atmospherics as a Marketing Tool," *Journal of Retailing,* Winter 1973–1974, pp. 48–64.

12. Sidney J. Levy, *Promotional Behavior* (Glenview, IL: Scott, Foresman, 1971), ch. 4.

13. Paul Wang and Lisa Petrison, "Integrated Marketing Communications and Its Potential Effects on Media Planning," *Journal of Media Planning* 6, no. 2 (1991): 11–18.

14. See Don E. Shultz, Stanley I. Tannenbaum, and Robert F. Lauterborn, *Integrated Marketing Communications: Putting It Together and Making It Work* (Lincolnwood, IL: NTC Business Books, 1992); and Ernan Roman, *Integrated Direct Marketing: The Cutting-Edge Strategy for Synchronizing Advertising, Direct Mail, Telemarketing, and Field Sales* (Lincolnwood, IL: NTC Business Books, 1995).

15. The definitions of advertising, sales promotion, and public relations are adapted from Peter D. Bennett, ed., *Dictionary of Marketing Terms* (Chicago: American Marketing Association, 1995).

16. See William L. Wilkie and Paul W. Farris, "Comparison Advertising: Problem and Potential," *Journal of Marketing,* October 1975, pp. 7–15.

17. See Donald E. Schultz, Dennis Martin, and William P. Brown, *Strategic Advertising Campaigns* (Chicago: Crain Books, 1984), pp. 192–97.

18. "The Best Awards: Retail/Fast-Food," *Advertising Age,* May 18, 1998, p S8; Karen Benezra, "Taco Bell Pooch Walks the Merch Path," *Brandweek,* June 8, 1998, p. 46; Bob Garfield, "Perspicacious Pooch Scores for Taco Bell," *Advertising Age,* March 9, 1998, p. 53; "Consumer 2000: Generation X," *American Demographics,* September 1999, www.mediacentral.com; "No 'Quiero' " in Future Taco Bell Advertising," *Advertising Age,* October 8, 1999, www.adage.com.

19. Dik Warren Twedt, "How to Plan New Products, Improve Old Ones, and Create Better Advertising," *Journal of Marketing,* January 1969, pp. 53–57.

20. See William A. Mindak and H. Malcolm Bybee, "Marketing Application to Fund Raising," *Journal of Marketing,* July 1971, pp. 13–18.

21. James B. Amdorfer, "Absolut Ads Sans Bottle Offer a Short-Story Series," *Advertising Age,* January 12, 1998, p. 8.

22. Yumiko Ono, "Bulletins from the Battle of Baldness Drug—Sports Figures Tout Rogaine for Pharmacia," *Wall Street Journal,* December 19, 1997, p. B1.

23. For further reading, see Dorothy Cohen, Legal Issues in Marketing Decision Making (Cincinnati, OH: South-Western, 1995).

24. Kevin Goldman, "Advertising: From Witches to Anorexics: Critical Eyes Scrutinize Ads for Political Correctness," *Wall Street Journal,* May 19, 1994, p. B1.

25. Adapted from Sandra Cordon, "Where High Road Meets Bottom Line: Ethical Mutual Funds Avoid Companies Deemed Socially Irresponsible," *The London Free Press,* October 9,

1998, p. D3; "Ethical Funds Launches 4 New Mutual Funds," *Ethical Funds,* January 17, 2000, www.ethicalfunds.com.

26. Schultz et al., *Strategic Advertising Campaigns,* p. 340.

27. See Herbert E. Krugman, "What Makes Advertising Effective?" *Harvard Business Review,* March-April 1975, p. 98.

28. Roland T. Rust and Richard W. Oliver, "Notes and Comments: The Death of Advertising," *Journal of Advertising,* December 1994, pp. 71–77.

29. See also Hani I. Mesak, "An Aggregate Advertising Pulsing Model with Wearout Effects," *Marketing Science,* Summer 1992, pp. 310–26; and Fred M. Feinberg, "Pulsing Policies for Aggregate Advertising Models," *Marketing Science,* Summer 1992, pp. 221–34.

30. See J. O. Peckham, *The Wheel of Marketing* (Scarsdale, NY: printed privately, 1975), pp. 73–77.

31. From Robert C. Blattberg and Scott A. Neslin, *Sales Promotion: Concepts, Methods, and Strategies* (Upper Saddle River, NJ: Prentice-Hall, 1990).

32. Roger A. Strang, "Sales Promotion—Fast Growth, Faulty Management," *Harvard Business Review,* July-August 1976 pp. 116–19.

33. See John C. Totten and Martin P. Block, *Analyzing Sales Promotion: Text and Cases,* 2d ed. (Chicago: Dartnell, 1994), pp. 69–70.

34. For a good summary of the research on whether promotion erodes the consumer franchise of leading brands, see Blattberg and Neslin, *Sales Promotion.*

35. See Paul W. Farris and John A. Quelch, "In Defense of Price Promotion," *Sloan Management Review,* Fall 1987, pp. 63–69.

36. For a model for setting sales promotions objectives, see David B. Jones, "Setting Promotional Goals: A Communications Relationship Model," *Journal of Consumer Marketing* 11, no. 1 (1994): 38–49.

37. See Paul W. Farris and Kusum L. Ailawadi, "Retail Power: Monster or Mouse?" *Journal of Retailing,* Winter 1992, pp. 351–69.

38. Strang, *Sales Promotion,* p. 120.

39. Adapted from Scott M. Cutlip, Allen H. Center, and Glen M. Broom, *Effective Public Relations,* 8th ed. (Upper Saddle River, NJ: Prentice-Hall, 1997).

40. For an excellent account, see Thomas L. Harris, *The Marketer's Guide to Public Relations* (New York: John Wiley, 1991). Also see *Value-Added Public Relations* (Chicago: NTC Business Books, 1998)

41. For further reading on cause-related marketing, see P. Rajan Varadarajan and Anil Menon, "Cause-Related Marketing: A Co-Alignment of Marketing Strategy and Corporate Philanthropy," *Journal of Marketing,* July 1988, pp. 58–74.

42. Material adapted from Thomas L. Harris, "PR Gets Personal," *Direct Marketing,* April 1994, pp. 29–32.

Chapter 16

Managing the
Sales Force

In this chapter, we will address the following questions:

■ What decisions do companies face in designing a sales force?

■ How do companies recruit, select, train, supervise, motivate, and evaluate a sales force?

■ How can salespeople improve their skills in selling, negotiating, and relationship-building?

Personal selling is a mainstay of nonprofit as well as for-profit organizations. College recruiters are the university's sales force arm; the U.S. Agricultural Extension Service uses specialists to sell farmers on new farming methods. On the business side, no one debates the importance of the sales force in the marketing mix. However, companies are sensitive to the high and rising costs (salaries, commissions, bonuses, travel expenses, and benefits) of maintaining a sales force. Because the average cost of a personal sales call ranges from $250 to $500, and closing a sale typically requires four calls, the total cost to complete a sale can range from $1,000 to $2,000.[1]

Not surprisingly, savvy companies are learning how to substitute other selling methods—including mail, phone, fax, and e-mail—to reduce field sales expenses. They also are working to increase sales force productivity through better selection, training, supervising, motivation, and compensation. *Sales force automation (SFA)* is playing an ever-larger role in personal selling, as more firms equip reps with laptop computers, software, and Web access to better manage customer and prospect contacts, display product specifications and availability, run presentations or demonstrations, and book orders.[2]

DESIGNING THE SALES FORCE

Personal selling is a key element in promotion, one of the four Ps in the marketing mix. But not all sales representatives do exactly the same kind of selling. In business settings, McMurry has distinguished these six types of sales representatives, ranging from the least to the most creative types of selling:[3]

1. Deliverer: A salesperson whose major task is the delivery of a product (milk, bread, or fuel).

2. Order taker: A salesperson who acts predominantly as an inside order taker (the salesperson standing behind the counter) or outside order taker (the soap salesperson calling on the supermarket manager).

3. Missionary: A salesperson whose major task is to build goodwill or to educate the actual or potential user, rather than to sell (the medical "detailer" representing an ethical pharmaceutical firm).

4. Technician: A salesperson with a high level of technical knowledge (the engineering salesperson who is primarily a consultant to client companies).

5. Demand creator: A salesperson who relies on creative methods for selling tangible products (vacuum cleaners or siding) or intangibles (insurance or education).

6. Solution vendor: A salesperson whose expertise lies in solving a customer's problem, often with a system of the firm's goods and services (such as computer and communications systems).

In general, salespeople perform one or more of the following tasks:

➤ *Prospecting:* Searching for prospects, or *leads,*

➤ *Targeting:* Deciding how to allocate their time among prospects and customers,

➤ *Communicating:* Communicating information about the company's products and services,

➤ *Selling:* Approaching, presenting, answering objections, and closing sales,

➤ *Servicing:* Providing various services to customers—consulting on problems, rendering technical assistance, arranging financing, expediting delivery,

➤ *Information gathering:* Conducting market research and doing intelligence work, and

➤ *Allocating:* Deciding which customers will get scarce products during shortages.

As this list suggests, the sales representative serves as the company's personal link to its customers and prospects while bringing back much-needed information about customers, markets, and competitors. Therefore, smart companies look carefully at the design of the sales force, including the development of sales force objectives, strategy, structure, size, and compensation (see Figure 16.1).

Sales Force Objectives and Strategy

Each company needs to define the specific objectives its sales force will achieve. Increasingly, companies are setting objectives for sales reps based not only on sales volume and profitability targets, but also on their ability to create customer satisfaction.

Consider Tiffany, the famous retailer of expensive jewelry. A purchase in this store can be like an investment, so management trains its retail sales staff to be consultants rather than strictly salespeople. Salespeople are trained to offer advice and information about the quality and cut of stones, the suitability of various settings, and the choices available in various price ranges. Even when selling less expensive items, salespeople know that part of the purchase is the experience and prestige of shopping at Tiffany. They also know that a satisfied customer is a potential repeat customer. In addition to its retail sales staff, Tiffany has 155 field reps, a catalog, and a Web presence (www.tiffany.com) to serve corporate customers. Training for new corporate sales

Figure 16.1   Designing a Sales Force

reps lasts for 6 to 8 weeks, and only when new hires have mastered the skills, knowledge, and products are they allowed to deal with customers.[4]

To implement the firm's sales objectives, a common strategy is for sales representatives to act as "account managers," arranging fruitful contact among various people in the buying and selling organizations. Selling increasingly calls for teamwork requiring the support of other personnel, such as top management, especially when national accounts or major sales are at stake; technical people, who supply technical information and service to the customer before, during, or after product purchase; customer service representatives, who provide installation, maintenance, and other services; and an office staff, consisting of sales analysts, order expediters, and administrative personnel. An example of a successful sales team orientation is provided by DuPont. Finding that corn growers needed a herbicide that could be applied less often, DuPont appointed a team of chemists, sales and marketing executives, and regulatory specialists to tackle the problem. Working together, they created a product that captured $57 million in sales during its first year.[5]

Once the company decides on objectives and strategy, it can use either a direct or a contractual sales force. A *direct (company) sales force* consists of full- or part-time paid employees who work exclusively for the company. This sales force includes *inside sales personnel,* who conduct business from the office using the telephone, fax, and e-mail, and receive visits from prospective buyers, and *field sales personnel,* who travel and visit customers. A *contractual sales force* consists of manufacturers' reps, sales agents, and brokers, who are paid a commission based on sales.

Sales Force Structure

The sales force strategy has implications for the sales force structure. If the company sells one product line to one end-using industry with customers in many locations, it would use a territorial sales force structure. If the company sells many products to many types of customers, it might need a product or market sales force structure. Table 16.1 summarizes the most common sales force structures.

Major accounts (also called key accounts, national accounts, global accounts, or house accounts) are typically singled out for special attention. The largest accounts may have a *strategic account management team* consisting of cross-functional personnel who are permanently assigned to one customer and may even maintain offices at the customer's facility. For example, Procter & Gamble assigned a strategic account team to work with Wal-Mart at its Bentonville, Arkansas, headquarters. This arrangement has saved P&G and Wal-Mart $30 billion jointly through supply chain improvements, while boosting profit margins by about 11 percent.[6]

Established companies need to revise their sales force structure as market and economic conditions change. IBM, for instance, lost market share in the computing industry because its marketing and sales organization had lost touch with customers. The company's worldwide marketing and sales were organized geographically, with sales reps covering customers in a wide range of industries. Although IBM was known for educating customers about technology—focusing solely on IBM's products—its "one-size-fits-all" presentations became a turn-off to increasingly computer-savvy customers. Ultimately, lost market share and the huge cost of maintaining its sales force made IBM slim down and reorganize its sales force vertically along 14 industry-specific lines, such as finance, petroleum, retail, and e-businesses.[7] This step created a mix of industry and product specialists. In another change, IBM sales reps have taken on an active role as consultant and now seek to create customer solutions, even if doing so sometimes means recommending a competitor's technology.

Table 16.1   Sales Force Structures

Territorial: Each sales representative is assigned an exclusive territory. This structure results in a clear definition of responsibilities and increases the rep's incentive to cultivate local business and personal ties. Travel expenses remain relatively low, because each rep travels within a small area.

Product: The importance of sales reps' knowing their products, together with the development of product divisions and product management, has led many companies to structure their sales forces along product lines. Product specialization is particularly useful for product lines that are technically complex, highly unrelated, or very numerous. Kodak uses one sales force for its film products that are intensively distributed, and another sales force to sell complex products that require technical support.

Market: Companies often specialize their sales forces along industry or customer lines. IBM set up a sales office for finance and brokerage customers in New York, another for GM in Detroit, and still another for Ford in Dearborn. Market specialization helps the sales force become knowledgeable about specific customer needs, but the major disadvantage is that customers are scattered throughout the country, requiring extensive travel.

Complex: When a company sells a diverse product line to many types of customers over a broad geographical area, it often combines several structures, with sales forces specialized by territory-product, territory-market, product-market, and so on. A sales representative might then report to one or more line and staff managers. Motorola has four types of sales forces: (1) a *strategic market sales force* composed of technical, applications, and quality engineers and service personnel assigned to major accounts; (2) a *geographic sales force* calling on customers in different territories; (3) a *distributor sales force* calling on and coaching Motorola distributors; and (4) an *inside sales force* handling orders via phone and fax.

Sales Force Size and Compensation

Once the company clarifies its sales force strategy and structure, it is ready to consider sales force size, based on the number of customers it wants to reach. One widely-used method for determining sales force size is the five-step *workload approach:* (1) group customers into size classes by annual sales volume; (2) establish call frequencies, the number of calls to be made per year on each account in a size class; (3) multiply the number of accounts in each size class by the call frequency to arrive at the total yearly sales call workload; (4) determine the average number of calls a sales rep can make per year; and (5) divide the total annual calls (calculated in step 3) required by the average annual calls made by a rep (calculated in step 4) to see how many reps are needed.

Suppose the company has 1,000 A accounts and 2,000 B accounts; A accounts require 36 calls a year (36,000 calls yearly), and B accounts require 12 calls a year (totaling 24,000 calls). The company therefore needs a sales force that can make 60,000 sales calls a year. If the average rep can make 1,000 calls a year, the company would need 60,000/1,000, or 60 sales representatives.

Many companies are shrinking their sales forces because the sales department is costly to maintain. Consider the situation of Coca-Cola Amatil, the Australian Coke franchisee. Amatil used to maintain an army of reps to call on small milk bar (corner store) accounts. These reps would often make up to 30 sales calls per day, staying just long enough to take an order and perhaps show one new product. When Amatil looked at the costs of sending these reps out to milk bars, it saw a good deal of wasted time and money. Now Amatil contacts these small accounts through a regular schedule of tele-marketing, freeing up its field reps to concentrate on larger accounts. This move has resulted in a much lower cost per order and made small accounts financially feasible.

The compensation package is a critical element in attracting top-quality sales reps, starting with the level and components. The level of compensation must bear some relation to the "going market price" for the type of sales job and required abilities. If the market price for salespeople is well defined, the individual firm has little choice but to pay the going rate. However, the market price for salespeople is seldom well defined. Published data on industry sales force compensation levels are infrequent and generally lack sufficient detail.

The company must next determine the four components of sales force compensation—a fixed amount, a variable amount, expense allowances, and benefits. The *fixed amount,* a salary, is intended to satisfy the sales reps' need for income stability. The *variable amount,* which might be commissions, a bonus, or profit sharing, is intended to stimulate and reward greater effort. *Expense allowances* enable sales reps to meet the expenses involved in travel, lodging, dining, and entertaining. *Benefits,* such as paid vacations, sickness or accident benefits, pensions, and life insurance, are intended to provide security and job satisfaction. Fixed compensation receives more emphasis in jobs with a high ratio of nonselling to selling duties and in jobs in which the selling task is technically complex and involves teamwork. Variable compensation receives more emphasis in jobs in which sales are cyclical or depend on individual initiative.

Fixed and variable compensation give rise to three basic types of compensation plans—straight salary, straight commission, and combination salary and commission. Only one-fourth of all firms use either a straight-salary or straight-commission method, while three-quarters use a combination of the two, though the relative proportion of salary versus incentives varies widely.[8]

Straight-salary plans provide sales reps with a secure income, make them more willing to perform nonselling activities, and give them less incentive to overstock customers. From the company's perspective, they provide administrative simplicity and lower turnover. Straight-commission plans attract higher sales performers, provide more motivation, require less supervision, and control selling costs.

Combination plans offer the benefits of both plans while reducing their disadvantages. Such plans allow companies to link the variable portion of a salesperson's pay to a wide variety of strategic goals. One trend is toward deemphasizing volume measures in favor of factors such as gross profitability, customer satisfaction, and customer retention. For example, IBM now partly rewards salespeople on the basis of customer satisfaction as measured by customer surveys.[9]

MANAGING THE SALES FORCE

Effective management of the sales force is needed to implement the company's chosen sales force design and achieve its sales objectives. Sales force management covers the steps in recruiting and selecting, training, supervising, motivating, and evaluating representatives (see Figure 16.2).

Recruiting and Selecting Sales Representatives

At the heart of a successful sales force is the selection of effective representatives. One survey revealed that the top 27 percent of the sales force brought in over 52 percent of the sales. Beyond differences in productivity is the great waste in hiring the wrong people. The average annual turnover rate for all industries is almost 20 percent. When a

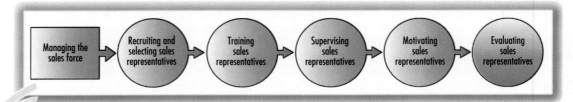

Figure 16.2   Managing the Sales Force

rep quits, the costs of finding and training a new rep, plus the cost of lost sales, can run into the high five figures—and a sales force with many new hires is less productive.[10]

In selecting sales reps, the company can start by asking customers what traits they prefer in salespeople. Most customers want honest, reliable, knowledgeable, and helpful reps. Another approach is to look for traits that are common to successful salespeople. Charles Garfield concluded that supersales performers exhibit risk taking, a powerful sense of mission, a problem-solving bent, care for the customer, and careful planning.[11] Mayer and Greenberg noted that the effective salesperson has *empathy,* the ability to feel as the customer does, and *ego drive,* a strong personal need to make the sale.[12]

After management develops suitable selection criteria, the next step is to recruit applicants by various means, including soliciting names from current sales reps, using employment agencies, placing print and on-line job ads, and contacting graduating college students. Selection procedures can vary from an informal interview to prolonged testing and interviewing. Although test scores are only one information element in a set that includes personal characteristics, references, past employment history, and interviewer reactions, they are weighted quite heavily by such companies as IBM, Prudential, Procter & Gamble, and Gillette. Gillette claims that tests have reduced turnover by 42 percent and have correlated well with the subsequent progress of new reps in the sales organization.

Training Sales Representatives

Today's customers expect salespeople to have deep product knowledge, offer ideas to improve customer operations, and be efficient and reliable. These demands have required companies to make a much higher investment in training their sales reps.

Companies use training to help sales reps: (1) Know and identify with the company; (2) learn about the company's products; (3) know customers' and competitors' characteristics; (4) make effective sales presentations; and (5) understand sales procedures and responsibilities. Training time varies with the complexity of the selling task and the type of person recruited into the sales organization. The median training period is 28 weeks in industrial-products companies, 12 in service companies, and 4 in consumer-products companies. At IBM, new reps receive extensive initial training and may spend 15 percent of their time each year in additional training.

Training often involves a variety of methods, including role playing, audio- and videotapes, CD-ROMs, and Web-based distance learning. For instance, reps at the Tandem division of Compaq used to complain that they could not keep up with the printed information and training materials the company sent them. Now field reps carry their own miniature training rooms with them—they simply slip a CD-ROM disk into their laptop computers.[13]

Supervising Sales Representatives

New sales representatives need more than a territory, a compensation package, and training—they also need proper supervision. Reps paid mostly on commission generally receive less supervision, while those who are salaried and must cover definite accounts are likely to receive substantial supervision. In the course of supervising sales reps, successful companies set norms for calls on customers and prospects, and they help reps make the most efficient use of sales time.

Norms for Customer Calls

In the early 1980s, the average salesperson made five calls a day; by 1989, that number had dropped to just 4.2 sales calls a day.[14] Today salespeople make even fewer in-person sales calls because they are using phone, fax, and e-mail to sell. In addition, more firms are using automated ordering systems to reduce reliance on sales calls.

How many calls should a company make on a particular account each year? Research shows that additional calls generally produce more sales, but companies still need to determine whether the increase in sales justifies the increase in sales costs. Some studies—and experiences such as those of Amatil, discussed earlier—suggest that sales reps may be spending too much time selling to smaller, less profitable accounts when they should be focusing more of their efforts on selling to larger, more profitable accounts.[15] Therefore, in setting norms, management needs to weigh the cost of a customer sales call against the sales and profit payback for that account.

Norms for Prospect Calls

Knowing the high cost of sales calls, companies often specify how much time reps should spend prospecting for new accounts. Spector Freight, for instance, wants its sales representatives to spend 25 percent of their time prospecting and to stop calling on a prospect after three unsuccessful calls. Other companies set prospect and customer norms based on product sales, specifying, for example, that reps spend 80 percent of their time selling established products and 20 percent selling new products.

Companies set up prospecting standards because many reps, left to their own devices, will spend most of their time with current customers, who are known quantities, rather than with prospects, who might never buy. In general, selling to prospects tends to be more difficult and more time-consuming than selling to established accounts, yet it is the road to customer base expansion and closing more sales. This is why some firms deploy a special missionary sales force to open new accounts (see Chapter 6).

Using Sales Time Efficiently

Not surprisingly, studies confirm that the best sales reps are those who manage their time effectively.[16] One popular efficiency tool is configurator software to automate the order preparation process. This type of program is offered by Massachusetts-based Concentra Corporation, among others. On a sales call, reps can use configurator software to present product specifications and pricing information, show customization options, and handle scheduling. Integrating all of this information, the configurator software can virtually write up the order in minutes. This software not only saves time; it also builds goodwill by reducing errors and letting both customer and supplier see the same information from the same source. Concentra's customers say this software has helped them increase sales and reduce cancellations.[17]

Another tool is *time-and-duty analysis,* which helps reps understand how they spend their time and how they might increase their productivity. In general, sales reps spend time in (1) preparation (getting information and planning call strategy); (2) travel (which can be more than 50 percent of total time); (3) food and breaks (some portion of every workday); (4) waiting (to see buyers); (5) selling (time spent with the buyer); and (6) administration (writing reports, billing, attending sales meetings, and so on).

With so many duties, it is no wonder that actual face-to-face selling time can amount to as little as 25 percent of total working time![18] To improve sales force productivity, many companies train their reps in the use of "phone power," simplify record-keeping, and use computerized methods to develop call and routing plans and to supply reps with customer and competitive information.

Seeking to reduce the time demands on their outside sales force, many firms have increased the size and responsibilities of their inside sales force. Inside salespeople are of three types. *Technical support people* provide technical information and answers to customers' questions. *Sales assistants* provide clerical backup for the outside reps by confirming appointments, carrying out credit checks, following up on deliveries, and answering customers' questions. *Telemarketers* use the phone to find new leads, qualify and sell to them, reactivate former accounts, and give more attention to neglected accounts.

The best sales reps spend time getting to know their customers' preferences, needs, and buying patterns so they can plan their calls accordingly. Technology speeds up this process. For example, before telecommunications reps at TimePlex go on a sales call, they use their laptops to dial into the firm's data network and retrieve status reports on that account's previous orders and other background information. When deals are struck, the reps use their laptops to record each order, double-check for errors, and then transmit everything electronically to the firm's New Jersey headquarters.[19]

In addition, Internet technology is helping to make prospecting more efficient. Company Web sites provide an introduction to self-identified potential customers and, for some businesses, may lead to on-line orders. For more complex transactions, the site provides a way for the buyer to contact the seller—for example, through a link to an e-mail address. The Pall Corporation, which makes fluid filtration and purification technologies, has all e-mail directed to company headquarters, with leads going directly to the appropriate sales rep. The quality and quantity of leads generated by its Web site (www.pall.com) has prompted the firm to promote its home page more aggressively.[20]

As another example, Lucent Technologies (www.lucent.com) combines e-mail with Web marketing to generate more qualified sales leads. A typical campaign starts with an e-mail inviting prospects to learn more about a particular offer (and qualify for a free gift) by visiting a customized Web page. Once there, prospects answer a few qualifying questions and can then request information to be sent by mail. Lucent's automated system separates these leads based on product needs, and contacts the best prospects 2 weeks later, offering free, downloadable software for analyzing total product costs. Prospects who choose the download are considered hot leads, so the system sends Lucent's sales force complete contact data on these prospects for immediate follow-up. "We never had to pick up the phone, and we've already established a relationship with them," notes Lucent's senior manager of marketing services.[21]

Motivating Sales Representatives

Some ambitious sales representatives are self-starters who will put forth their best effort without any special coaching. The majority of reps, however, require more encouragement and special incentives. This is especially true of field selling, which can be frustrating because reps usually work alone, keep irregular hours, are often away from home, frequently lack the authority to do what is necessary to win an account, and sometimes lose large orders they have worked hard to obtain. Most people, moreover, require incentives, such as financial gain or social recognition, to operate at full capacity.

Studying sales rep motivation, Churchill, Ford, and Walker developed a model indicating that the higher the salesperson's motivation, the greater his or her effort.[22] Greater effort will lead to greater performance, greater performance will lead to greater rewards, greater rewards will lead to greater satisfaction, and greater satisfaction will reinforce motivation. The model thus implies that sales managers must be able to convince salespeople that (1) *They can sell more by working harder or by being trained to work smarter,* and (2) *the rewards for better performance are worth the extra effort.*

According to this research, the most-valued reward was pay, followed by promotion, personal growth, and sense of accomplishment. The least-valued rewards were liking and respect, security, and recognition. Thus, salespeople seem highly motivated by pay and the chance to get ahead and satisfy their intrinsic needs, and less motivated by compliments and security. The researchers also found that the importance of motivators varied with demographic characteristics. Financial rewards were mostly valued by older, longer-tenured people and those who had large families, while higher-order rewards such as recognition were more valued by young salespeople who were unmarried or had small families and usually more formal education. However, motivators can vary across countries. Whereas money is the number-one motivator of 37 percent of U.S. salespeople, only 20 percent of salespeople in Canada feel the same way. Salespeople in Australia and New Zealand were the least motivated by a fat paycheck.[23]

Sales Quotas

Many companies set sales quotas prescribing what reps should sell during the year. Quotas can be set on dollar sales, unit volume, margin, selling effort or activity, and product type. After setting quotas, management often ties salesperson compensation to degree of quota fulfillment.

Sales quotas are developed from the annual marketing plan. As described in Chapter 3, management first prepares a sales forecast, which becomes the basis for planning production, workforce size, and financial requirements. Then the firm can establish sales quotas for regions and territories, often setting the total of all quotas higher than the sales forecast to encourage managers and salespeople to perform at their best level. If they fail to make their quotas, the company nevertheless might make its sales forecast.

In turn, each area sales manager divides that area's quota to arrive at an individual quota for each sales rep. A common approach to individual quotas is to set the individual rep's quota at least equal to the person's previous year's sales plus some fraction of the difference between area sales potential and previous year's sales. The more the rep reacts favorably to pressure, the higher the fraction should be.

Supplementary Motivators

Companies use additional motivators to stimulate sales force effort. One motivator is the periodic *sales meeting,* a social occasion that also serves as an important tool for education, communication, and motivation. Many companies sponsor *sales contests* to spur the sales force to a special selling effort above what is normally expected. The contest should present a reasonable opportunity for enough salespeople to win. At IBM, about 70 percent of the sales force qualifies for the 100 percent Club; the reward is a 3-day trip capped off by a recognition dinner and a special pin.

Whether a sales contest is focused on selling a specific product or products during a limited time period or is a more general recognition of top revenue earners for the period, the reward should be commensurate with the achievement. Reps who are well paid and whose earnings are based in large part on commissions are more likely to be motivated by a trip, a trophy, or merchandise than by a check of equal value. At the same time, some firms are successfully using less conventional rewards to motivate sales personnel. Ann Machado, founder and owner of Creative Staffing (an employment services firm), rewards both sales and nonsales employees with expensive dinners, parties, flowers, spa sessions, cooking lessons, and extra vacation time. Her secret is letting people pick the reward they want and outline what they will do to earn it. Then all she has to do is approve it. "Letting people choose their own rewards and goals empowers them," says Machado.[24]

Evaluating Sales Representatives

We have been describing the *feed-forward* aspects of sales supervision—how management communicates what sales reps should be doing and motivates them to do it. But good feed-forward requires good *feedback*, which means getting regular information from reps to evaluate their performance.

Sources of Information

Management can obtain information about reps in several ways, including sales reports, personal observation, customer letters and complaints, customer surveys, and conversations with other sales representatives. Many companies require their representatives to develop an annual *territory marketing plan* in which they outline their program for developing new accounts and increasing business from existing accounts. This type of report casts sales reps into the role of market managers and profit centers. Sales managers study these plans, make suggestions, and use them to develop sales quotas.

Sales reps write up completed activities on *call reports* and, in addition, submit expense reports, new-business reports, lost-business reports, and reports on local business and economic conditions. These reports provide raw data from which sales managers can extract key indicators of sales performance: (1) average number of sales calls per rep per day, (2) average sales call time per contact, (3) average revenue per sales call, (4) average cost per sales call, (5) entertainment cost per sales call, (6) percentage of orders per hundred sales calls, (7) number of new customers per period, (8) number of lost customers per period, and (9) sales force cost as a percentage of total sales.

Formal Evaluation

Sales reports, along with other observations, supply the raw materials for evaluation. There are several approaches to conducting evaluations. One type of evaluation compares the rep's current performance to that individual's past performance and to overall company averages on key sales performance indicators. These comparisons help management pinpoint specific areas for improvement. For example, if one rep's average gross profit per customer is lower than the company's average, that rep could be concentrating on the wrong customers or not spending enough time with each customer.

Evaluations can also assess the rep's knowledge of the firm, products, customers, competitors, territory, and responsibilities; relevant personality characteristics; and any problems in motivation or compliance.[25] As indicated earlier, an increasing number of companies are measuring customer satisfaction not only with their product and customer support service, but also with their salespeople. The sales manager can also check that salespeople know and observe the law. For example, under U.S. law, salespeople's statements must match the product's advertising claims. In selling to businesses, salespeople may not offer bribes to purchasing agents or others influencing a sale; they may not obtain or use competitors' technical or trade secrets through bribery or industrial espionage. Finally, salespeople must not disparage competitors or competing products by suggesting things that are not true.[26]

PRINCIPLES OF PERSONAL SELLING

Personal selling is an ancient art that has spawned many principles. Among these are three major aspects we will examine here: sales professionalism, negotiation, and relationship marketing (see Figure 16.3).[27]

Sales Professionalism

In the course of instilling professionalism, all sales-training approaches try to convert a salesperson from a passive order taker into an active order getter. *Order takers* operate on the assumption that customers know their own needs, resent attempts to influence them, and prefer courteous and self-effacing salespersons. There are two basic approaches in training salespersons to be *order getters*—a sales-oriented approach and a customer-oriented approach. The *sales-oriented approach* trains the person in the stereotyped high-pressure techniques traditionally used in selling automobiles. This form of selling assumes that customers are not likely to buy except under pressure, that they are influenced by a slick presentation, and that they will not be sorry after signing the order—or, if they are, that it doesn't matter.

The *customer-oriented approach* trains salespeople in customer problem solving. The rep learns to listen and ask questions in order to identify customer needs and come up with sound product solutions. This approach assumes that customers have latent needs that constitute opportunities, that they appreciate constructive suggestions, and that they will be loyal to sales reps who have their long-term interests at heart. Clearly, the professionalism of this customer-orientation is more in keeping with the marketing concept (discussed in Chapter 1) than are the hard-sell and order-taker approaches.

No approach works best in all circumstances. Yet most professional sales-training programs agree on the major steps involved in any effective sales process (see Figure 16.4).

Here is how these steps are applied in industrial selling:[28]

> ➤ *Prospecting and qualifying.* The first step in selling is to identify and qualify prospects. Companies can generate leads by examining data sources (newspapers, directories, CD-ROMs, Web sites); exhibiting at trade shows to encourage drop-bys; inviting

Figure 16.3   Managing the Sales Force: Improving Effectiveness

Figure 16.4   Major Steps in Effective Selling

customers to suggest the names of prospects; cultivating referral sources such as suppliers, dealers, and bankers; contacting trade associations; engaging in speaking and writing activities that draw attention; using the telephone, mail, and the Internet to find leads; and dropping in unannounced (cold canvassing). Companies can then qualify the leads (by contacting them by mail or phone) to assess their level of interest and financial capacity. The hottest prospects are turned over to the field sales force, while the merely warm prospects are turned over to the telemarketing unit for follow-up.

➤ *Preapproach.* The salesperson needs to learn as much as possible about the prospect company (what it needs, who is involved in the purchase decision) and its buyers (their personal characteristics and buying styles) by consulting trade and database sources. The salesperson can then set call objectives: to qualify the prospect, gather information, make an immediate sale. Another task is to decide on the best approach, which might be a personal visit, a phone call, or a letter. The best timing should also be considered because many prospects are busy at certain times. Finally, the salesperson should plan an overall sales strategy for the account.

➤ *Approach.* In this step, the salesperson decides how to get the relationship off to a good start. The salesperson might consider wearing clothes similar to what the buyers typically wear, show courtesy and attention to the buyer, and avoid distracting mannerisms. When meeting with the prospect, the rep should open with a positive statement and then concentrate on understanding the buyer's needs through careful questioning and active listening.

➤ *Presentation and demonstration.* Having listened to the buyer's needs, the salesperson now tells the product "story," being careful not to overemphasize product features (a product orientation) at the expense of a discussion of benefits and value (a customer orientation). Companies have developed three different styles of sales presentation. The oldest is the *canned approach,* a memorized sales talk covering the main points. It is based on stimulus-response thinking; that is, the buyer is passive and can be moved to purchase by the use of the right stimulus words, pictures, and actions. The *formulated approach* is also based on stimulus-response thinking but first identifies the buyer's needs and buying style and then uses an approach formulated to this type of buyer. The *need-satisfaction approach* starts with a search for the customer's real needs, after which the salesperson takes on the role of a knowledgeable consultant to help the customer save or make more money.

➤ *Overcoming objections.* Customers almost always pose objections during the presentation or when asked for the order. To handle these objections, the salesperson maintains a positive approach, asks the buyer to clarify the objection, asks questions that lead the buyer to answer his or her own objection, denies the validity of the objection, or turns the objection into a reason for buying. Handling and overcoming objections is a part of the broader skills of negotiation, which are discussed in the next section.

➤ *Closing.* Now the salesperson attempts to close the sale using one of several closing techniques. The rep can ask for the order, recapitulate the points of agreement, offer to help the buyer write up the order, ask whether the buyer wants A or B, get the buyer to make minor choices such as the color or size, or indicate what the buyer will lose if the order is not placed now. In addition, the rep might offer the buyer an inducement to close, such as a special price, an extra quantity, or a token gift.

➤ *Follow-up and maintenance.* Follow-up and maintenance are necessary to ensure customer satisfaction and repeat business. Immediately after closing, the salesperson should cement any necessary details on delivery time, purchase terms, and other matters that are important to the customer. The salesperson should schedule a follow-up call when the initial order is received to check on proper installation, training, and servicing. The purpose is to detect any problems, assure the buyer of the salesperson's interest, and reduce any cognitive dissonance that might have arisen. The salesperson should also develop a maintenance and growth plan for the account.

Negotiation

Salespeople involved in business-to-business deals, in particular, need negotiating skills as they work with customers to reach agreement on price and other terms of sale without making concessions that will hurt profitability. Although price is the most frequently negotiated issue, other issues include contract completion time; quality of goods and services; purchase volume; responsibility for financing, risk taking, promotion, and title; and product safety.

To be effective in sales negotiation, reps must be well prepared and have planning skill, knowledge of subject matter being negotiated, the ability to think clearly and rapidly under pressure and uncertainty, the ability to express thoughts verbally, listening skill, judgment and general intelligence, integrity, the ability to persuade others, and patience.[29] These attributes come into play when it is appropriate to negotiate with a customer or prospect—which is not in every situation.

When to Negotiate

According to Lee and Dobler, negotiation is an appropriate procedure for concluding a sale when (1) many factors bear not only on price, but also on quality and service; (2) business risks cannot be accurately predetermined; (3) a long period of time is required to produce the product purchased; (4) production is interrupted often because of numerous change orders.[30]

There is an obvious advantage in knowing the other party's reservation price and in making one's own reservation price seem higher (for a seller) or lower (for a buyer) than it really is. The openness with which buyers and sellers reveal their reservation prices depends upon the bargainers' personalities, the negotiation circumstances, and expectations about future relations.

Formulating a Negotiation Strategy

Successful salespeople prepare a strategic plan before meeting their buyers and making tactical decisions during negotiation sessions. A **negotiation strategy** is a commitment to an overall approach that has a good chance of achieving the negotiator's objectives.

Some negotiators pursue a "hard" strategy, whereas others maintain that a "soft" strategy yields more favorable results. Fisher and Ury propose a strategy of "principled negotiation." In this strategy, the parties (1) actively listen to each other's viewpoint, (2) focus on their interests rather than on their personal differences or positions, (3) search for options that offer mutual gain, and (4) insist on objective criteria to assess the solution.[31]

In line with this strategy, Fisher and Ury offer this advice about negotiation tactics: If the other party is more powerful, the best tactic is to know one's BATNA—Best Alternative to a Negotiated Agreement. By identifying the alternatives if a settlement is not reached, the company sets a standard against which any offer can be measured. Knowing its BATNA protects the company from being pressured into accepting unfavorable terms from a more powerful opponent.

What should a firm's negotiators do when the other side uses a take-it-or-leave-it tactic or seats them with the sun in their eyes? The firm's negotiators should recognize the tactic, raise the issue explicitly, and question the tactic's legitimacy and desirability—in other words, negotiate over it. If negotiating fails, the company should resort to its BATNA and terminate the negotiation until the other side ceases to employ these tactics. Meeting such tactics with defending principles is more productive than counterattacking with tricky tactics.

Relationship Marketing

The principles of personal selling and negotiation thus far described are *transaction-oriented* because their purpose is to close a specific sale. However, in many cases, the company is not seeking an immediate sale but rather to build a *long-term supplier-customer relationship* by demonstrating that it has the capabilities to serve the account's needs in a superior way over the long run.

More companies today are therefore emphasizing *relationship marketing* rather than transaction marketing, as discussed in Chapter 1. This has come about because larger customers are often global and prefer suppliers that can (1) sell and deliver a coordinated set of products and services to many locations; (2) quickly solve problems that arise in different locations; and (3) work closely with customer teams to improve products and processes.

However, some suppliers are still not set up to meet these requirements; their products are sold by separate sales forces that do not work together easily, and their technical people may not be willing to spend time to educate a customer. To succeed in winning and maintaining accounts in today's demanding environment, firms must encourage sales teamwork and reward it with appropriate compensation for work on shared accounts. They also need to establish better goals and measures for their sales force and reinforce the importance of teamwork in their training programs, even while honoring individual initiative.[32]

When a relationship management program is properly implemented throughout the organization—coordinating company efforts in marketing and sales and beyond—the organization will begin to focus as much on managing its customers as on managing its products. At the same time, smart companies realize that while there is a strong and warranted move toward relationship marketing, it is not effective in all situations. Ultimately, companies must judge which specific segments and customers will respond profitably to relationship management.

EXECUTIVE SUMMARY

Salespeople—the company's link to its customers—perform one or more of these tasks: prospecting, targeting, communicating, selling, servicing, information gathering, and allocating. Designing the sales force requires making decisions regarding objectives, strategy, structure, size, and compensation. Determining objectives and strategy requires defining the specific objectives the sales force will achieve and selecting the approaches and type of sales force that will be most effective.

Choosing the sales force structure entails dividing territories by geography, product, or market (or some combination of these). Estimating how large the sales force needs to be involves estimating the total workload and how many sales hours (and hence, salespeople) will be needed. Compensating the sales force entails determining what types of salaries, commissions, bonuses, expense accounts, and benefits to give, and how much weight customer satisfaction should have in determining total compensation.

There are five steps involved in managing the sales force: (1) recruiting and selecting sales representatives; (2) training reps in sales techniques and in the company's products, policies, and customer-satisfaction orientation; (3) supervising the sales force by establishing norms for customer and prospect calls and helping reps to use their time efficiently; (4) motivating the sales force, balancing quotas, monetary rewards, and supplementary motivators; and (5) evaluating individual and group sales performance through effective feedback.

Three major aspects of personal selling are sales professionalism, negotiation, and relationship marketing. Most trainers see professional selling as a seven-step process: prospecting and qualifying customers, preapproach, approach, presentation and demonstration, overcoming objections, closing, and follow-up and maintenance. Especially in business-to-business deals, professional selling requires negotiation, the art of arriving at transaction terms that satisfy both parties. Today's most successful firms are deemphasizing transaction-oriented marketing in favor of relationship marketing, which focuses on developing long-term, mutually beneficial relationships between two parties.

NOTES

1. For estimates of the cost of sales calls, see *Sales Force Compensation* (Chicago: Dartnell's 27th Survey, 1992), and *Sales & Marketing Management*'s 1993 sales manager's budget planner (June 28, 1993), pp. 3–75.
2. For more on sales force automation issues, see Doug Bartholomew, "Hard Sell?" *Industry Week*, March 1, 1999, www.industryweek.com; James LaVoy, "So, Did You Get What You Paid For?" *Sales & Field Force Automation*, February 1999, pp. 48–54.
3. Adapted from Robert N. McMurry, "The Mystique of Super-Salesmanship," *Harvard Business Review*, March–April 1961, p. 114. Also see William C. Moncrief III, "Selling Activity and Sales Position Taxonomies for Industrial Salesforces," *Journal of Marketing Research*, August 1986, pp. 261–70.
4. Sarah Lorge, "A Priceless Brand," *Sales & Marketing Management*, October 1998, pp. 102–10; "The Wall Street Transcript Publishes Retail Holiday Spending Report," *PRNewswire*, December 30, 1999, www.hoovers.com.
5. Christopher Power, "Smart Selling: How Companies Are Winning Over Today's Tougher Customer," *Business Week*, August 3, 1992, pp. 46–48.
6. For further reading, see John F. Martin and Gary S. Tubridy, "Major Account Management," in *AMA Management Handbook*, 3d ed. ed. John J. Hampton (New York: Amacom, 1994), pp. 3-25–3-27; Sanjit Sengupta, Robert E. Krapfel, and Michael A. Pusateri, "The Strategic Sales Force," *Marketing Management*, Summer 1997, pp. 29–34; Robert S. Duboff and Lori Underhill Sherer, "Customized Customer Loyalty," *Marketing Management*, Summer 1997, pp. 21–27; Tricia Campbell, "Getting Top Executives to Sell," *Sales & Marketing Management*, October 1998, p. 39.
7. Ira Sager, "Inside IBM: Internet Business Machines," *Business Week*, December 13, 1999, pp. EB20–EB38.

8. Luis R. Gomez-Mejia, David B. Balkin, and Robert L. Cardy, *Managing Human Resources* (Upper Saddle River, NJ: Prentice-Hall, 1995), pp. 416–18.

9. "What Salespeople Are Paid," *Sales & Marketing Management,* February 1995, pp. 30–31; Christopher Power, "Smart Selling: How Companies Are Winning Over Today's Tougher Customer," *Business Week,* August 3, 1992, pp. 46–48; William Keenan Jr., ed., *The Sales & Marketing Management Guide to Sales Compensation Planning: Commissions, Bonuses & Beyond* (Chicago: Probus Publishing, 1994).

10. George H. Lucas Jr., A. Parasuraman, Robert A. Davis, and Ben M. Enis, "An Empirical Study of Sales Force Turnover," *Journal of Marketing,* July 1987, pp. 34–59.

11. See Charles Garfield, *Peak Performers: The New Heroes of American Business* (New York: Avon Books, 1986); "What Makes a Supersalesperson?" *Sales & Marketing Management,* August 23, 1984, p. 86; "What Makes a Top Performer?" *Sales & Marketing Management,* May 1989; and Timothy J. Trow, "The Secret of a Good Hire: Profiling," *Sales & Marketing Management,* May 1990, pp. 44–55.

12. David Mayer and Herbert M. Greenberg, "What Makes a Good Salesman?" *Harvard Business Review,* July–August 1964, pp. 119–25.

13. Robert L. Lindstrom, "Training Hits the Road," *Sales & Marketing Management,* June 1995, pp. 10–14.

14. *Sales Force Compensation* (Chicago: Dartnell's 25th Survey, 1989), p. 13.

15. Michael R. W. Bommer, Brian F. O'Neil, and Beheruz N. Sethna, "A Methodology for Optimizing Selling Time of Salespersons," *Journal of Marketing Theory and Practice,* Spring 1994, pp. 61–75.

16. See Thomas Blackshear and Richard E. Plank, "The Impact of Adaptive Selling on Sales Effectiveness Within the Pharmaceutical Industry," *Journal of Marketing Theory and Practice,* Summer 1994, pp. 106–25.

17. "Automation Nation," *Marketing Tools,* April 1997; Scott Hample, "Made to Order," *Marketing Tools,* August 1997.

18. "Are Salespeople Gaining More Selling Time?" *Sales & Marketing Management,* July 1986, p. 29.

19. John W. Verity, "Taking a Laptop on a Call," *Business Week,* October 25, 1993, pp. 124–25.

20. Charles Waltner, "Pall Corp. Wins Business with Info-Driven Web Site," *Net Marketing,* October 1996.

21. "The Second Annual SMA Customer Interaction Awards," *Sales and Marketing Automation,* January 2000, www.sma.com.

22. See Gilbert A. Churchill Jr., Neil M. Ford, and Orville C. Walker Jr., *Sales Force Management: Planning, Implementation and Control,* 4th ed. (Homewood, IL: Irwin, 1993). Also see Jhinuk Chowdhury, "The Motivational Impact of Sales Quotas on Effort," *Journal of Marketing Research,* February 1993, pp. 28–41; Murali K. Mantrala, Prabhakant Sinha, and Andris A. Zoltners, "Structuring a Multiproduct Sales Quota-Bonus Plan for a Heterogeneous Sales Force: A Practical Model-Based Approach," *Marketing Science* 13, no. 2 (1994): 121–44; Wujin Chu, Eitan Gerstner, and James D. Hess, "Costs and Benefits of Hard-Sell," *Journal of Marketing Research,* February 1995, pp. 97–102.

23. "What Motivates U.S. Salespeople?" *American Salesman,* February 1994, pp. 25, 30.

24. "A Gift for Rewards," *Sales & Marketing Management,* March 1995, pp. 35–36.

25. See Philip M. Posdakoff and Scott B. MacKenzie, "Organizational Citizenship Behaviors and Sales Unit Effectiveness," *Journal of Marketing Research,* August 1994, pp. 351–63.

26. For further reading, see Dorothy Cohen, *Legal Issues in Marketing Decision Making* (Cincinnati, OH: South-Western, 1995) and Henry R. Cheeseman, *Contemporary Business Law,* 3rd edition (Upper Saddle River, NJ: Prentice-Hall, 2000).

27. For an excellent summary of the skills needed by sales representatives and sales managers, see Rolph Anderson and Bert Rosenbloom, "The World Class Sales Manager: Adapting to Global Megatrends," *Journal of Global Marketing* 5, no. 4 (1992): 11–22.

28. Some of the following discussion is based on W. J. E. Crissy, William H. Cunningham, and Isabella C. M. Cunningham, *Selling: The Personal Force in Marketing* (New York: John Wiley, 1977), pp. 119–29.

29. For additional reading, see Howard Raiffa, *The Art and Science of Negotiation* (Cambridge, MA: Harvard University Press, 1982); Max H. Bazerman and Margaret A. Neale, *Negotiating Rationally* (New York: Free Press, 1992); James C. Freund, *Smart Negotiating* (New York: Simon & Schuster, 1992); Frank L. Acuff, *How to Negotiate Anything with Anyone Anywhere Around the World* (New York: American Management Association, 1993); and Jehoshua Eliashberg, Gary L. Lilien, and Nam Kim, "Searching for Generalizations in Business Marketing Negotiations," *Marketing Science* 14, no. 3, pt. 1 (1995): G47–G60.

30. See Donald W. Dobler, *Purchasing and Materials Management,* 5th ed. (New York: McGraw-Hill, 1990).

31. Adapted from Roger Fisher and William Ury, *Getting to Yes: Negotiating Agreement Without Giving In,* rev. ed. (Boston: Houghton Mifflin, 1992), p. 57.

32. See Frank V. Cespedes, Stephen X. Doyle, and Robert J. Freedman, "Teamwork for Today's Selling, *Harvard Business Review,* March–April 1989, pp. 44–54, 58. Also see Cespedes, *Concurrent Marketing: Integrating Product, Sales, and Service* (Boston: Harvard Business School Press, 1995).

Managing Direct and On-Line Marketing

In this chapter, we will address the following questions:

■ What are the benefits of direct marketing?
■ How can companies use integrated direct marketing for competitive advantage?
■ What public and ethical issues are raised by direct marketing techniques?
■ What channels can direct marketers use to reach individual prospects and customers?
■ What marketing opportunities do on-line channels provide?

Today, the explosion of media is enabling many more companies to sell their products and services directly to customers without intermediaries, using traditional media (print and broadcast media, catalogs, direct mail, and telephone marketing) plus fax machines, e-mail, the Internet, and on-line services. Innovative marketers are creatively combining traditional and new media to make direct, individualized offers to existing customers, to identify their best prospects, to better target their offers, and to measure their results more accurately.

Despite the myriad marketing opportunities, this new-media world has also increased the level of competitive pressure, forcing small and large companies to battle for customers around the clock and around the world. Long-term customer relationship management is therefore driving the most successful direct and on-line marketing initiatives. Based on the information in their customer databases, companies can now customize their offers, messages, and media for more effective and efficient *one-to-one marketing*. The ultimate goal: stronger, more profitable bonds with targeted customers.

THE GROWTH AND BENEFITS OF DIRECT MARKETING

According to the Direct Marketing Association (DMA), **direct marketing** is defined as an interactive marketing system that uses one or more advertising media to effect a measurable response and/or transaction at any location. This definition emphasizes a measurable response, typically a customer order. Thus, direct marketing is sometimes called *direct-order marketing*.

Many direct marketers see direct marketing as playing a broader role these days, that of building a long-term relationship with the customer (*direct relationship marketing*).[1] In building relationships, some direct marketers send out birthday cards, information materials, or small premiums to select customers in their customer base. On the service side, airlines, hotels, and other businesses are strengthening customer relationships through frequency award programs and club programs.

Growth of Direct Marketing and Electronic Business

Sales produced through traditional direct-marketing channels (catalogs, direct mail, and telemarketing) have been growing rapidly. Whereas U.S. retail sales grow around 3 percent annually, catalog and direct-mail sales are growing about 7 percent annually. These sales include sales to consumers (53 percent), business-to-business sales (27 percent), and fundraising by charitable institutions (20 percent). Annual catalog and direct-mail sales are estimated at over $318 billion, with per capita direct sales of $630.[2]

The extraordinary growth of direct marketing is the result of many factors. Market "demassification" has resulted in an ever-increasing number of market niches with distinct preferences. Higher costs of driving, traffic and parking headaches, lack of time, a shortage of retail sales help, and queues at checkout counters all encourage at-home shopping, as do 24-hour toll-free telephone order hotlines and Web sites. Convenient next-day delivery via Federal Express, Airborne, and UPS has made ordering fast and easy. In addition, many chain stores have dropped slower-moving specialty items, creating an opportunity for direct marketers to promote these items directly to interested buyers. Also, direct marketers now have the computer power and the detailed data to cost-effectively single out the best prospects for their products. Increasingly, business marketers have turned to direct mail and telemarketing as an alternative to the rising costs of reaching business markets through the sales force.

Electronic communication is showing explosive growth, with Internet traffic doubling every 100 days. Millions of Web sites are already open for business, with more coming on-line every day. *Electronic business* is the general term for buyers and sellers using electronic means to research, communicate, and potentially transact with one another. *Electronic markets* are sponsored Web sites that (1) describe the products and services offered by sellers, and (2) allow buyers to search for information, identify what they need or want, and place orders using a credit card. The product is then delivered physically (to the customer's residence or office) or electronically (software and music can be downloaded to a customer's computer).

The Benefits of Direct Marketing

Direct marketing (on-line and off-) benefits customers in many ways. Shopping from home is fun, convenient, and hassle-free; it saves time and introduces consumers to a larger selection of merchandise. Shoppers can compare products and prices easily by browsing through mail catalogs and on-line shopping services, then order goods for themselves or others. Business customers also benefit by learning about available products and services without tying up time meeting with salespeople.

Sellers gain valuable benefits, as well. Direct marketers can buy a mailing list containing the names of almost any group (left-handed people, overweight people, millionaires), then personalize and customize their messages to build a continuous relationship with each customer. Direct marketing can also be timed to reach prospects at the right moment. The material sent by direct marketers receives higher readership because it is sent to more interested prospects. Direct marketing permits the testing of alternative media and messages in search of the most cost-effective approach, and it makes the direct marketer's offer and strategy less visible to competitors. Finally, direct marketers can measure responses to determine which campaigns have been the most profitable.

The Growing Use of Integrated Direct Marketing

Companies are increasingly recognizing the importance of integrating their marketing communications. Some companies are appointing a chief communications officer (CCO) to supervise specialists in advertising, sales promotion, public relations, and direct on-line marketing. The aim is to establish the right overall communication budget and the right allocation of funds to each communication tool. This movement has been variously called *integrated marketing communications (IMC), integrated direct marketing (IDM),* and *maximarketing.*[3]

How can direct marketing be integrated into campaign planning? Imagine a marketer using a single tool in a "one-shot" effort to reach and sell a prospect. An example of a single-vehicle, single-stage campaign is a one-time mailing offering a cookware item. A single-vehicle, multiple-stage campaign would involve successive mailings to the same prospect. Magazine publishers, for example, send about four renewal notices to a household before giving up. A more powerful approach is the multiple-vehicle, multiple-stage campaign. Consider the following sequence:

News campaign about a new product → Paid ad with a response mechanism →
Direct mail or e-mail → Outbound telemarketing → Face-to-face sales call →
Ongoing communication

For example, Compaq might launch a new laptop computer by first arranging news stories to stir interest. Then the firm might place media ads as well as Internet banner ads offering a free booklet on "How to Buy a Computer." Next, Compaq would mail the booklet to those who responded, along with an offer to sell the new computer at a special discount before it arrives in retail stores. Suppose 4 percent of those who receive the booklet order the computer. Compaq telemarketers then phone the 96 percent who did not buy to remind them of the offer. Suppose another 6 percent now order the computer. Those who do not place an order are offered a face-to-face sales call or demonstration in a local store. Even if the prospect is not ready to buy, there is ongoing communication.

Customer Databases and Direct Marketing

More marketers are harnessing information technology to build sophisticated customer databases and shift from mass marketing to highly targeted, one-to-one marketing (see Table 17.1).[4] As discussed in Chapter 4, a *customer database* is an organized collection of comprehensive data about individual customers or prospects that is current, accessible, and actionable for such marketing purposes as lead generation, lead qualification, sale of a product or service, or maintenance of customer relationships. **Database marketing** is the process of building, maintaining, and using customer databases and other databases (products, suppliers, resellers) for the purpose of contacting and transacting.

Database marketing is mostly frequently used by business marketers and service retailers, although Nabisco and other consumer packaged-goods companies have been experimenting with it. Armed with the information in its database, a company can achieve more target market precision than it can with mass marketing, segment marketing, or niche marketing. Companies use their databases in four ways:

Table 17.1   Mass Marketing versus One-to-One Marketing

Mass Marketing	One-to-One Marketing
Average customer	Individual customer
Customer anonymity	Customer profile
Standard product	Customized market offering
Mass production	Customized production
Mass distribution	Individualized distribution
Mass advertising	Individualized message
Mass promotion	Individualized incentives
One-way message	Two-way messages
Economies of scale	Economies of scope
Share of market	Share of customer
All customers	Profitable customers
Customer attraction	Customer retention

Source: Adapted from Don Peppers and Martha Rogers, *The One-to-One Future* (New York: Doubleday/Currency, 1993). See their Web site: www.1to1.com/articles/subscribe.html.

1. *To identify prospects:* Many companies generate sales leads by advertising their product or offer and building a database from the responses that come in. The firm can sort through this database to identify the best prospects and then contact them by mail, phone, e-mail, or personal sales call in an attempt to convert them into customers.

2. *To decide which customers should receive a particular offer:* Companies set up criteria describing the ideal target customer for an offer, then search their customer databases for those most closely resembling the ideal type. Companies such as The Limited and U S West are also comparing the marketing and servicing costs that go into retaining each customer versus the revenues he or she represents. Twice a year, for example, U S West sifts through its database looking for customers with more profit potential. By looking at demographic profiles, the mix of local versus long-distance calls, and the mix of services used, U S West can estimate potential spending. Next, the company determines how much of the customer's likely telecom budget is already coming its way. Armed with that knowledge, U S West sets a cutoff point for marketing spending on this customer.[5]

3. *To deepen customer loyalty:* Companies can build interest and enthusiasm by remembering customer preferences and by sending gifts, coupons, and special information. Consider Mars, a market leader not only in candy but also in pet food. In Germany, Mars has compiled the names of virtually every cat-owning German family by contacting veterinarians and by advertising a free cat-care booklet to consumers who fill out a questionnaire. As a result, Mars knows the cat's name, age, and birthday. Mars now sends a birthday card to each cat in Germany each year, along with a new-cat-food sample or money-saving coupons for Mars brands.

4. *To reactivate customer purchases:* Companies can use automatic mailing programs to send customers birthday or anniversary cards, holiday shopping reminders, off-season promotions, or other timely offers. For example, Streamline is a Boston-based on-line delivery service (www.streamline.com) that contracts with local groceries, video stores, and dry cleaners to fill and deliver orders when customers send in their shop-

ping lists. Streamline also keeps a database on what customers buy and when. Based on each customer's past behavior, the firm's software creates a profile and automatically sends e-mail reorder reminders when a customer is probably low on certain items. The result: Streamline's customers, who spend an average $6,000 a year, come back for more 90 percent of the time.[6]

Public and Ethical Issues in Direct Marketing

Although direct marketers and their customers usually enjoy mutually rewarding relationships, a darker side occasionally emerges. Key public and ethical issues include:

➤ *Irritation:* Many people find the increasing number of hard-sell, direct-marketing solicitations by phone, television, and e-mail to be a nuisance.

➤ *Unfairness:* Some direct marketers take advantage of impulsive or less sophisticated buyers. Television shopping channels and *infomercials*—extended-length, direct-response commercials that appear to be television shows demonstrating or discussing a product—may be the worst culprits. They feature smooth-talking hosts, elaborate demonstrations, claims of drastic or short-time price reductions, and easy purchasing to capture buyers who have low sales resistance.

➤ *Deception and fraud:* The Federal Trade Commission receives thousands of complaints annually about scams and frauds. Some direct marketers exaggerate claims about products and performance, some political fundraisers use questionable gimmicks such as envelopes that resemble official documents, and some nonprofit organizations pretend to conduct surveys when they are actually trying to identify donors.

➤ *Invasion of privacy:* Critics worry that marketers may know too much about their customers' lives, and that they may use this knowledge to take unfair advantage. American Express, long regarded as a leader on privacy issues, does not sell information on specific customer transactions. However, Amex found itself the target of consumer outrage when it announced a deal to make data on 175 million Americans available to any merchant who accepts AmEx cards. The uproar prompted Amex to kill the plan. America Online, also targeted by privacy advocates, wound up junking a plan to sell subscribers' telephone numbers.[7]

People in the direct-marketing industry are working on addressing these issues. They know that, left untended, such problems will lead to increasingly negative consumer attitudes, lower response rates, and calls for stricter government regulation. In the final analysis, most direct marketers want the same thing that consumers want: honest and well-designed marketing offers targeted only to those consumers who appreciate hearing about the offer.

MAJOR CHANNELS FOR DIRECT MARKETING

Direct marketers can use a number of channels for reaching prospects and customers. These include face-to-face selling, direct mail, catalog marketing, telemarketing, television and other direct-response media, kiosk marketing, and on-line channels.

Face-to-Face Selling

The original and oldest form of direct marketing is the field sales call. Today, most industrial companies rely heavily on a professional sales force to locate prospects, develop them into customers, and grow the business. Or they hire manufacturers' representatives and agents to carry out the direct-selling task. In addition, many consumer companies use a direct-selling force: insurance agents; stockbrokers; and distributors working for direct-sales organizations such as Avon, Amway, Mary Kay, and Tupperware.

Direct Mail

Direct-mail marketing involves sending an offer, announcement, reminder, or other item to a person at a particular address. Using highly selective mailing lists, direct marketers send out millions of mail pieces each year—letters, flyers, foldouts, and other "salespeople with wings." Some direct marketers mail audiotapes, videotapes, CDs, and computer diskettes to prospects and customers. The company that produces the Nordic Track Cardiovascular Exerciser advertises a free videotape showing the equipment's uses and health advantages. Ford sends a computer diskette called "Disk Drive Test Drive" to consumers who respond to its ads in computer publications. The diskette's menu provides technical specifications and attractive graphics about Ford cars and answers frequently asked questions.

Direct mail is a popular medium because it permits target market selectivity, it can be personalized, it is flexible, and it allows early testing and response measurement. Although the cost per thousand people reached is higher than with mass media, the people reached are much better prospects. The power of a well-designed direct-mail piece to garner contributions can be seen in a recent campaign for WFYI, an ailing public TV-radio station in Indianapolis. The results of a pair of startlingly graphic support pieces, created by the ad agency Young and Laramore for WFYI, outpaced all internal projections. The capital improvement campaign raised $3.5 million in its first 9 months, when the 5-year goal was $5 million. Only 500 pieces were mailed, so the average per piece return was $7,000.[8]

Three newer forms of mail delivery are *fax mail*, sending announcements of offers, sales, and events to fax machines or computers set up to receive faxes; *e-mail* (short for electronic mail), sending a message, file, image, or Web page electronically from one user to the e-mailbox of another individual (or to groups); and *voice mail*, leaving voice messages on recipients' voice mailboxes.

In constructing an effective direct-mail campaign, successful direct marketers follow the five steps shown in Table 17.2.

Catalog Marketing

Catalog marketing occurs when companies mail product catalogs (*full-line merchandise* catalogs, *specialty consumer* catalogs, or *business* catalogs in print, on CD, or on-line) to selected mail or electronic addressees. The Direct Marketing Association estimates there are currently up to 10,000 mail-order catalogs of all kinds. Catalog marketing has gotten a big boost from the Internet—about three-quarters of catalog companies also do business on-line. The Lands' End Web site (www.landsend.com), for example, gets 180,000 e-mail queries a year, surpassing the firm's print-mail response.[9]

The success of a catalog business depends on the company's ability to manage its customer lists so carefully that there is little duplication or bad debts, to control its inventory carefully, to offer quality merchandise so that returns are low, and to project a distinctive image. Some companies distinguish their catalogs by adding literary or information features, sending swatches of materials, sending gifts to their best customers, or donating a percentage of the profits to good causes. Other firms invite customers to view their Web-based catalogs for more information or to check on product availability.

Table 17.2   Steps in Developing a Direct-Mail Campaign

Step	Description
1. Set objectives	Establish objectives by which campaign success will be measured, such as producing orders from prospects, generating prospect leads, strengthening customer relationships, and informing and educating customers for later offers. An order-response rate of 2 percent is considered good for many products.
2. Identify target markets and prospects	The best customer targets are those who bought most recently, who buy frequently, and who spend the most. Consumer prospects can be identified on the basis of such variables as age, sex, income, education, previous mail-order purchases, purchase occasions, and lifestyle; business prospects can be identified on the basis of buying center role and other variables. Once the target market is defined, the direct marketer needs to obtain specific names by acquiring mailing lists and building databases.
3. Define the offer	According to Nash, the offer strategy consists of five elements: the product, the offer, the medium, the distribution method, and the creative strategy. Fortunately, all of these elements can be tested. In addition to these elements, the direct-mail marketer has to decide on five components of the mailing itself: the outside envelope, sales letter, circular, reply form, and reply envelope.
4. Test the elements	Direct marketing allows companies to test, under real marketplace conditions, the efficacy of different elements, such as product features, copy, prices, media, or mailing lists.
5. Measure results	By adding up the campaign costs, the firm can determine in advance the needed break-even response rate, net of returned merchandise and bad debts. Even when a specific campaign fails to break even, it can still be profitable over the customer lifetime, because of increased awareness and future intention to buy. A customer's ultimate value is not revealed by a purchase response to a particular mailing but by the expected profit made on all future purchases, net of acquisition and maintenance costs.

Sources: Based, in part, on information in Bob Stone, *Successful Direct Marketing Methods*, 6th ed. (Lincolnwood, IL: NTC Business Books, 1996); and Edward L. Nash, *Direct Marketing: Strategy, Planning, Execution,* 3d ed. (New York: McGraw-Hill, 1995).

Global consumers in Asia and Europe are also catching on to the catalog craze. A full 90 percent of L.L. Bean's international sales, for instance, come from Japan. One reason why Bean and other American catalog firms have flourished in Japan is that they offer high-quality merchandise aimed at specific groups. Consumer catalog companies such as Tiffany & Co., Patagonia, and Eddie Bauer are also entering Europe, as are business catalog firms such as Viking Office Products.[10]

Of course, by putting their catalogs on the Internet, catalog companies have better access to global consumers than ever before. They also save considerable printing and mailing costs while being able to offer unique services. In its latest attempt to build its brand over the Internet, Seattle-based casual apparel maker Eddie Bauer (www.eddiebauer.com) is letting customers enter a "virtual dressing room." Although visitors to Eddie bauer.com will find the same apparel that is shown in the catalog and in the stores, the site is more than just an electronic sales flyer: Customers can just click and drag different items to see how they look together. Because half of the consumers who visit the Web site have never shopped at Eddie Bauer before, their experience on-line is an important first contact with the company.[11]

Telemarketing

Telemarketing describes the use of telephone operators to attract new customers, to contact existing customers to ascertain satisfaction levels, or to take orders. In the case of routinely taking orders, it is called telesales. Many customers routinely order goods and services by telephone. The telephone has also spawned *home banking*. First Direct, set up by Britain's Midland Bank, operates entirely by telephone (as well as fax and Internet at www.firstdirect.com), with no branches to serve customers.[12]

Telemarketing has become a major direct-marketing tool, and is responsible for annual sales of $482 billion worth of products and services to consumers and businesses. The average household receives 19 telemarketing calls each year and makes 16 calls to place orders, although businesses are placing and receiving more telemarketing calls, as well. For example, Raleigh Bicycles uses telemarketing to reduce the amount of personal selling needed for contacting its dealers. In the first year, sales force travel costs were reduced by 50 percent and sales in a single quarter went up 34 percent.

Effective telemarketing depends on choosing the right telemarketers, training them well, and providing performance incentives. Telemarketers should have pleasant voices and project enthusiasm; after initial training with a script, they should move toward more improvisation. The call should be made at the right time, which is late morning and afternoon to reach business prospects, and evening hours between 7 and 9 P.M. to reach households. Given privacy issues and the higher cost per contact, precise list selection is critical.

Direct-Response Television Marketing

Although magazines, newspapers, and radio are all used to make direct offers to potential buyers, two forms of direct-response television marketing have become prominent in recent years:

1. *Direct-response TV advertising:* Some companies have been successful with 30- and 60-minute infomercials, which resemble documentaries and include testimonials and a toll-free number for ordering or getting further information. One example is the "Chrysler Showcase," a 30-minute infomercial touting Chrysler's brand heritage and the exterior design, performance, handling, and premium features of selected new models. This infomercial aired on national cable networks as well as United Airlines SkyTV. Infomercials generate an estimated $1.5 billion in annual sales.[13]

2. *Home shopping channels:* Several television channels are dedicated to selling goods and services. For example, on the 24-hour Home Shopping Network (HSN), hosts offer bargain prices on such products as jewelry, lamps, collectible dolls, and power tools. Viewers call in their orders on a toll-free number and receive delivery within 48 hours.

Kiosk Marketing

Some companies have designed "customer-order-placing machines" called *kiosks* (in contrast to vending machines, which dispense actual products) and placed them in stores, airports, and other locations. For example, the Florsheim Shoe Company includes a machine in selected stores to allow the customer to indicate the type of shoe he or she wants (dress, sport), along with the color and size. Pictures of Florsheim shoes that meet the criteria appear on the screen. If the particular shoes are not available in that store, the customer can order by dialing an attached phone and typing in a credit-card number and an address where the shoes should be delivered.

MANAGING ELECTRONIC COMMERCE AND ON-LINE MARKETING

Technology is expanding direct marketing into new electronic arenas. *Electronic commerce (e-commerce)* describes a wide variety of electronic platforms, such as the sending of purchase orders to suppliers via electronic data interchange (EDI); the use of fax and e-mail to conduct transactions; the use of ATMs, electronic point-of-sale terminals, and smart cards to facilitate payment and obtain digital cash; and the use of the Internet and on-line services. All of these involve doing business in a "marketspace" as compared to a physical "marketplace."[14] Although consumer buying over the Internet is growing rapidly—driven by purchases of computers and related products, books, CDs, toys, and videos—the volume of business Internet transactions is growing even faster: By 2003, U.S. business-to-business e-commerce is projected to reach $2.8 trillion.[15]

Commercial on-line services offer on-line information and marketing services to paid subscribers. The largest and best-known is America Online (AOL), which has 19 million subscribers and holds 50 percent of the market.[16] AOL and other on-line services offer proprietary channels featuring information (news, libraries, education, travel, sports, reference), entertainment (fun and games), shopping services, dialogue opportunities (bulletin boards, forums, chat rooms), and e-mail capabilities.

The *Internet* is an international web of computer networks that has made instantaneous and decentralized global communication possible. Internet usage has surged with the development of the user-friendly World Wide Web and browser programs such as Netscape Navigator and Microsoft Internet Explorer. Internet users can now experience fully integrated text, graphics, images, and sound; send e-mail and visit chat rooms to exchange views; shop for products; and find information of all kinds.

To target and reach these Internet users, marketers need to understand the characteristics and behavior of the on-line consumer.

The On-Line Consumer

As a whole, the Internet population is younger, more affluent, and better educated than the general population, with an almost equal number of men and women.[17] But as more people find their way onto the Internet, the cyberspace population is becoming more mainstream and diverse. Internet users in general place greater value on information and tend to respond negatively to messages aimed only at selling. They want to decide what marketing information they will receive about which products and services and under what conditions. In on-line marketing, it is the consumer, not the marketer, who gives permission and controls the interaction.

Internet consumers have around-the-clock access to varied information sources, making them better informed and more discerning shoppers. They can (1) get objective information about multiple brands, including costs, prices, features, and quality, without relying on manufacturers or retailers; (2) initiate requests for advertising and information from manufacturers and retailers; (3) design the offerings they want; and (4) use shopping agents to search for and invite offers from multiple sellers.

These new on-line buyer capabilities mean that the exchange process has become largely customer initiated and controlled; marketers must be invited to participate in the exchange. Even after marketers enter the exchange process, customers define the rules of engagement, and insulate themselves with the help of agents and intermediaries. Customers define what information they need, what offerings they want, and what prices they will pay—reversing, in many ways, time-honored marketing practices.

On-Line Marketing: Advantages and Disadvantages

On-line marketing is popular because it provides three major benefits to potential buyers:[18]

➤ *Convenience.* Customers can order 24 hours a day with a few keystrokes. At the Lands' End site (www.landsend.com), for example, buyers register their billing and shipping information only once; after that, whenever they make a purchase, their data will appear on the order form automatically.

➤ *Information.* Customers can quickly and easily find comparative information about companies, products, competitors, and prices. Consumer World (www.consumerworld.org), for example, offers access to dozens of comparison-shopping sites, consumer protection sites, and many other Internet resources to help shoppers make more informed buying choices.

➤ *Fewer hassles.* Customers don't have to deal with salespeople or wait in line. This is the special appeal of Autobytel (www.autobytel.com) and similar sites, which offer on-line car shopping so buyers can avoid haggling with salespeople over price and options.

At the same time, on-line marketing provides a number of benefits to marketers: (1) *quick adjustments to market conditions* (companies can quickly add products and change prices or descriptions), (2) *lower costs* (firms avoid the costs of maintaining a store and can create digital catalogs for much less than the cost of printing and mailing paper catalogs), (3) *relationship building* (firms can dialogue with consumers and invite them to download useful data or free demos), and (4) *audience sizing* (marketers can learn how many people visited their on-line site and how many stopped at particular places on the site).

Furthermore, on-line marketing is affordable for both small and large firms. There is no real limit on advertising space, in contrast to print and broadcast media, and information access and retrieval are nearly instantaneous. On-line marketers can reach anyone anyplace in the world, at any time, offering private yet speedy buying for consumers and business customers alike.[19]

Consider Wine.com (www.wine.com), the brainchild of master sommelier Peter Granoff and Silicon Valley engineer Robert Olson. Formerly known as Virtual Vineyards, this popular site features over 300 wines from 100 wineries plus hundreds of food and gift items for personal and corporate customers. One way the site adds value—without extra cost—is by providing detailed information on the characteristics of each wine, along with suggested food pairings. Customers can also join a wine club and enjoy the convenience of automatically receiving special wine or champagne selections to sample every month.[20]

Conducting On-Line Marketing

Marketers can get involved in on-line marketing by creating an electronic presence on the Internet; placing ads on-line; participating in forums, newsgroups, bulletin boards, and Web communities; and using e-mail to targeted audiences.

Electronic Presence

A company can establish an electronic presence on the Web in three ways:

1. *Buying space on a commercial on-line service.* This involves renting storage space on the on-line service's computer or establishing a link from the company's own computer to the on-line service's shopping mall. For example, the retailer JCPenney (www.jcpenney.com) has links to America Online and Prodigy. The on-line services typically design the storefront for which the company pays an annual fee plus a small percentage of its on-line sales.

2. *Selling through another site.* Amazon.com (www.amazon.com) broke new marketing ground by starting zShops, a special section on its Web site where manufacturers and retailers can sell their products. For less than $10 per month and a small percentage of on-line revenues, businesses of any size—even competitors—can reach out to Amazon's 12 million customers.[21]

3. *Opening its own Web site.* On a *corporate Web site,* the firm can offer basic information about its history, mission and philosophy, products and services, and locations; in addition, it may post current events, financial performance data, and job opportunities. One example is McDonald's (www.mcdonalds.com), which announces new promotions, helps visitors find the nearest outlet, posts news about its charitable works, and generally builds the firm's image—even though the site does not actually sell any food. On a *marketing Web site,* the firm seeks to bring prospects and customers closer to a purchase or other marketing outcome by offering a catalog, shopping tips, and possibly promotional features such as coupons or contests. The Garden site (www.garden.com), for example, offers a "garden planner" that lets visitors create and save their own ideal garden designs, then buy the plants and tools they need.

Business marketing is actually the driving force behind the e-commerce juggernaut. Major corporations such as Chevron, Ford Motor Company, General Electric, and Merck have invested millions in Web procurement systems to automate corporate purchasing. The result: Invoices that used to cost $100 to process now cost as little as $20. General Electric now requires its partners to join its Web procurement network (www.geis.com), which could save GE as much as $200 million per year by 2003.

Many companies are also developing "microsites"—small, specialized Web sites for specific occasions or products. For instance, the big motion picture studios are setting up separate sites for new films rather than sending people to the studios' main Web sites. Now other companies are using microsites for new-product launches, promotional campaigns, contests, recruiting, crisis communication, specific product information, and media relations. Frito-Lay, for example, has both a corporate Web site (www.fritolay.com) and a microsite (www.gosnacks.com) where consumers can place large orders for Cheetos and other snacks in special resealable containers. Companies should consider developing a microsite for any situation in which specific, detailed information needs to be made available quickly and easily.[22]

Advertising On-line

Companies can place on-line ads in three ways: (1) in special sections offered by the major commercial on-line services; (2) in selected Internet newsgroups that are set up for commercial purposes; and (3) using ads that pop up while subscribers are surfing on-line services or Web sites, including banner ads, pop-up windows, "tickers" (banners that move across the screen), and "roadblocks" (full-screen ads that users must click through to get to other screens).

Despite the ubiquity of banner ads, the "click-through rate" (the number of users who click on an ad to get more information) has plummeted below 1 percent. However, users who don't click may still see and absorb the banner ad message, notes Christopher Escher of Talk City (www.talkcity.com), an on-line community site: "Our focus groups tell us that people see our banner ads. Sometimes they click. Sometimes they don't. But the banner ads make them more likely to visit at another time."[23] Accustomed to measurement techniques for traditional media, advertisers want better measures of on-line advertising impact. For now, Web advertising is playing a supporting role in the promotion mixes of most advertisers.[24]

Forums, Newsgroups, Bulletin Boards, and Web Communities

On-line buyers increasingly create product information, not just consume it. They participate in Internet interest groups to share product-related information, with the result that "word of Web" is joining "word of mouth" as an important buying influence. To benefit from this trend, companies may participate in or sponsor Internet forums, newsgroups, and bulletin boards that appeal to special interest groups.

Forums are discussion groups that are usually located on commercial on-line services. A forum may operate a library, a "chat room" for real-time message exchanges, and even a classified ad directory. Some firms are adding proprietary chat rooms where visitors can go to discuss that company's offerings or interact with customer service reps. IGoGolf.com (www.igogolf.com), for example, made a $12,000 sale after a customer (who logged onto the U.S. site from Egypt) chatted with a customer service rep who recommended the right golf equipment.[25]

Newsgroups, the Internet version of forums, are limited to people who post and read messages on a specified topic. Thousands of newsgroups deal with every imaginable topic: healthy eating, caring for Bonsai trees, exchanging views about the latest soap opera happenings.

Bulletin board systems (BBSs) are specialized on-line services that center on a specific topic or group. Over 60,000 BBSs deal with numerous topics, such as vacations and hobbies. Marketers that participate in newsgroups and BBSs must take care to avoid a commercial tone in their messages.

Web communities are commercially sponsored Web sites where members congregate on-line and exchange views on issues of common interest. One such community is Agriculture Online (www.agriculture.com), where farmers and others can find commodity prices, recent farm news, and chat rooms of all types.

E-mail

The most targeted method a company can use to communicate directly with prospects and customers is via e-mail. Using inbound e-mail, the firm can invite people to e-mail the firm with questions, suggestions, and even complaints so customer service reps can respond and cultivate the relationship. E-savvy companies also develop Internet-based electronic mailing lists for outbound e-mail, sending out customer newsletters, special product or promotion offers based on purchasing histories, reminders of service requirements or warranty renewals, and announcements of special events.

However, in using e-mail as a direct-marketing vehicle, companies must be extra careful not to develop a reputation as a "spammer." *Spam* is the term for unsolicited e-mail. Consumers who are accustomed to receiving junk mail in their real mailboxes are often enraged to find unsolicited marketing pitches in their e-mail boxes. In fact, several states, as well as the federal government, have proposed legislation to limit or prohibit spam broadcasting.

Despite the possibility of being perceived as a spammer, savvy marketers are racing to take advantage of the potential of e-mail marketing.[26] One effective approach is *permission-based marketing,* a term coined by Seth Godin to describe the e-mail marketing model in which marketers ask for the customer's permission before sending e-mail offers. Amazon.com, for instance, invites customers to receive free newsletters with editors' recommendations for books in specific categories such as business and cooking. Targeted "opt-in marketing messages" are an increasingly important part of online marketing strategy because they can yield impressive response rates of 18–25 percent, compared with the average banner ad's response rate of 1 percent (or less).[27]

The Promise and Challenges of On-Line Marketing

On-line marketing is bringing profound changes to various sectors of the economy. Consumers' ability to order direct threatens to seriously hurt certain groups, particularly travel agents, stockbrokers, insurance salespeople, car dealers, and bookstore owners. These middlemen will be *disintermediated* by on-line services.[28] At the same time, some *reintermediation* will take place in the form of new on-line intermediaries, called *infomediaries,* which help consumers shop more easily and obtain lower prices.[29]

Consider mySimon (www.mysimon.com), which acts as an intelligent shopping agent for consumers looking for the best buys in categories such as books, toys, and computers. A shopper seeking a digital camera can go to mySimon, click on cameras, then digital cameras, scan the listing of makes and models, and locate the merchant offering a particular camera at the lowest price. Similarly, DealPilot (www.dealpilot.com) helps buyers compare prices of books, videos, DVDs, and CDs, while Point.com (www.point.com) helps buyers compare cellular phone service offerings.

Among other changes, Quelch and Klein believe that the Internet will lead to the more rapid internationalization of small- to medium-size enterprises.[30] The advantages of scale economies will be reduced, global advertising costs will be less, and smaller enterprises offering specialized products will be able to reach a much larger world market.

At the same time, on-line marketers continue to face a number of challenges:

➤ *Encouraging more buying:* The major on-line buyers today are businesses rather than individual consumers. Web marketers such as Priceline.com (www.priceline.com) are among the many sites using techniques such as special pricing to encourage more consumers to buy on-line. At auction sites such as eBay (www.ebay.com), many buyers return because they like bidding for what they want and getting a bargain.

➤ *Skewed user demographics and psychographics:* On-line users are more upscale, younger, and more Web-savvy than the general population, making them ideal prospects for computers, electronics, and financial services. The challenge now is to expand the on-line market and find ways of reaching diverse targeted segments. Eyeing the assets of younger, wealthier investors who frequent on-line brokerage firms, for example, Charles Schwab (www.schwab.com) acquired U.S. Trust so it could offer a wider range of services, such as private banking, to this attractive segment.[31]

➤ *Chaos and clutter:* The Internet offers millions of Web sites and a staggering volume of information. Navigating the Web can be frustrating. Many sites go unnoticed and even visited sites must capture visitors' attention within 8 seconds or lose them to another site.

➤ *Security:* Consumers worry about the security of credit-card numbers and other data sent to Internet sites, while companies worry about systems espionage or sabotage. The Internet is becoming more secure, but the race continues between new security measures and new code-breaking measures. To allay users' fears, Lending Tree (www.lendingtree.com)—a site that helps consumers shop for mortgages, credit cards, and other financial services—displays seals of approval from Verisign and other firms that monitor site security.

➤ *Ethical concerns:* As noted earlier, consumers who buy from direct marketers worry about companies making unauthorized use of their personal data, such as selling it to others. Threats of government intervention have spurred an increasing number of Web marketers to post privacy policies. Travelocity (www.travelocity.com), a one-stop-shopping site for travel and vacation-related purchases, is one of many sites that reassure visitors by displaying a seal of approval from the Better Business Bureau or other organizations and sites that examine Web privacy policies.

➤ *Consumer backlash.* Just as the Web has shifted power to consumers by giving them more product information, it has given them a more potent, effective means of expressing disgruntlement or even outrage. Rogue Web pages such as "Down with Snapple," often launched by irate consumers or former employees, can be seen by millions. They may contain valid information, but they can also spread unfounded rumors. Some companies shrug off these pages, but others are concerned enough to hire firms to monitor activity at these sites.[32]

 ## EXECUTIVE SUMMARY

Direct marketing is an interactive marketing system that uses one or more advertising media to effect a measurable response or transaction at any location. Direct marketing is now widely used in consumer markets, business-to-business markets, and markets for charitable contributions. Many companies have begun practicing integrated marketing communications, also called integrated direct marketing (IDM), using a multimedia approach to advertising that is generally more effective than single-media programs.

One of the most valuable direct-marketing tools is the customer database, an organized collection of comprehensive data about individual prospects or customers. Companies use their databases to identify prospects, decide which customers should receive an offer, deepen customer loyalty, and reactivate customer purchases.

Direct marketers and their customers usually enjoy mutually rewarding relationships. However, marketers must avoid campaigns that irritate consumers, are perceived as unfair, are deceptive or fraudulent, or invade customers' privacy.

Today, direct marketers can use a wide variety of channels to reach prospects and customers: sales calls; direct-mail marketing (sending an offer, announcement, reminder, or other item to a person at a particular address); catalog marketing; telemarketing; offers made by radio, magazine, and newspaper, direct-response television advertising; home shopping channels; kiosks; and on-line channels.

Electronic commerce describes a wide variety of electronic platforms. Commercial on-line services offer on-line information and marketing services to paid subscribers; the Internet is an international web of computer networks that makes instantaneous and decentralized global communication possible. Companies can go on-line by buying space on an on-line service; by selling through another site; by opening their own Web sites; by placing ads on-line; by participating in forums, newsgroups, bulletin boards, and Web communities; and by using e-mail to targeted audiences. Direct e-mailers that want to avoid being perceived as a spammer can use permission-based marketing, requesting the customer's permission before sending any e-mail offers. On-line marketing is leading to disintermediation of certain middlemen, even as infomediaries are starting to establish themselves as new on-line intermediaries.

NOTES

1. The terms *direct-order marketing* and *direct relationship marketing* were suggested as subsets of direct marketing by Stan Rapp and Tom Collins in *The Great Marketing Turnaround* (Upper Saddle River, NJ: Prentice-Hall, 1990).

2. Figures are for 1997, supplied by National Mail Order Association, tel: 612-788-1673.

3. Don E. Schultz, Stanley I. Tannenbaum, and Robert F. Lauterborn, *Integrated Marketing Communications* (Lincolnwood, IL: NTC Business Books, 1993); Ernan Roman, *Integrated Direct Marketing: The Cutting Edge Strategy for Synchronizing Advertising, Direct Mail, Telemarketing, and Field Sales* (Lincolnwood, IL: NTC Business Books, 1995); Stan Rapp and Thomas L. Collins, *The New Maxi-Marketing* (New York: McGraw-Hill, 1996), and *Beyond Maximarketing: The New Power of Caring and Daring* (New York: McGraw-Hill, 1994).

4. See Don Peppers and Martha Rogers, *The One-to-One Future* (New York: Doubleday/Currency, 1993).

5. "What've You Done for Us Lately?" *Business Week*, September 14, 1998, pp. 142–48.

6. Nicole Harris, "Spam That You Might Not Delete," *Business Week,* June 15, 1998, pp. 115–18.

7. Jennifer Tanaka, "Getting Personal," *Newsweek,* November 22, 1999, pp. 101–2; Bruce Horovitz, "AmEx Kills Database Deal After Privacy Outrage," *USA Today,* July 15, 1998, p. B1.

8. Debra Ray, "'Poor Mouth' Direct Mail Brochure Nets $3.5 Million in Contributions," *Direct Marketing*, February 1998, pp. 38–39.

9. Bruce Horovitz, "Catalog Craze Delivers Holiday Deals," *USA Today*, December 1, 1998, p. 3B.

10. Mari Yamaguchi, "Japanese Consumers Shun Local Catalogs to Buy American," *Marketing News*, December 2, 1996, p. 12; Cacilie Rohwedder, "U.S Mail-Order Firms Shake Up Europe—Better Service, Specialized Catalogs Find Eager Shoppers," *Wall Street Journal*, January 6, 1998; Kathleen Kiley, "B-to-B Marketers High on Overseas Sales," *Catalog Age*, January 1997, p. 8.

11. De'Ann Weimer, "Can I Try (Click) That Blouse (Drag) in Blue?" *Business Week*, November 9, 1998, p. 86.

12. See David Woodruff, "Twilight of the Teller?" *Business Week*, European Edition, July 20, 1998, pp. 16–17.

13. "Infomercial Offers Multiple Uses," *Direct Marketing*, September 1998, p. 11; Tim Hawthorne, "When and Why to Consider Infomercials," *Target Marketing*, February 1998, pp. 52–53.

14. See Jeffrey F. Rayport and John J. Sviokla, "Managing in the Marketspace," *Harvard Business Review*, November–December, 1994, pp. 75–85. Also see their "Exploiting the Virtual Value Chain," *Harvard Business Review*, November–December 1995, pp. 141–50.

15. "Online Holiday Shoppers to Triple," *CyberAtlas*, November 9, 1999, cyberatlas.internet.com/markets/retailing; "New BCG Study Re-Evaluates Size, Growth and Importance of Business-to-Business E-Commerce," *Boston Consulting Group,* December 21, 1999, www.bcg.com/practice/ecommerce/press_coverage_subpage4.asp.

16. Carol Pickering, "The First Online Business," *Business 2.0,* January 2000, p. 170.

17. Joanna Glasner, "Gender Gap? What Gender Gap?" *Wired Online*, November 8, 1999, www.wired/com/news/ebiz; "Numbers: Who's Online," *Business 2.0,* January 2000, pp. 251–52.

18. See Daniel S. Janal, *Online Marketing Handbook 1998 Edition: How to Promote, Advertise and Sell Your Products and Services on the Internet* (New York: John Wiley, 1998).

19. Robert Mullins, "E-Mail Marketing Puts Small Firms on Equal Footing with Big Business," *Milwaukee Business Journal*, January 3, 2000, www.amcity.com.

20. Gerald D. Boyd, "Cyberspace Caters to Wine Buffs," *San Francisco Chronicle,* May 8, 1998, p. 4.

21. Robert D. Hof, "Amazon.com Throws Open the Doors," *Business Week,* October 11, 1999, p. 44.

22. Greg Hansen, "Smaller May Be Better for Web Marketing," *Marketing News,* January 19, 1998, pp. 10, 13. For an excellent discussion of ways to attract viewers to Web sites, see Richard T. Watson, Sigmund Akselsen, and Leyland F. Pitt, "Attractors: Building Mountains in the Flat Landscape of the World Wide Web," *California Management Review,* Winter 1998, pp. 36–56.

23. "Advertise the Proven Way: Don't Bad-Mouth the Banner," *PC Computing,* January 2000, pp. 93–94.

24. See George Anders, "Internet Advertising, Just Like Its Medium, Is Pushing Boundaries," *Wall Street Journal,* November 30, 1998, p. 1.

25. "Case Study: Sell More Stuff," *PC Computing,* January 2000, p. 108.

26. Jay Winchester, "Point, Click, Sell," *Sales & Marketing Management,* November 1998, pp. 100–101.

27. "Take Advantage of the Free Market: Give Away the Store," *PC Computing,* January 2000, pp. 93, 98; Matthew Mills, "Vital Signs," *PC Computing,* August 1999, p. 14.

28. See Joseph Alba, John Lynch, Barton Weitz, Chris Janiszewski, Richard Lutz, Alan Sawyer, and Stacy Wood, "Interactive Home Shopping: Consumer, Retailer, and Manufacturer Incentives to Participate in Electronic Marketplaces," *Journal of Marketing,* July 1997, pp. 38–53.

29. See John Ellis, "'People Need a Haven from the Web That's on the Web,'" *Fast Company,* January–February 2000, pp. 242–46.

30. J. A. Quelch and L. R. Klein, "The Internet and International Marketing," *Sloan Management Review,* Spring 1996, pp. 60–75.

31. Amy Kover, "Schwab Makes a Grand Play for the Rich," *Fortune,* February 7, 2000, p. 32.

32. Stephanie Armour, "Companies Grapple with Gripes Posted on Web," *USA Today,* September 16, 1998, p. 5B.

Glossary

Advertising any paid form of nonpersonal presentation and promotion of ideas, goods, or services, by an identified sponsor (p. 281)

Attitude person's enduring favorable or unfavorable evaluations, emotional feelings, and action tendencies toward some object or idea (p. 96)

Belief descriptive thought that a person holds about something (p. 95)

Brand name, term, sign, symbol, or design, or a combination of these, intended to identify the goods or services of one seller or group of sellers and to differentiate them from those of the competitors (p. 188)

Business Services short-lasting goods and services that facilitate developing or managing the finished product (p. 186)

Capital Items long-lasting goods that facilitate developing or managing the finished product (p. 186)

Company Demand company's estimated share of market demand at alternative levels of company marketing effort in a given time period (p. 73)

Company Sales Forecast expected level of company sales based on a chosen marketing plan and an assumed marketing environment (p. 73)

Convenience Goods products purchased frequently, immediately, and with a minimum of effort (p. 185)

Customer Database organized collection of comprehensive data about individual customers, prospects, or suspects that is current, accessible, and actionable for marketing purposes such as lead generation, lead qualification, sales, and maintenance of customer relationships (p. 67)

Customer Delivered Value difference between total customer value and total customer cost (p. 20)

Database Marketing process of building, maintaining, and using customer databases and other databases (products, suppliers, resellers) for the purpose of contacting and transacting (p. 319)

Differentiation act of designing a set of meaningful differences to distinguish the company's offering from competitors' offerings (p. 175)

Direct Marketing interactive marketing system that uses one or more advertising media to effect a measurable response and/or transaction at any location (p. 317)

Environmental Threat challenge posed by an unfavorable external trend or development that would lead, in the absence of defensive marketing action, to deterioration in sales or profit (p. 47)

Image set of beliefs, ideas, and impressions that a person holds regarding an object (p. 273)

Learning changes in an individual's behavior that arise from experience (p. 95)

Lifestyle person's pattern of living in the world as expressed in activities, interests, and opinions (p. 92)

Market set of all actual and potential buyers of a market offer (p. 71)

Market Demand total volume that would be bought by a defined customer group in a defined geographical area in a defined time period in a defined marketing environment under a defined marketing program (p. 72)

Marketing societal process by which individuals and groups obtain what they need and want through creating, offering, and exchanging products and services of value freely with others (p. 4)

Marketing Audit comprehensive, systematic, independent, and periodic examination of a company's (or SBU's) marketing environment, objectives, strategies, and activities to identify problem areas and opportunities and recommend a plan of action for improving the company's marketing performance (p. 59)

Marketing Channels   sets of interdependent organizations involved in the process of making a product or service available for use or consumption (p. 236)

Marketing Concept   holds that the key to achieving organizational goals consists of the company being more effective than its competitors in creating, delivering, and communicating customer value to its chosen target markets (p. 12)

Marketing Decision Support System (MDSS)   coordinated collection of data, systems, tools, and techniques with supporting software and hardware by which an organization gathers and interprets information from business and environment and turns it into a basis for marketing action (p. 71)

Marketing Information System (MIS)   people, equipment, and procedures that gather, sort, analyze, evaluate, and distribute needed, timely, and accurate information to marketing decision makers (p. 64)

Marketing Implementation   process that turns marketing plans into action assignments and ensures that such assignments are executed in a manner that accomplishes the plan's stated objectives (p. 55)

Marketing Intelligence System   set of procedures and sources used by managers to obtain everyday information about developments in the marketing environment (p. 64)

Marketing Management   process of planning and executing the conception, pricing, promotion, and distribution of ideas, goods, services to create exchanges that satisfy individual and organizational goals (p. 4)

Marketing Mix   set of marketing tools that the firm uses to pursue its marketing objectives in the target market (p. 9)

Marketing Opportunity   area of buyer need in which a company can perform profitably (p. 46)

Marketing Process   analyzing market opportunities, researching and selecting target markets, designing market strategies, planning marketing programs, and organizing, implementing, and controlling the market effort (p. 50)

Marketing Research   systematic design, collection, analysis, and reporting of data and findings that are relevant to a specific marketing situation facing the company (p. 65)

Market-Oriented Strategic Planning   managerial process of developing and maintaining a viable fit among the organization's objectives, skills, and resources and its changing market opportunities (p. 40)

Market Potential   limit approached by market demand as industry marketing expenditures approach infinity for a given marketing environment (p. 73)

Materials   goods that enter the manufacturer's product completely (p. 185)

Media Selection   finding the most cost-effective media to deliver the desired number of exposures to the target audience (p. 285)

Negotiation Strategy   commitment to an overall approach that has a good chance of achieving the negotiator's objectives (p. 311)

Organizational Buying   decision-making process by which formal organizations establish the need for purchased products and services and identify, evaluate, and choose among alternative brands and suppliers (p. 108)

Packaging   activities of designing and producing the container for a product (p. 195)

Parts   goods that enter the manufacturer's product completely (p. 185)

Perception   process by which an individual selects, organizes, and interprets information inputs to create a meaningful picture of the world (p. 94)

Personality   distinguishing psychological characteristics that lead to relatively consistent and enduring responses to environment (p. 93)

Positioning   act of designing the company's offering and image to occupy a distinctive place in the target market's mind (p. 178)

Product Assortment   set of all products and items that a particular marketer offers for sale (p. 186)

Product Concept   holds that consumers favor those products that offer the most quality, performance, or innovative features (p. 11)

Production Concept   holds that consumers prefer products that are widely available and inexpensive (p. 11)

Product Mix   set of all products and items that a particular marketer offers for sale (p. 186)

Product Value Analysis   approach to cost reduction in which components are carefully studied to determine if they can be redesigned or standardized or made by cheaper methods of production (p. 118)

Profitable Customer a person, household, or company that over time yields a revenue stream that exceeds by an acceptable amount the company's cost stream of attracting, selling, and servicing that customer (p. 32)

Prospect Database organized collection of comprehensive data about individual customers, prospects, or suspects that is current, accessible, and actionable for marketing purposes such as lead generation, lead qualification, sales, and maintenance of customer relationships (p. 67)

Public any group that has an actual or potential interest in or impact on a company's ability to achieve its objectives (p. 292)

Public Relations (PR) variety of programs that are designed to promote or protect a company's image or its individual products (p. 292)

Reference Groups all the groups that have a direct (face-to-face) or indirect influence on a person's attitudes or behavior (p. 89)

Retailer any business enterprise whose sales volume comes primarily from retailing (p. 254)

Retail Store any business enterprise whose sales volume comes primarily from retailing (p. 254)

Sales Budget conservative estimate of the expected sales volume, and is used primarily for making current purchasing, production, and cash-flow decisions (p. 73)

Sales Promotion key ingredient in many marketing campaigns, consists of a diverse collection of incentive tools, mostly short term, designed to stimulate trial, or quicker or greater purchase, of particular products or services by consumers or the trade (p. 288)

Sales Quota sales goal set for a product line, company division, or sales representative (p. 73)

Satisfaction a person's feelings of pleasure or disappointment resulting from comparing a product's perceived performance (or outcome) in relation to his or her expectations (p. 21)

Selling Concept holds that consumers and businesses, if left alone, will ordinarily not buy enough of the organization's products (p. 11)

Service any act or performance that one party can offer to another that is essentially intangible and does not result in the ownership of anything (p. 200)

Shopping Goods products that the customer, in the process of selection and purchase, characteristically compares on the basis of suitability, quality, price, and style (p. 185)

Societal Marketing Concept holds that the organization's task is to determine the needs, wants, and interests of target markets and to deliver the desired satisfactions more effectively and efficiently than competitors in a way that preserves or enhances the consumer's and the society's well-being (p. 14)

Specialty Goods products with unique characteristics or brand identification (p. 185)

Supplies short-lasting goods and services that facilitate developing or managing the finished product (p. 186)

Total Customer Cost bundle of costs that customers expect to incur in evaluating, obtaining, using, and disposing of the product or service (p. 20)

Total Customer Value bundle of benefits that customers expect from a given product or service (p. 20)

Total Quality Management (TQM) an organization-wide approach to continuously improving the quality of all the organization's processes, products, and services (p. 33)

Trend direction or sequence of events that have some momentum and durability (p. 76)

Unsought Goods products that consumers do not know about or do not normally think of buying (p. 185)

Wholesaling all of the activities involved in selling goods or services to those who buy for resale or business use (p. 260)

Index